W9-BTJ-868

Stressful Life Events :

Their Nature and Effects

Edited by

Barbara Snell Dohrenwend
The City College of the
City University of New York

Bruce P. Dohrenwend
College of Physicians and Surgeons
Columbia University

A Wiley-Interscience Publication
John Wiley & Sons New York London Sydney Toronto

Library of Congress Cataloging in Publication Data

Conference on Stressful Life Events: Their Nature and
Effects, City University of New York, 1973.
Stressful life events.

"A Wiley-Interscience publication."
1. Stress (Psychology)—Congresses. I. Dohrenwend,
Barbara Snell, ed. II. Dohrenwend, Bruce Philip,
1927– ed. III. Title.

BF575.S75C64 1973 616.8'9'071 74-6369
ISBN 0-471-21753-0

Printed in the United States of America

10 9 8 7 6 5 4 3 2 1

Contributors

Aaron Antonovsky, Ph.D.

Lunenfeld-Kunin Professor of
Medical Sociology
The Regional Center for Health Sciences
Ben Gurion University of the Negev
Beer-Sheva, Israel and
The Israel Institute of Applied Social Research
Jerusalem, Israel

J. F. Aponte, Ph.D.

Assistant Professor of Psychology
Department of Psychiatry
University of North Carolina
Chapel Hill, North Carolina

W. K. Bentz, Ph.D.

Associate Professor of Sociology
Department of Psychiatry
University of North Carolina
Chapel Hill, North Carolina

D. R. Brogan, Ph.D.

Assistant Professor of Biostatistics
Department of Biostatistics
Emory University
Atlanta, Georgia

George W. Brown, Ph.D.

Professor of Sociology
Bedford College
Regents Park
University of London
London, England

Sidney Cobb, M.D.

Head, Psychiatric Epidemiology Research Unit
Butler Hospital
Providence, Rhode Island

Barbara Snell Dohrenwend, Ph.D.

Professor of Psychology
The City College of the City University of
New York
New York, New York

Bruce P. Dohrenwend, Ph.D.

Professor of Social Science
Department of Psychiatry
College of Physicians and Surgeons
Columbia University
New York, New York

Jeanne G. Eisenberg, M.A.

Senior Staff Associate
Columbia University School of Public Health
New York, New York

Rachel Favero, M.D.

Visiting Psychiatrist, Center for Epidemiologic
Studies
Division of Extramural Research Programs
National Institute of Mental Health
Rockville, Maryland

Joanne C. Gersten, Ph.D.

Assistant Professor of Epidemiology
Columbia University School of Public Health
New York, New York

Lawrence E. Hinkle, Jr., M.D.

Professor of Medicine and Professor of
Medicine in Psychiatry
Director of Division of Human Ecology
Departments of Medicine and Psychiatry
Cornell University Medical College
New York, New York

Thomas H. Holmes, M.D.

Professor of Psychiatry and Behavioral Sciences
University of Washington School of Medicine
Seattle, Washington

Richard W. Hudgens, M.D.

Associate Professor of Psychiatry
Washington University School of Medicine
St. Louis, Missouri

Sheppard G. Kellam, M.D.

Director Community Mental Health Assessment and Evaluation Unit and
Chief Psychiatric Consultant
Woodlawn Mental Health Center and
Associate Professor of Psychiatry
University of Chicago
Chicago, Illinois

Thomas S. Langner, Ph.D.

Professor of Epidemiology
Columbia University School of Public Health
New York, New York

Jacob J. Lindenthal, Ph.D.

Associate Professor of Sociology
Rutgers University
Newark, New Jersey

Robert E. Markush, M.D., M.P.H.

Chief, Center for Epidemiologic Studies
Division of Extramural Research Programs
National Institute of Mental Health
Rockville, Maryland

Minoru Masuda, Ph.D.

Professor of Psychiatry and Behavioral Sciences
University of Washington School of Medicine
Seattle, Washington

David Mechanic, Ph.D.

Professor of Sociology
University of Wisconsin
Madison, Wisconsin

F. T. Miller, Ph.D.

Associate Professor of Psychology
Department of Psychiatry
University of North Carolina
Chapel Hill, North Carolina

Jerome K. Myers, Ph.D.

Professor of Sociology
Yale University
New Haven, Connecticut

Lida Orzeck, Ph.D.

Research Associate
Columbia University School of Public Health
New York, New York

E. S. Paykel, M.D., M.R.C.P., M.R.C. Psych.

Consultant Psychiatrist
St. George's Hospital
London, England

Max P. Pepper, M.D.

Professor of Community Medicine
St. Louis University School of Medicine
St. Louis, Missouri

Richard H. Rahe, M.D., Commander, MC, USNR

Head, Biomedical Correlates Division
U.S. Navy Medical Neuropsychiatric Research Unit
San Diego, California and
Associate (adjunct) Professor of Psychiatry
University of California at San Diego and Los Angeles

Töres Theorell, M.D.

Assistant Professor of Internal Medicine
Department of Medicine Serafimerlasarettet
Karolinska Institute
Stockholm, Sweden

Preface

It is a remarkable thing when researchers from different disciplines converge on a common problem. This is what has been happening over the last 10 years with the problem of how to conceptualize and measure stressful life events. The interests of the researchers have varied. Some have been concerned mainly with physical illnesses; some mainly with psychiatric disorders. Some have focused more on how data on life events can aid prediction; others are more concerned with the possible role of life events in etiology. It is our impression, based we suppose partly on our own experience, that investigators from different disciplines have tended to begin their research on life events quite oblivious to relevant work of others. We tend to use different terms and read different journals than our colleagues in other disciplines. It is all too easy to miss their work or to be far less informed about it than would be useful.

Our own interest in stressful life events started with a more general interest in the relation of environmentally induced stress to psychopathology (Dohrenwend, 1961; Dohrenwend & Dohrenwend, 1965). We became especially concerned with life events on the basis of results from a panel study of about 150 adult respondents sampled from the general population of Washington Heights in New York City. In the first interview conducted in 1960–1961, we asked a small battery of widely used symptom questions touching on various aspects of anxiety, depression, and somatic complaint thought to be psychophysiological in nature. During the second interview we not only repeated these symptom questions but also asked whether there had been any serious illness or health problems since the previous interview about two years ago and about changes in work or job status. We found that just the relatively small sample of changes that we were able to elicit with these few questions were highly predictive of fluctuations in the psychological and physiological symptoms from the first to the second interview (Dohrenwend, 1966; Dohrenwend & Dohrenwend, 1969). We were sufficiently impressed to expand our procedures for eliciting life events in our further research efforts; some of this work is reported in this book. As we began to describe our work at various meetings of researchers from different disciplines, both in this country and abroad, we discovered that we were hardly alone in our interest in stressful life events.

It was out of a growing realization that a great deal of interesting and important work on stressful life events was going on that we decided to hold the Conference on Stressful Life Events: Their Nature and Effects.

Our personal motivation in holding the conference was to say something about what we had been doing and, more important, to learn about the work of others. Additionally, we felt that the time was ripe for stock-taking and that a careful and thorough job of it could be not only an immediate help to those working on the problem but also a platform from which major new advances could be launched. It was our feeling that different investigators had made different advances in conceptualization and measurement of life events but that there was no one approach that had scored a breakthrough. Moreover, as more researchers have begun to learn of each other's work, some interesting and useful controversies have begun to emerge. Since the advances and the controversies have developed in the context of what is now a substantial and fascinating body of empirical relationships between various measures of life events and such important matters as heart disease, depression, and attempted suicide, their implications are considerably more than academic.

This book is the direct result of the June 1973 conference. Excepting the introductory and final chapters, each chapter is based on a paper or formal discussion of a group of papers presented at the conference. Our own editorial attempts to put these chapters into historical perspective, relate them to each other, and to underline or spell out trends, problems, and prospects owe much more to both the informal and formal discussions during the conference than it is at all possible for us to acknowledge in any detail or specificity. Where we have missed or mangled major points, arguments, or nuances, we hope that a participant at the conference will be stimulated to develop the matter himself. For our part, we are most grateful to the participants—both those who presented papers and formal discussions and those who spoke from the floor or gave us comments and reactions in private. We learned a great deal.

Neither the conference nor this book would have been possible without financial support from the Center for Epidemiologic Studies of the National Institute of Mental Health (Grant MH-23379). The NIMH grant was supplemented by funds from Roche Laboratories, and we would like to express our appreciation to them. The work of preparing the conference was facilitated by the able assistance of Mrs. Marylin Horowitz. Important supporting services and extraordinarily pleasant settings for the conference were provided by the Graduate School and University Center of the City University of New York. Finally, Gerald Adler and Carla Conrad provided important editorial help for which we are most grateful.

REFERENCES

Dohrenwend, B. P. The social psychological nature of stress: A framework for causal inquiry. *Journal of Abnormal and Social Psychology,* 1961, **62,** 294–302.

Dohrenwend, B. P. Social status and psychological disorder: An issue of substance and an issue of method. *American Sociological Review,* 1966, **31,** 14–34.

Dohrenwend, B. P., & Dohrenwend, B. S. The problem of validity in field studies of psychological disorder. *Journal of Abnormal Psychology,* 1965, **70,** 52–69.

Dohrenwend, B. P., & Dohrenwend, B. S. *Social Status and Psychological Disorder*. New York: John Wiley & Sons, 1969.

BARBARA SNELL DOHRENWEND
BRUCE P. DOHRENWEND

New York, New York
March 1974

Contents

CHAPTER 1

A Brief Historical Introduction to Research on Stressful Life Events

BARBARA SNELL DOHRENWEND

BRUCE P. DOHRENWEND

"Stress" is a term that has been linked to varied concepts and operations (cf. Appley & Trumbull, 1967; Dodge & Martin, 1970; Hinkle, 1973; Janis, 1958; Lazarus, 1966; Levine & Scotch, 1970; Moss, 1973; McGrath, 1970). For some researchers it is a stimulus, sometimes more, sometimes less complex; for others it is an inferred inner state; and for still others it is an observable response to a stimulus or situation. Thus the use of the term is somewhat hazardous because of the lack of consensus that prevails in stress research. The contributors to this book, however, share two sets of concerns that give their work more unity than exists in stress research in general. First, they focus mainly on a class of stressful stimuli or situations to which everyone is exposed to a greater or lesser extent in the natural course of life. These stimuli or situations, which we call "life events," include experiences such as marriage, birth of a child, divorce, and death of a loved one.

The second focus shared by the contributors to this book is the general hypothesis that stressful life events play a role in the etiology of various somatic and psychiatric disorders. By way of introducing their chapters, in which they report some of the most extensive and challenging research that has been generated by this hypothesis, let us see how the hypothesis emerged historically from experimental and clinical approaches to the study of stress.

HISTORICAL ANTECEDENTS OF CURRENT RESEARCH ON STRESSFUL LIFE EVENTS

The foundation for systematic experimental research on the effects of stress was laid by Cannon in his detailed observations of bodily changes related to pain, hunger, and the major emotions. From these observations he concluded:

". . . the strong emotions, as fear and anger, are rightly interpreted as the concomitants of bodily changes which may be of utmost service in subsequent action. These bodily changes are so much like those which occur in pain and fierce struggle that, as early writers on evolution suggested, the emotions may be considered as foreshadowing the suffering and intensity of actual strife. On this general basis, therefore, the bodily alterations attending violent emotional states would, as organic preparation for fighting and possible injury, naturally involve the effects which pain itself would produce. And increased blood sugar, a larger output of adrenalin, an adapted circulation, greater number of red corpuscles and rapid clotting would all be favorable to the preservation of the organism that could best produce them" (1929, pp. 219–220).

Although his thinking focused on the survival functions of internal physiological adjustments produced by stressful conditions and strong emotions, Cannon felt compelled to respond to critics who accused him of failing to understand the pathogenic potential of relations between emotional arousal and bodily changes. To this end he posited:

". . . the persistent derangement of bodily functions in strong emotional reactions can be interpreted as due to persistence of the stimuli which evoke the reactions. They may persist because not naturally eliminated by completion of the emotional impulse, or because completion of the impulse is made impossible by circumstance . . ." (1929, p. 261).

To illustrate this proposition he cited a number of striking clinical cases. One demonstrated the termination of disturbance in a bodily function with the termination of a stressful event:

". . . A case of persistent vomiting which started when an income tax collector threatened punishment if a discrepancy in the tax statement was not explained, and which ceased as soon as [the clinician] went to the collector, as a therapeutic measure, and straightened out the difficulty" (1929, pp. 253–254).

In contrast, several cases of pathological thyroid condition illustrated the circumstances leading to persistent derangement of function; for example:

"A wife . . . saw her husband walking arm in arm with a strange woman and acting in such a way as to rouse jealousy and suspicion" (1929, p. 255).

". . . a married woman who had had two illegitimate children and whose husband committed suicide in her presence as a rebuke to her manner of living" (1929, p. 256).

Cannon's experimental work provided a necessary link in the argument that stressful life events can prove harmful. That is, he showed that stimuli associated with emotional arousal cause changes in basic physiological processes. However, his admittedly speculative attempt to forge a further link by specifying the conditions under which these physiological changes develop into pathological conditions, while pointing to life events, left it to others to grapple with the complexity of these events and their effects.

A major contribution to this task was made by Adolf Meyer in the 1930s through his advocacy of the life chart as a tool in medical diagnosis. Describing this technique, he wrote:

"We begin with the entering of date and year of birth . . . ; we next enter the periods of disorders of the various organs, and after this the data concerning the situations and reactions of the patient" (1951, p. 53).

His illustrations of the situations that he considered important to note were:

". . . the changes of habitat, of school entrance, graduations or changes, or failures; the various 'jobs'; the dates of possibly important births and deaths in the family, and other fundamentally important environmental incidents" (1951, p. 53).

Thus Meyer taught that life events may be an important part of the etiology of a disorder and that they need not be bizarre or catastrophic to be pathogenic. Instead, he suggested that even the most normal and necessary life events are potential contributors to the development of a pathological condition.

His teaching was reflected in the 1949 conference of the Association for Research in Nervous and Mental Diseases: Life Stress and Bodily Disease. The extent of the research that had accumulated by then is suggested by the range of diseases covered in ten specialized sessions on effects of life stress: disorders of growth, development and metabolism; disease of the eye; disease of the airways; headache; diseases of the stomach; diseases of the colon; disease of the muscles, joints, and periarticular structures; cardiovascular disease; disease of the skin; genital disorders.

In his review of the research presented at this conference, Harold Wolff attempted to account for the complexity of the effects of life stress that had by then become apparent. To this end he presented three propositions:

"1. Regardless of the apparent magnitude, the capacity of a given stress to evoke a protective reaction is a function of its significance to the implicated individual.

"2. The significance of a given stress for the individual determines, according to his temperament and past experiences, the characteristics of the protective reactions.

"3. When an individual exhibiting a given protective reaction pattern with co-existing symptoms is confronted by a situation which, through its new and different meaning evokes correspondingly different protective reactions, the latter may so overshadow the former as to cause the symptoms to disappear temporarily" (1950, p. 1079).

The hypotheses embodied in these propositions have proved controversial, but the issues that they imply have been central to subsequent research on stressful life events.

TWO CENTRAL ISSUES IN RESEARCH ON STRESSFUL LIFE EVENTS

One of these issues is suggested by an apparent paradox posed, for example, by Selye's conclusion from his influential physiological research that "Stress is part of life. It is a natural by-product of all our activities" (1956, p. 299). Hinkle has also noted the resemblance between ordinary life activities and laboratory studies of stress:

"The ordinary activities of daily life—the ingestion of food, or the failure to ingest food; muscular activity, or the absence of muscular activity; breathing, or not breathing; sleeping, or not sleeping;—all affect the dynamic steady state. Their effects are not qualitatively different from those of the 'stressors' that are used in the laboratory. It has been aptly said that 'to be alive is to be under stress' " (1973, p. 43).

Although we do not doubt the truth of this generalization, it is nevertheless a highly abstract truth. Even if every life event is stressful to some degree, it does not follow that all life events must be stressful to the same degree and, in fact, investigators have assumed that life events vary in stressfulness. One of the central issues that has guided research on stressful life events is therefore: What are the properties or conditions that distinguish more stressful from less stressful life events?

The second issue in research on stressful life events follows directly from the hypothesis that stressful life events play a role in the etiology of various somatic and psychological disorders. The questions derived from this hypothesis are sometimes concerned with specific disorders and sometimes with health changes in general, sometimes with particular types of stressful life event and sometimes with stressful life events in general, but all revolve around one issue: What are the pathological effects of stressful life events?

CURRENT RESEARCH ON STRESSFUL LIFE EVENTS

The studies and programs of research reported in this book were carried out in the years following the 1949 Conference on Life Stress and Bodily Disease. They represent varied approaches to the central issues concerning stressful life events. Some of these studies and programs have relied on clinical methods of research, whereas others have been epidemiological. Some have focused on the issue of what properties or conditions distinguish more stressful from less stressful life events, whereas others have emphasized questions related to the effects of stressful life events. As will be seen in the following chapters, in their different ways they have provided important advances in our understanding of these issues.

REFERENCES

Appley, M. H., & Trumbull, R. (Eds.) *Psychological Stress*. New York: Appleton-Century-Crofts, 1967.

Cannon, W. B. *Bodily Changes in Pain, Hunger, Fear and Rage*. New York: D. Appleton and Company, 1929.

Dodge, D. L., & Martin, W. T. *Social Stress and Chronic Illness*. Notre Dame, Ind.: University of Notre Dame Press, 1970.

Hinkle, L. E., Jr. The concept of "stress" in the biological and social sciences. *Science, Medicine, and Man,* 1973, **1,** 31–48.

Janis, I. L. *Psychological Stress*. New York: John Wiley & Sons, 1958.

Lazarus, R. S. *Psychological Stress and the Coping Process*. New York: McGraw-Hill Book Company, 1966.

Levine, S., & Scotch, N. A. (Eds.) *Social Stress*. Chicago: Aldine Press, 1970.

McGrath, J. E. (Ed.) *Social and Psychological Factors in Stress*. New York: Holt, Rinehart and Winston, 1970.

Meyer, A. The life chart and the obligation of specifying positive data in psychopathological diagnosis. In E. E. Winters (Ed.), *The Collected Papers of Adolf Meyer*, Vol. III, *Medical Teaching*. Baltimore: The Johns Hopkins Press, 1951. Pp. 52–56.

Moss, G. E. *Illness, Immunity, and Social Interaction*. New York: John Wiley & Sons, 1973.

Selye, H. *The Stress of Life*. New York: McGraw-Hill Book Company, 1956.

Wolff, H. G. Life stress and bodily disease—a formulation. In H. G. Wolff, S. G. Wolf, Jr., & C. C. Hare (Eds.), *Life Stress and Bodily Disease*. Baltimore: The Williams and Wilkins Company, 1950. Pp. 1059–1094.

Wolff, H. G., Wolf, S. G., Jr., & Hare, C. C. (Eds.) *Life Stress and Bodily Disease*. Baltimore: The Williams and Wilkins Company, 1950.

PART 1

Research Programs on Relations Between Stressful Life Events and Episodes of Physical Illness

The four chapters comprising Part 1 focus mainly although not exclusively on episodes of physical illness. In the first, Lawrence E. Hinkle, Jr., of the Cornell University Medical College provides an overview of retrospective and prospective studies of Bell Telephone employees, refugees from Mainland China, migrants who fled Europe during the Hungarian uprising in 1956, and United States servicemen when prisoners during the Korean War. Beginning in 1952, this remarkable series of studies was conducted to investigate how changes in the lives of people affect their health.

A few years earlier, Thomas H. Holmes and his colleagues at the University of Washington began their work on developing Adolf Meyer's concept of the "life-chart" into a systematic set of procedures for measuring the magnitude of stressful life events such as marriage, birth of a first child, and death of a loved one. Their use of psychophysical procedures for scaling such events—a major contribution to the field—is described in this chapter by Holmes and his co-author, Minoru Masuda. In addition, they summarize the use of the resulting measure of life events in retrospective and prospective investigations of illness in such varied groups as medical patients, resident physicians, and football players.

Richard H. Rahe, formerly one of Holmes' co-workers at the University of Washington, has extended these investigations into military settings. In his chapter, Rahe summarizes 10 years of research with Navy and Marine personnel—including an intriguing investigation of men undergoing hazardous training for service as underwater demolition experts. He presents a theoretical synthesis of his findings in the form of an impressive model of how stressful life events may exert their impact on health.

David Mechanic provides a critical discussion of the three preceding chapters. In addition to making a number of points about methodology he focuses attention on the relation of illness behavior to the study of stressful life events, drawing on his own current work on this topic to illuminate his discussion.

CHAPTER 2

The Effect of Exposure to Culture Change, Social Change, and Changes in Interpersonal Relationships on Health *

LAWRENCE E. HINKLE, JR.

INTRODUCTION

This chapter is a summary of some findings from studies that have been carried out by the Division of Human Ecology at Cornell University Medical College and by the Human Ecology Study Program which preceded it. These investigations were directed at the question of how the health of people is affected by changes in their cultural or social milieu or by changes in their interpersonal relationships. They began in 1952 and have continued to the present. All of them have been collaborative efforts, involving the parallel activities of physicians, psychiatrists, epidemiologists, psychologists, sociologists, anthropologists, and in some instances political scientists. In each investigation the representatives of the various disciplines have applied their own methods and concepts to the subject matter and the findings have been interrelated as the study proceeded. The investigators involved in each study were different; the names of the participants are listed in the bibliography as coauthors of the papers which described the research in which they took part.

Since physicians first began to observe and describe illness, they have been aware that occurrences which affect the supply of food, the character of the diet, the exposure of people to infectious or toxic agents or to opportunities for injury profoundly influence the amount and kind of illness that they experience. From the earliest times, War, Famine, and Pestilence have been three of the Four Horsemen of the Apocalypse. In the last few centuries less dramatic phenomena, such as technological changes and changes in general economic conditions, have been recognized as influencing patterns of illness. More recently

* This research was supported in part by grants from the Russell Sage Institute of Pathology.

there has been much concern about the effects that may be produced by rapid culture change, social dislocation, and changes in interpersonal relations. It has been recognized that each of these phenomena may be associated with changes in diet and habits, changes in physical activity, and changes in the opportunity for exposure to infection, toxic agents, or trauma; but beyond this there has been a special concern about whether the effects of such changes may be mediated directly by the central nervous system through its influence on the internal biochemical and physiological processes of the individual.

By the end of the decade of the 1940s, it was appreciated that changes in the relation of people to their social group, and in their relation to other people of importance in their lives, might represent stimuli sufficient to cause the central nervous system to initiate physiological reactions that could influence the course of disease. By then, experimental evidence indicated that the mediation of such neurally initiated reactions could be by way of the glands of internal secretion as well as by the effects of the autonomic and voluntary nervous systems (Cannon, 1929; Selye, 1946; Wolff, Wolf, & Hare, 1950). Although the precise details of the processes of this mediation were not yet clear, the evidence already uncovered made it apparent that probably any biochemical process within the cell could be influenced in some manner and to some degree by the central nervous system. Therefore it seemed evident that there would probably be no aspect of human growth, development, or disease that would in theory be immune to the influence of the effect of a man's relation to his social and interpersonal environment. Subsequent experimental investigations over the course of the 1950s and 1960s have filled in many details of the mechanisms involved and have strongly supported the conclusion suggested by the evidence that was available in 1949 (Hinkle, 1969).

During the same period a great deal was learned about the fundamental features of the higher functions of the central nervous system that are relevant to such neurally initiated organic reaction patterns (Hinkle, 1968, 1973). It became quite clear that the substrate for the operations of the nervous system is ''information'' in the technical sense. With the organs of special sense acting as ''sensors,'' the nervous system acquires information from the environment, evaluates this against ''memory'' using a combination of innate and acquired programmatic processes, and elaborates highly organized patterns of response designed to serve the biological needs of the organism. The process is communicative in nature, and the response of the organism is to the biological meaning to the information that it has acquired (Hinkle, 1973). One might say therefore that from a physiological point of view a man may be expected to react to the ''meaning'' of information he obtains from his social environment and not necessarily to the ''objective'' features of it that are discernible by others.

However, to postulate that a man's relation to his social environment, and especially to the important people in his life, may have an important influence on his health is not to say that it actually does so. The relative importance of such relationships as determinants of health and the effect of social change, culture change, and changes in interpersonal relations on the patterns of health of members of human populations must be determined by the direct observation of the effect of such variables on humans. It was an attempt to learn more about this that led us to the study of the effects of the social environment on human populations and induced me to organize, with Dr. Harold Wolff, The Human Ecology Study Program at Cornell University Medical College in 1954. Dr. Wolff and I used the term ''human ecology,'' which was then unfamiliar to the general public, in its literal sense to mean the study of the relationships between men and their environment, our specific interest being the effect of these relationships on human health.

STUDIES OF GROUPS OF SIMILAR PEOPLE IN RELATIVELY UNCHANGING ENVIRONMENTS

Our initial investigations were directed at two population groups whose members shared a very similar and stable social environment (Hinkle & Plummer, 1952; Hinkle & Wolff, 1958). The first of these was a group of career telephone operators in New York City (Hinkle & Plummer, 1952; Hinkle, Plummer, Metraux, Richter, Gittinger, Thetford, Ostfeld, Kane, Goldberg, Mitchell, Leichter, Pinsky, Goebel, Bross, & Wolff, 1957; Hinkle & Wolf, 1958). This was essentially a population of steadily employed semiskilled working women. Most of the women in this population originated from ''blue-collar'' families and had, on the average, a grammar school or part of a high school education. When they married, their husbands were likely to be steadily employed blue-collar workers. Generally they became telephone operators at the age of 17 or 18. The great majority of those who started in this employment dropped out after a few months or several years, but approximately 10% continued to work as telephone operators for 20 years or more. During this time they were covered by a sickness benefit program which enabled them to afford an average level of medical care for members of the community in which they lived. It also provided detailed and continuous records of all of their episodes of illness and all of their days of sickness absences throughout their careers. They were examined initially at the time of their employment, and most of them were examined from time to time after that for any one of a number of reasons. Any illness lasting a few days was covered by a physician's report, and often by a report from a hospital or from an attending physician as well as by diagnostic examinations carried out in the company's medical department. One could therefore obtain quite complete records of the number of days of illness and the number of episodes of sickness disability experienced by these women as well as information about the nature and the cause of the illnesses and the injuries that they had incurred.

For the purposes of our investigation we selected all of the 1327 telephone operators who were employed in one "division" of the company in eastern Manhattan (Hinkle & Plummer, 1952). Within this group there were 336 who had been employed continuously for more than 20 years. We investigated the frequency and the kinds of illness that each of these women had experienced over a 20-year period from her mid-twenties to her mid-forties. When the distribution of illness within the group had been determined, we selected the 20 women who had had the greatest number of days of sickness disability during the 20-year period and the 20 women who had had the smallest number of days of sickness disability. We examined each of these women in detail and we interviewed each at length.

We used a similar procedure to study 1527 blue-collar workmen who represented all of the men employed as installers, repairmen, and skilled workmen concerned with inside telephone equipment who were on the payroll of a similar division of the company on January 1, 1953 (Hinkle, Pinsky, Bross, & Plummer, 1956). These men also came from blue-collar families. On the average they were somewhat better educated than the women, having all or part of a high school education. They had been employed at a somewhat later age, in their early twenties. Approximately 90% of them had remained on the payroll

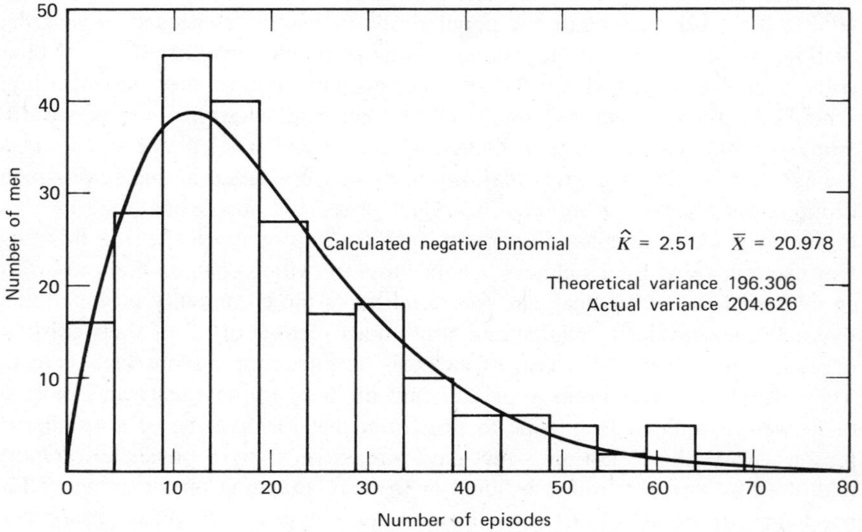

Figure 1. Distribution of 226 American working men by episodes of disabling illness during 20 years, age 20 to 40. (Data from records.)

from the time of their initial employment. The same kinds of medical and attendance records were available for these men. By a random sampling procedure we selected 226 with 20 or more years of service and studied their illnesses over a 20-year period from their mid-twenties to their mid-forties. After rank ordering the men in this sample according to the total number of days of disability during the observation period, we designated for intensive study the 20 men with the greatest number of disabilities and the 20 men with the smallest.

Since the findings from these two populations of men and women were similar, they may be summarized together. Within each of these groups of similar people who had been employed in a similar occupation in the same city over a similar period of life, there had been a marked difference in the amount of illness experienced by the individual members (Hinkle et al., 1956; Hinkle, Plummer, et al., 1957; Hinkle & Plummer, 1952; Hinkle & Wolff, 1957,

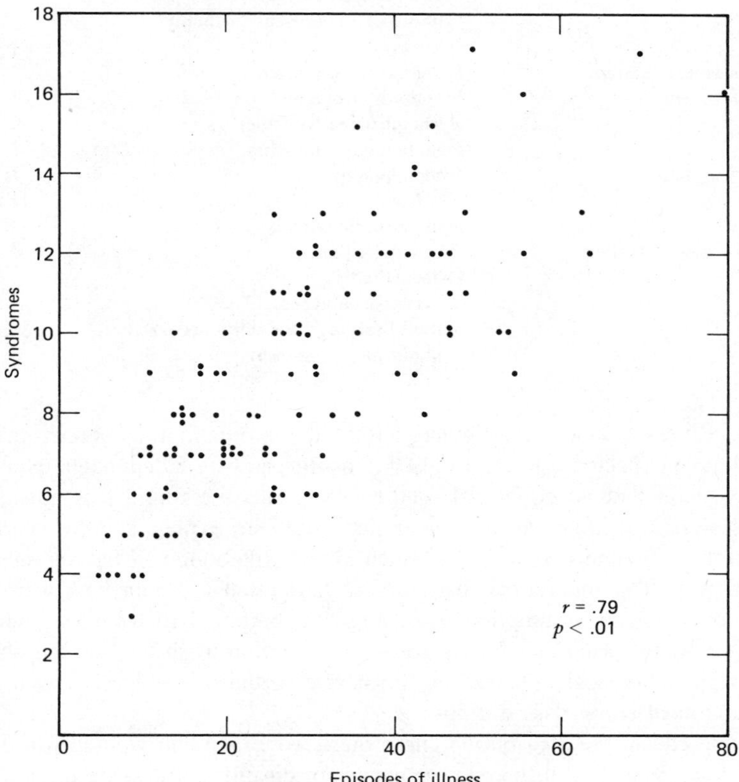

Figure 2. Episodes of illness versus syndromes of 116 American working men during 20 years, age 20 to 40.

Table 1. An "Ill" American Working Woman; Illnesses Experienced from Age 16 to Age 51

"Body System"	Syndrome	Episodes of Disability
Respiratory system	Influenza	1
	Pertussis	1
	Minor upper respiratory infections (approx.)	44
	Severe tonsillitis	2
Gastrointestinal system	Cholecystitis and cholelithiasis	2
	Diaphragmatic hernia	5
	Duodenal diverticulum	0
	Postoperative biliary symptoms	4
	Mucous colitis	4
	Infectious gastroenteritis (chronic, nondisabling constipation, low abdominal pain, "gas," and nausea, present for many years)	3
Cardiovascular system	Essential hypertension	0
Genital system	Myomata of uterus	0
	Dysmenorrhea (chronic)	0
	Postmenopausal flushes, severe	1
Urinary system	Pyelonephritis	1
	Cystitis	1
Blood	Hypochromic anemia	0
Musculoskeletal system	"Low back pain"	4
	Osteoarthritis	1
Head	Vascular headaches (nondisabling headaches occurred about once a month)	2

1958). Illness was not distributed within the group in the manner that one would have expected it to be if episodes of illness were independent events and every person had an equal risk of becoming ill. We found that episodes of illness were distributed in a manner that could be explained only on the assumption that some people had a much greater likelihood of having an illness than others. The theoretical distributions that fitted the data best were those based on such an assumption. The negative binomial distribution, which is based on the assumption of a chi-square distribution of risk, fitted the observations reasonably well, whereas the Poisson distribution, which is based on the assumption of equal risk, did not.

At one end of the distribution curve there were men and women who had no days of sickness disability and no episodes of disabling illness during a 20-year period. There were many men and women who had fewer than five days of

"Body System"	Syndrome	Episodes of Disability
Ears	Otitis media	2
	Ménière's syndrome	1
Eyes	Conjunctivitis	1
Teeth	Dental caries (total extractions)	3
Skin	Urticaria	2
	Cellulitis	1
Breast	Fibroma	1
Metabolic	Obesity	
Mood, thought, behavior	Moderately severe depressions	3
	Anxiety-tension states (symptoms of anxiety, tension, depression chronically present)	5
Accidents	Contusions	8
	Lacerations	3
	Sprains	1
Operations	Cholecystectomy	
	Hysterectomy and oophorectomy	
	Excision of fibroma of breast	
	Total dental extractions	
	Summary	
Total days disabled		1041
Disabling episodes of illness		95
"Major" illnesses		9
Disabling disturbances of mood, thought, and behavior		8
"Body systems" involved		15
Accidents		12
Operations		4

sickness absence and only one or two episodes of disabling illness each year. At the other end of the distribution there were men and women whose total period of sickness disability during the 20 years, from age 20 to 40, amounted to more than 1000 days, or almost three calendar years. Some of these people had had approximately 100 episodes of disabling illness during this time. There was a strong positive correlation between the number of days of sickness disability that a person had experienced, the number of episodes of disabling illness that he had experienced, and the number of different kinds of illnesses he had experienced. The people with the greater amount of disability had had more disease syndromes, more of their organ systems primarily involved in disease, and diseases arising from a greater number of apparent causes. Those with more sickness disability had had more brief illnesses of minor consequences and also more prolonged and life-endangering illnesses. The coefficients of correlation between these different aspects of illness (Spearman's rho) was of the order of +.4 to +.6 in most instances and was significant at the 1% level or beyond.

The direct examination of the most frequently disabled members of these populations confirmed that they were sick people in almost every respect. Table 1 is an example of the medical history of a frequently disabled woman, and Table 2 presents the medical history of a "healthy man."

The illnesses that occurred among the members of these populations generally were not isolated during a few years of the observation period. They tended to occur from time to time throughout the entire 20-year period. If a person had few episodes of illness, these were likely to be scattered over the 20

Table 2. A "Healthy" American Working Man; Illnesses Experienced to Age 59

Birth and early development	Normal
Illnesses experienced before age 12	"Very few colds" "Few childhood diseases" "Mild"
Estimated days of disability before age 12	<12
Illnesses experienced, age 12–24	One minor laceration "Maybe a few colds"

Illnesses by Record and History, Age 24–59

"Organ System"	Syndrome	Episodes
Respiratory	Minor upper respiratory infections	9
Gastrointestinal	Acute gastroenteritis	2
	Hemorrhoid	1
Genitourinary	Varicocele	1
Skin	Furuncle	1
Eyes	Hyperopia	1
Teeth	Caries	1
Accidents	Minor contusions and lacerations	5
Mood, Thought, and Behavior	Anxiety, acute	1

Summary

Total days disabled, 35 years	7
Total episodes of illness	22
"Major" episodes	0
Disabling episodes	5
Episodes of disturbance of mood, thought, and behavior	1
"Organ systems" involved	8
Operations	0

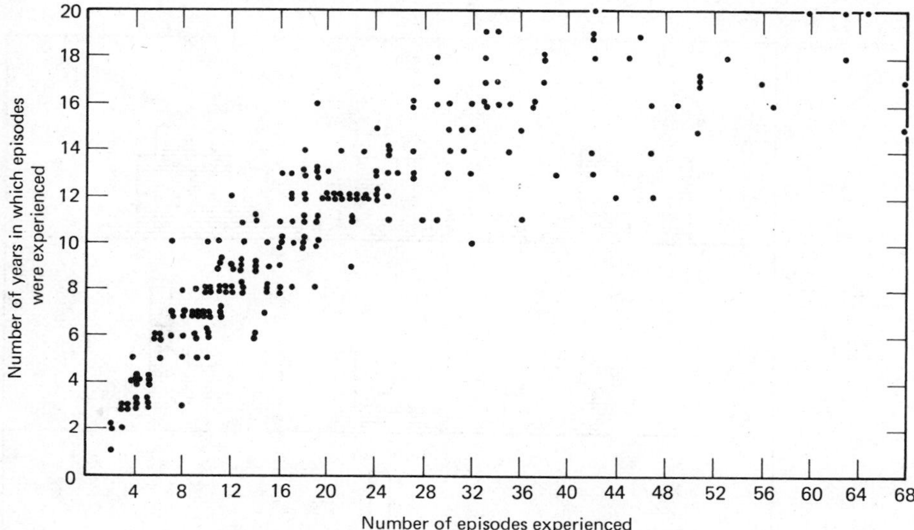

Figure 3. Number of episodes of disabling illness experienced by 226 American working men versus number of years of the 20-year observation period during which the informant experienced a disabling illness. (Data from records.)

years rather than being located within 1 or 2 years. If a person had many episodes of illness, he also was likely to have had some episodes in almost every year of the 20 years. This finding was so consistent that the amount of illness experienced by a subject during one 5-year period could be used to predict the frequency of his illness during the next 15- or 20-year period.

In spite of the overall constancy of patterns of illness, the frequency of the illness experienced by each individual did fluctuate to some extent. Men and women with higher levels of disability did have some years in which they experienced a great many episodes of illness and other years in which they experienced fewer episodes. During periods in which they had many episodes of illness, these illnesses included both "minor" and "major" illness, illnesses involving several organ systems, and illnesses arising from several different primary causes. We referred to these as "clusters of illness." This "clustering" phenomenon was also seen among people who had a moderate level of disability and a moderate frequency of illness and those who had relatively little disability and a low frequency of illness. Those with moderate levels of illness had clusters of moderate size, and those with low levels of illness had clusters of small size; in each instance the clusters contained illnesses of several kinds and of several apparent causes, and sometimes they contained major illness as well as minor illness.

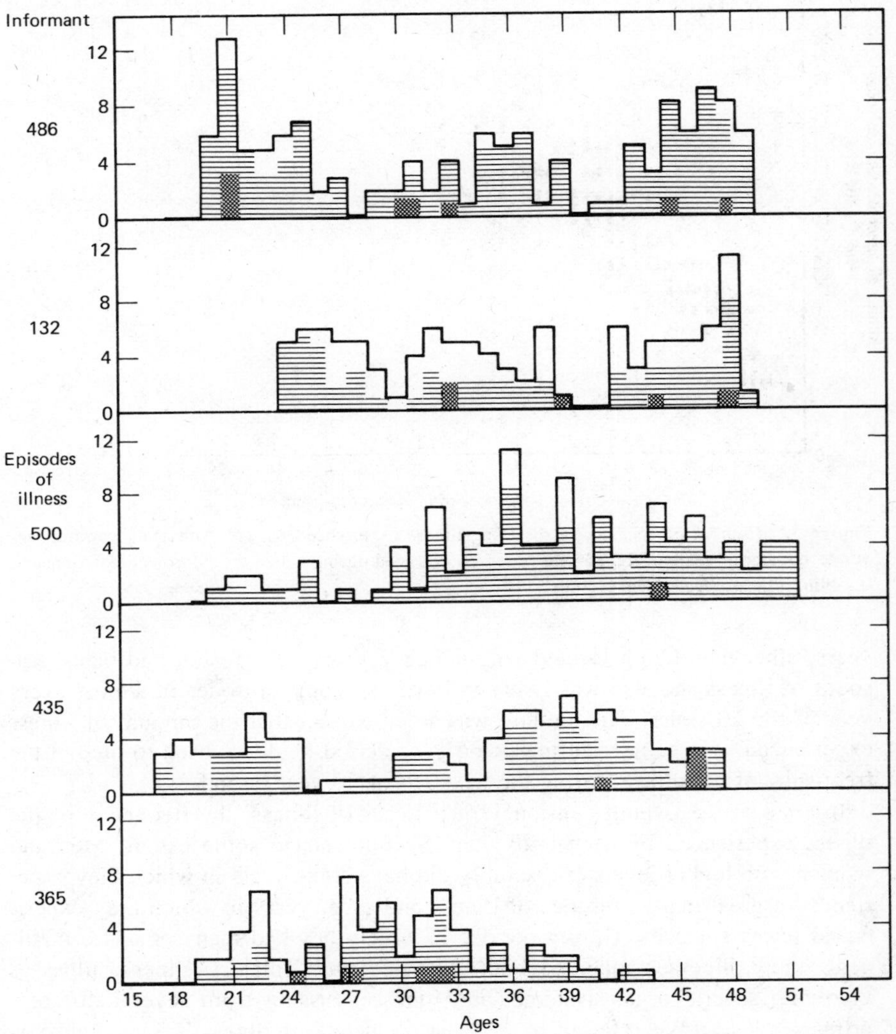

Figure 4. Number of episodes of illness occurring annually in each of five frequently ill American men. The "observation period" begins at time of employment (age 15 to 24 years) and continues to the mid-forties. Major disabling illnesses are in black; minor disabling illnesses are hatched; nondisabling illnesses are in white.

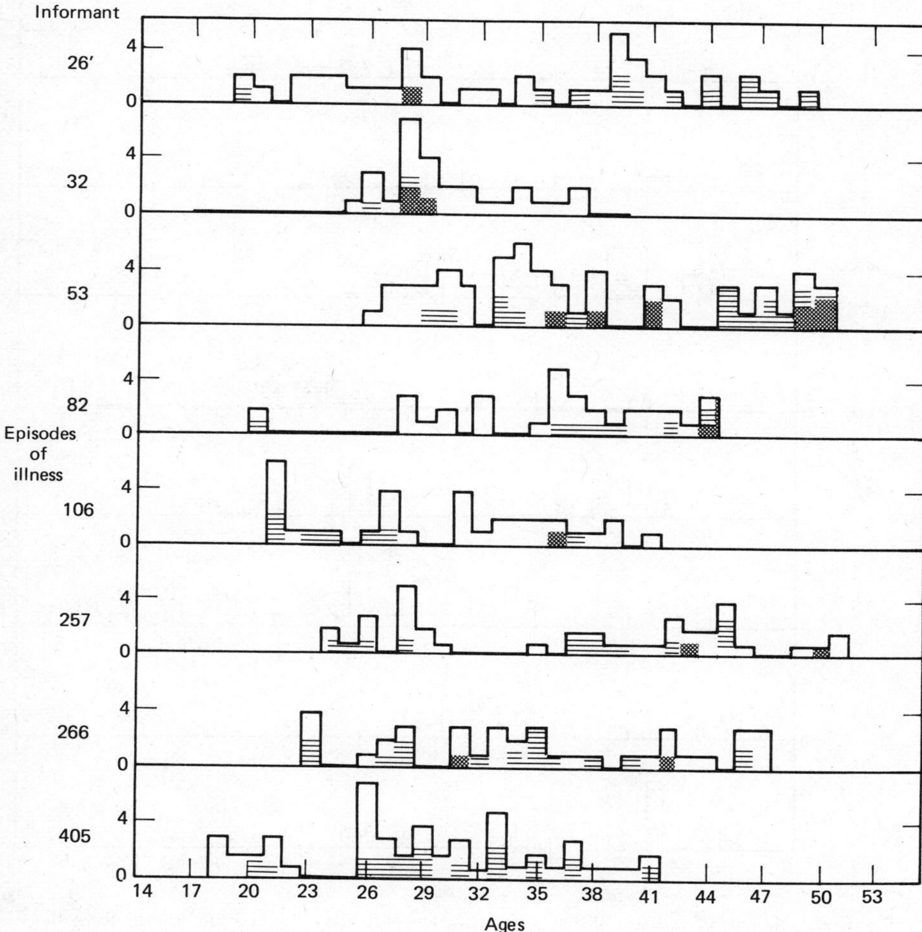

Figure 5. Number of episodes of illness occurring annually in each of eight American men with a moderate frequency of illness.

In summary, we observed that within these two populations, made up of similar people engaged in similar activities in a similar environment over a similar period of life, each individual tended to have his own mean level of frequency of episodes of illness and of sickness disability over a 20-year period, around which his observed episodes of illness fluctuated from year to year. To explain this observation one could set up a null hypothesis that the variations in illness were simply random fluctuations around a mean arising from the interaction of

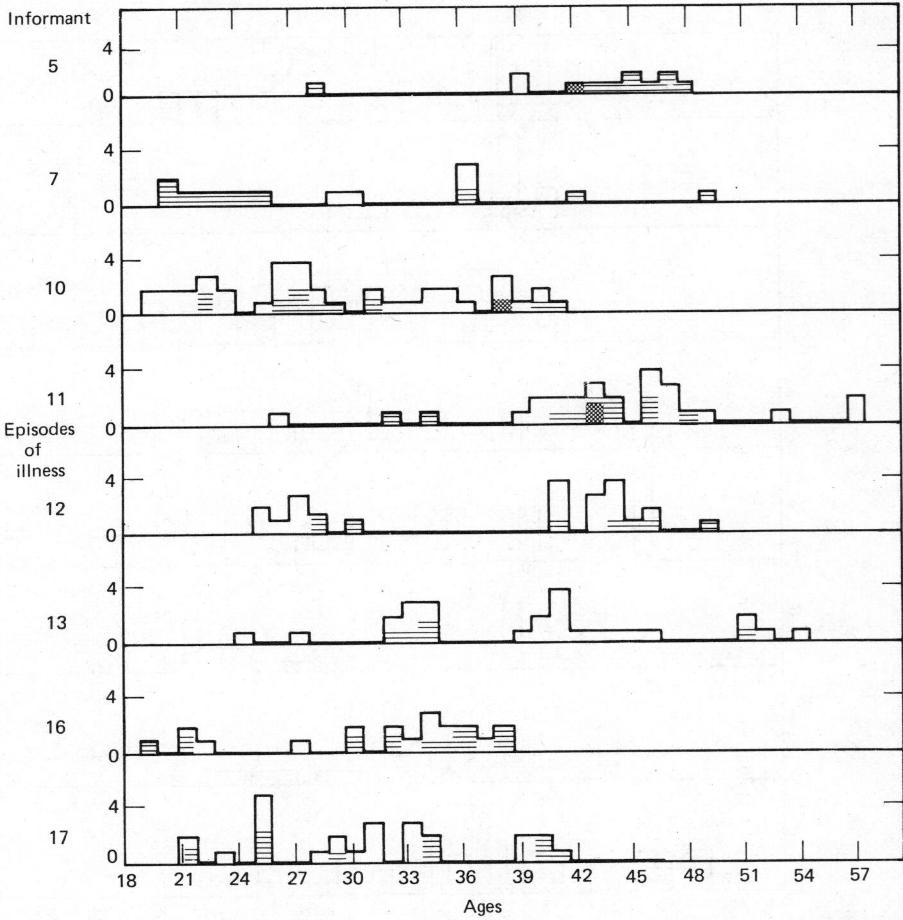

Figure 6. Number of episodes of illness occurring annually in each of eight American men with a low frequency of illness.

many factors. By the statistical analyses of these data alone, we were not able to establish that the null hypothesis is not correct. The explanation for the apparent clustering of illness therefore might simply be the random fluctuation of the many factors that determine the occurrence of any given episode of illness. One does not necessarily have to postulate that the clustering phenomenon has any special significance in any given instance. However, it is also possible that each cluster represents a response of the individual to significant changes in his environment.

We found that the healthy subjects generally were people whose social backgrounds, personal aspirations, and interests coincided with the circumstances in which they found themselves, whereas this often was not the case among those who were frequently ill (Hinkle, 1959; Hinkle, Christenson, Kane, Ostfeld, Thetford, & Wolff, 1958). In other words, the ''healthy'' telephone operators were women of blue-collar backgrounds, with grammar school educations, who liked their work, found it easy and satisfying, liked their families and associates, and were generally content and comfortable with their lot in life. This was often not the case with the frequently ill telephone operators. A number of these were women of disparate backgrounds—for example, women of white-collar background who had had a high school or even part of a college education—and many of them were working at this job not because they liked it but from necessity. They often described it as confining or boring. For various reasons these women were unhappy with their lot in life, with their families, their associates, and their communities. However, we observed that there were some members of the frequently ill group who did not express dissatisfaction with important aspects of their lives, and conversely there were a considerable number of women in the healthy group whose life histories were full of deprivation and difficulties, and whose social backgrounds and aspirations did not show a close fit with their present life situation. We made similar observations within the group of men.

The longitudinal and retrospective life histories obtained from the frequently ill and the moderately ill usually suggested that a cluster of illness coincided with a period when the individual was experiencing many demands and frustrations arising from his social environment or his interpersonal relations. These histories suggested that significant changes in the relations of ill people to their social group and in their relations to other important people in their lives were significantly associated with changes in their health. Retrospectively, the association between ''stressful'' life situations ''perceived'' as ''difficult'' or ''unsatisfying'' was quite consistent within the group of ill people.

On the other hand, some of the information obtained from the ''healthy people'' indicated that a significant proportion of these people had encountered many social demands and difficulties during the observation period and had endured important changes in their lives and in their interpersonal relations without developing illness. For example, one of the ''healthiest'' telephone operators was a woman who had been an effective and well-liked worker throughout the entire period of her employment. As evidenced by medical examinations and interviews, by the testimony of friends and employees, and by the testimony of unbroken records covering the entire period, she had been healthy all of this time. Her history indicated that she was the daughter of an alcoholic longshoreman and a teenaged immigrant girl. She had been born into a household of great poverty, constant conflict, and much turmoil. Four of her nine siblings had died in infancy of infection and apparent malnutrition. When she

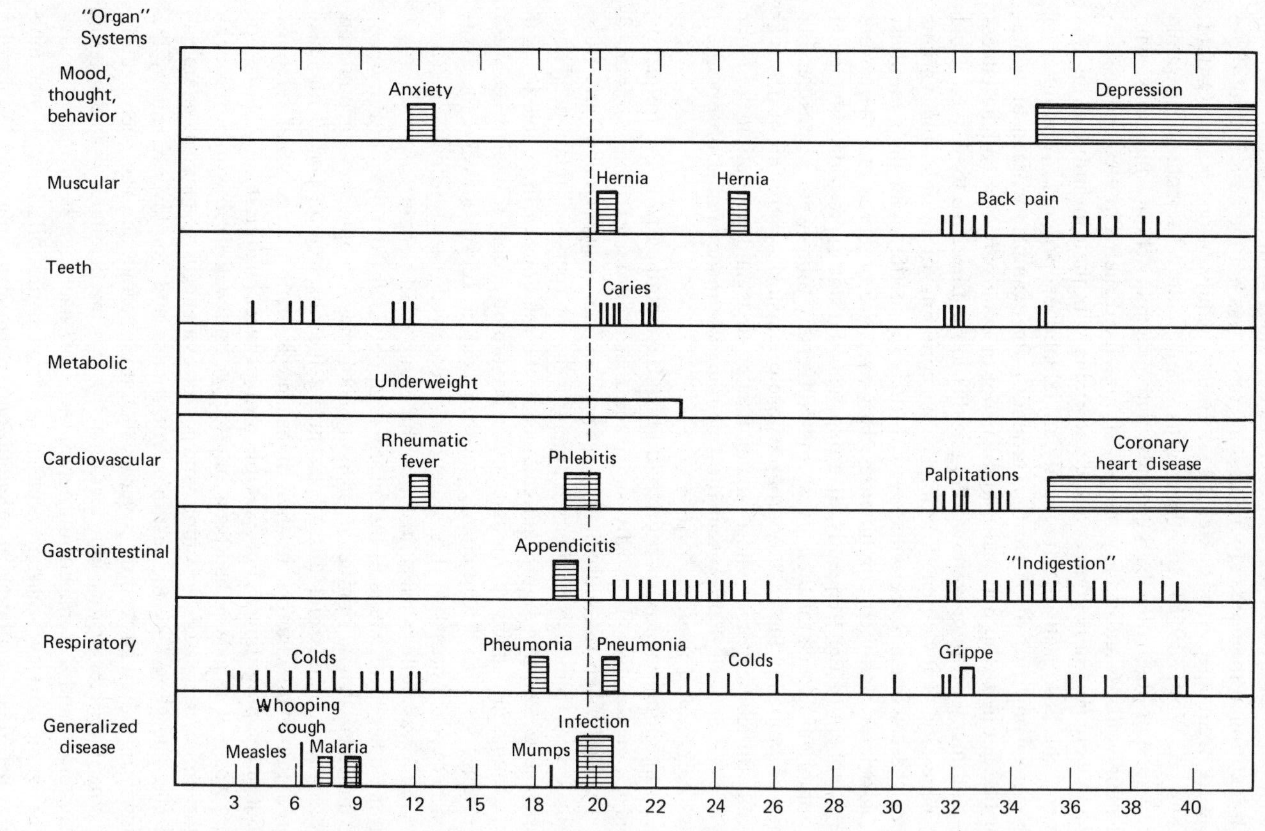

Figure 7. Two "clusters" of illness of American working men—one between ages 18 and 24; the other between ages 32 and 40.

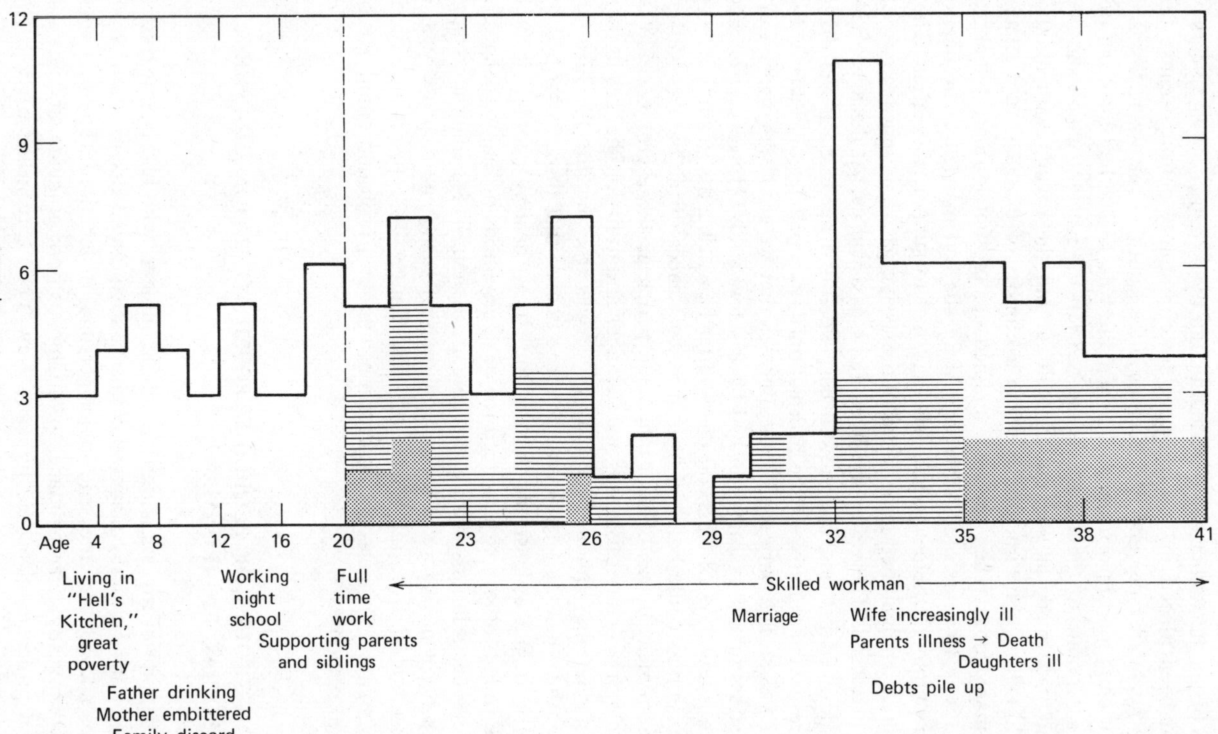

Figure 8. The relation between life situations and clusters of illness of the American working man. The major disabling illnesses are in black; minor disabling illnesses are hatched; nondisabling illnesses are in white.(This figure is reprinted with the permission of the author from L. E. Hinkle, Jr., and H. G. Wolff. Ecological investigations of the relationship between illness, life experience, and the social environment. *Annals of Internal Medicine,* 1958, **49,** 1373–1388.)

was 3 years of age her father had deserted his family. When she was 5 years of age she had been placed in an orphanage by community action because her mother was neglecting her and had been adjudged unfit to raise her. She had had a barren childhood in orphanages. When she was 13 she had been put out to work as a servant. At the age of 16 she had left the place at which she was working and had lived, as she put it, "all around the town" with another teenage girl. During this time she had had a number of casual sexual attachments and many jobs. When she had obtained her present job as a telephone operator she was 23 years old. At the age of 27 she had married a chronically ill, neurotic plumber's helper, whom she had had to support thereafter. They had no children. He had died in her arms of a massive gastric hemorrhage when she was 44 years old. Thereafter she lived alone as a widow. At the age of 54, when we examined her and interviewed her, we found her to be a well-liked and highly respected employee. She had had only two episodes of sickness disability in 31 years. The only significant illnesses that we could uncover on extensive questioning and examination had been a few colds. However, she said she did have a few days of "nervousness" after her husband's death.

Similar examples could be cited from the experiences of the men as well as those of the women. It was evident that some people in these groups could be exposed to major social deprivations and demands and to major changes in their interpersonal relations without becoming ill. It was true that the life histories described by the "healthy" tended to be more benign that those described by the frequently ill, but at least one-third of the "most healthy people" in both groups were found to have experienced major deprivations or major changes in their interpersonal relations during the course of their lives. Interviews suggested that a frequent feature of the personalities of such healthy people was a relative "insulation" from the effects of such changes—a capacity to experience social change, and personal deprivation without a profound emotional or psychological response.

STUDIES OF GROUPS OF PEOPLE EXPOSED TO MAJOR CHANGES IN THEIR SOCIAL ENVIRONMENT

For our next group of investigations we sought subjects who had been exposed to major social and cultural changes and who had experienced separations from their families and communities and major personal dislocations. The first such group that we investigated was made up of Chinese-born graduate students and technical and professional people living in New York City in the early 1950s (Hinkle, Plummer et al., 1957; Hinkle & Wolff, 1957, 1958; Hinkle, Gittinger, Goldberger, Metraux, Ostfeld, Richter, & Wolff, 1957). The members of this group had all been reared in China, in the Chinese cultural milieu. Most of them were the sons or daughters of upper-class Chinese who had been adherents of the Chinese Nationalist Government of Chiang Kai-shek. Most of them had been born between 1910 and 1930. During the course of their lives they had been exposed to the effects of the disruption of the old Chinese culture, the rapid change in Chinese society, the social upheavals, and the geographic dislocation which characterized the first half of the twentieth century in China. Many of them had had personal experience with wars, revolutions, new customs, and technological changes in their homelands. In China they had received, or had been in the process of receiving, a modern Western college education, and in this context they had had to make a personal adaptation to features of two dissimilar cultures.

With few exceptions, they had to come to the United States in the period after World War II, between 1946 and 1949, in pursuit of further educational or professional training, leaving their families behind and planning on returning to careers in China. They had been unable, or unwilling, to return to China after the Chinese Communist accession to power in 1948–1949. Stranded in the United States, most of them had since been in a situation of uncertainty, without assurance of their future status, their occupations, or their careers, and often with no knowledge of the fate of their families, friends, and possessions in China. They were therefore a group who had experienced many major changes in their lives and who had had to make many major adaptations to new social relationships.

When our investigation was initiated in the fall of 1954, there were several thousand such Chinese in the United States. The 100 that we selected for our study were obtained from a list of these people in the New York City area. Our sample was intended to cover the major variables of age, background, intellectual and professional interests within this population. Participants were recruited by a widely respected member of this Chinese group, who selected their names from various lists that were available. He asked those selected to participate in a study that was designed to investigate the personal experiences and problems of adjustment of the members of this group. He told them that they would not be paid for their participation, but that they would receive $25 to cover their expenses during the day that they were with us. Since most of the members of this group were highly interested in making their problems and difficulties better known, and many were, in addition, in financial straits, we were informed that very few of those designated were unwilling to participate. Health was not one of the variables that was considered in the selection of participants and the recruiter was not himself aware that the health of those recruited was one of our major interests. We did not detect any evidence of a major "health bias" in the sample during the course of the examination, but the possibility that there was some bias in relation to health cannot be excluded.

Most of the participants were in their twenties or thirties at the time that we saw them. Medical information was obtained from them by means of a systematic medical history and by examinations carried out by a physician. Each member of the group was also studied with a number of psychological tests, with interviews with psychiatrists, and with interviews with an anthropologist. There were 69 men and 31 women among them.

Of the men, 60 were more than 32 years of age. The distribution of illness among these men during the 20-year period from age 12 to 32 was studied in the same way that we had studied the distribution of illness in the two groups of American working people. This distribution exhibited the same features that we had observed in the two American groups. A small proportion of the group had experienced the greater proportion of the sickness disability and of the episodes of illness. Episodes of illness were distributed within the group in a manner which indicated that some members had a much greater likelihood of experiencing an episode than others. The data rather closely fitted a negative binomial distribution. Those who had had the greatest number of illnesses had the greatest variety of illnesses involving a greater number of their organ systems and a greater number of possible etiological agents. The frequently ill people had had many illnesses throughout the 20-year observation period, whereas the healthy had had few or none. The clustering of illness episodes was less apparent among these Chinese, although it could be seen among the more ill members of the group. It was felt that the retrospective or recall nature of the medical data might have tended to obscure this phenomenon because of the difficulty in recalling relatively minor illnesses and the time of their occurrence.

All of these Chinese had been exposed to culture change, to major social dislocations, and to disruptions of some of their important interpersonal relationships. Since most of them were of upper-class origin, they had been more protected from the physical aspects of the Chinese environment than one would have expected had they been poor, but some of the experiences that they had encountered during wars, revolutions, and other disruptions of their lives had probably provided them with more opportunity for exposure to infectious disease and trauma then one might have expected in a similar group of middle-upper-class Americans. These two factors may have accounted for the relatively greater average frequency of major evidences of disease among the Chinese than among the Americans at a similar age.

Among these Chinese, as among the Americans, there were some who had experienced remarkably little illness during the period from age 12 to 32. An example is a man who was the son of a successful Nationalist officer. Because of civil warfare he had been sent, at the age of 3 with his mother, to live with his grandparents in a rural village. From that time to the age of 10 he had been reared in a traditional Chinese village setting with all that this implied in terms of sanitation and opportunity for infection. He then rejoined his father's household and was sent to modern Chinese primary schools and "middle schools." During World War II he continued his education at Chung-king with great difficulty, experiencing many bombings and much privation and fatigue. Later in the war he left China and accompanied his father to Europe. There, without friends, and in a cultural setting quite strange to him, he entered a medical school, which he attended for three years. In the late 1940s he was taken by his father to the United States and was left alone while his father returned to China. He had tried to get into an American medical school but had failed. After that he made no further attempt to attain an education or to find a job. He lived on the money his father had left with him until this gave out. In the meantime, the Nationalist government on the Chinese mainland collapsed. His father was imprisoned, some of his funds were cut off, and he lost all contact with his relatives in China. Shortly after that his last few thousand dollars were stolen from him. He then moved to another American city and finally obtained a full-time job of a routine nature in a field entirely unrelated to medicine. He found this work dull, but he continued to do it out of necessity. At the time that we saw him, he was living alone in a strange city with no relatives and with few associates of his own background. Throughout all of this he had remained essentially healthy.

Both the psychiatrists and the psychologists who participated in the Chinese study commented upon the apparent "emotional insulation" of the more healthy members of the Chinese group. Major "life changes," which they had expected to create profound emotional reactions in these people, seemed to have rather little effect on them.

We next studied a group of people who were in the midst of a major social and geographic dislocation at the time that we saw them: the refugees from the Hungarian revolution of 1956 (Hinkle, 1956; Hinkle, Kane, Christenson, & Wolff, 1959). In the early summer of 1956 the Hungarian political and social situation had seemed to these people to be much as it had been during the previous 10 years. For most of our future subjects, life then had the rather monotonous and gray flavor of a society in which a state-run economy and a rigid bureaucracy provided an adequate but meager living for most people at the cost of many annoying shortages, delays, and inconveniences, and much perceived limitation of individual initiative. In August and early September of that year an unexpected series of political events led to an uprising in which many young people of the cities, many workers, and a good many soldiers took a leading role. As a result of this uprising the state police and the ruling regime were temporarily overthrown. For several weeks it appeared as if a new and more liberal government would be established; but then an intervention by the Russian army restored the original party group to control. During the period of the revolution, and for some time after the Russian intervention, the border between Hungary and Austria was open. Many people who had been out of sympathy with the Communist state took the opportunity to flee as soon as this opportunity appeared. Others, including many who participated in the revolution, found it necessary to flee for their own safety when the revolution was crushed. By November 1956, approximately 60,000 Hungarians were refugees in Austria. During November and December some 30,000 of them were flown to the United States in a massive airlift. These Hungarians, who had been going about their daily lives in their accustomed manner in July 1956, found themselves in January 1957 to be refugees in a foreign country, in the meantime having passed through a period of profound disturbances of their usual daily routine, a major social upheaval, and a long journey to a new society and a new culture, in which they were separated from their families and from most of the important social groups and interpersonal relationships that they had previously enjoyed.

In the period from December 1956 to June 1957, we studied a group of these people. The demographic characteristics of the population of Hungarian refugees were not specifically known at that time, and it was not possible to draw a probability sample from the group. Therefore we used a procedure like that which we had used with the Chinese. We designated a group of informants who represented the major demographic segments of the refugee population as we knew them and who appeared to be more or less representative of the group from which they were taken. The 69 subjects included students, professionals, teachers and other intellectuals, skilled and semiskilled workers, and young people between the ages of 15 and 25 from the large cities. The procedures used to study these people included a careful and extensive chronological life history, a detailed history of all illnesses, medical examinations, interviews with sociologists, psychologists, and a cultural anthropologist, and a series of psychological tests. The whole investigation required two days of each subject's time.

We found that during the previous 10 years, the rate at which these Hungarians had experienced episodes of illness of many types, both physical and psychological, was higher than that which we had seen in any other comparable group including the Chinese. These people also expressed a profound degree of insecurity and frustration about the social environment in which they had been living. The personal historical evidence suggested that when these people had had difficulty in making a satisfactory adaptation to their social environment in the past, and most notably during the periods when they felt insecure, frustrated, or threatened, they had had an increased number of episodes of many varieties of illness. This again had been especially true of those who had been frequently ill.

On the other hand, the physical dislocation and the social, emotional, and psychological changes that they had experienced during the revolution and subsequent flight had been accompanied by an improvement in their general health and well-being in most instances. In spite of the difficulties they had encountered, there was an element of pleasurable excitement and anticipation—in some instances amounting almost to a euphoria—in their attitude toward their recent and present experiences. When each person's medical condition during the six months of recent acute change was compared with his own previous medical history, the majority of these people were found to have experienced a period of relative or absolute well-being during the period of their acute dislocation in the months before we saw them.

Among these Hungarians, as among the members of the groups that we studied previously, we found that individuals differed markedly in their general susceptibility to illness. Those having the greatest number of episodes had experienced more types of illness involving more of their organ systems, falling into more "causal" categories. The frequently ill people also had experienced a greater number of disturbances of mood, thought, and behavior.

There were some members of this group who had lived through remarkably diverse and demanding life situations, including significant changes in their social position, their physical environment, and their family relationships, with very little illness. There were others who had experienced many illnesses in settings which appeared to be much more benign. Such differences in susceptibility to illness appeared to be dependent in part on the physical characteristics of the individual, including both his genetically determined susceptibilities to disease and his previous experience with the infectious, traumatic, toxic, and other damaging agents from the physical environment which had helped to create the various kinds of illness that he had experienced. In this, as in the other investigations, there was also evidence from the personality studies which indicated that those who had experienced the greater amount of illness had, in general, perceived their environment as more threatening, challenging, demanding, and frustrating than the healthier people. The more healthy members of the group tended to describe their life situations in a much more benign manner, even though these experiences "objectively," in the eyes of the examiner, seemed to be very like the experiences of the frequently ill.

During the period from 1954 to 1956 we had the opportunity to observe a third group of people who had experienced extreme degrees of social dislocation and deprivation, threat and insecurity, often in a setting of extreme physical hardship. This opportunity was provided by a review of the experience of American prisoners of war in North Korea at the time of the Korean conflict, and by a review of the methods that were used by the state police systems of Eastern European countries, and in China, for the arrest and interrogation of people suspected of political crimes, for their subsequent preparation for trial, and the process of their "reeducation" during their imprisonment (Hinkle, 1961; Hinkle & Wolff, 1956). This was not a study of a population sample but an opportunity to review data from many sources and to see and study in detail some people who had experienced these procedures or had helped to carry them out.

The evidence from all sources indicated that the sudden arrest of a person suspected of a political crime and his total isolation and systematic interrogation in a setting of great fear and uncertainty predictably produced, in many subjects, serious signs of disorganization of the highest integrative functions of the brain, accompanied by confusion, pliability, and suggestibility, sleep disturbance, and evidence of disturbances of various bodily functions. The effect of this procedure could be greatly enhanced if it was accompanied by the deliberate manipulation of the subjects' position or activity, his food and fluid intake, his sleep cycle, the temperature of his surroundings, or painful or damaging physical harassment.

The psychological effects of these procedures were not dependent on the manipulation of the physical environment of the prisoner or the infliction of pain or injury. A substantial disorganization might occur quite in the absence of any of these, provided the total social isolation and the other features of the interrogation procedure were carried out. On the other hand, the physical manipulation of the subject or of his environment, if sufficiently intense and prolonged, had certain unavoidable physiological consequences, whereas the manipulation of the social and psychological milieu, taken alone, did not necessarily have such consequences. Subjects who were familiar with the procedures of the state police, who had experienced social isolation and interrogation before, and who felt fairly secure about what could and could not be done to them under the circumstances might endure the interrogation process with all of the isolation and threat that accompanied it indefinitely without adverse effect (Bone, 1957).

PROSPECTIVE INVESTIGATIONS OF THE RELATION BETWEEN DISCRETE AND DEFINABLE LIFE CHANGES AND SPECIFIC MANIFESTATIONS OF ILLNESS

Our next investigations were aimed at obtaining information by the use of ongoing "prospective" observations of carefully defined population groups under circumstances in which both the manifestations of illness and the nature of the change in social relationships or interpersonal relationships could be defined in advance and observed as the events occurred. The first of these efforts was aimed at the short-term observation of factors affecting the occurrence of acute episodes of illness (Hinkle, Christenson, Benjamin, Kane, Plummer, & Wolff, 1961). We undertook to study the common cold and acute gastroenteritis, illnesses that take the form of discrete episodes and occur with great frequency in the general population of the United States.

To study these phenomena we designated at random 24 telephone operators from a group of 737 who worked in close proximity with each other in two large air conditioned rooms of a building on East 56th Street in New York City. Since they were associated with each other closely and traveled to work in winter on crowded public buses and subways, there was good reason to believe that all of these women would have a widespread exposure to any of the 70 or more viruses that were then known to cause the common cold syndrome and might be prevalent in the community. Having designated our subjects, we persuaded them to be examined and to allow us to observe them at weekly intervals, while photographing their nasal mucus membranes, observing the redness, engorgement, and secretion in their noses and throats, obtaining bacterial cultures and throat washings for viral agents, and obtaining serum samples for antibody determinations once a month.

Each subject kept a diary of her symptoms and of her important activities during the week. At each weekly visit this was reviewed with her. The 24 women were observed for six months throughout the winter of 1959–1960, from mid-October to mid-April.

At the time of the first examination we found the same skewed distribution of illness among the women in this sample that we observed in other population groups. Records indicated that during the 10 years prior to our study a small proportion of these women had had a great many illnesses of many varieties and that a much larger proportion of them had had few or no illnesses. This distribution applied to respiratory illnesses as well as to other kinds of illness. During the six-month observation period all of the women were closely exposed to each other and to the other women in the building. Presumably they had equal exposure to the respiratory pathogens that were present in the community at large. In spite of this, respiratory illnesses were not randomly distributed among them. Past experience with respiratory illness predicted present and observed experience to an unexpected degree. Those women who had had a great many respiratory illnesses in the past had several respiratory illnesses during the observation period, and most of those who had had few such illnesses in the past had few episodes of illness during the observation period. The same held for episodes of acute gastroenteritis.

When an epidemic of the A2 or "Asian" strain of influenza virus appeared in the city during the winter, it caused a marked increase in the number of respiratory illnesses among all the women who worked in the building. The women in our study group experienced an increased frequency of illness at the same time. A number of those who had had many respiratory illnesses in the past came down with acute florid episodes of pneumonia or of the common cold syndrome. Those who had had fewer illnesses in the past developed colds or gastroenteritis and some others had minor symptoms; some developed antibodies indicating that they had been infected by the virus but had no evidence of illness at all.

The events and situations that these women encountered during the course of

Table 3. Response to Infection with Asian Strain of Influenza Virus

Informant	Disabling Respiratory Illnesses		Serological Evidence of Infection	Illness Observed		
	Previous Five Years	Observation Period		Disabling Episodes	Episodes not Disabling	No Episodes
3F	CCCCCCCCCCCFFGG	CFF				
4F	CCCCCCCCCCCGGGG	FG				
15F	CCCCCCCCFGGGGGG	CF				
14F	CCCCCCFFGGG	CFF	•	F		
13F	CCCCCGGGG	CCGG				
1F	CCCCFGG	C				
10F	CCCFGGG	CFF	•	F		
12F	CCCGGG	GG	•	G		
17F	CCFFGG					
2F	CCCG		•		C	
16F	CCFG					
19F	CCCG	C	•	C		
20F	CCCF	C	•	C		
44F	CFGG		•		C	
47F	CCCF		•			O
40F	CFG	CG	•	G		
45F	CCF		•			O
7F	F	C				
9F	G		•			O
21F	C					
11F						
22F						
23F						
24F			•		C	

C = common cold.
F = influenza.
G = gastroenteritis.

the winter were, for the most part, the mundane and various changes in interpersonal relations and in ordinary activities that people usually encounter during their daily lives: minor conflicts with other members of their families, disputes with landlords, breakdowns of plumbing or electrical appliances, or a "crisis" when the dog had puppies on the living room rug. Occasionally there was a sickness, a death in the family, or, conversely, a vacation trip or a happy Christmas reunion. From the reports of the women given at the time of these events, it appeared that those which caused sadness or weeping or periods of sexual excitement (either of which might cause an increase in the engorgement and secretion of the nasal mucosa) were likely to be followed by an acute respiratory illness, provided an adequate exposure to a viral agent occurred at the same time. Other kinds of pleasurable excitement and arousal, like that created by the preparation for a long-anticipated winter vacation, also seemed to set the stage for the occurrence of an acute respiratory illness. However, the number of instances of these phenomena was too small to allow one to draw any firm conclusions from the data.

It was clearly desirable to study a larger population over a longer period of time, to have a large proportion of the members of this population systematically exposed to clearly definable and potentially major changes in social and interpersonal relations, and to have a clearly identifiable major illness as the dependent variable. Therefore we turned to the population of 270,000 men employed by the Bell System throughout the continental United States. These men, mostly of northern and western European stock, in the age range of 20 to 65, are employed in a limited number of highly specifiable jobs. Almost all of them are career employees who enter this system in their early twenties. Most of them continue in its employment until they retire or die. They are covered by a uniform system of sickness and retirement benefits, and records of their health, attendance, and occupational experiences are maintained in a standard manner throughout the system.

The Bell System employs men of two sorts: 250,000 of its male employees have all or part of a high school education. The great majority of these men enter the system as semiskilled blue-collar workers and soon become skilled craftsmen who install, repair, or maintain telephone equipment; but some of them enter as white-collar clerical employees. As nonmanagement employees, they earned up to $8000 a year at the time that our study began. Approximately half of these "no-college" men become foremen or other first-line supervisors before they retire, and a great many of them become second level supervisors. Only a relatively small proportion attain the highest levels of management, but the number from which they are drawn is so great and the system is so large that 321 men, or approximately one-fifth, of all the managers and executives of level five and above were of no-college background in 1963. These managers and executives earned from $33,000 to more than $45,000 per year at that time, and they presided over organizations of considerable technical complexity, employing thousands of men, and capitalized at many millions of dollars. By the commonly accepted criteria for American social class, men who have attained such managerial or executive positions have attained upper-middle-class or upper-class status.

The remaining 20,000 employees of the Bell System are recruited as young men who have recently graduated from college after four years of education beyond secondary school. They are hired by the System with the expectation that they will become managers, but with no guarantee that they will do so. These college men start out in nonmanagement jobs alongside the no-college workmen as trainees. Within a few years most of them have attained the first level of management. From this point on the System makes no formal distinction between them and the no-college men. College and no-college men compete for the same managerial jobs. At least half of the college men ultimately attain the third level of management, and a disproportionate number of them become senior managers and executives. As a result, they constitute four-fifths of the upper level managers of the Bell System.

The Bell System population thus can be used to study men of two different social backgrounds who are engaged in similar occupations throughout the nation. Some men from each background are upwardly and geographically mobile, whereas others are not. This system also keeps records of the causes of death and the sickness absences of all men in the employee group. One of the most clearly definable major causes of death and disability in this system is coronary heart disease. Death rates and attack rates for coronary heart disease among these men are comparable to those for all American men. It is therefore possible to investigate the extent to which the experiences of mobile men might influence the incidence and prevalence of coronary heart disease among them, as well as to estimate what effect the social class backgrounds and present social categories of men might have on their likelihood of developing this disease.

Our first effort in this direction was the investigation of the relation between certain highly specific occupational experiences and the occurrence of coronary heart disease in an age cohort of men selected from a typical Bell System company (Hinkle, Benjamin, Christenson, & Ullmann, 1966; Lehman, Schulman, & Hinkle, 1967). For this purpose we selected the New Jersey Bell Telephone Company, which is near the median for all companies in the industry in size, in rural-urban distribution, in the age of its employees, and in the proportion of those on the payroll who are men. The cohort was selected by obtaining a complete payroll from the company for January 1, 1935, and designating all men on this list who had been born between January 1, 1902, and December 31, 1908, and had been hired between January 1, 1923, and December 31, 1930. Of the 1160 men so designated, 274 were college men and 886 were no-college men. On January 1, 1935, the median age of the men in this cohort was 30 years. With perhaps one or two exceptions, every man in the group could be considered to be "at risk" for the development of clinical coronary heart disease at that time. We were able to trace 1152 of these men from 1935 to 1965, that is, from age 30 to age 60, and to determine who among them had died from coronary heart disease during this period.

From occupational records we were able to abstract data on nine categories of experience bearing on the organizational and social mobility of these men: the highest rank attained, the number of promotions, the number of job changes, the number of different job titles, the number of demotions, the number of company departments served in, the number of work location changes, the number of transfers to other companies in the industry, and the line-staff managerial experience. The basic unit of measurement was the number of changes that had occurred per unit time. To determine the possible relationship between these indicators of organizational mobility and death due to coronary heart disease, the mobility experience of those who died from this disease before age 60 was compared with the experience of otherwise similar men in the cohort who had equivalent lengths of exposure within the company. The details of this matching procedure were described elsewhere (Hinkle, et al., 1966). Each man who died of coronary heart disease was matched with a man who died of another cause and whose age at death and year of death was closest to that of the coronary man. He was also matched to another man who survived and the survivor's experience over the same period of years was compared with that of the man who died. The "matched trios" were contrasted in terms of the nine dimensions of organizational mobility discussed above.

A "principal component analysis" was used in the study of the data. Two factors were isolated which accounted for approximately 60% of the observed variation in mobility. The first, or mobility factor, was made up of five highly intercorrelated dimensions: final level attained, number of promotions, number of job changes, number of job titles, and line-staff experience. The second, or immobility factor, was composed of four dimensions: number of demotions, number of job changes, number of job location changes, and number of job title changes. This accounted for about 15% of the variation.

Two hypotheses were tested: (1) Those who died from coronary heart disease had experienced a greater amount of organizational mobility than either the men who died from other causes or the survivors; (2) Those who died from coronary heart disease had experienced a greater amount of immobility than either those who died from other causes or survivors. Neither of these hypotheses was substantiated. The mobility and the immobility scores of the men who died from coronary heart disease were not significantly different from the scores of those who died of other causes or from the scores of those who survived. When the three groups of men were compared on each dimension of experience singly, the findings were the same. In no case had the coronary men had mobility experiences significantly different from the experiences of men who died of other causes or of those who survived.

The relation between the development of coronary heart disease and exposure to organizational, social, and geographic mobility, and to the "life experiences" and changes in interpersonal relationships which accompany these, was also investigated by the prospective study of the entire Bell System population of 270,000 men (Hinkle, Whitney, Lehman, Dunn, Benjamin, King, Plakun, & Flehinger, 1968; Hinkle, 1972).

In 1961 arrangements were made so that the clinical data on each new illness and death of a man in the System that was reported under Rubric 420 of the seventh edition of the *International Classification of Diseases** was investigated and reviewed by a company physician according to a prearranged schedule, and these data were reported each quarter to our staff. Elaborate arrangements were made to assure the accuracy and completeness of the reporting and the uniform classification of the episodes (Hinkle et al., 1968). For five years, from January 1, 1962, to December 31, 1966, all events of coronary heart disease that occurred in the System were analyzed. There were 4306 first events (new cases) and 1839 deaths.

When specific attack rates and death rates for men in various categories were computed, the data indicated that the most upwardly mobile men, those men without college education who had risen to the highest managerial and executive levels of the organization, had coronary attack rates no higher than those of men of the same age and length of service who had remained as workmen and foremen. Even men who had come into the system without a college education and who had obtained a college education by going to school at night, while at the same time rising to become managers before the age of 40, had overall attack rates no higher than other men—although there was a suggestion that they may have experienced a small excess of new events and death during the period when they were age 30 to 40, at a time when they were actually going to college and working nights as well as days.

Certain categories of occupational experience which could be clearly identified and were generally regarded as highly demanding for those exposed to them were studied in more detail. The effect of promotion to a higher level of responsibility was studied by examining the coronary attack rates among managers in relation to the amount of time that had passed since they were last promoted. It was found that men who had been promoted to new responsibilities within the past year had had no higher attack rates than those who had been promoted less recently. The effect of transfer from one department to

* Rubric 420, Seventh Edition of International Classification of Diseases: *Arteriosclerotic Heart Disease, Including Coronary Disease*. Included under this Rubric are coronary occlusion, coronary insufficiency, and angina pectoris, as well as other manifestations of coronary heart disease.

another, which is regarded as requiring a major adaptation for many men, was also not associated with an increase in the attack rate. The effect of transfer from one company to another, which was looked upon as probably the most demanding sort of occupational experience that one might encounter, since it required the transfer of families to new locations, and the uprooting of family and community relationships, as well as changes in working relationships and new responsibilities, was studied also. It was found that this was not associated with any increase in the coronary attack rate.

STUDIES NOW IN PROGRESS

Since 1962 we have been following prospectively 838 men between the ages of 40 and 65 (Hinkle, 1972; 1973). Each of these men was examined intensively at the time of entry into the study, and each has been followed carefully at intervals since that time. Of these men, 301 were a stratified sample selected from the cohort of men in the New Jersey Bell Telephone Company described in the preceding section. Another 127 men were in their late thirties and early forties designated from other companies in the Bell System in other parts of the country. The most recent 400 are men from 21 industries and 3 labor unions in the New York metropolitan area. The social categories of these men range from lower blue-collar, unskilled workmen to upper white-collar executives and professional men. The medical data include intensive diagnostic procedures to determine the presence of evidence of coronary heart disease, hypertensive disease, pulmonary disease, and such metabolic abnormalities as diabetes mellitus, gout, and hyperlipidemia as well as complex efforts to determine the abnormalities of the cardiac conduction system which may be involved in the phenomenon of sudden death. Social and psychological data have been obtained by interview schedules developed by our sociological associates and carried out by them. Psychological testing has been carried out through the use of large batteries of standard, clinical, psychological tests of a paper-pencil variety, administered by the psychological associates. In all groups, data on daily activities and events were obtained from round-of-life schedules, from employment records, and from questionnaire-guided interviews at frequent intervals.

The observations of the people in these groups up to the present indicate the following:

1. New cases of coronary heart disease rarely if ever occur except among men who have some combination of hyperlipidemia, abnormalities of carbohydrate metabolism, hypertension, cigarette smoking, and a family history of this disease. In many instances these people also have preexisting evidence of arteriosclerosis in other vessels.

2. Unexpected sudden death rarely if ever occurs to men who do not have preexisting evidence of coronary heart disease, hypertensive heart disease, pulmonary disease with cardiac involvement, or alcoholism, especially if they are heavy cigarette smokers.

3. The life experiences of people who develop new events of coronary heart disease and of those who die suddenly are quite similar to the life experiences of their matched controls who do not develop the disease or die.

4. Acute events of coronary heart disease and sudden death often occur in a setting of hard work, difficult interpersonal relations, and fatigue. They often are precipitated by activities such as arguments or emotional upsets, unexpected exertion, or sexual intercourse. These activities do appear to precipitate acute events of myocardial infarction in people with preexisting metabolic abnormalities, atherosclerosis, hypertension, or heart disease, and they seem to precipitate fatal events in people with preexisting serious heart disease: but when people are without evidence of predisposing factors or cardiovascular disease, such activities seem to have no untoward consequences.

CONCLUSIONS AND COMMENTS

The observations that I have described suggest several conclusions. The first conclusion is that in populations of similar people who share similar experiences over comparable periods of one or two decades, between the ages of 10 and 50, there will be a few people who have a great many episodes of disabling illness and days of disability, some who have a moderate number, many who have very little, and some who have none. The manifestations of illness will be distributed among the members of these populations in a manner which indicates that some people have a much greater risk of becoming ill than others. The people at greatest risk will have more days of disability, more episodes of disability, more kinds of illness (more ''disease syndromes''), involving more organ systems, attributable to a greater variety of causal agents, and including more major and life-endangering illnesses as well as more minor and transient episodes. The patterns of illness created by differences in risk are likely to continue over periods as long as 20 years or more, with the frequently ill continuing to have much illness and the less frequently ill continuing to be relatively healthy.

The explanations for these phenomena appear to arise partly from the biological characteristics of ''illness'' and partly from arbitrary and empirical procedures that are used to define and classify the manifestations of illness. Diseases or disease syndromes, as these are commonly defined medically, are not discrete and independent entities. Some diseases such as coronary heart disease are manifestations of other diseases such as generalized arteriosclerosis. Some acute illnesses such as congestive heart failure may be manifestations of any one of a number of diseases. The occurrence of an episode of one disease increases the likelihood that episodes of other diseases will occur. Thus obesity increases the likelihood that latent diabetes mellitus will become manifest; the presence of diabetes mellitus increases the likelihood that infections of the urinary tract will occur; infections of the urinary tract increase the likelihood that serious kidney disease will occur; kidney disease increases the likelihood that hypertension will occur; hypertension increases the likelihood that coronary heart disease will occur; and so on. Thus the presence of one disease may imply the presence of other diseases and beget yet other diseases.

The classification of diseases by their organ system of primary occurrence is an arbitrary and convenient way of grouping diseases, but it is artificial. Few if any disease processes are confined to only one organ system. Diabetes mellitus, for example, which is commonly classified as a disease of the metabolic system, is a biochemical disorder that involves cells in every part of the body and produces major manifestations in the kidneys, the blood vessels, the peripheral nerves, the eyes, and the gastrointestinal tract. The result of this arbitrary method of classification is that anyone who has many syndromes, or episodes of illness, will almost by definition have manifestations of illness that involve many organ systems, and the number of organ systems will increase as the number of episodes of illness increases.

The division of diseases according to their primary causes is also arbitrary and artificial. Every disease has more than one cause. Diabetes mellitus is a genetic disease in the sense that the capacity to have it is based upon a genetic susceptibility; however, it is also a dietary disease because often it does not become manifest unless the subject becomes obese, and its manifestations may disappear if the total calories and the carbohydrates in the diet are restricted. Diabetes is also a degenerative disease in the sense that it often becomes manifest only as old age approaches, and with increasing age more and more people show evidence of its presence. It is not an infectious disease, but it increases the likelihood that infections will occur. It is not a disorder of mood, thought, or behavior, but it may first appear in the setting of a depressive illness and may become very much worse in people who are upset by profound interpersonal conflict, and so on. People who have many episodes of illness are thus likely to have illnesses of many apparent primary causes.

The occurrence of minor and transient episodes of illness increases the likelihood that major and life-endangering episodes of illness will occur. The common cold, for example, is a minor and transient episode of illness. A person may experience several hundred colds in his life without any adverse effect. However, when people have colds, they are distinctly more likely to develop major and potentially life-endangering illnesses such as bronchial pneumonia, lobar pneumonia, asthma, or congestive heart failure. Even a very benign condition such as a migraine headache carries a small but real increase in the risk of having a stroke.

Finally, many people have congenital, or acquired, predispositions to have disorders of one or another of their organ systems—for example, a propensity for hyperfunction of the nasorespiratory mucosa, with repeated episodes of vasomotor rhinitis, ''allergic'' rhinitis, profuse and prolonged colds, and bronchitis, or even bronchial pneumonia. Others have comparable phenomena involving their gastrointestinal tracts, skin, or other organ systems.

The second conclusion that may be drawn is that when people have preexisting susceptibilities to illness, or have established patterns of illness, the frequency of their illnesses and the number and kind are likely to change when there are significant changes in their social or interpersonal relationships.

The apparent reasons for this have been mentioned several times. Changes in significant social or interpersonal relationships are very often accompanied by changes in habits, changes in patterns of activity, changes in the intake of food and medication, and changes in exposure to potential sources of infection or trauma. They are also frequently associated with changes in mood and with physiological changes directly mediated by the central nervous system. Any or all of these might affect the frequency or severity of illness.

Our observations also lead to the conclusion that some people live through major changes in social relationships, major deprivations and dislocations, and major changes in interpersonal relations and exhibit little if any overt evidence of illness. This phenomenon appears to have two explanations. First, some of these people do not appear to have the preexisting patterns of illness or the necessary physical factors of susceptibility which render them vulnerable to the occurrence of illness. Acute changes in social or interpersonal relationships are much more likely to be accompanied by acute episodes of illness when subjects have preexisting and well-established susceptibilities to illness for other reasons. Apparently the physiological concomitants of adaptations to social and interpersonal change are of such magnitude that they may easily precipitate illness among people in whom illnesses are already quite likely to occur, but they do not readily precipitate illness in others who have no special preexisting susceptibilities.

Moreover, some people who remain free from illness in the face of major life changes appear to have psychological characteristics which help to ''insulate'' them from the effects of some of their life experiences. The anthropologists, psychiatrists, psychologists, sociologists, and physicians who were involved in our various studies of American working people, of Chinese, of Hungarians, and of political prisoners were very different, yet they all commented on the fact that the healthiest members of our samples often showed little psychological reaction to events and situations which caused profound reactions in other members of the group. The loss of a husband or wife, the separation from one's family, the isolation from one's friends, community, or country, the frustration of apparently important desires, or the failure to attain apparently important goals produced no profound or lasting reaction. They seemed to have a shallow attachment to people, goals, or groups, and they readily shifted to other relationships when established relationships were disrupted. There was an almost "sociopathic" flavor to some of them. Others endured prolonged deprivations, boredom, or sustained hard work without obvious adverse effects.

Many of these people displayed a distinct awareness of their own limitations and their physiological needs. They behaved as if their own well-being were one of their primary concerns. They avoided situations that would make demands on them if they felt they could not, or did not want to meet these demands. An employed man or woman might refuse a promotion because he did not want the increased responsibility, refuse a transfer because it was "too much trouble," or refuse to work overtime because it might be too tiring—despite the fact that each of these changes might have increased his income, increased his prestige, or increased his opportunity to get ahead in his occupation. As family members, such people might refuse to take the responsibility for an aged or ill parent or sibling, giving as an explanation a statement implying that it would be "too much for me." If such a person learned that family members or relatives in a foreign country were in need, or were being oppressed, he might give little evidence of concern about this, and he might explain, if asked, that he saw no reason to worry about it since there was nothing he could do about it. If it was the lot in life of such a person to be poor, or to live alone, he seemed to feel no need to be unhappy about this or to rebel against it. Such psychological characteristics, and the attitudes that accompanied them, appear to play a role in the "immunity" of some people to the effects of deprivation and change.

A fourth conclusion is that the effect of a social change, or a change in interpersonal relations, on the health of an individual cannot be defined solely by the nature of the change itself. The effect depends on the physical and psychological characteristics of the person who is exposed to the change and on the circumstances under which it is encountered.

This has been observed in every population that we studied. The explanation appears to lie in the many biological, social, and psychological phenomena that we have been discussing. Changes that have been associated with important fluctuations of the health of some people in each group have had little or no effect on the health of others. Exposure to profound and sustained culture change, social change, and change in interpersonal relations of the type that was seen among the Chinese was not necessarily associated with any manifestations that could be described as illness. Acute major dislocations of the type experienced by the Hungarians did not necessarily produce illness. Even the profound social isolation, insecurity, threats, demands, and deprivations that were thrust upon political prisoners and prisoners of war did not always produce major adverse physiological or psychological reactions if they were not accompanied by physical injury or serious manipulation of the physical environment. Systematic occupational and social changes in the American populations have not produced major episodes of illness, except among those who were especially susceptible.

Our findings point to the following general conclusions:

1. Exposure to culture change, social change, and change in interpersonal relations may lead to a significant change in health if (*a*) a person has preexisting illness or susceptibility to illness, and he perceives the change as important to him, or (*b*) there is a significant change in his activities, habits, ingestants, exposure to disease-causing agents, or in the physical characteristics of his environment.

2. Exposure to culture change, social change, and change in interpersonal relations may lead to *no* significant change in health if (*a*) a person has no significant preexisting illness or susceptibility to illness, or if he does not perceive the change as important to him, and (*b*) there is no significant change in his activities, habits, ingestants, exposure to disease-causing agents, or in the physical characteristics of his environment.

3. If a culture change, social change, or change in interpersonal relations is not associated with a significant change in the activities, habits, ingestants, exposure to disease-causing agents, or in the physical characteristics of the environment of a person, then its effect upon his health cannot be defined solely by its nature, its magnitude, its acuteness or chronicity, or its apparent importance in the eyes of others.

REFERENCES

Bone, E. *Seven Years Solitary*. New York: Harcourt, Brace, 1957.

Cannon, W. B. *Bodily Changes in Pain, Hunger, Fear and Rage, An Account of Recent Research into the Function of Emotional Excitement*, Second Edition. New York: D. Appleton and Company, 1929.

Hinkle, L. E., Jr. The concept of "stress" in the biological and social sciences. Invited paper before the Third International Conference on Social Science and Medicine, August 14–18, 1972, Elsinore, Denmark. To be published in *Science and Medicine*.

Hinkle, L. E., Jr. The effects of "social" and "behavioral" aspects of the environment on human health. Background document prepared for NIEHS Task Force on Research Planning in the Environmental Health Sciences. Deposited in the National Library of Medicine. (Copies available on request to: National Library of Medicine, 8600 Rockville Pike, Bethesda, Md. 20014.)

Hinkle, L. E., Jr. An estimate of the effects of ''stress'' on the incidence and prevalence of coronary heart disease in a large industrial population in the United States. *Proceedings of the II Congress of the International Society on Thrombosis and Haemostasis, July 13, 1971, Oslo, Norway.* Stuttgart, Germany: F. K. Shattaur Verlag, 1972.

Hinkle, L. E., Jr. Motivations of the individuals who took part in the uprising. In *Second Seminar on the Hungarian Revolution of October, 1956.* Forest Hills, N.Y.: Society for the Investigation of Human Ecology, 1958.

Hinkle, L. E., Jr. Physical health, mental health, and the social environment: Some characteristics of healthy and unhealthy people. In R. H. Ojemann (Ed.), *Recent Contributions of Biological and Psychological Investigations to Preventative Psychiatry.* Iowa City: State University of Iowa, 1959.

Hinkle, L. E., Jr. The physiological state of the interrogation subject as it affects brain function. In A. D. Biderman & H. Zimmer (Eds.), *The Manipulation of Human Behavior.* New York: John Wiley & Sons, 1961.

Hinkle, L. E., Jr. Relating biochemical, physiological and psychological disorders to the social environment. *Archives of Environmental Health,* 1968, **16,** 77–82.

Hinkle, L. E., Jr. A study of the precursors of acute and fatal coronary heart disease. Public Annual Report, Cornell University Medical College, NHLI 70-2069, February 1, 1972. Copies available from National Technical Information Services (NTIS), Springfield, Va.

Hinkle, L. E., Jr. A study of the precursors of acute and fatal coronary heart disease. Public Annual Report, Cornell University Medical College, NHLI 70-2069, February 1, 1973. Copies available from National Technical Information Services (NTIS), Springfield, Va.

Hinkle, L. E., Jr., Benjamin, B., Christenson, W. N., & Ullman, D. S. Coronary heart disease: The thirty-year experience of 1,160 men. *AMA Archives of Environmental Health,* 1966, **13,** 312–321.

Hinkle, L. E., Jr., Christenson, W. N., Benjamin, B., Kane, F. D., Plummer, N., & Wolff, H. G. The occurrence of illness among 24 ''normal'' women: Evidences of differences in susceptibility to acute respiratory and gastrointestinal syndromes. With the Collaboration of Morris Schaefer, M.D. and Daniel Widelock, Ph.D. of the Department of Health of New York City. Unpublished. Presented before the American College of Physicians, Annual Scientific Meeting, Miami Beach, May 10, 1961.

Hinkle, L. E., Jr., Christenson, W. N., Kane, F. D., Ostfeld, A., Thetford, W. N. & Wolff, H. G. An investigation of the relation between life experience, personality characteristics, and general susceptibility to illness. *Psychosomatic Medicine,* 1958, **20,** 278–295.

Hinkle, L. E., Jr., Gittinger, J. W., Goldberger, L., Ostfeld, A., Metraux, R., Richter P., & Wolff, H. G. Studies in human ecology: Factors covering the adaptation of Chinese unable to return to China. In *Experimental Psychopathology.* New York: Grune & Stratton, 1957.

Hinkle, L. E., Jr., Kane, F. D., Christenson, W. N., & Wolff, H. G. Hungarian refugees: Life experiences and features influencing participation in the revolution and subsequent flight. *American Journal of Psychiatry,* 1959, **116,** 16–19.

Hinkle, L. E., Jr., Pinsky, R. H., Bross, I. D. J., & Plummer, N. The distribution of sickness disability in a homogeneous group of "healthy adult men." *American Journal of Hygiene,* 1956, **64,** 220–242.

Hinkle, L. E., Jr., & Plummer, N. Life stress and industrial absenteeism in one segment of a working population. *Industrial Medicine and Surgery,* 1952, **21,** 363–375.

Hinkle, L. E., Jr., Plummer, N., Metraux, R., Richter, P., Gittinger, J. W., Thetford, W. N., Ostfeld, A. M., Kane, F. D., Goldberger, L., Mitchell, W. E., Leichter, H., Pinsky, R., Goebel, D., Bross, I. D. J., & Wolff, H. G. Studies in human ecology, factors relevant to the occurrence of bodily illness and disturbances in mood, thought, and behavior in three homogeneous population groups. *American Journal of Psychiatry,* 1957, **114,** 212–220.

Hinkle, L. E., Jr., Whitney, L. H., Lehman, E. W., Dunn, J., Benjamin, B., King, R., Plakun, A., & Flehinger, B. Occupation, education and coronary heart disease. *Science, 1968,* **161,** 238–246.

Hinkle, L. E., Jr., & Wolff, H. G. Communist interrogation and indoctrination of "enemies of the state." Analysis of methods used by the Communist state police (a special report). *Archives of Neurology & Psychiatry,* 1956, **76,** 115–174.

Hinkle, L. E., Jr., & Wolff, H. G. Ecologic investigations of the relationship between illness, life experiences and the social environment. *Annals of Internal Medicine,* 1958, **49,** 1373–1388.

Hinkle, L. E., Jr., & Wolff, H. G. Health and social environment: Experimental investigations. In A. H. Leighton, J. A. Clausen, & R. N. Wilson (Eds.), *Explorations in Social Psychiatry.* New York: Basic Books, 1957.

Hinkle, L. E., Jr. & Wolff, H. G. The methods of interrogation and indoctrination used by the Communist state police. *Bulletin of the New York Academy of Medicine,* 1957, **33,** 600–615.

Lehman, E. W., Schulman, J., & Hinkle, L. E., Jr. Coronary deaths and organizational mobility: The 30-year experience of 1,160 men. *Archives of Environmental Health,* 1967, **15,** 455–461.

Selye, H. The general adaptation syndrome and the diseases of adaptation. *Journal of Clinical Endocrinology,* 1946, **6,** 117–230.

Wolff, H. G., Wolf, S. G., and Hare, C. C. (Eds.) *Life Stress and Bodily Disease.* Baltimore: The Williams and Wilkens Company, 1950.

CHAPTER 3

Life Change and Illness Susceptibility *

THOMAS H. HOLMES

MINORU MASUDA

The purpose of this report is to document the development and pilot application of the Social Readjustment Rating Scale (SRRS). The method for scaling the life-event and life-style items under study was derived from psychophysics, which is the division of psychology that deals with man's ability to make subjective magnitude estimations about certain of his experiences (Stevens & Galanter, 1957; Stevens, 1966). The scale has been used as a tool to investigate the similarities and differences among cultures, to study recall of life events, and to evaluate the relationship of life change to the occurrence of disease. Here *disease* applies to change in health status and includes a broad spectrum of medical, surgical, and psychiatric disorders.

BACKGROUND OF THE STUDY

Placed in a historical perspective, this research evolved from the chrysalis of psychobiology generated by Adolf Meyer (Lief, 1948). His invention of the "life chart," a device for organizing the medical data as a dynamic biography, provided a unique method for demonstrating his schema of the relationship of biological, psychological, and sociological phenomena to the processes of

* This research was supported in part by Public Health Service Undergraduate Training in Human Behavior Grant No. 5-T2-MH-7871-03, Undergraduate Training in Psychiatry Grant No. 5-T2-MH-5939-13, and Graduate Training in Psychiatry Grant No. 5-T1-MH-5557-14 from the Institute of Mental Health; P.H.S. General Research Support Grant No. 1-S01-FR-5432-04; O'Donnell Psychiatric Research Fund; Scottish Rite Committee for Research in Schizophrenia; and Stuht Psychiatric Research Fund. This chapter except for minor revisions was previously published in: John Paul Scott and Edward C. Senay (Eds.), *Separation and Depression: Clinical and Research Aspects,* Washington, D. C.: American Association for The Advancement of Science (Publication number 94).

health and disease in man. The importance of many of the life events used in this research was emphasized by Meyer: ". . . changes of habitat, of school entrance, graduations or changes or failures; the various jobs; the date of possibly important births and deaths in the family, and other fundamentally important environmental influences" (Lief, 1948, p. 420).

More recently in Harold G. Wolff's laboratory,* the concepts of Pavlov, Freud, Cannon, and Skinner were incorporated in the Meyerian schema. The research that resulted from this synthesis adduced powerful evidence that "stressful" life events, by evoking psychophysiological reactions, played an important causative role in the natural history of many diseases (Holmes, Goodell, Wolf, & Wolff, 1950; Wolff, Wolf & Hare, 1950; Grace, Wolf & Wolff, 1951; Wolf, Cardon, Shepard, & Wolff, 1950; Wolf, 1965). Again, many of the life events denoted "stressful" were enumerated by Meyer and in Table 1 of this report.

Beginning in our laboratory in 1949, the life-chart device has been used systematically in more than 5000 patients to study the quality and quantity of life events empirically observed to cluster at the time of disease onset. Table 1 reveals that each item derived from this study is unique. There are two categories of items: those indicative of the life style of the individual, and those indicative of occurrences that involved the individual. Evolving usually from ordinary, but sometimes from extraordinary, social and interpersonal transactions, these events pertain to major areas of dynamic significance in the social structure of the American way of life. These include family constellation, marriage, occupation, economics, residence, group and peer relationships, education, religion, recreation, and health.

During the developmental phase of this research, the interview technique was used to assess the meaning of the events for the individual. As expected, the psychological significance and emotions varied widely with the patient. Also, it will be noted that only some of the events are negative or "stressful" in the conventional sense, that is, are socially undesirable. Many are socially desirable and consonant with the American values of achievement, success, materialism, practicality, efficiency, future orientation, conformism, and self-reliance.

There was identified, however, one theme common to all these life events. The occurrence of each event usually evoked, or was associated with, some adaptive or coping behavior on the part of the involved individual. Thus, each item was constructed to contain life events whose advent is either indicative of, or requires a significant change in, the ongoing life pattern of the individual. The emphasis is on change from the existing steady state and not on psychological meaning, emotion, or social desirability.

* Harold G. Wolff, M.D. (1898–1962), was Anne Parrish Titzell Professor of Medicine (Neurology), Cornell University Medical College and The New York Hospital.

The method for assigning a magnitude to the items was developed for use in psychophysics—the study of the psychological perception of the quality, quantity, magnitude, and intensity of physical phenomena. This subjective assessment of the observer plotted against the physical dimension being perceived (length of object, intensity of sound, brightness of light, number of objects, and so on) provides a reliable delineation of man's ability to quantify certain of his experiences (Stevens & Galanter, 1957; Stevens, 1966). Stevens and Galanter (1957) demonstrated that the subjective magnitude estimation was related to some power function of the physical stimulus.

This process for quantifying human perception has been carried further to study opinions and attitudes. Sellin and Wolfgang (1964) constructed a scale, utilizing the geometric mean, of the "seriousness" of juvenile delinquent acts. The validity of their conclusions was based on the logarithmic relationship between the category scales of "seriousness" and magnitude of scale scores, the power function of money that related scale scores to money thefts, and the logarithmic relationships between the delinquency scores and the maximum penalties provided by law.

Rashevsky (1964) analyzed the data from the Hollingshead and Redlich study on social class and mental illness and found a logarithmic relationship between social position and aspiration. The comprehensive review by Stevens (1966) concluded that human judgment of a social consensus was effectively quantifiable and recommended the use of the geometric mean as the best average statistic.

The present study, which generated the Social Readjustment Rating Scale, also extends Ekman's Law (Stevens, 1966) from the field of metric stimuli psychophysics into the nonmetric field of psychosocial phenomena. The fact that judgmental variability is proportional in a linear fashion to the magnitude estimation can be regarded as an adjunct to the general scientific law of relative variability. The extension of this law into the area encompassed by our investigation adds further support to the validity of subjective magnitude estimations.

METHOD FOR SCALING LIFE-EVENT ITEMS

During the evolution of their present form, the life-event items to be scaled were used in a series of studies summarized by Rahe, Meyer, Smith, Kjaer, and Holmes (1964) which established that a cluster of social events that require change in ongoing life adjustment is significantly associated with the time of illness onset. Similarly, the relationship of what has been called "life stress," "emotional stress," "object loss," and so forth, and illness onset was demonstrated by other investigations (Greene, 1954; Greene, Young, & Swisher, 1956;

Table 1. Social Readjustment Rating Questionnaire

	Event	Value
1.	Marriage	500
2.	Troubles with the boss	_____
3.	Detention in jail or other institution	_____
4.	Death of spouse	_____
5.	Major change in sleeping habits (a lot more or a lot less sleep, or change in part of day when asleep)	_____
6.	Death of a close family member	_____
7.	Major change in eating habits (a lot more or a lot less food intake, or very different meal hours or surroundings)	_____
8.	Foreclosure on a mortgage or loan	_____
9.	Revision of personal habits (dress, manners, associations, etc.)	_____
10.	Death of a close friend	_____
11.	Minor violations of the law (e.g., traffic tickets, jaywalking, disturbing the peace)	_____
12.	Outstanding personal achievement	_____
13.	Pregnancy	_____
14.	Major change in the health or behavior of a family member	_____
15.	Sexual difficulties	_____
16.	In-law troubles	_____
17.	Major change in number of family get-togethers (e.g., a lot more or a lot less than usual)	_____
18.	Major change in financial state (e.g., a lot worse off or a lot better off than usual)	_____
19.	Gaining a new family member (e.g., through birth, adoption, oldster moving in)	_____
20.	Change in residence	_____
21.	Son or daughter leaving home (e.g., marriage, attending college)	_____

Kissen, 1956; Hawkins, Davies, & Holmes, 1957; Weiss, Dlin, Rollin, Fischer, & Bepler, 1957; Greene & Miller, 1958; Kjaer, 1959; Smith, 1962; Graham & Stevenson, 1963; Stevenson & Graham, 1963; Fischer, Dlin, Winters, Hagner, Russell, & Weiss, 1964; Rahe & Holmes, 1965). It has been adduced from these studies that this clustering of social, or life, events achieves etiologic significance as a necessary, but not sufficient, cause of illness and accounts in part for the time of onset of disease.

Methodologically, the interview or questionnaire technique used in these studies has yielded only the number and types of events making up the cluster. Some estimate of the magnitude of these events was now required to bring greater precision to this area of research and to provide a quantitative basis for new epidemiological studies of diseases. The following method achieves this requisite (Holmes & Rahe, 1967).

A sample of convenience composed of 394 subjects completed the paper-and-pencil test (Table 1) (Holmes & Rahe, 1967). Table 2 contains the charac-

Event	Value
22. Marital separation from mate	______
23. Major change in church activities (e.g., a lot more or a lot less than usual)	______
24. Marital reconciliation with mate	______
25. Being fired from work	______
26. Divorce	______
27. Changing to a different line of work	______
28. Major change in the number of arguments with spouse (e.g., either a lot more or a lot less than usual regarding child-rearing, personal habits)	______
29. Major change in responsibilities at work (e.g., promotion, demotion, lateral transfer)	______
30. Wife beginning or ceasing work outside the home	______
31. Major change in working hours or conditions	______
32. Major change in usual type and/or amount of recreation	______
33. Taking on a mortgage greater than $10,000 (e.g., purchasing a home, business)	______
34. Taking on a mortgage or loan less than $10,000 (e.g., purchasing a car, TV, freezer)	______
35. Major personal injury or illness	______
36. Major business readjustment (e.g., merger, reorganization, bankruptcy)	______
37. Major change in social activities (e.g., clubs, dancing, movies, visiting)	______
38. Major change in living conditions (e.g., building a new home, remodeling, deterioration of home or neighborhood)	______
39. Retirement from work	______
40. Vacation	______
41. Christmas	______
42. Changing to a new school	______
43. Beginning or ceasing formal schooling	______

From Holmes and Rahe, 1967, Table 1, p. 214.

teristics of the sample. The items were the 43 life events that were empirically derived from clinical experience. The following written instructions were given to each subject who completed the Social Readjustment Rating Questionnaire (SRRQ).

1. Social readjustment includes the amount and duration of change in one's accustomed pattern of life resulting from various life events. As defined, social readjustment measures the intensity and length of time necessary to accommodate to a life event, *regardless of the desirability of this event.*

2. You are asked to rate a series of life events as to their relative degrees of necessary readjustment. In scoring, *use all of your experience* in arriving at your answer. This means personal experience where it applies as well as what you have learned to be the case for others. Some persons accommodate to change more readily than others; some persons adjust with particular ease or difficulty to only certain events. Therefore, strive to give your opinion of the

average degree of readjustment necessary for each event rather than the extreme.

3. The mechanics of rating are these: Event 1, Marriage, has been given an arbitrary value of 500. As you complete each of the remaining events think to yourself, "Is this event indicative of more or less readjustment than marriage?" "Would the readjustment take longer or shorter to accomplish?" If you decide the readjustment is more intense and protracted, then choose a *proportionately larger* number and place it in the blank directly opposite the event in the column marked "Values." If you decide the event represents less and shorter readjustment than marriage, then indicate how much less by placing a *proportionately smaller* number in the opposite blank. (If an event requires intense readjustment over a short time span, it may approximate in value an event requiring less intense readjustment over a long period of time.) If the event is equal in social readjustment to marriage, record the number 500 opposite the event.

The order in which the items were presented is shown in Table 1.

RESULTS

The Social Readjustment Rating Scale (SRRS) is shown in Table 3 (Holmes & Rahe, 1967). This table contains the magnitude of the life events that is derived when the mean score, divided by 10, of each item for the entire sample is calculated and arranged in rank order. That consensus is high concerning the relative order and magnitude of the means of items is demonstrated by the high coefficients of correlation (Pearson's r) (Guilford, 1965) between the discrete groups contained in the sample. Table 2 reveals that all the coefficients of correlation were above .90 with the exception of that between white and Negro, which was .82. Recalculation of the data using Spearman's rank order correlation coefficient (Siegel, 1956) yielded almost identical results. Kendall's coefficient of concordance (W) (Siegel, 1956) for the 394 individuals was .477, significant at $p < .005$.

Three measures of central tendency were systematically evaluated (Masuda & Holmes, 1967a): the arithmetic mean, the geometric mean (computed as the mean log of the scores) (Arkin & Colton, 1959, p. 26), and the median (calculated by using Edwards' correction for ties in the same set) (Edwards, 1958, p. 44).

The arithmetic mean scores were consistently higher than the scores of the other two measures of central tendency. Above the score of 120, the geometric mean was generally lower than the median; below 120, the median was consistently lower than the geometric mean. The geometric means and the medians were closer in magnitude to each other than to the arithmetic mean. There was

Table 2. Pearson's Coefficient of Correlation between Discrete Groups in a Sample of Subjects Who Completed the SRRQ ($N = 394$)

Group	Number in Group	. . . Versus . . .	Group	Number in Group	Coefficient of Correlation
Male	179		Female	215	.965
Single	171		Married	223	.960
Age < 30	206		Age 30–60	137	.958
Age < 30	206		Age > 60	51	.923
Age 30–60	137		Age > 60	51	.965
First generation	19		Second generation	69	.908
First generation	19		Third generation	306	.929
Second generation	69		Third generation	306	.975
< College	182		4 years of college	212	.967
Lower class	71		Middle class	323	.928
White	363		Negro	19	.820
White	363		Oriental	12	.940
Protestant	241		Catholic	42	.913
Protestant	241		Jewish	19	.971
Protestant	241		Other religion	45	.948
Protestant	241		No religious preference	47	.926

From Holmes and Rahe, 1967, Table 2, p. 215.

Table 3. Social Readjustment Rating Scale

Rank	Life Event	Mean Value
1	Death of spouse	100
2	Divorce	73
3	Marital separation	65
4	Jail term	63
5	Death of close family member	63
6	Personal injury or illness	53
7	Marriage	50
8	Fired at work	47
9	Marital reconciliation	45
10	Retirement	45
11	Change in health of family member	44
12	Pregnancy	40
13	Sex difficulties	39
14	Gain of new family member	39
15	Business readjustment	39
16	Change in financial state	38
17	Death of close friend	37
18	Change to different line of work	36
19	Change in number of arguments with spouse	35
20	Mortgage over $10,000	31
21	Foreclosure of mortgage or loan	30
22	Change in responsibilities at work	29
23	Son or daughter leaving home	29
24	Trouble with in-laws	29
25	Outstanding personal achievement	28
26	Wife begin or stop work	26
27	Begin or end school	26
28	Change in living conditions	25
29	Revision of personal habits	24
30	Trouble with boss	23
31	Change in work hours or conditions	20
32	Change in residence	20
33	Change in schools	20
34	Change in recreation	19
35	Change in church activities	19
36	Change in social activities	18
37	Mortgage or loan less than $10,000	17
38	Change in sleeping habits	16
39	Change in number of family get-togethers	15
40	Change in eating habits	15
41	Vacation	13
42	Christmas	12
43	Minor violations of the law	11

From Holmes and Rahe, 1967, Table 3, p. 216.

a close parallel in the rank order of all three measures of central tendencies. Kendall's coefficient of concordance (*W*) (Siegel, 1956) for the rank ordering of the three kinds of central measures was .992. The general principle that variability in scores is a function of the magnitude of scores (Ekman's Law) (Stevens, 1966) was clearly demonstrated by the linear relationship between the standard errors of the geometric mean and the geometric mean score (Figure 1). The distribution of the arithmetic mean scores was skewed, while distribution of the geometric mean scores tended more toward "normalization" (Figure 2).

Replication of the scaling method has been carried out on two American samples. Ruch and Holmes (1971) compared a college population (average age 18) with the original sample and found a very high coefficient of correlation (Spearman's rho .97). Pasley's work (1969) is of particular interest, since it reports on the youngest population yet studied. Intercorrelations between seventh-grade students (average age 13) and ninth- and eleventh-grade students, college freshmen, and the original sample of adults (Spearman's rho > .78) indicate that the remarkable consensus about life-change events is well established by the beginning of adolescence.

Ruch and Holmes (1971), in addition to replicating the study, compared the

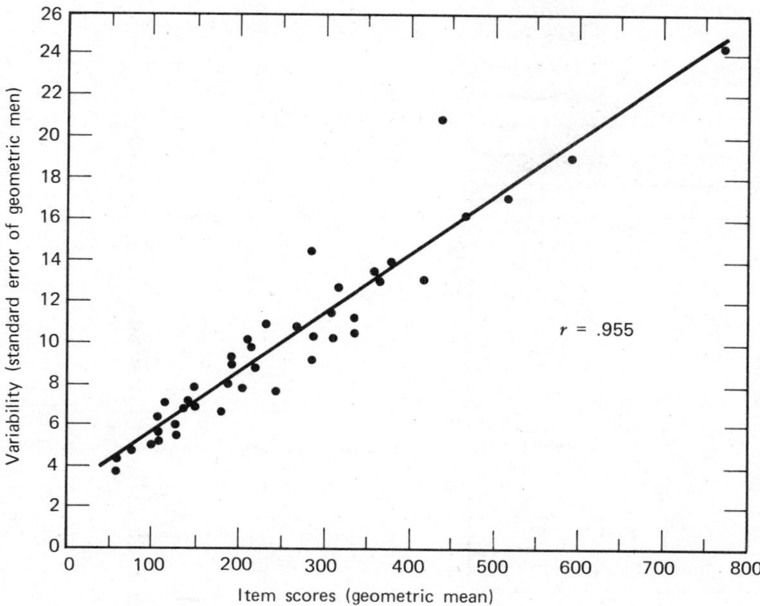

Figure 1. Linear relationship between variability (standard error) and subjective magnitude (item scores). (From Masuda & Holmes, 1967a, Fig. 3, p. 223.)

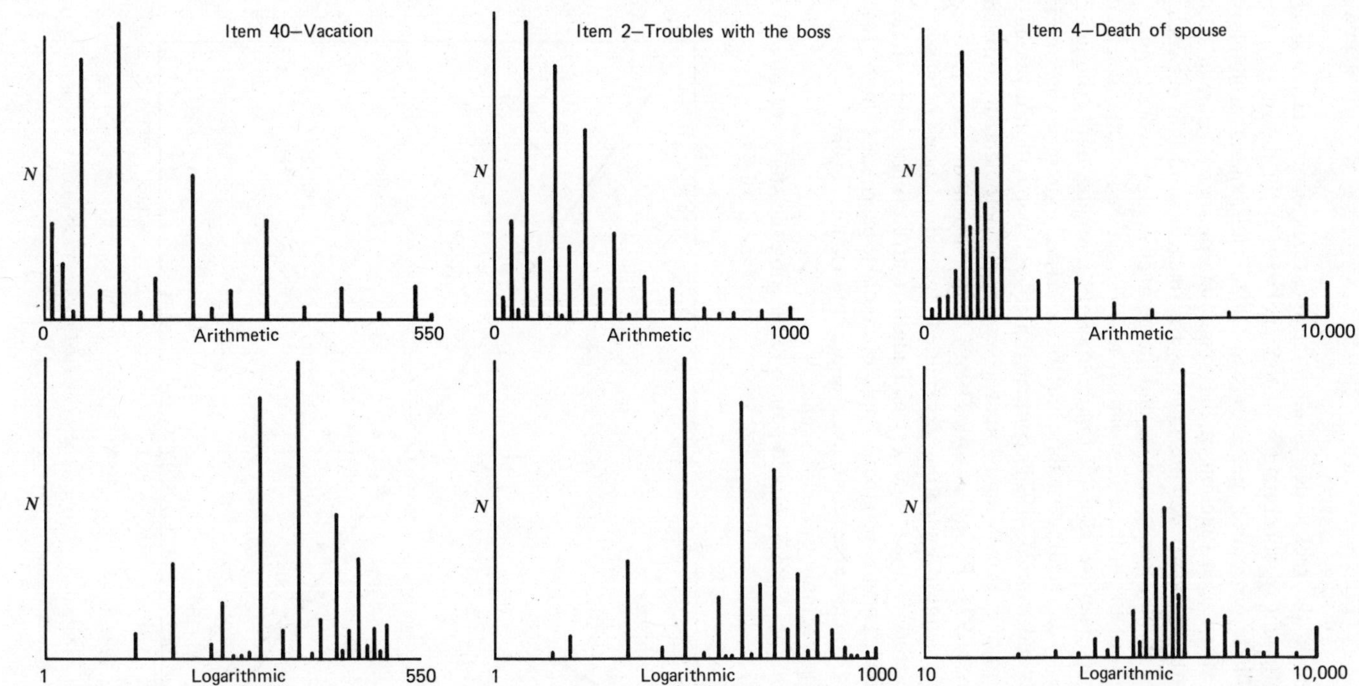

Figure 2. Distribution of scores on three items on the Social Readjustment Rating Questionnaire: comparisons on arithmetic and logarithmic scales (Americans, $N = 394$). (From Masuda & Holmes, 1967a, Fig. 2, p. 222.)

magnitude-estimation scaling method used in this research and Thurstone's method of paired comparisons (Torgerson, 1958). Of the original 43 life events, 11 items that were representative of the range were selected. The 11 items yielded 55 pairs by a procedure in which each item is paired with each of the other 10 items. Two hundred and eleven subjects were asked to compare and underline the member of each pair judged to be the more serious for the average person. The Thurstone (1959) method of paired comparisons (Case V) was used. Spearman's rank order correlation coefficient between the magnitude estimation and paired comparison scales was positive ($r_s = .93$) and the relationship between the two scales appeared to be linear.

In another methodological manipulation, the Social Readjustment Rating Scale was replicated by changing the module item with which the other items were compared (Bramwell, 1971). In this study, an attempt was made to develop a Social and Athletic Readjustment Rating Scale to be used in an evaluation of life change and injuries in college athletes. Thirty-eight of the 43 original items of the SRRS were retained in the new scale. Two items were revised and three (pregnancy, retirement from work, and Christmas) were deleted. A new module item, *entering college,* replaced marriage and was assigned a value of 500. Instructions for scaling similar to those issued in the original study were given to 80 college athletes. Again, Spearman's rank order correlation coefficient between the 38 items common to both scaling attempts was high ($r_s = .85$).

Coddington (1972a, 1972b) modified the Social Readjustment Rating Questionnaire to contain items specifically related to childhood life style. A different list of experiences was constructed for the preschool age group, elementary school age group, junior high school age group, and senior high school age group. The method for producing each age group scale was that used in generating the Social Readjustment Rating Scale. The people who did the rating were 131 teachers, 25 pediatricians, and 87 mental health workers. Inter-rater agreement was high with rank order correlations of .90 or greater. Using the new scale to quantify recent childhood experiences in 3500 children, Coddington constructed an age-related curve of average social readjustment scores.

Casey, Masuda, and Holmes (1967) used the SRRS to demonstrate that consistency of recall is related to the saliency of life events. The data suggested the inference that, if an event is recalled consistently, it is salient to the individual and may indirectly reflect validity of recall. The items of the SRRS were converted into a paper-and-pencil test, which allowed the respondent to indicate by year, during the previous decade, the occurrence of the life-event items. This permitted a quantitative definition of the life change per year. Fifty-five subjects completed the questionnaire twice, with Time 2 coming 9 months after Time 1. Comparison of the data from the two questionnaires indicated that the instrument was reliable. The stability coefficients (Pearson's r) for three representative years were .744 for 1 year before, .638 for 4 years before, and .669 for 7 years before. These findings viewed from Time 1 and Time 2 were significant at the .0005 level of confidence. Further, the data indicated that, although the amount recalled over time decreased, that which was recalled tended to be consistent. The decrement in amount recalled began after the first year. It was also observed that the relationship between the saliency of the life event and consistency of recall was highly significant. These conclusions are similar to those obtained from studies of recall of health events from interview data (Haggard, Brekstad, & Skard, 1960; U.S. National Health Survey, 1961, 1963; Wenar and Coulter, 1962; Mechanic and Newton, 1965).

CROSS-CULTURAL STUDIES

In the development of the SRRS, the high correlations between minority groups and the white population (Table 2) (Holmes & Rahe, 1967) suggested the desirability of extending the investigation further into the cross-cultural area. Table 4 summarizes some of the data from our laboratory (Masuda & Holmes, 1967b; Komaroff, Masuda, & Holmes, 1968; Celdrán, 1970; Harmon, Masuda, & Holmes, 1970). More recently, Seppa (1972) compared a sample from El Salvador, a Spanish-speaking Central American country, with the Spanish sample studied by Celdrán (1970) and found the consensus high. Rahe (1969), in addition to summarizing some of the aforementioned studies, cited data on literate populations from Denmark and Sweden and on a semiliterate sample from Hawaii. Woon (1971) compared a sample of Malaysians with Americans, and Janney and Holmes (unpublished) compared a Peruvian sample with Spanish-speaking samples and Americans. Again, the consensus was high, with Spearman's rank order correlation coefficients ranging from .629 to .943.

Table 4. Cross-Cultural Comparisons between American, Japanese, Western European, Spanish, Negro American, and Mexican American

Culture Group	Japanese	Western European	Spanish	Negro American	Mexican American
American	.752	.884	.847	.798	.735
Japanese		.844	.836	.816	.724
Western European [1]			.849	.772	.754
Spanish				.848	.767
Negro American					.892

[1] Western European is composed of French and French-speaking Swiss and Belgians.
Adapted from Masuda and Holmes, 1967b; Komaroff, Masuda, and Holmes, 1968; Celdrán, 1970; and Harmon, Masuda, and Holmes, 1970.

Table 5 reveals the remarkable consensus about the common life events obtained when Americans, whose culture is embedded in the democratic Western ethic of internalized Christian moral values, are compared with Japanese, whose Eastern culture is embedded in a particularistic, hierarchical system emphasizing family-oriented, externally sanctioned rules of ethical conduct (DeVos, 1960). In addition to documenting cross-cultural similarities, the SRRQ provides an equally powerful tool for delineating quantitatively and qualitatively cross-cultural differences (Table 5). These differences identify the cultural variants that distinguish one society from the other.

SOCIAL READJUSTMENT RATING SCALE AND ILLNESS ONSET

The life-event items contained in the SRRS were originally used in our laboratory to construct a Schedule of Recent Experience (SRE) * (Hawkins et al., Holmes, 1957; Rahe et al., 1964). This instrument, a self-administered questionnaire, allows the respondent to document over a 10-year period the year of occurrence of the life-event items. In retrospective studies carried out before the development of the SRRS, the SRE had been used to adduce data that the life events cluster significantly in the 2-year period preceding onset of tuberculosis, heart disease, skin disease, hernia, and pregnancy. These findings were reported by Rahe et al. (1964).

The development of the scale of magnitudes for the life-event items (SRRS) combined with the SRE provided a unique method for validation of the findings of the retrospective studies and for a quantitative definition of a life crisis.

Retrospective Studies

The following section addresses itself to the association of life changes and disease onset. In a pilot study by Rahe and Holmes (unpublished, a), the SRE was mailed to 200 resident physicians in the University of Washington integrated hospital system. The cover letter requested the participation of residents in a research project but did not disclose the project's purpose. The subjects were asked to list all "major health changes" by year of occurrence for the past 10 years. In this pilot study, it was assumed that the subjects were sophisticated in matters of health and disease, and no systematic attempt was made to verify the report of health changes. The 88 subjects (86 males, 2 females; age 22 to 33 years) who completed and returned the questionnaire

* Further information about the cost and use of the Schedule of Recent Experience (SRE) can be obtained from Thomas H. Holmes, M.D., Department of Psychiatry RP-10, University of Washington, Seattle, Washington 98195.

Table 5. Comparison of Ranking and Item Scores Derived from the SRRQ Between Japanese ($N = 112$) and American ($N = 168$) Samples

SRRQ Item Number	Item Name [1]	American Rank	American Geometric Mean	Japanese Rank	Japanese Geometric Mean
4	Death of spouse [2]	1	880	1	1079
26	Divorce	2	630	3	637
22	Marital separation [2]	3	541	7	459
1	Marriage	4	500	6	500
6	Death of close family member	5	483	4	573
3	Detention in jail [3]	6	474	2	721
35	Major personal injury or illness [3]	7	426	5	542
39	Retirement from work [4]	8	401	11	289
25	Being fired from work	9	384	8	373
24	Marital reconciliation [2]	10	362	15	272
15	Sexual difficulties	11	326	10	311
14	Major change in health of family	12	325	9	327
19	Addition of new family member [4]	13	311	23	181
36	Major business readjustment	14	305	12	284
18	Major change in financial state [3]	15	288	21	210
28	Major change in arguments with spouse [4]	16	281	33	118
10	Death of close friend	17	278	16	269
27	Changing to different line of work	18	276	13.5	274
13	Pregnancy	19	273	13.5	274
8	Mortgage foreclosure	20	248	19	225
29	Major change in work responsibilities	21	228	22	197
21	Son or daughter leaving home [2]	22	204	18	247
16	In-law troubles	23	195	20	221
30	Wife starting or ending work	24.5	192	25	165

provided retrospective data, which were analyzed for the relationship of health changes to life changes. The items subscribed to in the SRE by the subjects were assigned their values from the Social Readjustment Rating Scale (Table 3). The values were summed for each year and the total life-change units (LCU) derived were plotted for each subject for the decade under study. Upon this profile the reported health changes were superimposed. Data on one subject are presented in Figure 3.

A total of 96 diseases or changes in health status was reported by the 88 subjects for the previous 10 years. The 34 varieties reported were classified into seven categories: infectious and parasitic, allergic, musculoskeletal, psychosomatic, psychiatric, physical trauma, and miscellaneous. Infectious (45 percent), allergic (13 percent), musculoskeletal (11 percent), and psychosomatic (7 percent) composed the majority of reported health changes.

SRRQ Item Number	Item Name [1]	American Rank	American Geometric Mean	Japanese Rank	Japanese Geometric Mean
43	Start or end of formal schooling [4]	24.5	192	32	126
2	Troubles with boss	26	174	27	145
12	Outstanding personal achievement	27	161	24	166
33	Mortgage loan over $10,000 [4]	28	158	17	252
38	Major change in living conditions	29	153	26	162
31	Major change in working conditions	30	141	31	131
42	Changing to new school	31	126	34	108
9	Major revision of personal habits	32	124	29	135
20	Change in residence	33	114	37	91
32	Major change in recreation [2]	34	113	38	85
37	Major change in social activities [2]	35	105	39	72
23	Major change in church activities [4]	36	93	42	46
5	Major change in sleeping habits	37	83	35	94
7	Major change in eating habits	38.5	78	36	93
34	Mortgage loan less than $10,000 [4]	38.5	78	30	170
17	Major change in family get-togethers	40	75	40	60
40	Vacation	41	54	41	56
41	Christmas	42	40	43	40
11	Minor violations of the law [4]	43	34	28	138

[1] Items listed in order of descending rank on American geometric mean.
Items scored significantly different:
[2] $p < .05$
[3] $p < .01$
[4] $p < .001$.
From Masuda and Holmes, 1967b, Table 3, p. 232.

On the basis of the previous studies (Rahe et al., 1964), an arbitrary criterion was established for the temporal association of an illness or health change with life-change events: a reported change in health must occur within the 2-year period following the occurrence of a cluster of life changes. This 2-year period was the time when the subject was "at risk" after the life-change clustering. Eighty-nine of the 96 major health changes reported (93 percent) were associated temporally with a clustering of life changes whose values summed to at least 150 LCU per year. A life crisis was, thus, defined as any clustering of life-change events whose individual values summed to 150 LCU or more in 1 year. The health change itself was not counted as one of the life changes making up the life-change unit total for the year. In some instances, the life crisis peaks mounted to more than 500 LCU. The magnitude of most of the reported life changes was between 18 and 25 LCU (see Table 3). Although the number

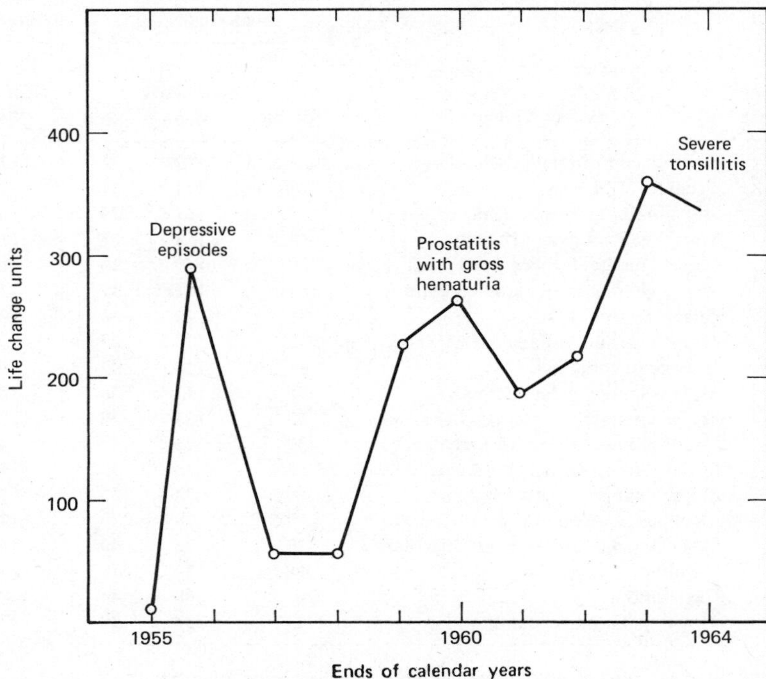

Figure 3. Temporal relationship of life crisis and disease occurrence. (From Rahe & Holmes, unpublished, 2a.)

of life changes making up a peak of 150–500 LCU ranged between 7 and 25, the duration of a life crisis was occasionally observed to persist longer than 2 years.

The relationship of the magnitude of the life crises to the proportion of life crises associated with major health changes is shown in Table 6 (Rahe & Holmes, unpublished, a).

The 93 percent association of reported health changes with a life crisis was significantly greater than chance association. Chance association was calculated as follows. The 130 reported life crises represented approximately one-third of the maximum number of possible life crises. The number of life crises possible for the sample would have been 4 for each of the 88 subjects, or 352. If the 96 reported health changes were distributed randomly over the 352 possible life crises, then approximately one-third of them would have fallen within the boundaries of the 130 reported life crises. The chi-square value for the difference between the observed (93 percent) and the expected (35 percent) association of health change with a life crisis was 95.9. This difference is significant at the .001 level.

Table 6. Relationship of Life Crisis Magnitude to Percentage of Life Crises Associated with Health Changes

	Number of Life Crises			
	Associated with Health Changes	Not Associated with Health Changes	Total Number of Life Crises	Life Crises Associated with Health Changes (%)
Mild life crisis (150–199 LCU)	13	22	35	37
Moderate life crisis (200–299 LCU)	29	28	57	51
Major life crisis (300+ LCU)	30	8	38	79
Total	72 [1]	58	130	55

[1] Some life crises were associated with more than one health change.
From Rahe and Holmes, unpublished, a.

Further analysis of the data in Table 6 indicated a direct relationship between the magnitude of the life crisis and the risk of health change. As the life-change units increased, so did the percentage of illness associated with the life crisis. Of the life crises between 150 and 199 LCU, 37 percent had an associated health change. This association rose to 51 percent for crises with scores between 200 and 299 LCU, and to 79 percent for crises with scores of 300 LCU or more. These three ranges of scores have been used to define a *mild* (150–199 LCU), *moderate* (200–299 LCU), and *major* (300+LCU) life crisis. In some subjects, two or more major health changes occurred during the time at risk. This accounts for the fact that in Table 6 the 89 health changes were associated with 72 life crises.

Figure 3 is an example of one subject's life-change unit profile during a 10-year period, and it illustrates graphically the relationship between life crises and major health changes. The solid line connects points that indicate yearly total life-change units. Reported health changes are indicated over their year of occurrence. The subject's depressive episodes in 1956 coincided with the appearance of a life crisis, whereas his episodes of prostatitis in 1960 and of tonsillitis in 1964 occurred about 1 year after the appearance of the life crisis with which they were associated. On the average, associated health changes followed a life crisis by about a year.

T. S. Holmes (1970) used the Schedule of Recent Experience and the Social Readjustment Rating Scale to define a qualitative and quantitative psychosocial history and to characterize certain aspects of the life style of 199 hospitalized patients on the medical wards of University Hospital and Veterans Administration Hospital in Seattle. Thirty-seven of the items reported by the patients were more frequent in the 0 to 5 years prior to hospitalization than in the 6 to 10

Table 7. Frequency Distribution of Life Changes Over 10 Years Prior to Hospitalization for 199 Patients

Item	Number of Occurrences	Occurrences per Subject	Magnitude
Vacation	894	4.492	13
Personal injury or illness	792	3.980	53
Change in residence	730	3.668	20
Mortgage or loan less than $10,000	328	1.648	17
Change in work hours or conditions	315	1.583	20
Change in financial state	313	1.573	38
Change in recreation	305	1.533	19
Change in social activities	279	1.402	18
Change to different line of work	275	1.382	36
Change in sleeping habits	266	1.337	16
Change in responsibilities at work	265	1.332	29
Change in eating habits	262	1.317	15
Change in health of family member	250	1.256	44
Minor violations of the law	245	1.231	11
Death of close friend	242	1.216	37
Gain of new family member	237	1.191	39
Death of close family member	229	1.151	63
Outstanding personal achievement	200	1.005	28
Revision in personal habits	199	1.000	24

years prior. The average frequency of each item in the 0 to 5 years prior to hospitalization was nearly twice that of the 6 to 10 years prior. The mean magnitude of the items reported was 29.1 LCU. However, the rank order of the items in each time period was substantially the same, as measured by $r_s = .882$ ($p < .001$). Because of this uniformity, the total 10-year ranking of item frequency was taken as the grand rank. These findings are shown in Table 7.

The most frequent items during the 10 years prior to hospitalization were vacation, personal injury or illness, and change in residence. Together these items accounted for 28 percent of all the reports. The least frequent were foreclosure of mortgage or loan, fired at work, and death of spouse. These accounted for only 0.5 percent of all the items reported. The three most frequent items were reported more than 50 times for each report of the three least frequent items.

Men and women displayed no significant difference in the average number of life changes per person. Single, married, and divorced-separated patients displayed an average of 50 percent more life changes per person than widowed pa-

Item	Number of Occurrences	Occurrences per Subject	Magnitude
Change in living conditions	196	0.985	25
Change in number of family get-togethers	159	0.799	15
Change in sex difficulties	159	0.799	39
Change in church activities	147	0.739	19
Wife begin or stop work	132	0.663	26
Change in number of arguments with spouse	125	0.628	35
Begin or end school	113	0.568	26
Marital separation	109	0.548	65
Business readjustment	107	0.538	39
Trouble with boss	102	0.513	23
Son or daughter leaving home	94	0.472	29
Mortgage over $10,000	83	0.417	31
Trouble with in-laws	77	0.387	29
Marriage	71	0.357	50
Change in schools	67	0.337	20
Jail term	62	0.312	63
Retirement	43	0.216	45
Divorce	34	0.171	73
Foreclosure of mortgage or loan	18	0.090	30
Fired at work	17	0.085	47
Death of spouse	12	0.060	100

From T. S. Holmes, 1970, Table III-11.

tients. Patients between 20 and 30 years old displayed about 50 percent more life changes per person than those between 45 and 60, and twice as many as those over 60 years old.

Retrospective studies carried out by Rahe and colleagues in Sweden have shown a positive relationship between mounting life change and sudden cardiac death (Rahe & Lind, 1971) and time of onset of myocardial infarction (Rahe & Paasikivi, 1971; Theorell & Rahe, 1971). Edwards (1971) has demonstrated a similar relationship between life change and myocardial infarction. Similar data have been adduced for the relationship of increasing amounts of life change and the occurrence of fractures (Tollefson, 1972), beginning of pregnancy (Knittel & Holmes, unpublished), and time of incarceration in a Federal prison (Cutler, Masuda, & Holmes, unpublished). Hong and Holmes (unpublished) used the Schedule of Recent Experience to quantify the magnitude of life change occurring during migration and the three-year period of acculturation in a case report of transient diabetes. Wold (1968) demonstrated that a life crisis was present in the family at the time of onset of leukemia in children.

The Schedule of Recent Experience has also been used as an instrument for research in two areas of academic performance. Harris (1972) investigated the relationship of life change to academic performance among selected college freshmen at varying levels of college readiness. He found that the grade point average is inversely proportional to the amount of life change experienced. This effect of life change on grade point average remained constant regardless of the level of college readiness.

Carranza (1972) examined the impact of life changes on high school teacher performance. He found a positive and significant correlation between teacher life-change magnitude and teacher absenteeism due to illness or injury and the number of times the teacher changed residence. There was a significant negative correlation between amount of life change and postgraduate education obtained by the teacher beyond the Bachelor of Arts degree. In essence, the overall evidence suggested that high life change is associated with less desirable aspects of teacher performance.

Prospective Studies

Rahe and Holmes (unpublished, b) followed up 84 of the 88 resident physicians described previously as subjects for a prospective study. In this study, the life changes for the previous 18 months were used as the quantitative base for predicting illness onset for the near future. When data about the disease occurrence were obtained 9 months later, 49 percent of the high-risk group (300+ LCU) reported illness; 25 percent of the medium-risk group (200–299 LCU) reported illness; and 9 percent of the low-risk group (150–199 LCU) reported illness.

T. S. Holmes (1970), using a somewhat different method, followed 54 medical students from the beginning of their freshmen year to the end of their sophomore year. Again, the SRE was used to collect data, and the life-change magnitude of the year before entrance to medical school was used to predict disease occurrence for a full 2-year period at risk. At the end of that time, the SRE was administered a second time, so that retrospective data could be compared with the prospective data. With the allowance of a few percentage points difference, the outcome of both approaches was essentially the same. Thus, in both the prospective and retrospective surveys, 52 percent of the subjects experienced major health changes during the 2-year period at risk. Of these, 86 percent with high life-change scores, 48 percent with moderate life-change scores, and 33 percent with low life-change scores experienced major health changes. Thus, individuals who remained in good health for the first year of the period at risk had the same chance of experiencing major health changes during the remainder of the period as they did at its beginning, depending on the magnitude of their life-change scores. The data also revealed that subjects with major health changes experienced more minor health changes than subjects without major health changes.

Thurlow (1971) also used the SRE to conduct both a retrospective and prospective study on one population. He divided the SRE items into "objective" and "subjective" categories, and found the latter to be the better predictors of illness.

Rahe (1968) expanded the studies to Naval personnel. With the previous 6-month period as the time base for establishment of the predictive life-change score, approximately 2500 officers and enlisted men aboard three U.S. Navy cruisers provided health-change data after 6 months at sea. The upper 30 percent of the life-change units provided the subjects for the high-risk group, and the lower 30 percent provided the subjects for the low-risk group. In the first month of the cruise, the high-risk group had nearly 90 percent more *first* illnesses than the low-risk group. The high-risk group consistently reported more illnesses each month for the 6-month cruise period and had one-third more illnesses during the follow-up period than did the low-risk group. Although the high-risk group, relatively speaking, had more serious illnesses than the low-risk group, the health changes reported in this study were considerably *less*

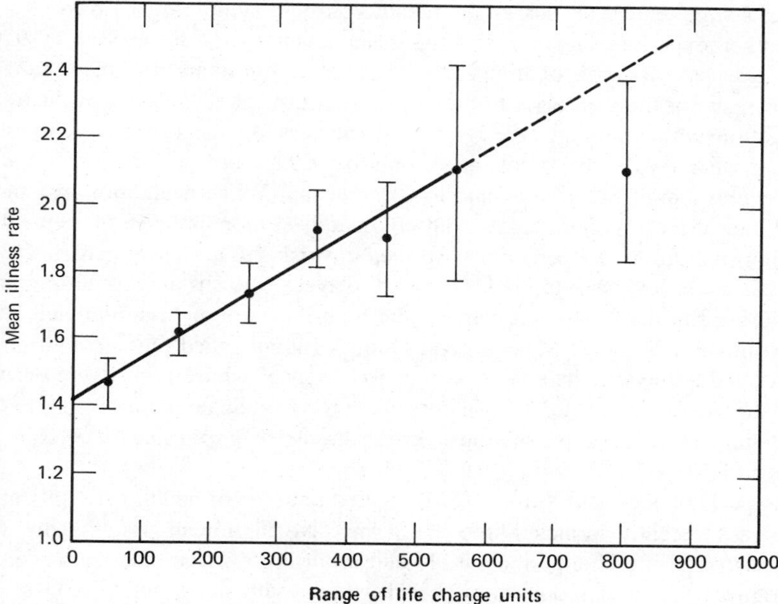

Figure 4. Mean illness rates and standard errors of the mean for equal divisions of the total range of life change units. (From Rahe, Mahan, & Arthur, 1970, Fig. 1, p. 404.)

serious than those reported when the at-risk period was 1 or 2 years, as was true in the aforementioned prospective studies by T. S. Holmes (1970) and Rahe and Holmes (unpublished, b).

In another study, Rahe, Mahan, and Arthur (1970) demonstrated a linear relationship between the mean illness rate of shipboard personnel and the magnitude of life change, as shown in Figure 4.

Rubin, Gunderson, and Arthur (1969) improved the ability of the SRE to predict illness onset in Naval personnel by deriving new scores with the statistical maneuver of stepwise multiple regression analysis. It was their judgment that empirical regression weights derived from a military population predicted future illness better than the prior weights derived from the civilian population.

Holmes and Holmes (1970) adduced data about the association of life change and minor health change. Minor health changes were defined as the signs and symptoms of everyday life, such as cuts, bruises, headaches, stomach aches, backaches, and colds, that do not cause time lost from work or require a visit to the doctor. The findings indicated that subjects were much more likely to experience the signs and symptoms of everyday life on days of greater-than-average life changes. Life changes tended to cluster significantly around health changes. The opposite also was confirmed: subjects were much less likely to experience signs and symptoms on days of less-than-average life change; and low amounts of life change tended to cluster significantly around symptom-free days.

Another experimental approach has been taken by T. H. Holmes (1970). With age, sex, and risk of injury used as relative constants, the magnitude of life changes for the year prior to the season was used as the base to evaluate the association with injury in college football players. In the one study, the 100 subjects were divided by thirds, according to the rank order of their life-change scores, into a high-, medium-, and low-risk group. When evaluation was made at the end of their athletic season, approximately 3 months later, 50 percent of the high-risk group, 25 percent of the medium-risk group, and 9 percent of the low-risk group had been injured. Of the 10 players who sustained multiple injuries during the season, seven were in the high-risk group. In subsequent studies, Bramwell, Wagner, Masuda, and Holmes (unpublished), using a specially constructed Athletic Schedule of Recent Experience, whose items were derived from the Social and Athletic Readjustment Rating Scale (Bramwell, 1971), found that the association of injury in the high-risk group had risen from 50 percent to 70 percent.

Casey, Thoresen, and Smith (1970) studied patterns of health care utilization in trainees recently inducted into the Army. No significant relationship was found between life-change magnitude and reporting on sick call. However, of the trainees who did report on sick call, those with the highest LCU scores were more likely to require sophisticated evaluation and treatment other than that offered at the dispensary level. Zilmer, Kogan, and Holmes (unpublished) also found no relationship between life-change magnitude and utilization of health care facilities in a large population of members of a prepaid health care clinic.

Association of Magnitude of Life Change with Seriousness of Illness

During the course of these investigations, inspection of the data suggested a positive relationship between the seriousness of illness judged intuitively and life-change magnitude for the year prior to the onset of disease. Since there was no satisfactory scale of the seriousness of individual illnesses (Hinkle, Redmont, Plummer, & Wolff, 1960; Rahe, 1968), Wyler, Masuda, and Holmes (1968, 1970) set themselves the task of constructing one. By use of a method similar to that employed in development of the Social Readjustment Rating Scale, 500 units were assigned to the "seriousness" of peptic ulcer. With this as the module item, 125 diseases were rated by two separate samples of physicians. The rank-order correlation (Spearman's rho) was .98. When physicians were compared with a sample of laymen, the correlation of .94 was almost as high. Also, the fact that comparison of Spanish, Irish, and American laymen yielded correlations of .90 or greater suggested a broad, cross-cultural consensus about the seriousness of illness (Celdrán, 1970; McMahon, 1971; Seppa, 1972).

Using the Seriousness of Illness Rating Scale, Wyler, Masuda, and Holmes (1971) assigned appropriate values to 42 diseases experienced by 232 patients. These values were compared with the life-change magnitude that occurred in the 2-year period of time preceding onset of disease. The correlation was highly significant (Spearman's rho .648) for chronic diseases. No significant relationship was found with infectious diseases of acute onset.

These data suggest that the greater the life change or adaptive requirement, the greater the vulnerability or lowering of resistance to disease, and the more serious the disease that does develop. The concept of a variable threshold of resistance and the necessity of having a special pathogen present may help to account for the differences observed in the acute infectious diseases. Thus, the concept of life change appears to have relevance to the causation of disease, time of onset of disease, and severity of disease. It does not seem to contribute much to an understanding of specificity of disease type (Graham & Stevenson, 1963).

SUMMARY

A method generated by psychophysics has been used to construct the Social Readjustment Rating Scale, which consists of 43 life-event items that require change in individual adjustment. Information about the time and frequency of occurrence of life-change events was gathered in several populations by a standardized paper-and-pencil test, the Schedule of Recent Experience. The magnitude of life change was observed to be highly significantly related to time of disease onset. The greater the magnitude of life change (or life crisis), the greater the probability that the life change would be associated with disease onset, and the greater the probability that the population at risk would experience disease. There was also a strong positive correlation between magnitude of life change (life crisis) and seriousness of the chronic illness experienced. The major health changes observed covered a wide range of psychiatric, medical, and surgical diseases.

It is postulated that life-change events, by evoking adaptive efforts by the human organism that are faulty in kind and duration, lower ''bodily resistance'' and enhance the probability of disease occurrence.

REFERENCES

Arkin, H., & Colton, R. R. *Statistical Methods,* Fourth Edition. New York: Barnes and Noble, 1959.

Bramwell, S. T. Personality and psychosocial variables in college athletes. Medical Thesis, University of Washington, Seattle, 1971.

Bramwell, S. T., Wagner, N. N., Masuda, M., & Holmes, T. H. Prediction of injury in college athletes. Unpublished.

Carranza, E. A study of the impact of life changes on high school teacher performance in the Lansing school district as measured by the Holmes and Rahe schedule of Recent Experience. Ph.D. thesis, Michigan State University, College of Education, East Lansing, 1972.

Casey, R. L., Masuda, M., & Holmes, T. H. Quantitative study of recall of life events. *Journal of Psychosomatic Research,* 1967, **11,** 239–247.

Casey, R. L., Thoresen, A. R., & Smith, F. J. The use of the schedule of recent experience questionnaire in an institutional health care setting. *Journal of Psychosomatic Research,* 1970, **14,** 149–154.

Celdrán, H. H. The cross-cultural consistence of two social consensus scales: The Seriousness of Illness Rating Scale and The Social Readjustment Rating Scale in Spain. Medical thesis, University of Washington, Seattle, 1970.

Coddington, R. D. The significance of life events as etiologic factors in the diseases of children. I. A survey of professional workers. *Journal of Psychosomatic Research,* 1972, **16,** 7–18. (a)

Coddington, R. D. The significance of life events as etiologic factors in the diseases of children. II. A study of a normal population. *Journal of Psychosomatic Research,* 1972, **16,** 205–213. (b)

Cutler, D. L., Masuda, M., & Holmes, T. H. The relationship between life change events and criminal behavior. Unpublished.

DeVos, G. The relationship of guilt towards parents to achievement and arranged marriage among the Japanese. *Psychiatry,* 1960, **23,** 287–301.

Edwards, A. E. *Statistical Analysis.* New York: Rinehart, 1958.

Edwards, M. K. Life crisis and myocardial infarction. Master of Nursing thesis, University of Washington, Seattle, 1971.

Fischer, H. K., Dlin, B. M., Winters, W. L., Hagner, S. B., Russell, G. W., & Weiss, E. Emotional factors in coronary occlusion. II. Time patterns and factors related to onset. *Psychosomatics,* 1964, **5,** 280–291.

Grace, W. J., Wolf, S., & Wolff, H. G. *The Human Colon.* New York: Hoeber, 1951.

Graham, D. T., & Stevenson, I. Disease as response to life stress. I. The nature of the evidence. In H. I. Lief, V. F. Lief, & N. R. Lief (Eds.), *The Psychological Basis of Medical Practise.* New York: Hoeber Medical Division, Harper and Row, 1963. Pp. 115–136.

Greene, W. A., Jr. Psychological factors and reticulo-endothelial disease. I. Preliminary observations on a group of males with lymphomas and leukemias. *Psychosomatic Medicine,* 1954, **16,** 220–230.

Greene, W. A., Jr., & Miller, G. Psychological factors and reticulo-endothelial disease. IV. Observations on a group of children and adolescents with leukemia: An interpretation of disease development in terms of the mother-child unit. *Psychosomatic Medicine,* 1958, **20,** 124–144.

Greene, W. A., Jr., Young, L. E., & Swisher, S. N. Psychological factors and reticulo-endothelial disease. II. Observations on a group of women with lymphomas and leukemias. *Psychosomatic Medicine,* 1956, **18,** 284–303.

Guilford, J. P. *Fundamental Statistics in Psychology and Education.* New York: McGraw-Hill Book Company, 1965.

Haggard, E. A., Brekstad, A., & Skard, A. G. On the reliability of the anamnestic interview. *Journal of Abnormal Social Psychology,* 1960, **61,** 311–318.

Harmon, D. K., Masuda, M., & Holmes, T. H. The Social Readjustment Rating Scale: A cross cultural study of Western Europeans and Americans. *Journal of Psychosomatic Research,* 1970, **14,** 391–400.

Harris, P. W. The relationship of life change to academic performance among selected college freshmen at varying levels of college readiness. Doctor of Education thesis, East Texas State University, Commerce, Texas, 1972.

Hawkins, N. G., Davies, R., & Holmes, T. H. Evidence of psychosocial factors in the development of pulmonary tuberculosis. *American Review of Tuberculosis and Pulmonary Diseases,* 1957, **75,** 768–780.

Hinkle, L. E., Jr., Redmont, R., Plummer, N., & Wolff, H. G. An examination of the relation between symptoms, disability, and serious illness in two homogeneous groups of men and women. *American Journal of Public Health,* 1960, **50,** 1327–1366.

Holmes, T. H. Psychologic screening. In *Football Injuries. Papers Presented at a*

Workshop. Sponsored by Subcommittee on Athletic Injuries, Committee on the Skeletal System, Division of Medical Sciences, National Research Council, February 1969. Washington, D.C.: National Academy of Sciences, 1970. Pp. 211–214.

Holmes, T. H., Goodell, H., Wolf, S., & Wolff, H. G. *The Nose. An Experimental Study of Reactions within the Nose in Human Subjects during Varying Life Experiences.* Springfield, Ill.: Charles C Thomas, 1950.

Holmes, T. H., & Rahe, R. H. The Social Readjustment Rating Scale. *Journal of Psychosomatic Research,* 1967, **11,** 213–218.

Holmes, T. S. Adaptive behavior and health change. Medical thesis, University of Washington, Seattle, 1970.

Holmes, T. S., & Holmes, T. H. Short-term intrusions into the life style routine. *Journal of Psychosomatic Research,* 1970, **14,** 121–132.

Hong, K. M., & Holmes, T. H. A case study of transient diabetes mellitus precipitated by cultural changes. Unpublished.

Janney, J. G., Masuda, M., & Holmes, T. H. Comparison of Social Readjustment Questionnaire in Callejon de Huaylas and Cuzco regions of Peru one year post-earthquake. Unpublished.

Kissen, D. M. Some psychosocial aspects of pulmonary tuberculosis. *International Journal of Social Psychiatry,* 1958, **3,** 252–259.

Kissen, D. M. Specific psychological factors in pulmonary tuberculosis. *Health Bulletin,* Edinburgh, 1956, **14,** 44–46.

Kjaer, G. Some psychosomatic aspects of pregnancy with particular reference to nausea and vomiting. Medical thesis, University of Washington, Seattle, 1959.

Knittel, W. C., & Holmes, T. H. Life change and onset of pregnancy. Unpublished.

Komaroff, A. L., Masuda, M., & Holmes, T. H. The Social Readjustment Rating Scale: A comparative study of Negro, Mexican and white Americans. *Journal of Psychosomatic Research,* 1968, **12,** 121–128.

Lief, A. (Ed.) *The Commonsense Psychiatry of Dr. Adolf Meyer.* New York: McGraw-Hill Book Company, 1948.

McMahon, B. J. Seriousness of Illness Rating Scale: A comparative study of Irish and Americans. Medical thesis, University of Washington, Seattle, 1971.

Masuda, M., & Holmes, T. H. Magnitude estimations of social readjustments. *Journal of Psychosomatic Research,* 1967, **11,** 219–225. (a)

Masuda, M., & Holmes, T. H. The Social Readjustment Rating Scale: A cross cultural study of Japanese and Americans. *Journal of Psychosomatic Research,* 1967, **11,** 227–237. (b)

Mechanic, D., & Newton, M. Some problems in the analysis of morbidity data. *Journal of Chronic Diseases,* 1965, **18,** 569–580.

Pasley, S. The Social Readjustment Rating Scale: A study of the significance of life events in age groups ranging from college freshmen to seventh grade. As part of Tutorial in Psychology, Chatham College, Pittsburgh, 1969.

Rahe, R. H. Life-change measurement as a predictor of illness. *Proceedings of the Royal Society of Medicine,* 1968, **61,** 1124–1126.

Rahe, R. H. Multi-cultural correlations of life change scaling: America, Japan, Denmark and Sweden. *Journal of Psychosomatic Research,* 1969, **13,** 191–195.

Rahe, R. H., & Holmes, T. H. Life crisis and disease onset: A prospective study of life crises and health changes. Unpublished. (b)

Rahe, R. H., & Holmes, T. H. Life crisis and disease onset: Qualitative and quantitative definition of the life crisis and its association with health change. Unpublished. (a)

Rahe, R. H., & Holmes, T. H. Social, psychologic and psychophysiologic aspects of inguinal hernia. *Journal of Psychosomatic Research,* 1965, **8,** 487–491.

Rahe, R. H., & Lind, E. Psychosocial factors and sudden cardiac death: A pilot study. *Journal of Psychosomatic Research,* 1971, **15,** 19–24.

Rahe, R. H., Mahan, J. L., & Arthur, R. J. Prediction of near-future health change from subjects' preceding life changes. *Journal of Psychosomatic Research,* 1970, **14,** 401–406.

Rahe, R. H., Meyer, M., Smith, M., Kjaer, G., & Holmes, T. H. Social stress and illness onset. *Journal of Psychosomatic Research,* 1964, **8,** 35–44.

Rahe, R. H., & Paasikivi, J. Psychosocial factors and myocardial infarction. II. An outpatient study in Sweden. *Journal of Psychosomatic Research,* 1971, **15,** 33–39.

Rashevsky, N. *Some Medical Aspects of Mathematical Biology.* Springfield, Ill.: Charles C Thomas, 1964.

Rubin, R. T., Gunderson, E. K. E., & Arthur, R. J. Life stress and illness patterns in the U.S. Navy. III. Prior life change and illness onset in an attack carrier's crew. *Archives of Environmental Health,* 1969, **19,** 753–757.

Rubin, R. T., Gunderson, E. K. E., & Arthur, R. J. Life stress and illness patterns in the U.S. Navy. V. Prior life change and illness onset in a battleship crew. *Journal of Psychosomatic Research,* 1971, **15,** 89–94.

Ruch, L. O., & Holmes, T. H. Scaling of life change: Comparison of direct and indirect methods. *Journal of Psychosomatic Research,* 1971, **15,** 221–227.

Sellin, T., & Wolfgang, M. E. *The Measurement of Delinquency.* New York: John Wiley & Sons, 1964.

Seppa, M. T. The Social Readjustment Rating Scale and the Seriousness of Illness Rating Scale: A comparison of Salvadorans, Spanish and Americans. Medical thesis, University of Washington, Seattle, 1972.

Siegel, S. *Nonparametric Statistics for the Behavioral Sciences.* New York: McGraw-Hill Book Company, 1956.

Smith, M. Psychogenic factors in skin disease. Medical thesis, University of Washington, Seattle, 1962.

Stevens, S. S. A metric for the social consensus. *Science,* 1966, **151,** 530–541.

Stevens, S. S., & Galanter, E. H. Ratio scales and category scales for a dozen perceptual continua. *Journal of Experimental Psychology,* 1957, **54,** 377–411.

Stevenson, I., & Graham, D. T. Disease as response to life stress. II. Obtaining the evidence clinically. In H. I. Lief, V. F. Lief, N. R. Lief (Eds.), *The Psychological Basis of Medical Practice.* New York: Hoeber Medical Division of Harper and Row, 1963. Pp. 137–153.

Theorell, T., & Rahe, R. H. Psychosocial factors and myocardial infarction. I. An inpatient study in Sweden. *Journal of Psychosomatic Research,* 1971, **15,** 25–31.

Thurlow, H. J. Illness in relation to life situation and sick-role tendency. *Journal of Psychosomatic Research,* 1971, **15,** 73–88.

Thurstone, L. L. *The Measurement of Values.* Chicago: University of Chicago Press, 1959.

Tollefson, D. J. The relationship between the occurrence of fractures and life crisis events. Master of Nursing thesis, University of Washington, Seattle, 1972.

Torgerson, W. S. *Theory and Methods of Scaling.* New York: John Wiley & Sons, 1958.

U.S. National Health Survey. June 1961. Health Interview Responses Compared with Medical Records, Series D-5, Public Health Service, Washington, D.C.

U.S. National Health Survey, January 1963. Comparison of Hospitalization Reporting in Three Survey Procedures, Series D-8, Public Health Service, Washington, D.C.

Weiss, E., Dlin, B., Rollin, H. R., Fischer, H. K., & Bepler, C. R. Emotional factors in coronary occlusion. *Archives of Internal Medicine,* 1957, **99,** 628–641.

Wenar, C., & Coulter, J. B. A reliability study of developmental histories. *Child Development,* 1962, **33,** 453–462.

Wold, D. A. The adjustment of siblings to childhood leukemia. Medical thesis, University of Washington, Seattle, 1968.

Wolf, S. *The Stomach.* New York: Oxford University Press, 1965.

Wolf, S., Cardon, P. V., Shepard, E. M., & Wolff, H. G. *Life Stress and Essential Hypertension.* Baltimore, Md.: The Williams and Wilkins Company, 1950.

Wolff, H. G., Wolf, S., & Hare, C. C. *Life Stress and Bodily Disease.* Baltimore, Md.: The Williams and Wilkins Company, 1950.

Woon, T., Masuda, M., Wagner, N. N., & Holmes, T. H. The Social Readjustment Rating Scale: A cross-cultural study of Malaysians and Americans. *Journal of Cross-Cultural Psychology,* 1971, **2,** 373–386.

Wyler, A. R., Masuda, M., & Holmes, T. H. Magnitude of life events and seriousness of illness. *Psychosomatic Medicine,* 1971, **33,** 115–122.

Wyler, A. R., Masuda, M., & Holmes, T. H. Seriousness of Illness Rating Scale. *Journal of Psychosomatic Research,* 1968, **11,** 363–374.

Wyler, A. R., Masuda, M., & Holmes, T. H. The Seriousness of Illness Rating Scale: Reproducibility. *Journal of Psychosomatic Research,* 1970, **14,** 59–64.

Zilmer, M. E., Kogan, W. S., & Holmes, T. H. An investigation into the existence and nature of a correlation between Schedule of Recent Experience scores and actual health care utilization. Unpublished.

CHAPTER 4

The Pathway Between Subjects' Recent Life Changes and Their Near-Future Illness Reports: Representative Results and Methodological Issues *

RICHARD H. RAHE

INTRODUCTION

In the Spring of 1972 some of my colleagues at the U.S. Navy Medical Neuropsychiatric Research Unit and I organized a North Atlantic Treaty Organization scientific symposium on the topic of life stress and illness. This conference, which was held in the pastoral setting of Beitostölen, Norway, brought together researchers who had studied life changes and physical illness with others who had worked with life changes and mental disease and highlighted the fact that it was indeed time that much of the life-change research done in separate corners of the world be brought together and viewed in its entirety. This book continues to develop the needed interresearcher communication in our rather specialized field. In keeping with this theme, my chapter is an attempt to present an overview of several important steps along the pathway between subjects' life changes and their near-future illness reporting. In addition, I will present some representative results from my work at the Navy unit to illustrate the nature of relationship between steps along this pathway. Finally, I wish to call attention to some key methodologic issues.

Dr. Thomas Holmes, in the preceding chapter (with Dr. Minoru Masuda), cogently presented our early life-change and illness studies done at the University of Washington. I will therefore not reiterate early methodologic studies but

* Report 73-47, supported by the Bureau of Medicine and Surgery, Department of the Navy, under Research Work Unit MF51.524.0025011DD5G. Opinions expressed are those of the author and are not to be construed as necessarily reflecting the official view or endorsement of the Department of the Navy.

assume you know what I mean whan I talk of life-change units (LCU). I begin therefore with my conceptualization of stressful life events and their effects.

Conceptualization of the Pathway between Stress and Illness

Figure 1 presents the pathway along which environmental stresses must ''travel'' and the transformations that occur before they may stimulate subjects' illness reports. This conceptualization utilizes optical lenses and filters to illustrate various steps along the pathway. In addition, a physiologic ''black box'' and an illness rule are depicted.

First, ''light rays'' of various intensities are drawn at the left edge of the figure symbolizing a subject's environmental input. In our schema we consider these lines to represent subjects' recent LCU ''exposure.'' Thus the solid black lines represent high LCU events; thinner solid lines represent moderate LCU events; the thin dotted lines represent low LCU events.

The first filter shown in the figure (step 1) is what we call the ''past experience filter.'' This filter, much like a polarizing filter, represents how one's past experience with various life change events may alter his LCU values; some LCU values may thereby be augmented while others are lessened. Hence the lines between steps 1 and 2 in the figure indicate an individual's ''filtered'' estimates of his recent environmental exposure.

The negative lens next indicated in the figure (step 2) represents an individual's psychological defenses. Some life-change events are ''diffracted away'' by various ego defense mechanisms and cease to be of significance; others pass through one's defenses with little ''deflection.''

A subject's physiological reactions to his recent life-change events occur only when those events ''penetrate'' his psychological defenses. Such physiological reactions figuratively occur inside the physiological black box (step 3). This black box subsumes the entire discipline of psychophysiology. A vast array of studies have shown that life-change events perceived by a subject result in physiological activation in many body systems. Solid and dotted lines emerging from the black box in Figure 1 now represent various intensities of physiological activation rather than life events.

The filter shown above step 4 represents a subject's coping abilities. Here we define coping rather narrowly as one's abilities to reduce his physiological activation. This filter is much like a color filter in that certain of the body's physiological activations are ''absorbed'' through one's coping abilities whereas others continue unaffected. A coping mechanism such as a subject's ability to relax and thereby alter his psychophysiologic activation may diminish a rapid pulse rate, for example, but may not affect an elevated output of catecholamines.

Finally, physiological activation continuing despite one's coping abilities

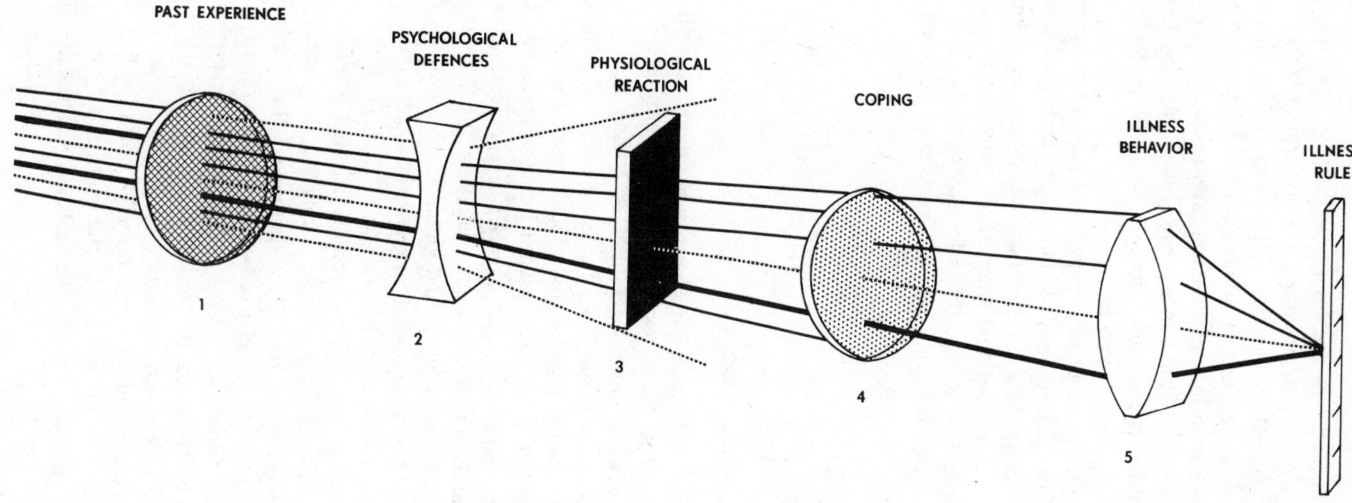

Figure 1. The pathway between subjects' exposure to recent life change and their near-future illness reports. Permission kindly granted by Archives of General Psychiatry.

may or may not be interpreted by the subject as body symptoms. Furthermore, even if an individual interprets his physiologic activation as body symptoms, he may or may not seek medical counsel regarding them. The positive lens shown above step 5 therefore symbolizes a subject's illness behavior—that is, his decision to focus attention on his perceived physiological activation and report these perceptions as body symptoms to a medical authority. Medical personnel may then diagnose these symptoms, along with possible pathologic tissue changes, as indicative of illness (step 6).

In sum, a subject's recent life-change experience passes through several steps of perception and defense before body symptoms are perceived and perhaps reported. Along this pathway there are several chances for the life-change input to be handled in such a manner that they never stimulate a subject's illness reporting. Despite these limitations, the selected research results that follow illustrate that significant correlations are still seen, even between distant steps along this pathway.

SELECTED RESULTS

Subjects' Past Experience Filter

Previous studies of subjects' recent life changes and their near-future illness experience reported from our Navy research unit have utilitzed LCU estimates derived from group scaling studies (Holmes & Rahe, 1967; Rahe, 1969b). These LCU values are mean (geometric) values of subjects' estimates which ignore wide variability found among individual reporters (Rahe, Lundberg, Theorell, & Bennett, 1971). In dealing with large samples one can use these mean LCU values and assume that the number of underestimations of various individuals' LCU values for one life-change event are balanced out by the number of overestimations of other individual's LCU values for the same event. In dealing with small groups of subjects, however, individual variation in LCU scaling may assume some importance.

Theorell, in his chapter in this book, points out that healthy subjects registered lower LCU estimates for life-change events they had actually experienced than did others who had not recently experienced these events. Other researchers found the opposite to be true—particularly with life-change events connoting separations (Horowitz, Shaefer, & Cooney, in press). In addition, subjects' LCU values for recent life changes are seen to decrease over time from the occurrence of the event (Horowitz et al., in press).

Currently we are experimenting at our research unit to define an individual's particular LCU estimates of his recent life-change events by using a slight modification of the LCU scaling method. We call this method the Subjective Life

Change Unit scaling system, or the SLCU method. The instructions for this scaling follow.

Instructions for Scoring Your Adjustment to Your Recent Life Changes

Persons adapt to their recent life changes in different ways. Some people find the adjustment to a residential move, for example, to be enormous, whereas others find very little life adjustment necessary. You are now requested to "score" each of the recent life changes that you marked with an X as to the amount of adjustment you needed to handle the event.

Your scores can range from 1 to 100 "points." If, for example, you experienced a residential move but felt it required very little life adjustment, you would choose a low number and place it in the blank to the right of the question boxes. On the other hand, if you recently changed residence and felt it required a near maximal life adjustment, you would place a high number, toward 100, in the blank to the right of that question's boxes. For intermediate life adjustment scores you would choose intermediate numbers between 1 and 100.

Please go back through your questionnaire and for each recent life change you indicated with an X choose your personal life change adjustment score (between 1 and 100) which reflects what you saw to be the amount of life adjustment necessary to cope with or handle the event. Use both your estimates of the intensity of the life change and its duration to arrive at your scores.

Psychological Defenses and Physiological Activation

Hinkle and Antonovsky illustrate in their chapters in this book how some subjects may experience life changes of intense magnitudes and appear to be little affected by them—at least they do not become demonstrably ill soon after their experiences. Hinkle comments that some of his subjects who remained healthy in spite of severe adversity appeared to show "emotional insulation" from their recent stresses.

A more recent study depicting how a subject's psychological defenses may prevent his recent life stresses from causing psychophysiologic activation was one of parents whose children were dying of leukemia (Wolff, Friedman, Hofer, & Mason, 1964). These parents' 17-hydroxycorticosteroid (17-OHCS) excretion was periodically measured over this stressful experience. Parents who handled this stress by adequate psychological defense mechanisms, chiefly characterized by repression of affect and projection of their concern onto cancer victims in general, showed normal 17-OHCS excretion rates. On the other hand, parents who were unable to psychologically defend themselves against the imminent death of their child and often admitted to feelings of despair demonstrated abnormally elevated 17-OHCS excretion rates.

Many of our current Navy investigations are directed toward an understanding of such psychophysiological phenomena. Only with such an understanding of physiological mechanisms along the pathway between life change and illness can we begin to objectively measure subjects' reactions to life stress.

Coping and Symptom Formation

Data concerning subjects' recent life changes, symptom recognition, and illness reports have been reported on four Naval populations (Rahe, Gunderson, & Arthur, 1970; Rahe, 1972; Rahe, Fløistad, Bergan, Ringdahl, Gerhardt, Gunderson, & Arthur, 1973). Subjects' recent life changes were gathered by the use of the Schedule of Recent Experience (SRE) questionnaire (Hawkins, Davies, & Holmes, 1957; Rahe, 1969a). Body symptom recognition was estimated by use of the Health Opinion Survey (HOS) (MacMillan, 1957). Subjects' illness reports were gathered *prospectively* over the ensuing six-month to one-year interval by physician reviews of their standard health records. Seventy to eighty percent of illness reports were seen to involve just four of the major body systems: gastrointestinal, genital-urinary, musculoskeletal, and dermal. Illnesses reported were generally minor in severity.

The SRE questionnaire presents subjects with a list of 42 representative life-change events previously listed in Holmes and Masuda's chapter. Respondents indicate which if any of these events occurred to them over the past few years and if events have occurred, when they happened. The timing of the events is generally indicated by the respondent marking the appropriate six-month interval(s) over the past two to three years. Thus for each subject a total number of life changes experienced over successive six-month intervals is calculated. Next subjects' recent life changes are given standard LCU scores. Each subject thereby attains a LCU total for 0–6 months prior to study, 7–12 months prior, 13–18 months prior, and so on.

The HOS questionnaire contains 20 questions about subjects' perceptions of body symptoms. For example: Are you ever bothered by your heart beating hard? Do you ever feel bothered by all sorts of pains or ailments in different parts of your body? Each question is scored on a 3-point continuum (except one dichotomously scored question). In our scoring system, which is the inverse of the system used by Myers (described in the Myers, Lindenthal, & Pepper chapter in this volume), the greater the subject's perception of body symptoms the higher his score. Macmillan was interested in utilizing these body symptom questions to arrive at estimations of subjects' tendencies toward psychoneurosis as indicated by their feelings of depression and anxiety over their current state of health. We have generally stayed away from the psychological diagnosis potential of the HOS and used it mainly as a measure of subjects' perceptions of their psychophysiologic activation.

Data presented below were gathered from nearly 2500 U.S. Navy enlisted men aboard three heavy cruisers and from slightly over 1000 Royal Norwegian Navy enlisted men serving aboard smaller ships and patrol boats. Average age of the U.S. Navy subjects was 22 years; average age of the Norwegians was 21 years. Men from both countries were usually unmarried and nearly all had attained the equivalent of a high school education.

Body Symptom Reporting

Table 1 presents data on subjects' six-month LCU estimates over the two and one-half years prior to study correlated with their perceptions of body symptoms at the time of study. It can be seen that for the U.S. Navy men aboard each of the cruisers—the U.S.S. St. Paul, the U.S.S. Canberra, and the U.S.S. Galveston—as well as for the Norwegians, the most recent six-month interval consistently showed highest correlation with currently perceived body symptoms. The further back in time was the six-month LCU report, the lower was the correlation seen between subjects' life changes and their current body symptoms. These findings suggest that it is the very recent life change events which predominantly influence currently perceived body symptomatology. Research by others has also shown correlations between subjects' immediately prior six-month LCU reports and their current or near-future body symptomatology of approximately .35 (Cline & Chosey, 1972; Dohrenwend, 1973).

As stated earlier, the coping filter (step 4) in Figure 1 connotes whether or not subjects successfully "absorb" their physiological activation. If they cope successfully with their physiological activation, symptoms cease. Subjects who

Table 1. Correlations between 3245 Subjects' Recent LCU Scores over Two and One-half Years prior to Study and Their Body Symptoms Scores Registered at the Time of the Study

	U.S. Navy			
Time Intervals prior to Study (months)	St. Paul ($N = 785$)	Canberra ($N = 893$)	Galveston ($N = 746$)	Norwegian Navy ($N = 821$)
0–6	0.35**	0.22**	0.36**	0.22**
7–12	0.25**	0.16**	0.28**	0.23**
13–18	0.21**	0.19**	0.20**	0.16**
19–24	0.18**	0.15**	0.24**	0.11*
25–30	0.18**	0.11*	0.17**	—

** $p < 0.001$.
* $p < 0.01$.

do not successfully cope with their psychophysiological activation still may not report their body symptoms to medical personnel. The correlation between our Navy subjects' body symptoms score and their illness reports over the following six months to one year was approximately .35, however.

Why some subjects decide to report body symptoms and others do not has been a subject of several studies by the author of the next chapter, Dr. David Mechanic. After noting that many persons with body symptoms do not report them to a medical facility, what is the order of correlation seen between subjects' recent LCU and their near-future illness reports?

Illness Reporting

Table 2 represents correlations found between U.S. and Norwegian Navy subjects' six-month LCU magnitudes over two and one-half years prior to study with their illness reports *prospectively* gathered over a 6- to 13-month follow-up period. Illness reporting was measured in terms of physician-evaluated new illness reports per 1000 men per day. As anticipated, the correlations seen were lower than those found between subjects' recent life-change magnitudes and their body symptom reports (Table 1). Although low in magnitude, many of the correlations in Table 2 still achieved statistical significance.

A direct relationship has been seen between subjects' immediately prior six-month LCU magnitude and the medical severity of their near-future illness reports (Rahe, McKean, & Arthur, 1967; Rahe, Bennett, Romo, Siltanen, & Arthur, 1973). In special groups of Navy men who frequently encounter serious illnesses, such as injuries, the correlation seen between the men's recent LCU

Table 2. Correlations between 3265 Subjects' Recent LCU Scores over Two and One-Half Years prior to Study and Their Number of Reported Illnesses over Six to Thirteen Months of Prospective Follow-Up

	U.S. Navy			
Time Intervals prior to Study (months)	St. Paul ($N = 802$)	Canberra ($N = 895$)	Galveston ($N = 747$)	Norwegian Navy ($N = 821$)
0–6	0.10*	0.12**	0.16**	0.12**
7–12	0.08*	0.03	0.16**	0.09*
13–18	0.06	0.08*	0.13**	0.08*
19–24	0.05	0.07	0.14**	0.05
25–30	0.07	0.02	0.09*	—

** $p \leq 0.001$.
* $p \leq 0.01$.

and their near-future illness reports was .50 (Rahe, Biersner, Ryman, & Arthur, 1972).

In shipboard studies, however, where the men primarily experience minor illnesses, the possibilities of the men successfully ignoring body symptoms and not reporting them to a medical facility are many. This option, of men not reporting perceived body symptoms, leads us to the topic of subjects' illness behavior.

Illness Behavior

In both the U.S. and the Norwegian Navy studies we saw that a subject's age, his marital status, and his job satisfaction exerted an influence on his illness behavior. Subjects with high body symptom reports but none or just one illness report tended to be older, married, and more satisfied with their work than did similarly symptomatic subjects who reported several illnesses.

Our current studies of shipboard populations also focus heavily on environmental factors influencing the men's illness behavior. For example, certain divisions of men aboard ship report illnesses between two to three times the rate of men in other divisions (Pugh, Gunderson, Erickson, Rahe, & Rubin, 1972). Environmental stresses, such as rank, responsibilities for others, and work overload have also been shown to significantly influence the men's illness reporting rates (Rahe, Gunderson, Pugh, Rubin, & Arthur, 1972).

DISCUSSION OF THREE METHODOLOGIC ISSUES

I now would like to discuss briefly three methodologic issues. First is the precarious nature of currently making any assumptions regarding the significance of socially desirable or "positive" life-change events in their influence on subjects' illness reporting. Second, magnitude scaling of subjects' recent life-change events appears to be unnecessary for populations chiefly experiencing low to moderately low LCU recent life-change events. Third, the incomplete state of our present knowledge of the validity and reliability of the SRE questionnaire needs to be outlined.

Positive versus Negative Events

Our original list of 42 life-change events was empirically derived from patient interviews carried out at the University of Washington. It simply proved to be the case that subjects occasionally reported socially desirable or "positive" life-change events prior to their illness onsets along with more frequently reported socially undesirable or "negative" events. Thus a few positive life events were included in our list. Moreover, in my several prospective studies at the Navy research unit, subjects' positive life-change events uniformly showed positive (direct) correlations with subjects' illness reports. Myers found similar results in his prospective studies. Thus it appears that subjects' positive life changes—marriage, promotion, vacation and so on—are frequently followed by illness reports.

Brown, Paykel, and Gersten and her co-authors report in their chapters that in their retrospective studies patients with depression and parents of mentally disturbed children reported an improvement in symptomatology following positive life changes. Would they have found the same results had their studies been prospective in design? More important, however, is the fact that none of us has yet presented subjects with a sufficiently long list of positive life events to be able to draw firm conclusions one way or the other as to how they affect subjects' illness reports.

The LCU Scale versus a Simple Unit Scale

An interesting problem which arises when using the LCU magnitude scale with samples of subjects who primarily report low to moderately low LCU events is that one can dispense with the LCU scale. In most of our Navy studies, for example, our subjects are young, single men who generally report low to moderately low recent life changes which range between 17 and 44 LCU. These events cluster around a mean of approximately 25 LCU. In other words, there generally proves to be very little difference in the LCU values of the men's recent life-change events. In fact, correlations run between subjects' LCU scores and simple unit scores for their recent life changes (scoring each life change event as 1) have reached as high as .89.

Rather than throw out the LCU method, one must simply become critical in identifying samples where its use is appropriate. For example, in some of our present Navy studies of persons developing coronary heart disease we are dealing with samples of middle-aged men and women who report such recent life-change events as changing jobs, falling into debt, buying a home, divorce, and death of spouse. It seems crucial here to treat an event such as divorce (73 LCU) differently from an event such as a recent residential move (20 LCU). As pointed out in Theorell's chapter in this book, only when his coronary heart disease subjects were analyzed in terms of their recent LCU values were their recent life-change data significantly different from those of control subjects; simple unit scaling did not differentiate between his heart disease and control samples.

Validity and Reliability of the SRE Questionnaire

In my studies of over 600 subjects with coronary heart disease, where subjects' recent life changes are gathered *both* by interview and by questionnaire, the interviewers have been invariably impressed that the information obtained by questionnaire is a valid although conservative estimate of subjects' recent life-change experience. When interviewers probed into respondents' answers, they found that subjects rarely if ever listed life-change events which they had not experienced. For one example of 140 patients the patients completed the questionnaire for themselves and their spouses completed a separate questionnaire "as if" they were the patient (Rahe, Romo, Bennett, & Siltanen, 1973). Realizing that spouses do not know all of their mate's recent life changes, interpair correlations still ran between .50 and .75 over the one to two years immediately prior to study. Brown, in his chapter, indicates that when the life events are carefully dated by interviewers and confined to those events that both husband and wife would know about, interpair correlations can be obtained as high as .78. Hence it appears that the SRE questionnaire is a moderately valid measure, but less valid and more conservative than an interview.

Reliability estimates of the questionnaire have varied from as high as .90 to as low as .26 (Thurlow, 1971; McDonald, Pugh, Gunderson, & Rahe, 1972; Casey, Masuda, & Holmes, 1967). This dramatic falloff in reliability seems to be related primarily to (1) the time interval between administrations of the questionnaire, (2) the education level, and probable intelligence level, of the subjects, (3) the time interval over which subjects' recent life changes are summed, (4) the wording and format of the various life event questions, and (5) the intercorrelations between various life-change events.

When the time interval between questionnaire administrations was two weeks, the test-retest correlation was .90; when the interval was eight months, the correlations ranged between .64 and .74; a ten-month interval gave correlations between .52 and .61; a two-year interval gave a correlation of .26. Highest correlations were obtained from graduate students in psychology (.90) and physicians (.64 to .74). Intermediate correlations were obtained from military enlisted men (.55 to .61). The extremely low correlation of .26 was obtained from brewery workers. When subjects reported life changes for yearly rather than six-month intervals, reliability increased. Questions with modifiers in them (e.g., "major" or "a lot more") and questions with intricate formats were less reliably answered than those without qualifiers and those more simply presented. Finally, since many of the life-change questions proved to be highly intercorrelated, test-retest reliability was seen to be enhanced by handling the questions by interrelated clusters rather than by LCU score.

Currently at the Navy research unit we are experimenting with changes in the format of the SRE questionnaire, the dropping of qualifiers from various questions, and have worked on a life-change cluster scoring technique (Rahe, Pugh, Erickson, Gunderson, & Rubin, 1971; Pugh, Erickson, Rubin, Gunderson, & Rahe, 1971; McDonald, 1973). Recently a simplified format SRE achieved a test-retest correlation (over one month) of .90 for Navy enlisted men (McDonald, 1973).

Since a questionnaire is the only practical device for use in large-scale epidemiological investigations, it is important to strive for highest reliability. Limiting factors such as intelligence of subjects or subjects' lack of motivation to cooperate in the questionnaire's completion will always lend questionnaire results somewhat lower reliabilities than that which might be achieved through solicitous interviews.

SUMMARY COMMENT

In closing I reiterate there are many intervening variables to be considered between a subject's recent exposure to life change and his perception of body symptoms as well as his possible near-future illness reports. The more proximal the steps depicted in Figure 1 are, the higher their correlation should be. For example, correlations seen for our Navy subjects between their recent LCU exposure (step 1) and their perceived body symptoms (step 4) were around .30; the correlations seen between these subjects' body symptoms (step 4) and their near-future illness reports (step 6) was .35; the correlations seen between these subjects' recent LCU (step 1) and their near-future illness reports (step 6) was around .12. Even skipping from subjects' recent LCU to their near-future illness reports (step 1 to step 6), it is impressive that something as simple as a brief questionnaire recording of subjects' recent life changes shows *any* significant correlation with a criterion as distant and unspectacular as subjects' minor illness reports up to a year later.

REFERENCES

Casey, R. L., Masuda, M., & Holmes, T. H. Quantitative study of recall of life events. *Journal of Psychosomatic Research,* 1967, **11,** 239–247.

Cline, D. W., & Chosey, J. J. A prospective study of life changes and subsequent health changes. *Archives of General Psychiatry,* 1972, **21,** 51.

Dohrenwend, B. S. Life events as stressors: A methodological inquiry. *Journal of Health and Social Behavior,* 1973, **14,** 167–175.

Gunderson, E. K. E., Rahe, R. H., & Arthur, R. J. The epidemiology of illness in naval environments. II. Demographic, social background, and occupational factors. *Military Medicine,* 1970, **135,** 453–463.

Hawkins, N. G., Davies, R., & Holmes, T. H. Evidence of psychosocial factors in the development of pulmonary tuberculosis. *American Review of Tuberculosis and Pulmonary Diseases,* 1957, **75,** 5.

Holmes, T. H., & Rahe, R. H. The social readjustment rating scale. *Journal of Psychosomatic Research,* 1967, **11,** 213–218.

Horowitz, M. J., Shaefer, C., & Cooney, P. Life event scaling for recency of experience. In E. K. E. Gunderson & R. H. Rahe (Eds.), *Stress and Illness*. (In press)

MacMillan, A. M. The health opinion survey: Technique for estimating prevalence of psychoneurotic and related types of disorder in communities. *Psychological Reports,* 1957, **2,** 325.

McDonald, B. W. Personal communication, 1973.

McDonald, B. W., Pugh, W. M., Gunderson, E. K. E., & Rahe, R. H. Reliability of life change cluster scores. *British Journal of Social and Clinical Psychology,* 1972, **2,** 407–409.

Pugh, W. M., Erickson, J., Rubin, R. T., Gunderson, E. K. E., & Rahe, R. H. Cluster analyses of life changes. II. Method and replication in Navy subpopulations. *Archives of General Psychiatry,* 1971, **25,** 333–340.

Pugh, W. M., Gunderson, E. K. E., Erickson, J., Rahe, R. H., & Rubin, R. T. Variations of illness incidence in Navy populations. *Military Medicine,* 1972, **137,** 224–227.

Rahe, R. H. Life change measurement as a predictor of illnesses. *Proceedings of the Royal Society of Medicine,* 1968, **61,** 1124–1126.

Rahe, R. H. Life crisis and health change. In Philip R. A. May & R. Whittenborn (Eds.), *Psychotropic Drug Response: Advances in Prediction*. Springfield, Ill.: Charles C Thomas, 1969. Pp. 92–125. (a)

Rahe, R. H. Multicultural correlations of life changes scaling: America, Japan, Denmark, and Sweden. *Journal of Psychosomatic Research,* 1969, **13,** 191–195. (b)

Rahe, R. H. Subjects' recent life changes and their near-future illness reports: A review. *Annals of Clinical Research,* 1972, **4,** 393–397.

Rahe, R. H., Bennett, L. K., Romo, M., Siltanen, P., & Arthur, R. J. Subjects' recent life changes and coronary heart disease in Finland. *American Journal of Psychiatry,* 1973, **130,** 1222–1226.

Rahe, R. H., Biersner, R. J., Ryman, D., & Arthur, R. J. Psychosocial predictors of illness behavior and failure in stressful training. *Journal of Health and Social Behavior,* 1972, **13,** 393–397.

Rahe, R. H., Fløistad, I., Bergan, T., Ringdahl, R., Gerhardt, R., Gunderson, E. K. E., & Arthur, R. J. Subjects' life changes, symptom recognition, and illness reports in the Norwegian Navy. Unit Report, U.S. Navy Medical Neuropsychiatric Research Unit, San Diego, 1973.

Rahe, R. H., Gunderson, E. K. E., & Arthur, R. J. Medical and psychiatric epidemiology in the reporting of acute illness. *Journal of Chronic Disease,* 1970, **23,** 245–255.

Rahe, R. H., Gunderson, E. K. E., Pugh, W., Rubin, R. T., & Arthur, R. J. Illness prediction studies. Use of psychosocial and occupational characteristics as predictors. *Archives of Environmental Health,* 1972, **25,** 192–197.

Rahe, R. H., Lundberg, U., Theorell, T., & Bennett, L. K. The social readjustment rating scale: A comparative study of Swedes and Americans. *Journal of Psychosomatic Research,* 1971, **15,** 241–249.

Rahe, R. H., McKean, J. D., & Arthur, R. J. A longitudinal study of life change and illness patterns. *Journal of Psychosomatic Research,* 1967, **10,** 355–366.

Rahe, R. H., Pugh, W. M., Erickson, J., Gunderson, E. K. E., & Rubin, R. T. Cluster analysis of life changes. I. Consistency of clusters across large Navy samples. *Archives of General Psychiatry,* 1971, **25,** 330–332.

Rahe, R. H., Romo, M., Bennett, L. K., & Siltanen, P. Finnish subjects' recent life changes, myocardial infarction, and abrupt coronary death. Unit Report 72-40, U.S. Navy Medical Neuropsychiatric Research Unit, San Diego, 1973.

Thurlow, H. J. Illness in relation to life situation and sick-role tendency. *Journal of Psychosomatic Research,* 1971, **15,** 73–88.

Wolff, C. T., Friedman, S. B., Hofer, M. A., & Mason, J. W. Relationships between psychological defenses and mean urinary 17-hydroxycorticosteroid excretion rates: Part I. A predictive study of parents of children with leukemia. *Psychosomatic Medicine,* 1964, **26,** 576–591.

CHAPTER 5

Discussion of Research Programs on Relations Between Stressful Life Events and Episodes of Physical Illness *

DAVID MECHANIC

INTRODUCTION

It is clear that stressful life events play some role in the occurrence of illness in populations. But any statement beyond this vague generalization is likely to stir controversy. The important issues in understanding how life events interact with social psychological, biological, and intrapsychic variables require specification of *what events* influence *what* illnesses under *what* conditions through *what* processes. A prerequisite for fruitfully addressing these questions is greater specification of dependent variables and the intervening links that explain associations between global measures of life events and various more specific indices of illness.

The three papers reviewed here summarize the work of investigators who have been on the forefront of efforts to expand our understanding of the role of life situations in adaptation and illness. We owe them much in the development of this area of inquiry, in stimulating our interest and curiosity, and in suggesting a variety of intriguing hypotheses based on the data they have collected. These investigations, charting new areas of concern, developed original perspectives and new forms of measurement. It is perhaps too easy to look back and raise one or another issue concerning the development of concepts, the precision of measurement, possible confounding variables, and the representativeness of samples.

Theory, if it is to be useful, must be tied to measurement in some fashion. Grand theory may evoke big ideas, but if they cannot in some fashion be translated into methods that are practical and communicable, understanding is

* Supported in part by grants from the National Institute of Mental Health (MH-20708) and the Robert Wood Johnson Foundation.

unlikely to go very far. The diffusion of instruments like the Schedule of Recent Experience or the Social Readjustment Rating Scale can be explained, I believe, by the need for a technology that allows research to go forward, and much of the failure in the developing study of the life-situation approach to disease in recent decades has been the absence of effective research methods that facilitate the translation of theoretical contentions into research questions. Even the most cursory acquaintance with the writings of Harold Wolff (1950), Franz Alexander (1950), Roy Grinker (1953), Michael Balint (1957), and many others would provide sufficient hypotheses to keep us busy for many years to come. The main difficulty has been our ability to pose the questions they raise in a fashion that allows verification or refutation, or that facilitates the exploration of alternative hypotheses that try to account for the same phenomena. The scales developed by Holmes and his co-workers are tools aimed at closing the gap between theory and research, and they provide an approach for beginning research in the area. But these tools have sometimes also been adopted in studies more because they were easy to use than because they adequately addressed the theoretical questions at issue.

However interesting it is to learn that stressful events precede the occurrence of illness more frequently than they occur in control populations, this observation does not take us very far either theoretically or from a practical standpoint. Since the illnesses of many individuals do not appear to be preceded by identifiable stressors, and since many people who are under stress do not become ill, meaningful statements must specify the conditions under which stress affects the occurrence of illness and consider how stress interacts with biological, psychological, and behavioral factors. Hinkle's chapter draws our attention to the complexity of this problem area, and the interactions between physical constitution, psychological states, and the impact of life events. His most impressive data pertain to coronary heart disease (Hinkle, 1968). We are hardly in a position to say that he has had the last word here, nor may we generalize to illnesses whose characteristics are quite different. Hinkle, in accounting for the association between life events and patterns of illness, concludes, "Changes in significant social or interpersonal relationships are very often accompanied by changes in habits, changes in patterns of activity, changes in the intake of food and medication, and changes in exposure to potential sources of infection or trauma. They are also frequently associated with changes in mood, and with physiological changes directly mediated by the central nervous system. Any or all of these might affect the frequency or severity of illness." But even this complex statement hardly begins to exhaust the reasonable possibilities, and as my discussion proceeds I will develop some others. As we move into new research efforts, we must begin to develop designs that allow us to examine the power of competing hypotheses.

Before moving directly into the substance of the debate, I would like to raise one more peripheral issue. Rahe concluded elsewhere that the value of defining precipitating factors "is that such temporal factors may prove to be more readily brought under control than predisposing ones, such as heredity" (in press). If such statements are to be more than platitudes justifying our research efforts, we will have to give serious attention to whether such contentions are correct and if so, what approach might be more likely to yield information of practical import. The disregard in medicine for the life-situation approach stems less from its lack of plausibility than from its failure to provide the physician who endorses its reasonableness with a viable approach to the patient. Life situations are enormously difficult to modify, even with the greatest of commitment, and thus very serious attention will have to be given to the development of viable practice models derived from growing understanding of how life situations interact with the occurrence of illness.

CONSIDERATION OF SOME ALTERNATIVE MODELS OF ILLNESS

Much of the stress literature deals with general concepts of illness. Since we have yet to develop global measures of health and illness, investigators depend on persons' perceptions of their health, their reports of illness, or examination of medical records during some defined time period. Not only do all of these sources of information have various measurement biases, but they are also affected by patterns of illness behavior, that is, differential propensities to recognize and respond to bodily indications, to define oneself as ill, and to seek medical assistance. In many instances, how persons perceive their health status and the extent to which they use medical services reflect patterns of illness behavior as much as they indicate the presence of illness.

Medical practitioners proceed from a theoretical perspective that is far removed from the typical conceptions of those who seek their help. Patients tend to form constructions of their state of health on an experiential and empirical basis modified by prior assumptions, cultural learning, and world views. Although patients come to emphasize symptoms that discomfort them, frighten them, or disrupt usual activities and routines, physicians are more likely to think in terms of symptoms for which their techniques of practice apply. Thus whereas practitioners tend for the most part to separate physical and mental illness, as does the medical care system, patients respond to the whole gamut of their experience, both physical and intrapsychic, although they may not necessarily adopt a vocabulary of distress that is consistent with their response.

It is instructive to examine the correlates of persons' perceptions of their health. We have carried out studies in which we ask respondents to rate their health, and we have examined these perceptions in relation to reports of stress as well as to medical histories. For example, in a study of 151 women living in London, we found that those who reported that their health was fair, below average, or poor were more likely than those indicating good health to report a variety of symptoms during the previous month such as pains, tiredness, difficulty sleeping, and poor appetite. They were also more likely than women reporting better health to have a history of high blood pressure, bronchitis, and other chronic conditions. The largest differences among women reporting good health and those reporting poor health, however, were in the reports of a health history involving emotional difficulties and "nerves." Moreover, the general perception of health was correlated with every stress measure we included in the study. Whereas 47% of those in the low stress group visited their general practitioner 11 or more times during the three previous years, 71% of those in the high stress group had 11 or more visits. Similar results were obtained for the year immediately preceding the study.

My colleague Jim Greenley and I are presently carrying out an epidemiological study of psychological distress and help-seeking among some 1700 students. In this study we ask students to rate their *physical health*. As we anticipated, such ratings are substantially correlated with measures of psychological distress. The index in the study most highly associated with reports of physical health status is Langner's 22-item scale. To arrive at a better conception of what the basis of estimates of physical health was, we examined these reports in relation to some 200 symptom items reflecting a wide range of measures of personal problems and psychological distress. It is clear from this analysis that specific symptoms most highly correlated with ratings of physical health are those very characteristic of the presenting complaints of many patients seeking medical care. The picture that emerges is one of underlying depression with many vague and diffuse symptoms. These include being bothered by all sorts of ailments, feeling weak all over, having undefined pains, lacking energy, feeling tense and nervous, feeling depressed, drowsiness, nervous stomach, having personal worries, being nervous, feeling blue, and having headaches. As in other studies, the dimension of interference with normal activities also is clear. Students reporting poor physical health are more likely to report that their problems prevent them from doing what they like to do. We are presently collecting data from a large sample in Milwaukee which will allow us to examine how perceptions of physical health status relate to social stress, psychological distress, and medical histories, and how these factors interact with illness behavior in affecting rates of utilization of medical care. The data from the studies we have carried out thus far suggest that medical history, life changes, psychological distress, and illness behavior interact in complex ways, and each contributes independently to perceptions of illness and medical care utilization. For the purposes of our discussion here, all I need emphasize is that reported illness, whether reported directly in a medical interview or obtained from patients' medical records, is a global outcome measure resulting from a variety of different factors. I will return to this issue later in another context.

CONCEPTIONS OF STRESSFUL LIFE EVENTS AND THEIR IMPACT

A major theoretical issue, which receives considerable attention in this book, concerns the advisability of focusing on life events requiring adaptive changes regardless of their social or personal desirability as compared with events which are experienced as threatening or distressing. Although the issue is one that requires an empirical resolution, the theoretical implications of each of these two approaches are very different. The life-change approach implies that the significance of stress events is that they demand adaptation, which in itself is costly to the organism as demands increase. This notion is somewhat like Hans Selye's (1956) concept of stress as a nonspecific bodily response that is wearing on the biological system. It is less consistent with various cognitive theories of stress that give emphasis to perceptions of threat, loss, and challenges to self-esteem. Whereas the life-change conception does not appear to require consideration of psychological intervening variables, the cognitive perspective depends on them. Thus each conception suggests different research models, and each model may be appropriate for different types of illness.

If, for the purposes of discussion, we assume that life changes, even desirable ones, contribute to illness, we still must resolve alternative interpretations of the impact of such events. One possibility already mentioned assumes some direct biological response to continuing demands to maintain adaptive balance in the face of changing circumstances and demands, that is, that the high need for reactivity itself increases vulnerability to illness. Still another view is that the types of life event usually included in such stress scales involve new demands, changes in life routines, and breaks in established patterns. Thus such events as moving into a new and better house might, however globally defined, include a variety of smaller adjustments that involve psychological threats such as establishing relationships with new neighbors, getting the house in order, dealing with possible financial demands resulting from the move, and problems in the children's adjustment to new friends and new schools. Or the activity itself may take time and attention away from protective and anticipatory coping and thus result in increased risks of illness and accidents. A promotion on the job may involve increases in status and income, but it also may elevate performance demands, lead the person to question his competence and performance, or in other ways threaten personal comfort or disrupt working routines. Despite years of research on life changes, we know very little more about the meaning of such events to individuals, what new life demands they make, and what types of adjustment they require from these individuals.

Most scales of life events include relatively few events or life changes that are clearly positive in their impact. Although such events as marriage and retirement are positively defined, they call forth tremendous personal adjustments and may involve a variety of perceptual challenges. The level of conceptualization of such items is quite different from items such as "someone complimented you today," "you had an interesting afternoon," "you won an award for excellence." The items on the life-change scales imply situations requiring complex responses; the items just mentioned characterize experiences of mastery. I am skeptical that experiences of mastery would relate to illness. It is fairly obvious that persons seek life changes that add to their experience and that they can control. If our concern is not with mastery but with challenges of different types, calling forth varying magnitudes of difficulty, then I would think that as we move into future studies we should characterize such demands more precisely. And I would further expect that the reaction to such demands would depend on the capacity of the person to deal with such life changes, and this in turn would depend on skills and preparation and social supports. As our research develops we need to give greater attention to such variables as coping skills and supportive relationships that may intervene between the occurrence of life events and the initiation of illness.

ILLNESS AND ILLNESS BEHAVIOR

The concept of illness usually used in life-change studies is one that confounds bodily conditions and behavior. Studies dealing with illness in general come to depend disproportionately on common instances of illness, particularly acute respiratory disease, which overshadow more important types of morbidity that occur with lower prevalence in the population. Such common instances of illness, such as respiratory disease, are also poor indicators because they are susceptible to extremely large biasing effects both in the reporting of morbidity and in seeking medical care. Measures of psychological distress are vulnerable to similar criticisms because of large biasing effects in reporting and seeking assistance.

Various prevalence studies of illness in the community which use short recall periods to insure reliability of memory find that only approximately one-third of those who report symptoms that are serious enough to do something about (such as restricting activities or self-medication) actually seek medical care (White, Williams, & Greenberg, 1961). Thus records of illness or work absenteeism are highly biased sources of information about illness and are a product of factors usually ignored in life-event studies. A careful morbidity interview would provide more reliable data if short recall periods were used, but I know of few life-event studies that have used sufficiently short recall periods to obtain reasonable measures of acute illness. In the area of psychological distress, the data on selective biases are even more impressive, and the selection factors in some instances may be as influential as the illnesses in accounting for seeking help.

One conception that has informed many stress studies is that the cumulation of life difficulties increases vulnerability to illness of all types and in all bodily systems. In characterizing the ''healthy'' and the ''ill'' telephone operators, Hinkle describes the healthy ones as women ''who liked their work, found it easy and satisfying, liked their families and associates, and were generally content and comfortable with their lot in life.'' In contrast, many of the ill operators ''were working at this job not because they liked it but from necessity. They often described it as confining or boring.'' Since illness is an attributional process, encompassing the person's total experience, it is plausible that the differences between those described as healthy and ill are in part differences in attributional behavior. Just as symptoms may be a cause of visiting the doctor or taking time off from work, they may also serve as an excuse to do so. It is fully consistent with this perspective that those who hate their activities, or find them confining, take refuge in the sick role, whereas those who find such activities pleasurable ignore nondisabling symptoms. Since most studies of life events are dependent on illness measures, predominantly weighted by respiratory and other acute self-limited conditions, it is not unreasonable to suggest that much of the association found between life events and illness is explainable in terms of manipulating illness definitions for the benefits they deliver. This is no trivial issue, either theoretically or practically speaking. Much of the work-absenteeism literature, for example, assumes that improvements in controlling respiratory disease will substantially diminish failure to report to work. But if respiratory diagnoses are the excuse rather than the cause, then we might posit alternative conceptions.

In short, people who are unhappy, bored, or otherwise discontented may focus on symptoms that have a very high prevalence in the population, but which are frequently normalized, as a way of managing life events. Some persons, indeed, may develop a career of such responses, managing their lives and others through a vocabulary of illness. The career may fluctuate depending on the difficulties of one's life, but the repertoire may be available whenever things become too tough. I am not suggesting that such processes are by any means an independent alternative theory of illness clustering or the association between life events and illness reporting, but I do maintain that any serious exploration of the issue cannot afford to neglect these considerations.

The complications of meaning in these situations are suggested by some of the stimulating work of Imboden and colleagues (Imboden, Canter, & Cluff, 1961; Imboden, Canter, Cluff, & Trever, 1959) on the course of various infectious diseases. They suggest that depression becomes intertwined and confused with the symptoms of infectious disease, resulting in chronicity. This can be seen as a problem in attribution of illness, and it relates to our earlier discussion of the diffuse and vague complaints associated with perceptions of physical health. For example, the usual course of influenza and brucellosis is likely to leave the patient fatigued, with a lack of energy and interest, with weakness and a variety of other somatic symptoms. These symptoms may also accompany depression and other emotional distress. The similarity in symptoms makes it reasonable for the patient to attribute the occurrence of these symptoms, after the infection is no longer objectively evident, to the continued persistence of the illness. The similarity that makes such attributions more likely also makes it difficult for the physician to determine when the symptoms are a product of an emotional problem and when they are complications of the physical illness.

In our research examining the use of ambulatory medical services, we find that those who seek medical care most frequently seek care for problems that occur very commonly in the population, but which frequently go untreated. Thus the presence of the problem itself is not an adequate explanation for the patient's complaint to the physician. The probability that the person will present such a problem is increased when he is under stress. Hence our data suggest that stress is a factor triggering the use of a medical facility, although I would not preclude the possibility that stress plays a more direct role in the occurrence of illness as well. Our data further suggest that the relationship between stressful events and the use of medical facilities is mediated by various sociocultural and situational factors. Persons, because of prior upbringing and experience, develop varying propensities to use medical care services, are more or less skeptical of the medical care process, and have different vocabularies for expressing distress. These interact in complicated ways. We find, for example, that stress is more influential in triggering medical utilization when persons have a high propensity toward the use of medical services, but it is less influential when the tendency to depend on medical services is lower. Stress thus must be seen as a general motivating influence; among persons with low propensity toward the use of medical services, stress may lead to the initiation of other forms of coping behavior (Mechanic, 1972a, pp. 203–222, 1972b; Mechanic & Volkart, 1961).

This might be an appropriate occasion to emphasize the importance of motivational concepts in studies of stress and illness. To the extent that people have modest aspirations and less intense commitments, they more easily insulate themselves from stress. I find Hinkle's description of impressions of healthy subjects extremely provocative and worthy of continued exploration. He suggests that the persons with the least illness often showed little psychological reaction to events; they readily shifted to other relationships when established ones were disrupted, and some of them had an "almost 'sociopathic' flavor." He indicates that these persons often avoided demanding situations and "behaved as if their well-being were one of their primary concerns." To some unknown extent these differences among people probably have a constitutional basis, but it is also possible that these were people who handled their affairs to avoid emotional arousal.

Persons who can successfully manage arousal may avoid many of the psychophysiological symptoms we discussed, and thus also attributions of illness and associated help-seeking. Whether such persons actually have lower prevalence of various specific conditions is an issue worth pursuing; there is some evidence beyond Hinkle's studies that this is the case. For example, Shepherd and his group (Kessel & Shepherd, 1965) found that persons who rarely use physicians are healthy and tend to ignore more common illnesses. Further it has been observed that persons who accept their environment, and who do not struggle against it, experience greater personal comfort and less psychophysiological symptomatology. It has also been noted that particularly effective copers are frequently persons who tend to be task oriented but who tend not to be introspective. Such persons appear to have much less interference from psychological arousal that may deter from attention to a task orientation, and they appear to suffer less from doubts and indecision. However, we have yet to untangle what is cause and what is effect, which aspects of these behaviors stem from physical constitution and heredity and which from cultural background and social preparation. As René Dubos (1959) has noted, disease reflects man's aspirations and strivings. The capacity to feel distress and *dis-ease* may be a reflection of man's humanity.

I earlier referred to the selective processes in help-seeking for respiratory conditions and other common complaints, and I would like to conclude my discussion by reporting on some of the work Jim Greenley and I have been carrying out on the prevalence of psychological distress and its relationship to help-seeking behavior. In this study we are comparing a random sample of a student population with a consecutive sample of students seeking psychiatric care. Our data show a very large overlap in symptoms between those in the population and those seeking psychiatric assistance. For example, whereas 22% of the students in the random sample received a score of 8 or higher on Langner's 22-item scale, only 54% of those seeking psychiatric care had an equally high score. Although the magnitude of symptoms is the best predictor of seeking psychiatric care, it explains only a very modest proportion of the variance in help-seeking. Such factors as religion, religiosity, social background, and social values have a considerable effect on seeking care. Such effects could be a consequence either of different patterns of illness behavior or of the fact that these factors affect in some fashion the differential distribution of psychological distress. We thus examined the influence of these factors controlling for varying levels of psychological distress, and we find that most of the selective influences persist. We anticipated that the selection effects would be greatest in the mild and moderate symptom groups and less in the most severe symptom groups. Although this hypothesis was generally confirmed, the data were surprising in the extent to which the selection effects persisted in severe symptom groups, suggesting that even among students with the most severe symptoms, sociocultural factors influenced those who sought psychiatric care (Greenley & Mechanic, 1973).

In this study we have not attempted to differentiate the occurrence of objective stressors from students' reports of problems, stress, difficulty, and symptoms. But unlike many other studies, we have had respondents rate the severity of each symptom reported so that this could be taken into account. Our results seem to confirm those reported by Langner (Langner & Michael, 1963) and others. Simple counts of symptoms and problems result in findings very similar to those based on weighted indices. This result appears to occur because those who have more severe problems or symptoms also tend to report many other problems or symptoms as well.

I have raised many more issues than I have resolved. Illness and the responses to it are extremely complex phenomena, and their illumination requires complex investigations and conceptual schemes. The study of life events and illness is now a viable field of investigation, having aroused the interests of many researchers. It is time for us to refine our hypotheses and methods of investigation so that our efforts begin to cumulate and establish the utility of this viewpoint in the practice of medicine.

REFERENCES

Alexander, F., *Psychosomatic Medicine: Its Principles and Applications,* New York: Norton, 1950.

Balint, M. *The Doctor, His Patient, and the Illness.* New York: International Universities Press, 1957.

Dubos, R. *Mirage of Health.* New York: Harper, 1959.

Greenley, J., & Mechanic, D. Social factors in seeking psychiatric care. Paper presented at the annual meetings of the American Psychiatric Association, 1973.

Grinker, R. R. *Psychosomatic Research.* New York: Norton, 1953.

Hinkle, L. E., Jr. Occupation, education and coronary heart disease. *Science,* 1968, **161,** 238–46.

Imboden, J. B., Canter, A., & Cluff, L. E. Symptomatic recovery from medical disorders. *Journal of the American Medical Association,* 1961, **178,** 1182–1184.

Imboden, J. B., Canter, A., Cluff, L. E., & Trever, R. W. Brucellosis. III. Psychologic aspects of delayed convalescence. *Archives of Internal Medicine,* 1959, **103,** 406–414.

Kessel, N., & Shepherd, M. The health and attitudes of people who seldom consult a doctor. *Medical Care,* 1965, **3,** 6–10.

Langner, T. S., & Michael, S. T. *Life Stress and Mental Health: The Midtown Manhattan Study*. New York: Free Press, 1963.

Mechanic, D. *Public Expectations and Health Care*. New York: John Wiley & Sons, 1972. (a)

Mechanic, D. Social psychologic factors affecting the presentation of bodily complaints. *New England Journal of Medicine,* 1972, **286,** 1132–1139. (b)

Mechanic, D., & Volkart, E. H. Stress, illness behavior, and the sick role. *American Sociological Review,* 1961, **26,** 51–58.

Rahe, R. H. Life change and subjects' subsequent illness reports. In E. K. E. Gunderson & R. H. Rahe (Eds.), *Life Stress and Illness*. Springfield, Ill.: Charles C Thomas, 1974. Pp. 134–163.

Selye, H. *The Stress of Life*. New York: McGraw-Hill Book Company, 1956.

White, K., Williams, T. F., & Greenberg, B. G. The ecology of medical care. *New England Journal of Medicine,* 1961, **265,** 885–892.

Wolf, S., & Goodell, H. *Harold G. Wolff's Stress and Disease,* Second Edition. Springfield, Ill.: Charles C Thomas, 1968.

Wolff, H. G. Life stress and bodily disease—a formulation. In H. G. Wolff, S. G. Wolf, & C. C. Hare (Eds.), *Life Stress and Bodily Disease*. Baltimore: The Williams and Wilkins Company, 1950. Pp. 1059–1094.

PART 2

Clinical Research on Relations Between Stressful Life Events and Particular Types of Physical and Psychiatric Disorder

The four chapters in this part of the book have in common the research strategy of comparing patients of particular types with controls in efforts to assess the significance of life events. For Töres Theorell, the concern is with coronary heart disease; for Richard W. Hudgens and for Eugene S. Paykel, the focus is mainly on psychiatric disorders involving depression.

These three papers are extraordinary for the critical concern the authors show for the methods and research strategy they employ. Questions are raised, for example, about the extent to which some life events are themselves symptoms or consequences of illness and the problems this raises when working with retrospective reports. Vivid findings on such important factors as the role of loss in depression and on assessment of subjective "upset" associated with events related to cardiovascular disease are tempered by such concern.

The discussion of the first three chapters by Sidney Cobb reinforces these methodological concerns and suggests a general model that might guide future studies of the effects of stressful life events.

CHAPTER 6

Life Events Before and After the Onset of a Premature Myocardial Infarction

TÖRES THEORELL

INTRODUCTION

"Premature" (before age 65) myocardial infarctions (MI) occur predominantly in persons with combinations of certain clinical characteristics, such as elevated blood lipids, elevated blood pressure, excessive cigarette smoking, and diabetes (Keys, 1970). Several authors have described social and psychological traits which seem to predispose subjects to early development of MI (Theorell & Rahe, 1972). Furthermore, MI patients themselves as well as their relatives tend to report retrospectively that the year before disease onset was characterized by unusually many concomitant important changes in the patient's life (Dunbar, 1943; Rahe & Lind, 1971; Rahe & Paasikivi, 1971; Rahe, Romo, Bennett & Siltanen, 1973a; Theorell & Rahe, 1971; van der Valk & Groen, 1967). When all these clinical observations are added to one another one may ask: Do certain genetic traits, early childhood experiences, and clinical characteristics cooperate in forming reactions to life experiences that are harmful to "sensitized hearts"?

In the present chapter some psychoendocrine mechanisms related to the heart are discussed briefly. Then the variability of one of these hormonal systems, the catecholamines, is described in relation to stressful life experiences in young previous victims of MI. Retrospective reports of life changes during lifetime and during the last year before MI onset are compared in various ways with reports from comparable healthy subjects. Finally, an ongoing prospective investigation in Stockholm is described.

PHYSIOLOGICAL BACKGROUND

Coronary atherosclerosis, the predisposing process in most MI patients, is known to be influenced by genetic factors (Liljefors, 1970), diet (Keys, 1970), and cigarette smoking and hypertension (Tibblin, 1970). There is an interplay between such "coronary risk factors" and psychosocial factors. The latter factors may influence diet, smoking, and hypertension. On the other hand, some psychological characteristics may be the consequence of illness or "subclinical" (not yet clinically overt) characteristics of a subject.

A myocardial infarction (necrosis) may be *precipitated* by the following mechanisms:

1. Sudden thrombosis in a coronary artery. A clot (thrombosis) is formed in a narrow part of the artery, thus preventing blood supply to an area of the myocardium. As a consequence, a myocardial necrosis may develop. This process is facilitated by enhanced stickiness of the thrombocytes, which initiate local thrombosis formation on the vessel wall. Aggregation of the thrombocytes is facilitated by catecholamines, which may thus mediate thrombosis formation (Ardlie, Glew, & Schwartz, 1966).

2. Sudden bleeding in a lipid deposit (atherosclerotic formation) in a coronary artery wall. Such a bleeding may be induced by heavy physical or psychological strain, which both induce elevated pulse rate and blood pressure and thus mechanical strain in the vessel wall. This may cause a total extinction of blood flow in the artery. In this mechanism catecholamines may also have significance since they belong to those hormones that elevate pulse rate and blood pressure.

3. Increased oxygen consumption in the myocardium. If one part of the myocardium is supplied by narrow coronary arteries, *sudden increased demands* on the heart, if sufficiently long-lasting, may induce so serious an oxygen deficit in this area that necrosis develops. Such demands may also be mediated by catecholamines.

Thus catecholamines—mainly epinephrine and norepinephrine—belong to those hormonal systems that may mediate the precipitation of a myocardial necrosis in a vulnerable heart. It is not yet possible to study *in vivo* the catecholamines in the human myocardium. Therefore in studies of humans we have to study the output of cathecholamines either in blood, which may also give a rough estimation of catecholamines in the myocardium, or in urine. The output of free catecholamines in the urine collected during several hours has been reported to reflect reasonably well the sympathoadrenomedullary activity in a subject during the same period. Epinephrine output has been demonstrated to reflect mainly psychological strain, whereas norepinephrine output reflects both physical and psychological strains (Levi, 1972).

LIFE EVENTS AND CATECHOLAMINES

To obtain some estimation of the importance of naturally occurring life events to catecholamine output in premature MI patients, the following study was performed: 21 male subjects below 67 years of age (range 45–66, mean 56), who had suffered a myocardial infarction 1 to 2 years before the investigation, participated in a week-to-week prospective study. An interviewer who was ignorant of the patient's somatic symptoms each time checked a revised version of the Schedule of Recent Experiences (SRE) with him and calculated a total adjustment score for the past week. The patient was instructed to collect urine during the busy part of the last day of this week. A subject always collected his urine during the same weekday and also during the same hours of this day (±1 hour). He was instructed to note the time of start and stop of his urine collection. Careful instructions as to smoking, alcohol, diet, and physical activity were given, with the aim of keeping extraneous factors influencing catecholamine output as constant as possible in the subject. Interviews concerning these factors were made

Table 1. Individual Regressions and Correlations Between Epinephrine Output and Total Life-Change Scores per Week in the Longitudinal Study

LCU per week—Epinephrine per Day ($m\mu g \times 10^{-1}$/min)			
Case Number	**Correlation Coefficient**	**Number Accepted Observations**	**Regression Coefficient**
1	0.120	10	0.037
2	0.073	4	0.077
3	0.709	9	0.344
4	0.185	8	0.060
5	−0.374	9	−0.102
6	−0.294	8	−0.106
7	0.010	9	0.003
8	0.847	7	0.724
9	0.838	6	0.486
10	0.415	6	−0.191
11	0.240	3	2.357
12	0.602	7	0.446
13	0.865	9	0.510
14	0.347	8	0.164
15	0.434	7	0.172
16	0.738	6	0.390
17	0.138	14	0.098
18	0.343	7	0.078
19	0.836	7	0.598
20	—	2	0.221
21	0.407	4	0.333
		Mean of regressions	0.320
		Standard error	0.115
		t	2.778
		p	$< .02$

Table 2. Intrasubject Correlations Between Physiological Measures and Total Life-Change Scores per Week in the Longitudinal Study (N = 130–147, each value corrected for variations in *mean levels* between subjects)

r	LCU per Week	Epinephrine Output	Norepinephrine Output
Epinephrine output	0.32***		
Norepinephrine output	0.21*	0.72***	
Serum cholesterol	0.06	− 0.07	− 0.05
Serum triglyceride [1]	− 0.15	− 0.08	− 0.09
Serum uric acid	− 0.02	− 0.17*	0.23**
Serum creatinine	0.16	0.03	0.10

[1] Only subjects who had at least 8 hours fasting before venous puncture. $N = 102$.
* $p < .05$.
** $p < .01$.
*** $p < .001$.

each time, and when the subject had not been able to follow the instructions the corresponding observation was discarded according to criteria made in advance.

Tables 1 and 2 indicate the intrasubject correlations that were computed. Both epinephrine and norepinephrine output correlated significantly with life-change units (LCU) based on the total amount of adaptation that the subject reported that he had experienced during the week. The same finding was made also when weeks with registered items during the last day of the week were excluded from the correlation analysis. This means that several life events had psychoendocrine effects lasting several days. In this sample a 200% increase in LCU corresponded very roughly to a 100% increase in adrenaline output. However, according to Table 1, the individual variation in correlation between LCU and adrenaline output was great. Two subjects, for instance, had very significant life changes going on during the period but their catecholamine output remained stable. Personality was also important since ''impulsiveness,'' measured according to Eysenck-Schalling, and mean epinephrine output were significantly correlated with one another ($r = .65, p < .01$) (Schalling & Holmberg, 1970).

The study did give the impression that life events may have considerable effects on the catecholamine output in most subjects, but these effects vary with personality. Life events were also important to the clinical symptoms in several patients.

In this study no significant correlations were found with other studied metabolic variables (serum cholesterol, uric acid, and triglycerides). However, it was observed that during weeks with signs of overt depression the serum triglyceride levels were significantly elevated when compared with those of other weeks.

In the catecholamine study no dichotomization was made between undesirable and desirable events. Indeed, desirable events were in several cases observed to be accompanied by elevated epinephrine output in the urine (Theorell, 1970; Theorell, Lind, Fröberg, Karlsson, & Levi, 1972).

LIFE EVENTS DURING THE TOTAL LIFE SPAN

Numerous retrospective and prospective studies have demonstrated that certain anxious, ambitious, dissatisfied, and aggressive personality traits precede the onset of premature myocardial infarctions (e.g., Bonami & Rimé, 1972; Brosek, Keys, & Blackburn, 1970; Dunbar, 1943; Medalie, 1972; Rosenman, 1971; Wolf, 1969). Syme, Hyman, and Enterline (1964) proposed the hypothesis that excessive *mobility* in jobs and residence may be a premorbid social characteristic in victims of premature myocardial infarctions. Related to this hypothesis is the finding of Shekelle, Ostfeld, and Paul (1969) that subjects with an abnormally high number of social discrepancies—in education, religion, and economic and ethnic background between the subject and his parents and/or spouse—could be predicted to have an elevated incidence of premature myocardial infarctions compared to others. Hinkle, however, could not verify the "mobility hypothesis" in his studies (Hinkle, Whitney, Lehman, Dunn, Benjamin, King, Plakun, & Flehinger, 1968). Studies of conventional social variables show that men in lower socioeconomic and educational groups tend to have an elevated incidence of premature myocardial infarctions compared to others (Hinkle, 1971).

Data obtained in extensive interviews of 106 male MI patients below 60 years of age who had been cared for at our hospital during a 2½-year period were compared with data obtained from 96 male subjects, 40–60 years of age, who had been selected from the greater Stockholm area in a representative way (Lind & Theorell, 1973). The mean ages of the two groups were 50.9 and 50.3 years, respectively. The dropout frequency was 18% (22/118) in the control group and 3% (3/107) in the patient group. It should be pointed out that the consecutive patient sample is more representative of infarction patients than most similar samples described in the literature. The inhabitants in Stockholm do not have a *free* choice of hospital care, and private beds for this kind of emergency care did not exist during the investigation period. Furthermore, hospital care is free and the possible significance of attacks of central chest pain is widely known in Stockholm. Therefore persons in Stockholm with such attacks, regardless of socioeconomic group, more readily than in many other countries tend to seek help at the hospitals. One source of error, however, is created by those who die outside hospitals. Prospective investigations, however, have shown that those MI patients who die outside hospitals do not differ strikingly in personality traits from those who survive the first hours and get into hospital (Jenkins, Zyzanski, Rosenman, & Cleveland, 1971; Medalie, 1972).

The interviews comprised questions about childhood, number of and order among siblings, and education; about conflicts with parents, children, spouse, teachers at school, and superiors during military service and at work; about number of changes of residence and job throughout the total life span; about number of work hours per week; and also about attitudes toward work and family. Marital conditions were covered in several questions.

The following variables did discriminate patients from controls significantly: having grown up as a late child in a large family; reports of conflicts with teachers at school; low educational level; having been classified as not completely fit for military service; reports of conflicts with superiors at work; and excessive overtime work. The first variable, having grown up as a late child in a large family, is probably related to "low socioeconomic group." Socioeconomic status is very difficult to measure in Sweden. All these factors were significantly more frequent in the patient group than in the control group ($p < .05$). This tendency was constant in different income subgroups and also when mode of living was held constant. Patients below 50 years differed more from their control group than patients between 50 and 60 differed from theirs. The interviewer's possible knowledge or ignorance of the patient's diagnosis did not make any difference to these results.

Among those variables that did *not* discriminate the groups from one another the following should be mentioned: number of job changes throughout the total life span. In a questionnaire study of the nation-wide cooperative chain where most employees live outside Stockholm and the majority belongs to lower socioeconomic groups, however, premature MI patients were found to have had significantly more changes of residence after age 15 than a randomized sample of subjects in the cooperative chain individually matched according to age, sex, and kind of employment (Theorell, Lind, & Lundberg, 1973).

Thus when the mobility variable is studied in premature MI patients in Sweden conflicting results are obtained. Our studies, however, support the hypothesis that the typical premature MI patient has frequently been a "non-adapter" long before his coronary heart disease becomes manifest.

RECENT LIFE EVENTS

In 1968 two pilot studies were preformed retrospectively, with SRE technique (Rahe & Paasikivi, 1971; Theorell & Rahe, 1971), of survivors of myocardial infarctions who had been taken care of at our department. These studies showed that the patients frequently report a significant life-change buildup during the last half-year before disease onset compared to the corresponding half-year one or two years before and one year after. The magnitude of this increase measured by life-change units (LCU) was about two times baseline levels. In a sample of subjects who had died coronary deaths outside hospital, this life-change buildup, according to reports of close relatives, had a magnitude of three to four times baseline levels (Rahe & Lind, 1971). These findings have recently been replicated in Finland (Rahe, Romo, Bennett, & Siltanen, 1973b).

Swedish studies of life-change frequencies in healthy samples have not been published. Therefore the following study was performed. All subjects employed in the nation-wide Swedish cooperative chain who had been in full work in 1969 and 1970 but then developed a myocardial infarction during one of these years were individually matched to normal subjects according to age, sex, and kind of employment in the cooperative chain. All subjects ($N=69$ in both groups) were asked to fill out extended SRE questionnaires for the *year before infarction* (patients) and 1970 or 1971 (controls). A number of life-change items were retested in a second questionnaire since we suspected that the time instruction (12 months before disease onset or control year) might have been misunderstood. In the 20 cases where differences were found in life change registering between the first and second questionnaires, telephone interviews were performed. Due to deaths and serious illnesses in the patient sample the participation rate was somewhat lower in this group. Fifty-six and sixty-five subjects, respectively, participated in all the three stages of the study.

Table 3 shows the frequency of reported items in the two groups. Some items concerning work—change of work schedule, conflicts with superiors or colleagues, and increased responsibility—were more frequent among the patients. If the number of subjects who reported *any* of *eight work items* were registered, 41% of the patients compared to 17% of control subjects ($p<.01$) were found to have reported changes at work during the year investigated. Those eight items were: change to different line of work; retirement from work; major change in work schedule; increased responsibility; decreased responsibility; trouble with boss; trouble with colleagues; unemployed for more than one month. Also it was noted that accidents causing work absenteeism of at least three weeks' duration were more frequent in the patient group during the year (5 compared to 0). On the whole, however, as Figure 1 shows, the *number* of reported items was quite similar in the two groups.

It is obvious that the fact that the patient knew about the disease may have contaminated the answers to the questions. It should be pointed out, however, that overt illness *before* the MI onset could not explain the results. Table 4 shows the reported rates of illness of more than three weeks' duration in the two groups. They are similar in the two groups.

Table 3. Number of Subjects Who Reported Life-Change Items during 12 Months before Onset of Myocardial Infarction (patients) and during Control Year (control subjects) [1]

	Patient	Control
1. Change to different line of work	2	1
2. Retirement from work	0	0
3. Major change in working schedule	7	1
4. Increased responsibility in work	6	2
5. Decreased responsibility in work	2	2
6. Trouble with boss	7	2
7. Trouble with colleagues	8	4
8. Being unemployed for more than one month	0	3
9. Other major change in working conditions	10	7
10. Start or stop of extra work	5	4
11. Taking a course of studying at home for work purposes	6	15
12. Change of income	15	26
13. Other changes in economy	9	8
14. Marriage	0	0
15. Marital separation	0	1
16. Divorce	1	1
17. Conflicts with wife/husband	3	3
18. Conflicts with family	5	3
19. Conflicts with other relatives	3	1
20. Separation from wife/husband more than one month due to work, traveling, etc.	0	2
21. Wife/husband start or stop working	9	3
22. Birth or adoption of child	0	0
23. Change in sexual habits	13	13
24. Wife/husband seriously ill	5	5
25. Death of spouse	0	0
26. Son/daughter seriously ill	1	2
27. Death of son/daughter	0	0
28. Close relative seriously ill	14	14
29. Death of close relative	4	4
30. Close friend seriously ill	6	7
31. Death of close friend	3	3
32. Change of residence	2	2
33. Addition of new member to household (e.g., relative)	0	0
34. Family member leaving home	9	11
35. Other changes in living conditions	15	17
36. Major change in social habits	12	7

[1] The original samples consisted of 69 subjects each. Due to deaths and serious diseases in the patient group, the participation rate was lower in the patient group than in the control group, 56 and 65, respectively.

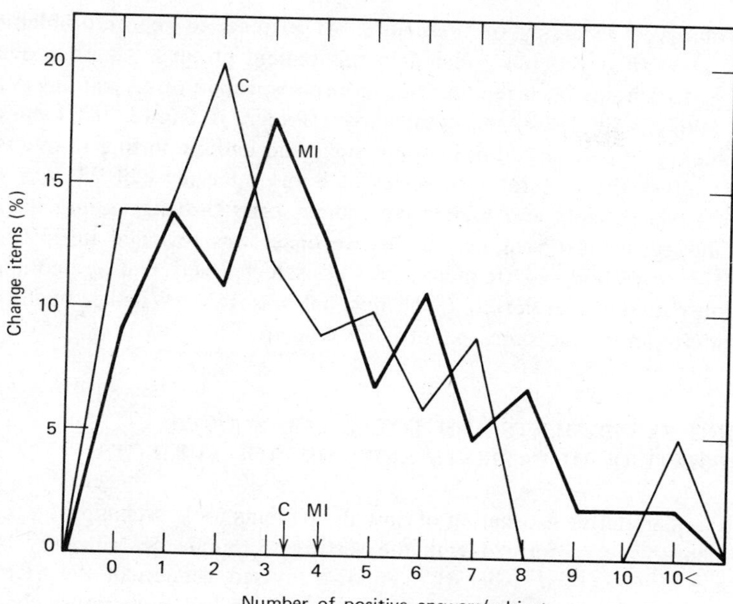

Figure 1. Distribution of subjects in myocardial infarction (MI) patient ($N = 56$) and control (C) ($N = 65$) groups according to *number* of registered life change items.

Table 4. Comparison Between Reported Rates of Different Illnesses of More than Three Weeks' Duration in Patients during Last Year before MI Onset and in Control Subjects during Corresponding Year

Illness	MI Patients ($N = 56$)	Control Subjects ($N = 65$)
Accidents	5	0
Cardiovascular	4	1
Uretherolithiasis	1	1
Arthritis, etc.	1	2
"Nervous"	1	0
Cancer of skin	0	1
Pneumonia	0	1
Low back pain	1	1
Tonsilitis	0	1

The observed tendency of premature MI patients to report problems and changes at work is probably related to this patient group's "work addiction" tendency, which has been reported in both retrospective (e.g., van der Valk & Groen, 1967; Wolf, 1969) and prospective (Bonami & Rimé, 1972) studies.

A tendency of overreporting in some areas and underreporting in others may further confuse the picture. In a series of home interviews of 23 *nonselected* premature MI patients and their wives some serious change going on in the family during the last year before disease onset was revealed in 35% of the cases. The corresponding frequency in a nonselected series of age-comparable infarction patients interviewed at the hospital was 16%. Whether healthy subjects underreport to the same extent is not known.

SCALING EXPERIMENTS AND TOTAL LCU SCORES IN PREMATURE MI PATIENTS AND CONTROL SUBJECTS

To find a quantitative estimation of how the patients look at changes, a series of experiments were performed with the scaling technique described by Holmes and Rahe (1967). First a list of events—a revised version of the SRE—was given to the MI patients and their control group in the cooperative chain (see above). The same list was also given to patients, derived in an analogous way, with *low back pain* and *neurosis* of more than three months' duration belonging to the same population. These latter two groups also had control groups, derived from randomized but individually age-, sex-, and employment-matched healthy subjects in the cooperative chain. All these subjects were asked to rate graphically with a cross on a straight horizontal line the severity of each event from 0 to 100 in relation to a standard event—more serious to the right, less serious to the left of the standard. One randomized fourth of the control groups was asked to rate the amount of *adjustment* that the event would require to him/her and another fourth was asked to rate the amount of *upsettingness* that the event would cause. Randomized halves of the patient groups were requested to perform the same procedures.

This experiment showed that neurosis patients tend to rate the events as requiring more adjustment and causing more upsettingness than their controls ($p < .01$ for both comparisons), whereas infarction patients tended to rate the events' amount of *upsettingness* but *not their amount of adjustment* higher than their controls ($p < .01$ for upsettingness). Low back pain patients did not differ in their scaling means from controls (Lundberg & Theorell, 1973a).

When adjustment and upsettingness scales were applied to the events reported for the investigated year in the two groups the following result was obtained: If the relative *readjustment* weights obtained from mean scores of the control subjects were used, the infarction group had a mean total score of 155, whereas the mean total score of the control group was 135. If relative *upsetting* weights were used with the same procedure, the corresponding mean total scores were 136 and 115, respectively. None of these differences between group means was significant, neither adjustment nor upsetting scores.

If the mean scores of *each group* were applied—the infarction group's mean scores for patients and the control group's mean scores for control subjects—the mean total *adjustment* score difference between the groups was of the same magnitude and nonsignificant (161 for patients and 135 for control subjects), whereas the mean total *upset* score difference between the groups was greater and significant (161 and 115, respectively, $p < .05$). These results are shown in Table 5 and Figure 2.

When weights that had been obtained from events the subjects had experienced themselves during the period were applied, the differences between obtained mean total scores were greater than with previously mentioned methods. As to *adjustment,* patient and control group mean total scores were 168 and 105 (the difference nonsignificant), respectively. As to *upsetting,* the corresponding means were 143 and 63, respectively ($p < .05$). Table 5 and Figure 3 present these results. Thus *individual* quality and perception of the changes were important. Upsettingness was more important than adjustment.

Finally, the effect of the experience of an event during the last year was stud-

Table 5. Mean Total Change Scores with Different Techniques in Patient and Control Groups

	Infarction Group			Control Group				
	Mean	Standard Deviation	N	Mean	Standard Deviation	N	t	$p<$
Readjustment								
Control group's mean item scores for both groups	155	115	56	135	123	65	0.91	n.s.
Group mean item scores for each group	161	118	56	135	123	65	1.19	n.s.
Individual scores	168	186	24	105	81	18	1.45	n.s.
Upset								
Control group's mean item scores for both groups	136	108	56	115	114	65	1.06	n.s.
Group mean item scores for each group	161	115	56	115	114	65	2.14	.05
Individual scores	143	135	25	63	67	13	2.37	.05

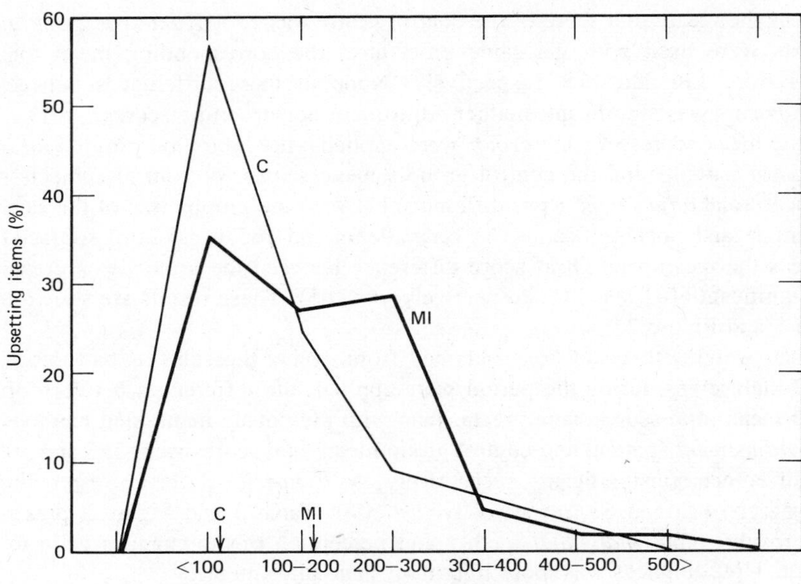

Figure 2. Distribution of subjects in MI patient (*N* = 56) and control (*N* = 65) groups according to total upset score per 12 months. The total scores based on each group's mean item scores.

Table 6. Mean Values of Total Life-Change Scores for Infarction Patients and Control Subjects

	Scores Based on Scales of Recently Experienced Items		Scores Based on Scales of Recently Nonexperienced Items	
	Controls	**Infarctions**	**Controls**	**Infarctions**
			Adjustment	
Mean	**92.82 * ***	**158.37 * ***	**141.39**	**160.15**
Standard error	**8.89**	**16.61**	**15.93**	**15.69**
N	**65**	**56**	**65**	**56**
			Upsettingness	
Mean	**71.69 * * ***	**155.46 * * ***	**109.47 ***	**160.86 ***
Standard error	**7.63**	**16.01**	**13.47**	**16.31**
N	**65**	**56**	**65**	**56**

* $p < .05$.
* * $p < .01$.
* * * $p < .001$.

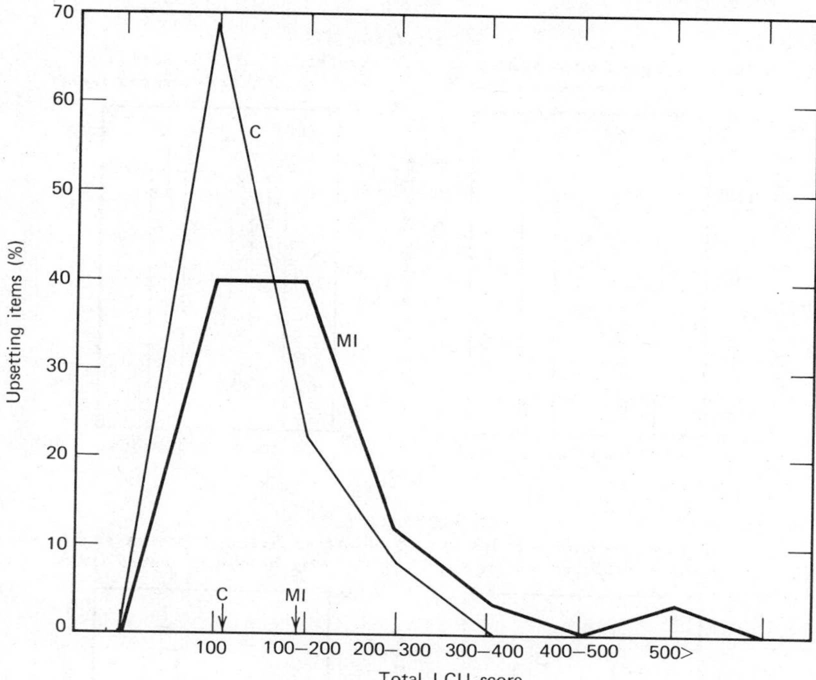

Figure 3. Distribution of subjects in MI patient ($N = 25$) and control ($N = 13$) groups according to total upset score per 12 months. The total scores based upon each individual's score of his/her own changes during the period.

ied. Event ratings obtained from patients who had experienced the events during the last year were compared with ratings obtained from those who had no such fresh experience. The same procedure was performed with control subjects. The results indicate that with regard both to adjustment and upsettingness the *normal* way of reacting in scaling performance to a fresh experience of an event is to give it a *lower* score. This tendency, however, is not observed in the MI patient groups where the fresh experience did not affect the weights given to the events significantly, as shown in Table 6. Thus the patients seemed to have a more rigid way of scaling changes. The effect of using "nonexperienced" scales versus "experienced" scales for calculating LCU totals in the two groups is shown in Figure 4. Hence when "experienced" scales are used both adjustment and upsettingness total scores are strikingly different in the two groups (Lundberg & Theorell, 1973b).

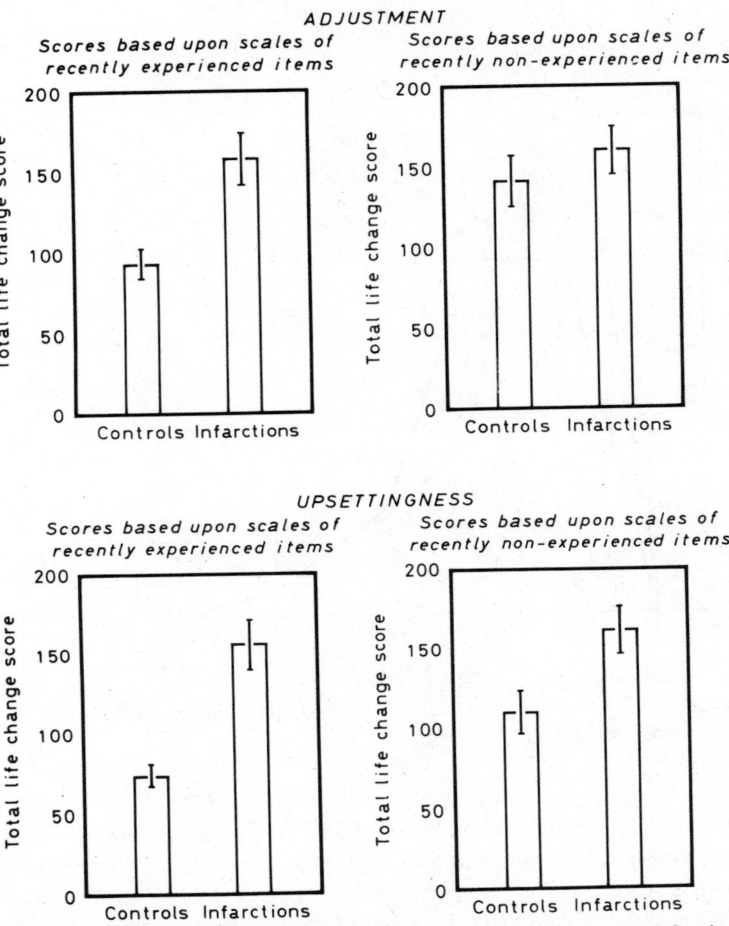

Figure 4. Mean values of total life-change scores for control subjects and infarction patients regarding "adjustment" and "upsettingness." The scores have been based upon scales of recently experienced and nonexperienced items, respectively.

PROSPECTIVE STUDY

The bias created by the patient's own knowledge about his or her illness cannot be ruled out without a prospective study. Such a study has recently been started. Seven thousand building construction workers, aged 40–60, representing about 80% of available members of the trade union in this age group in the greater Stockholm area, have filled out a questionnaire comprising an extended version of the SRE for the last year and questions about social background and attitudes. ECG, blood pressure, and smoking data will be available from an ongoing health survey. Detailed information concerning work absenteeism and possible diagnoses during the studied period will be obtained at the national insurance company to which all working Swedes belong. ECG's will be rechecked by the health survey in two years. For each five-year age cohort a "CHD personality risk group" will be selected. In this group the subjects with high total upset scores will be selected as an "extra high risk group." The mortality and morbidity data during the coming two years in the studied samples will be collected and compared. By using large samples and a relatively short follow-up period we shall be able to study the effects of *change* on health data. People who are ill at the start of the examination will be analyzed separately.

What kind of diseases shall we predict with the described strategy? Suicides? Ulcers? Alcoholism? Myocardial infarctions? Coronary deaths? None at all?

If we find prospectively that high total life-change scores do not predict the onset of a myocardial infarction, does that mean that the retrospective studies lie? It should be remembered that the reports of subjects who do not know that they are going to develop a myocardial infarction in the near future are not necessarily "more true" than the retrospective analysis of the situation afterward. "I ignored my work situation" is a common remark from infarction patients.

In any patient with a myocardial infarction the mere knowledge of how the patient looks at his general situation before and after disease onset is of great value in the rehabilitation process. The SRE is an example of a tool which can be easily and rapidly used by any clinician in this analysis.

The crucial psychosocial difference between young victims of myocardial infarction and comparable healthy subjects may thus be the patient's inability to adapt to changes. Whether this defective ability should be called "type A behavior," "Sisyphus syndrome," "work addiction," or "neuroticism," and whether we are dealing with genetic traits or behavior patterns formed by early childhood circumstances is not known. A combination of genetics and social circumstances may be operating. When heredity "is held constant," as in the retrospective study of CHD-discordant monozygotic twins by Liljefors and Rahe (1970), the social environment seems to be important for the development of premature coronary heart disease. The many important intervening variables such as diet and smoking further complicate the picture.

REFERENCES

Ardlie, N. G., Glew, G., & Schwartz, C. J. Influence of catecholamines on nucleotide-induced platelet aggregation. *Nature,* 1966, **212,** 415–417.

Bonami, M., & Rimé, B. Approche exploratoire de la personnalité precoronarienne par analyse standardisée de donnée projective thematique. *Journal of Psychosomatic Research,* 1972, **16,** 103–113.

Brozek, J., Keys, A., & Blackburn, H. Personality differences between potential coronary and noncoronary subjects. *Annals of the New York Academy of Science,* 1966, **134,** 1057–1064.

Dunbar, F. *Psychosomatic Diagnosis.* New York: Hoeber Medical Division of Harper and Row, 1973.

Hinkle, L. E., Jr. An estimate of the effects of ''stress'' on the incidence and prevalence of coronary heart disease in a large industrial population in the United States. Lecture at the Conference on Thrombosis, Oslo, 1971.

Hinkle, L. E., Jr., Whitney, H. L., Lehman, E. W., Dunn, J., Benjamin, B., King, R., Plakun, A., & Flehinger, B. Occupation, education and coronary heart disease. *Science,* 1968, **161,** 238–246.

Holmes, T. H., & Rahe, R. H. The social readjustment rating scale. *Journal of Psychosomatic Research,* **11,** 1967, 213–218.

Jenkins, C. D., Zyzanski, S. J., Rosenman, R. H., & Cleveland, G. L. Association of coronary-prone behavior scores with recurrence of coronary heart disease. *Journal of Chronic Disease,* 1971, **24,** 601–611.

Keys, A. (Ed.) Coronary heart disease in seven countries. *American Heart Association, Monograph 29.* New York, 1970.

Levi, L. *Stress and Distress in Response to Psychosocial Stimuli.* Stockholm: Almquist and Wiskell, 1972.

Liljefors, L. Coronary heart disease in male twins. *Acta Medica Scandinavia Supplumentum* 1970, **511**.

Liljefors, L., & Rahe, R. H. An identical twin study of psychosocial factors in coronary heart disease in Sweden. *Psychosomatic Medicine,* 1970, **32,** 523–543.

Lind, E., & Theorell, T. Sociological characteristics and myocardial infarctions. *Journal of Psychosomatic Research,* 1973, **17,** 59–73.

Lundberg, U., & Theorell, T. Life change scaling in psychosomatic research—recently experienced and non-experienced events. 1973 (In preparation) (b).

Lundberg, U., & Theorell, T. Life change scaling in three diagnostic groups. 1973. (In preparation.) (a)

Medalie, J. H. Factors associated with the first myocardial infarction: 5 years observation of 10,000 adult males. Lecture at the Symposium on Epidemiology and Prevention of Coronary Heart Disease, Helsinki, 1972.

Rahe, R. H., & Lind, E. Psychosocial factors and sudden cardiac death. A pilot study. *Journal of Psychosomatic Research,* 1971, **15,** 19–24.

Rahe, R. H., & Paasikivi, J. Psychosocial factors and myocardial infarction. II. An outpatient study in Sweden. *Journal of Psychosomatic Research,* 1971, **15,** 33–39.

Rahe, R. H., Romo, M., Bennett, L., & Siltanen, P. Subjects' recent life changes and myocardial infarction in Helsinki. *Archives of Internal Medicine,* 1973. (In press) (a)

Rahe, R. H., Romo, M., Bennett, L., & Siltanen, P. Subjects' recent life changes and sudden death in Helsinki. *Archives of Internal Medicine,* 1973. (In press) (b)

Rosenman, R. H. Assessing the risk associated with behavior patterns. *Journal of the Medical Association (Georgia),* 1971, **60,** 31–34.

Schalling, D., & Holmberg, M. Extraversion in criminals and the "dual nature" of extraversion. *Reports from the Psychological Laboratories no. 306.* University of Stockholm, 1970.

Shekelle, R. B., Ostfeld, A. M., & Paul, O. Social status and incidence of coronary heart disease. *Journal of Chronic Disease,* 1969, **22,** 381–394.

Syme, S. L., Hyman, M. M., & Enterline, P. E. Some social and cultural factors associated with the occurence of coronary heart disease. *Journal of Chronic Disease,* 1964, **17,** 277–289.

Theorell, T. Psychological factors in relation to the onset of myocardial infarction and to some metabolic variables. Academic thesis, Karolinska Institute, Stockholm, 1970.

Theorell, T., Lind, E., Fröberg, J., Karlsson, C. G., & Levi, L. A longitudinal study of 21 subjects with coronary heart disease: Life changes, catecholamine excretion and related biochemical reactions. *Psychosomatic Medicine,* 1972, **34,** 505–516.

Theorell, T., Lind, E., & Lundberg, U. Attityd-och bakgrunds-monster hos infarktneuros-och ryggpatienter i den svenska kooperationen. *Socialmedicinsk tidskrift,* 1973, (in press).

Theorell, T., & Rahe, R. H. Psychosocial factors and myocardial infarction. 1. An inpatient study in Sweden. *Journal of Psychosomatic Research,* 1971, **15,** 25–31.

Theorell, T., & Rahe, R. H. Psychosocial factors and myocardial infarction—Ongoing research in Stockholm. Prepared for NATO Conference on Stress and Disease. Beitöstolen, Norway, 1972.

Tibblin, G. Risk factors in coronary heart disease. In *Thrombosis and Coronary Heart Disease. Advances in Cardiology,* Volume 4. Basel: Karger, 1970.

van der Valk, J. M., & Groen, J. J. Personality and conflict situation in patients with myocardial infarction. *Journal of Psychosomatic Research,* 1967, **11,** 41–46.

Wolf, S. Psychosocial forces in myocardial infarction and sudden death. *Circulation,* 1969, **4:** Supp. 4, 74.

CHAPTER 7

Personal Catastrophe and Depression:

*A Consideration of the Subject with Respect to Medically Ill Adolescents, and a Requiem for Retrospective Life-Event Studies **

RICHARD W. HUDGENS

INTRODUCTION

There is no disputing the fact that many people who experience or anticipate personal catastrophe—for example, bereavement, imprisonment, or life-threatening illness—also experience severe emotional distress. They may call this distress anxiety, depression, terror, despair, or other words denoting dysphoric affect. There is also no disagreement that other people experiencing the same catastrophic events weather their storms with surprisingly little inner turmoil. Confronting this paradox, many investigators have postulated special factors of susceptibility in those who experience emotional breakdown under stress, and special protective factors in those who experience much less than the expected amount of distress under the blows of fate. But after at least 30 years of research in this area, there are still more questions than answers. In any case, we should remember that most people do not become severely disabled psychiatrically when terrible things happen to them, and that those who do become disabled regain their equilibrium in a reasonably short time. There is very little contention among psychiatric and sociologic researchers about these matters.

On the other hand, controversy has arisen concerning the reverse side of this issue—the role of stressful events in the genesis of sustained psychiatric disorders such as schizophrenia or in depressive illness with distorted judgment

* This work was supported in part by the following U.S. Public Health Service Grants MH-13002, MH-05804, MH-07081.

and a full panoply of vegetative symptoms. For many years there was widespread and uncritical acceptance of the thesis that nearly all disorders affecting the emotions could be traced to some meaningful personal experience or cluster of events, however far-fetched or temporally remote the connection between the experience and the illness might appear by standards of common sense. Currently, however, serious investigators do not take this for granted. In the past decade the entire issue of the connection between life events and psychiatric illness has been reopened for critical study. For example, Brown and his associates (Brown & Birley, 1968; Birley & Brown, 1970; Brown, 1972; Brown, Sklair, Harris, & Birley, 1973) in London have been diligent in seeking out pitfalls in the methodology of retrospective studies and applying in their own studies the lessons they have learned. And Clayton and her associates (Clayton, Halikas, & Maurice, 1971; Clayton, Halikas, & Maurice, 1972; Clayton, Halikas, Maurice, & Robins, 1973) and Holmes, Masuda, and Rahe (1967, 1970) have undertaken prospective studies which may ultimately be quite helpful in answering questions about the connections between life events and psychiatric illness.

As I interpret the results of recent studies done in St. Louis (Clayton et al., 1971, 1972, 1973; Hudgens, Morrison, & Barchha, 1967; Hudgens, Robins, & Delong, 1970; Morrison, Hudgens, & Barchha, 1968), London (Brown et al., 1968, 1973; Birley and Brown, 1970), New Haven (Paykel, Myers, Dienett, Klerman, Lindenthal, & Pepper, 1969; Paykel, Prusoff, & Ulenhuth, 1971), Seattle (Holmes and Rahe, 1967; Holmes and Masuda, 1970), and elsewhere, investigators have demonstrated a causal connection between stressful life events and subsequent worsening of conditions already under way, between life events and subsequent admission to psychiatric hospitals or clinics, and, in a substantial minority of bereaved persons, between bereavement and depressions of moderate degree for which psychiatric care was rarely sought. It does not seem to me that investigators have yet convincingly demonstrated that life stress can cause madness in a person previously of sound mind, nor can it cause a severe depression sustained for many months and attended by multiple disturbance of physical and mental function.

The present chapter deals with the issues I have raised in this introduction. I present data concerning the association between personal catastrophe and moderately serious depression in adolescents hospitalized for medical and surgical disorders, then deal with the issue of susceptibility. Then I discuss some pitfalls of retrospective studies which make it likely that segments of the scientific community may remain unconvinced when such studies produce evidence for a causal connection between life events and the onset of sustained psychiatric disorders.

METHODS

At the Washington University Medical Center in St. Louis we have undertaken an extensive study of hospitalized adolescents whom we intend to follow up after an interval of 10 to 12 years. We selected 110 psychiatric inpatients, 12 through 19 years of age, chosen by methods described elsewhere (Stevenson, Hudgens, Held, Merideth, Hendrix, & Carr, 1972). They were 37% of the teenagers admitted to Renard Hospital between February 1, 1965, and February 27, 1968. As controls for this sample we selected 110 adolescents hospitalized on nonpsychiatric services of the same medical center, each of whom was paired with a psychiatric subject with whom he was matched for age, sex, race, and staff-care or private-care status. It is the control group with which this chapter is concerned. They were selected during three separate study periods in 1968 and 1969. During those study periods 730 patients, ages 12 through 19, were admitted to nonpsychiatric services in the medical center. Of these, 156 were identified on the daily hospital admission rosters as prospective controls, since each matched a specific psychiatric inpatient for the factors studied. Fortuitously, none of the 156 had ever been hospitalized for psychiatric symptoms, which would have been our only reason for excluding them from the study. Of the 156 prospective controls, 46 were not interviewed: 4 because they were unconscious, 3 because their physicians refused to let us see them, and 39 because they were discharged before the interviewer could talk to them, usually within 48 hours.

The 110 controls selected for study differed significantly from the 620 other teenagers on nonpsychiatric services in that the mean age was 6 months older, and a significantly greater proportion of the studied sample was white (84 versus 74%).

Each subject received a research interview which contained both open-ended and structured parts, during which we obtained extensive information about psychiatric, medical, social, family, and scholastic histories. The interview required from 90 minutes to 5 hours to administer. A relative of each subject,

Table 1. Depression Criteria

1. An onset, whether rapid or gradual, after which there was a difference from usual self, manifested predominantly by a dysphoric mood.
2. The change included at least two of the following symptoms: self-blaming or self-negating attitude, diminished interest, excessive worrying, death wishes.
3. The change included at least four of the following symptoms: anorexia, insomnia, decreased libido, tired, trouble thinking or concentrating, diminished or impaired activity, not keeping self well-groomed, crying, or other agitated behavior.
4. No disturbance of consciousness.
5. No other diagnosis likely to explain symptoms.

usually a parent, was interviewed separately using the same protocol. After discharge the Washington University Medical Center hospital records were reviewed, school records were collected for 94% of the patients, and medical information from other institutions was collected for 64% of the patients. All information was coded and punched on IBM cards.

The subjects were given diagnoses according to specific criteria. The only disorder with which the current report is concerned is depression, the criteria for which are given in Table 1.

RESULTS

Among the adolescent controls there were 78 patients without psychiatric illness by our definition; 8 controls had depression by our criteria; and 13 were called "undiagnosed, most like depression." They differed from the 8 with definite depression only in that they had too few symptoms to meet our strict

Table 2. Principal Psychiatric Research Diagnoses among Adolescent Psychiatric Inpatients and Nonpsychiatric Inpatients

	Psychiatric Inpatients (N = 110)	Controls (Nonpsychiatric Inpatients) (N = 110)
Depresssion	19	8
Mania	11	0
Schizophrenia	6	0
Antisocial personality	7	2
Epilepsy	0	6
Mental deficiency	1	3
Organic brain syndrome	1	0
Alcoholism	1	0
Anxiety neurosis	0	1
Anorexia nervosa	1	0
Undiagnosed psychiatric illness:		
Most like depression	14	13
Most like antisocial personality	7	3
Most like hysteria	2	1
Most like schizophrenia	1	0
Most like anxiety neurosis	0	1
Between depression and other diagnosis	2	0
Schizoaffective	7	0
Unclassifiable	29	1
No psychiatric illness ever	1	71

Table 3. Stress and Depression among Controls Hospitalized for Nonpsychiatric Disorders (all controls fulfilling the criteria for depression are included)

Subject	Age and Sex	Type Stress	Interval Between Onset of Stress and Onset of Depression	Was Stress Still Present at Time of Onset of Depression?	Duration of Depression	Has Stress Continued Throughout Depression?
C-002	18 F	1. Onset lupus eryth.	7 years	Yes	6 months	Yes
		2. Steroid treatment	6 months	Yes		Yes
C-004	19F	None known	(no stress)	(no stress)	5 months	(no stress)
C-025	19 F (age 11 when depressed)	1. Parents separated	Immediate	Yes	9 months	Yes
C-027	15 F	1. Obesity	Unknown	Yes	1 year	Yes
		2. Moved to strange city	Immediate	Yes		No (single event)
C-032	14 M	1. Rheumatoid arthritis	2 years	Yes	2 months	Yes
		2. Steroid treatment	10 months	Yes		Yes
C-035	19 F	1. Childbirth by Caesarian section	Immediate	Yes	3 weeks	No (single event)
C-057	18 F	1. Injuries suffered in accident	Immediate	Yes	10 months	Yes
		2. Boyfriend killed in same accident	Immediate	Yes		No (single event)
C-058	15 F	1. Asthma	Immediate	Yes	6 months	Yes

Table 4. Relation Between Stress and Symptoms Among Controls "Undiagnosed, Most Like Depression"

Subject	Age and Sex	Type Stress	Interval between Onset of Stress and Onset of Symptoms	Was Stress Still Present when Symptoms Began?	Duration of Symptoms	Did Stress Continue throughout Persistence of Symptoms?
C-030	19 F (14 when depressed)	Hepatitis, ulcer, missed year of school	Immediate	Yes	1–3 years	?
C-037	18 M	None known	No stress	No stress	8 months	No stress
C-038	17 F	Hodgkins disease, worsened	Hodgkins present 3½ years, worsening occurred immediately prior to depression	Yes	3 weeks	Yes
C-040	18 F	Husband entered armed forces	Immediate	Yes	3 months	Yes
C-042	18 F	Epilepsy, recurrence	Epilepsy present 6 months, recurrence occurred immediately prior to depression	Yes	1 month	Yes
C-043	16 F	Ulcerative colitis, recurred. "Self-depreciating all her life."	Colitis first began 6 years before, recurrence immediately prior to depression	Yes	5 months	Yes
C-046	13 F	Congenital heart disease, worsened	Disabled for 3½ years, worsening of cardiac status immediately prior to depression	Yes	4–5 months	Yes

C-051	17 M	Hodgkins disease, forced to drop school	Hodgkins present 3 years, forced to drop school immediately prior to depression	Yes	8 months	Yes
C-053	18 F (12 when first depressed)	Parents divorced (moody, easily upset ''all her life'' before that)	Chronic depressive symptoms worsened immediately	Yes	Episodic throughout life	No
C-070	18 F (14 when first depressed)	Encephalitis (paraplegic since then). Repair of decubiti	Immediate, worsened symptoms in association with hospitalization for decubiti	Yes	Episodic, associated with hospitalizations	Yes
C-086	15 F	Sarcoma	Immediate	Yes	9 months	Yes
C-096	19 M (17 when depressed)	Killed girl in auto accident	Immediate	Yes	1 year	No
C-102	19 M (17 when depressed)	Burned in accident, physical disabilities	Immediate	Yes	''Several months''	Yes
C-111	19 M (15 when depressed)	Brother died	Immediate	Yes	Uncertain	No

criteria for the diagnosis. An additional patient had been admitted to the neurologic service for epilepsy, his most important diagnosis, but he was discovered to have a depressive syndrome as well. We included him among those with probable depression, bringing the total to 14. In this report the 14 patients with probable depression and the 8 with definite depression are considered together, and all 22 are compared with respect to various items to the 78 psychiatrically well controls. Thus 100 control subjects are considered, and the 10 controls with psychiatric diagnoses other than depression are omitted from consideration.

In the depressive group were 6 boys and 16 girls. Of these, 21 were white, 1 was black. Of the 22 subjects, 15 had depressive episodes at the time of our study, while 7 had been depressed only in the past. The age of first onset of depression ranged from 11 to 19, with a mean of 15.9 years and a median age of onset of 16. It was possible to ascertain the duration of affective disorder in 17 of the 22 patients. The briefest depressions were of 3 weeks' duration in 2 patients who were ill at the time of the study, and who may, of course, have continued to be sick for some time thereafter. The longest duration of depression was 1 year. Only 1 patient had seen a psychiatrist as an outpatient during his depression, but he had received no medication. Three others had received tranquilizers from nonpsychiatric physicians. Thus the depressions were not particularly severe.

Tables 3 and 4 illustrate a striking finding among our 22 adolescent controls with affective disorder. In Table 3 it is seen that in 7 of the 8 patients with definite depression, onset was preceded by stress that was both objectively serious and meaningful to the patients. None of the 7 had had depressions prior to the stresses. In 5 cases the patients and their families dated the onsets as immediately following the stresses, whereas in 2, whose depressions occurred while they were receiving steroid medication, onsets were delayed (though they may nevertheless have been caused by the steroids).

In Table 4 the same pattern is observed for the 14 patients with probable depression, for all but 1 of whom objectively severe and personally upsetting stress immediately preceded the depressions. Only 2 of these subjects had ever had depressive symptoms prior to the stresses, having been previously described as moody, self-depreciating, and overly reactive.

Thus for 20 of the 22 depressed controls marked stress or worsening of ongoing stress was reported prior to the onset of psychiatric symptoms, immediately prior to onset in 18 of the 20. In the 5 instances where the stresses were not continuous throughout the course of the depressions, they were nevertheless occurrences of marked significance whose psychological impact continued long after the events themselves.

COMPARISON OF DEPRESSED AND PSYCHIATRICALLY WELL PATIENTS

We compared the 22 depressed controls and the 78 psychiatrically well (but medically ill) controls with respect to a large number of demographic items and factors in the medical, social, family, and scholastic histories. The depressed patients were a mean of 17.3 years of age at the time of the study, one year older than the well patients. This may be of some importance in that they had been at risk one year longer than those without depression. But the two factors that markedly distinguished the depressed adolescents from those that were well are a significantly higher incidence of psychiatric disorders in the histories of the biological parents of depressed patients and significantly more severe nonpsychiatric illnesses preceding the onsets of their depressions.

With respect to the first factor, the 22 depressives had 8 mothers with a history of psychiatric illness (6 depressed, 1 alcoholic, and 1 hysteric) and 7 fathers with such histories (6 alcoholics and 1 undiagnosed). Thus 15 (34%) of the parents were ill, currently or in the past, compared with 17 (11%) of the parents of well controls, a difference significant at the .05 level. We found 3 depressed patients who had both mothers and fathers with a history of psychiatric illness, while 9 had only one ill parent. The 17 well controls with a history of parental psychopathology each had only 1 sick parent. Thus 55% of the depressed group had at least 1 sick parent, compared to 22% of the well group ($p < .01$). Although we obtained information about psychiatric illness in siblings, too few had entered the age of risk for most psychiatric disorders to make meaningful calculations about incidence. Information about remote relatives was also gathered, but we would not venture to make diagnoses or calculate incidence on the basis of third-hand information.

With respect to the second factor, to ascertain the severity of medical disorder, it had been recorded for each control whether the probable outcome of his nonpsychiatric disorder was complete recovery without defect, persistent defect without disability, chronic disability, or death. This judgment had been made independently of the knowledge of patients' psychiatric diagnoses, or of the knowledge as to whether or not they had a psychiatric illness. Among the depressed controls 68% had a probable outcome of chronic disability or death compared to only 37% of the well controls ($p < .05$). The depressed patients also differed from the controls with respect to other indices of severity of their nonpsychiatric disorders. For example, significantly more (77 versus 54%, $p < .05$) had been hospitalized more than once for nonpsychiatric illness; the currently depressed patients were in the nonpsychiatric hospitals almost twice as long as the well controls, an average of 24 versus 13 days; and the parents' hopes for the patients' future, ascertained by independent questioning, had been changed for the worse by the presence of the medical illnesses in 36% of the depressed patients and 7% of those who were psychiatrically well.

The 22 depressed adolescents and 78 psychiatrically well patients did not differ significantly with respect to sex, race, place of residence, socioeconomic background, future career goals, history of head injury, intelligence quotient, academic and disciplinary scholastic history, amount of antisocial behavior, birth order, size of sibship, bereavement experiences, history of parental divorce or separation, or duration of medical disability.

The next question that arises concerns the nature of the association between the two factors found to be significantly more common in the depressives, parental psychopathology and severe medical disorder, and between each of these factors and the subsequent occurrence of depression. First we discovered that the presence of both factors together strongly predicted depression in our sample of teenagers. Among the total group of adolescents considered in this chapter, 50% of those with a psychiatrically ill parent and a medical prognosis of chronic disability or death developed depression, whereas only 9% with neither of those disadvantages ($p < .01$) did.

Next, to ascertain the possible independence of the two factors associated with depression, we eliminated from our calculations those patients with psychiatrically ill parents and considered only those without parental psychopathology. We found that 23% of those with poor prognoses developed depressions, compared to 9% of those with better prognoses. Chi-square corrected is 1.7, $p < .20$, not significant. Looking at it the other way, when we eliminated those subjects with a probable outcome of disability or death and considered only those with better prognoses: 27% of those with parental psychopathology but only 9% of those without a sick parent had depression. Chi-square corrected is 1.3, $p < .30$, again not significant at the 5% level. Thus from a sample of this size we cannot say with confidence that these two factors, severe illness and parental psychopathology, operated independently of each other in their association with depression. There is an indication, however, that each may have increased our adolescents' susceptibility to the affective disorder. When both

Table 5. Interaction among Adolescents' Medical Prognosis, Psychiatric Illness in Parents, and Depression in Adolescents

	Psychiatric Disorder in Parent	
Adolescents' Medical Prognosis	Yes	No
Poor	50% had depression	23% had depression
Good	27% had depression	9% had depression

factors occurred in the life of the same unfortunate youngster, the odds were 50:50 that depression would ensue, though not, it should be recalled, a depression that would require psychiatric hospitalization. And only one of the subjects had even seen a psychiatrist as an outpatient. Table 5 illustrates the interaction of the two factors: having a medical illness with poor prognosis and having a psychiatrically ill parent.

DISCUSSION

Our findings suggest that there might have been a cause-effect relationship between stress and subsequent depression in 20 of 22 adolescents hospitalized on medical and surgical wards for nonpsychiatric disorders. The stresses in all cases were severe by objective standards and personally important to the patients themselves. In addition, there was evidence that two factors might have influenced susceptibility to depression, having a psychiatrically ill parent and having a medical disorder whose probable outcome was chronic disability or death. The depressions that followed the stresses in the 20 adolescents were of only moderate severity. None of the 20 had required psychiatric hospitalization, only one had seen a psychiatrist as an outpatient, and only two with antecedent stress and one with no prior stress had been treated with mild tranquilizers by nonpsychiatric physicians.

These findings are similar to Clayton's (1971, 1972). In a prospective study of 109 randomly selected widows and widowers she and her co-workers found that 38 (35%) had a "depressive symptom complex" one month after the death of the spouse. Of the entire group of 109 widowed subjects only 15% had seen or called a physician for problems related to grieving. Those with depression were not significantly more likely to request such consultation than those without depression (18 versus 13%). Only one subject saw a psychiatrist, and this was at the insistence of one of the investigators.

The main difference between our findings and those of Clayton was that she found no difference between her depressed widows and nondepressed widows with respect to a family history of psychiatric disorder. One possible explanation for this may be that relatives were not interviewed in her study, whereas in our investigation one parent, usually the mother, was interviewed directly about her psychiatric health and that of the other parent in 89% of the cases.

Concerning our own findings, we do not know whether the depressive syndrome in our medically ill subjects was, in some essential way, a milder variety of the same disorder as severe depressive illness with vegetative symptoms, delusions of worthlessness, and high suicidal risk seen among psychiatric inpatients. In support of this possibility was the high incidence (34%) of psychiatric illness among the parents of our depressed patients on the nonpsychiatric wards, similar to the incidence found among the parents of depressives in our psychiatric inpatient group (45%). In fact, definite depression itself was more common among the parents of the depressed patients on the medical and surgical wards (14%) than among the parents of the adolescents on the psychiatric inpatient service (6%). Certainly the relative mildness of the depressions among the subjects discussed in this chapter does not indicate that this was essentially a different disorder from severe depressive illness, since this finding may have been an artifact of selection. Severely depressed patients may have shown up in psychiatric hospitals, not on medical wards, despite the concurrence of medical disorders. The projected follow-up of our control sample and their relatives, and the longitudinal comparison of their course with that of our psychiatric inpatients, may prove an answer to this question.

Our other findings, that both parental psychopathology and very severe medical illness may render an adolescent susceptible to the development of depression, are in accordance with common sense and with the findings of others. First, it is well established that psychiatric disorders run in families. The nature of the possible causal link between psychiatric illness in the parents and psychiatric illness in their offspring may have been genetic, environmental, or a combination of both. We were not able to ascertain the relative importance of heredity and life experience in the depressions of our adolescent subjects.

Second, much anecdotal information over the years, as well as systematic findings of George Brown (1973) and others, suggest that severe stress is more likely than milder stress to lead to marked mood changes. Again we should remember that the nature of the connection between disruptive life events and subsequent emotional turmoil has not yet been discovered, since we do not yet understand the biological "essence" of depression (either the mood or the syndrome) or many of the physiological concomitants of depression in the brain and the rest of the body. Clinical studies alone will obviously not provide sufficient clarification of this issue.

What is my excuse for presenting a retrospective study of life events and depression, when I would prefer to bury such investigations rather than to praise them? It is simply that candor compels me to report findings that so strikingly suggest an immediate temporal connection between severe stress and subsequent affective disorder, especially since I have so often argued on the skeptic's side of this issue. I make no claim that we have proven a cause-effect relationship, for in the long run the claims of retrospective life-event studies will leave a number of readers unsatisfied, whatever the findings. A consideration of some methodological necessities of a valid study of the relationship between stress and illness will demonstrate why there are so many difficulties in the interpretation of results:

1. A valid study must date the onset of illness within a reasonable time span. This is extremely difficult to do, especially retrospectively, not only because

the essence of a psychiatric illness cannot be specified, but also because early symptoms may be subtle or forgotten.

2. Events must be dated, and anyone who has tried to do this retrospectively knows how difficult it is.

3. History must be replicated by informants. Our study comparing patients and their close relatives with respect to independent reporting of recent, specified stresses, showed significant discrepancies between informants' and patients' histories (Hudgens et al., 1970).

4. There should be a quantification of the importance of each type of event for each patient: What is stressful for one person may be of little consequence to another.

5. Diagnostically cohesive groups must be studied if any statement is to be made about precipitation of a specific syndrome.

6. A representative sample of people with a given syndrome must be considered if anything is to be said about the causes of such a disorder. Hospitalized patients are clearly not a representative sample of those with a given type illness; neither are outpatients, since care-seeking is often determined by factors other than the occurrence of the illness; neither are cases found in house-to-house surveys, since in such surveys house-bound persons and women will be overrepresented, and institutionalized persons will be missed.

7. The illness studied should be one that is demarcated, by symptom-type severity, or duration, from everyday emotional reactions that make sense in the context of the putatively causative events.

8. The same kind of event or cluster of circumstances which allegedly triggers an illness at one time in a patient's life should precipitate a recurrence later if the events recur in a similar context of emotional distress.

9. Suitable control groups must be selected. There are possible problems with every type of control group; for exampe, it can be objected that medically ill controls for a psychiatric study sample may themselves have illnesses precipitated by life stress. And it can be argued that general population controls for a psychiatric sample are *too* well, that the fact of illness and care-seeking have not been held constant between the experimental and control groups, or that well controls are likely to underreport life stress because they worry less than psychiatric patients or have not had their memory refreshed by the repeated interviewing that is the fate of many psychiatric patients.

10. Events that are possible consequences of the illnesses in question should be excluded from consideration as possible precipitants of the illness. For example, by my count, 29 of 43 events on Holmes' Social Readjustment Rating Scale (Holmes & Rahe, 1967) are events that are often the symptoms or consequences of illness. The same is true of 32 of 61 events on Paykel's (Paykel et al., 1971) long scale of events and 18 of 33 events on his short scale.

Thus the problems involved in studying, retrospectively, the relationship between multiple types of life events and the onset of psychiatric disorders are so great that it may not be worthwhile doing such studies.

By contrast, the prospective study of the effect of a specific event, generally believed stressful, on a high risk population might have value. For example, Winokur, Clayton, and Reich (1969) have reported that among their female manic-depressive patients, if a woman had ever had a postpartum episode, she invariably had a subsequent affective episode when she had another baby. The numbers were very small—three patients, six subsequent childbirths, and six recurrences of postpartum episodes—but the data suggest that it would be worthwhile to study this relationship prospectively in a large group of manic-depressive women of childbearing age. A testable hypothesis could be formed. If it were disproven, it would not need repeated testing. If not disproven, this could lead to further studies, for example, on the nature of the event, parturition: emotional, endocrinological, or so forth. These might someday lead to a discovery of ''bridges'' between the causative event and the essential internal changes that constitute affective disorder, whatever they may turn out to be.

SUMMARY

In this study 110 adolescents hospitalized on medical and surgical wards for nonpsychiatric disorders were selected as a control group for 110 psychiatric inpatients, age 12 through 19. The two groups were matched for age, sex, race, and socioeconomic status of the families. Each patient was extensively interviewed concerning psychiatric, medical, social, scholastic, and family histories; a relative of each patient (the parent in 89% of the cases) was interviewed separately with the same protocol. Medical and scholastic records were subsequently obtained from hospitals, physicians, and schools.

Of the 110 controls, 22 were found to have a current or past depressive syndrome. Two-thirds were depressed at the time of the study, one-third only in the past. The depressions were of only moderate severity; none of the patients had been hospitalized for this disorder, and only 1 had seen a psychiatrist. Of these 22 subjects, the depression had been preceded by objectively severe and personally significant life stress in 20 cases. In 18 of the 20 cases, the depressions ensued immediately after the stresses began.

When the depressed patients were compared with 78 psychiatrically well (but medically ill) controls the two groups were found to differ significantly with respect to only two of a large number of factors. Of the depressives, 55% had at least one biological parent with a history of psychiatric disorder, compared to 22% of the controls ($p < .01$); and 68% of the depressed patients had a medical disorder with a probable prognosis of chronic disability or death, compared with 37% of the psychiatrically well patients ($p < .05$). When both these factors were present a subject had a 50% chance of developing depression. When neither factor was present the chance was only 9%. When we controlled for the presence of each factor, the other was found in a higher proportion of depressed subjects than well subjects. But the number of patients was too small to demonstrate that these factors operated independently of each other to a statistically significant degree.

These findings are discussed in the light of other prospective and retrospective studies of life events. A cause-effect connection between life stress and disabling psychiatric illness, not present at the time of stress, has yet to be convincingly demonstrated, in this author's opinion. There are indications that such connections may exist for some illnesses, but there is a great need for prospective studies in this area. The author enumerates some pitfalls and criticisms of retrospective life-event studies which make it likely that the findings of such studies, whether positive or negative, will continue to provoke skepticism.

REFERENCES

Birley, J. L. T., & Brown, G. W. Crises and life changes preceding the onset or relapse of acute schizophrenia: Clinical aspects. *British Journal of Psychiatry,* 1970, **116,** 327–333.

Brown, G. W., Life events and psychiatric illness: Some thoughts on methodology and causality. *Journal of Psychosomatic Research,* 1972, **16,** 311–320.

Brown, G. W., & Birley, J. L. T. Crises and life changes and the onset of schizophrenia. *Journal of Health and Social Behavior,* 1968, **9,** 203–214.

Brown, G. W., Harris, T. O., & Peto, J. Life events and psychiatric disorders. Part II: Nature of causal link. *Psychological Medicine.* (In press)

Brown, G. W., Sklair, F., Harris, T. O., & Birley, J. L. T. Life events and psychiatric disorders. Part I: Some methodological issues. *Psychological Medicine,* 1973, **3,** 74–87.

Clayton, P. J., Halikas, J. A., & Maurice, W. L. The bereavement of the widowed. *Diseases of the Nervous System,* 1971, **32,** 597–604.

Clayton, P. J., Halikas, J. A. & Maurice, W. L. The depression of widowhood. *British Journal of Psychiatry,* 1972, **120,** 71–77.

Clayton, P. J., Halikas, J. A., Maurice, W. L., & Robins, E. Anticipatory grief and widowhood. *British Journal of Psychiatry,* 1973, **122,** 47–51.

Holmes, T. H., & Mausuda, M. Life change and illness susceptibility. Presented at Symposium on Separation and Depression: Clinical and Research Aspects, at the annual meeting of the American Association for the Advancement of Science. Chicago, Illinois, December 26–30, 1970.

Holmes, T. H., & Rahe, R. H. The Social Readjustment Rating Scale. *Journal of Psychosomatic Research,* 1967, **2,** 213–218.

Hudgens, R. W., Morrison, J. R., & Barchha, R. G. Life events and onset of primary affective disorders. *Archives of General Psychiatry,* 1967, **16,** 134–145.

Hudgens, R. W., Robins, E., & Delong, W. B. The reporting of recent stress in the lives of psychiatric patients. *British Journal of Psychiatry,* 1970, **117,** 635–643.

Morrison, J. R., Hudgens, R. W., & Barchha, R. G. Life events and psychiatric illness. *British Journal of Psychiatry,* 1968, **114,** 423–432.

Paykel, E. S., Myers, J. K., Dienelt, M. N., Klerman, G. L., Lindenthal, J. J., & Pepper, M. P. Life events and depression: A controlled study. *Archives of General Psychiatry,* 1969, **21,** 753–760.

Paykel, E. S., Prusoff, B. A., & Ulenhuth, E. H. Scaling of life events. *Archives of General Psychiatry,* 1971, **25,** 340–347.

Stevenson, E. K., Hudgens, R. W., Held, C. P., Merideth, C. H., Hendrix, M. E., & Carr, D. L. Suicidal communication by adolescents. *Diseases of the Nervous System,* 1972, **33,** 112–122.

Winokur, G., Clayton, P. J., & Reich, T. *Manic Depressive Illness.* St. Louis, C. V. Mosby Company, 1969.

CHAPTER 8

Life Stress and Psychiatric Disorder:

Applications of the Clinical Approach *

E. S. PAYKEL

INTRODUCTION

The contents of this book present an intriguing mix of epidemiological and clinical research. In this spectrum the present report falls definitely at the clinical end. It summarizes a series of studies, carried out in collaboration with colleagues, into the relationship of life events and clinical psychiatric disorders.

The classical clinical approach to eliciting life-event data is retrospective, and most of these studies used this approach. Retrospective studies present a number of well-known difficulties which are reviewed by Hudgens elsewhere in this book. In particular there are two major problems that must be overcome: the first is that the psychiatric patient may experience new events, such as loss of job, as a result of his disorder. Second, there may be inaccuracy of recall. The psychiatric patient may look hard for a cause of his illness in the past and may have his view of the world so distorted by psychiatric illness that he may overemphasize the significance of events which did occur. These problems are not confined to clinical studies. Most of the associations between events and illness found in epidemiological studies also depend on the retrospective reporting by the subject of events which occurred days, weeks, months, or years before.

These difficulties are, at least in part, surmountable. We have tried in our studies to confine our attention to events prior to symptomatic onset, and to minimize reporting distortions by careful interview technique and delaying in-

* Research studies reported in this chapter were supported by U.S. Public Health Service Grant MH 13738 and were carried out at Yale University where the author was formerly Associate Professor of Psychiatry. Collaborative investigators in these studies included Selby Jacobs, M.D., Gerald Klerman, M.D., Jerome Myers, Ph.D., Brigitte Prusoff, M.P.H., and E. H. Uhlenhuth, M.D.

terview until acute psychiatric disturbance has subsided. Despite its difficulties, the retrospective approach is useful, and I believe that Hudgens is premature in attempting a requiem for it. Indeed there are many areas that cannot be studied in any other way. Although prospective studies of event reactions are highly desirable, incidences of many psychiatric disorders, such as schizophrenia or suicide attempts, are very low in the general population, so that it would be difficult to generate adequate samples in any frame which was rigorously prospective with respect to life events.

COMPARISONS BETWEEN DEPRESSIVES AND GENERAL POPULATION CONTROLS

The studies to be reported were carried out primarily in New Haven. The first was a comparison between depressives and general population controls. Methods and findings have previously been described in detail (Paykel, Myers, Dienelt, Klerman, Lindenthal, & Pepper, 1969). One hundred and eighty-five depressed patients were obtained by screening all admissions to a representative variety of psychiatric facilities. Control subjects were derived from a concurrent general population epidemiological survey of 938 adults carried out in New Haven by Myers, Lindenthal, and Pepper (1971). From this large sample we selected a subsample of 185 subjects, each matched with one of the depressed patients on sex, age (in decades), marital status, race, and social class.

Information was obtained with a semistructured interview on the occurrence of 61 life events spanning a wide range of experiences. Since the life-events lists for patients and controls differed slightly, they were reduced for analysis to 33 identical events by condensation of some categories and omission of others. Occurrence of these events was recorded for the depressives in the six months immediately preceding the onset of depression. Onset was carefully defined in symptomatic terms at an initial interview without inquiry about life events. Life-event information was obtained by a separate interviewer some weeks later, after symptomatic improvement, to minimize reporting distortion due to presence of depression. Control subjects were interviewed in their homes concerning the six months prior to the interview.

Overall, the depressed patients were found to report about three times as many events as their matched controls. The increased total event frequency was reflected in increased frequencies of most of the individual events. For eight events the differences between depressives and general population reached statistical significance. These events were increased arguments with spouse, marital separation, changing to a new type of work or starting work, death of immediate family member, serious illness of family member, departure of family member from home, serious personal physical illness, and substantial change in work conditions. Most of the other events were also reported more frequently by the depressives, but they occurred too infrequently in either group for differences to achieve statistical significance.

We asked a further question of the data: Do all events, or only certain types of event, distinguish depressed patients from controls? This question is one of generality versus specificity of stress. Are there special connotations within some events which render them particularly liable to induce depression? To ex-

Table 1. Events Grouped by Area of Activity: Number of Individuals Reporting at Least One Event in Category

Category	Depressed Patients	Controls	Significance [1]	Events Included in Category
Employment	46	20	$< .01$	Begin New Job Changes at Work Demotion Fired Unemployment Promotion Retirement Business Failure
Health	53	24	$< .01$	Serious personal illness Serious illness of family member Pregnancy Childbirth Stillbirth
Family	22	11	N.S. ($p = .07$)	Child engaged Child married Son drafted Family member leaves home New person in home
Marital	63	5	$< .01$	Marriage Separation Divorce Increase in arguments with spouse
Legal	14	5	N.S. ($p = .06$)	Court appearance Lawsuit Jail

[1] X^2 (with Yates correction).

Modified from E. S. Paykel, J. K. Myers, M. N. Dienelt, G. L. Klerman, J. J. Lindenthal, and M. P. Pepper, Life events and depression: A controlled study, *Archives of General Psychiatry,* 1969, 21, 753.

amine this issue, events were grouped into categories according to several alternative but partly overlapping sets of criteria. For each category frequencies were calculated in terms of numbers of individuals reporting at least one event from that category.

The first grouping of events was according to the area of life endeavor they involved. Findings are shown in Table 1. Five categories were derived: employment, health, family, marital, and legal. Of the 33 events, 25 could be assigned to one of these. When frequencies were examined the results were somewhat similar in all categories, although some differences just failed to reach significance. In all categories at least twice as many events were reported by depressives as controls. This categorization would suggest a somewhat nonspecific view of the stress preceding depression.

Another way of looking at events is by a value dimension, based on cultural norms and social desirability. In terms of general shared values, some events are regarded as undesirable and other events as desirable. This view contrasts with a less specific approach which has tended to apply in the psychosomatic literature, and was adopted for instance by Holmes and Rahe (1967) in their scaling studies, which depended solely on the magnitude of life change necessitated by the event, irrespective of desirability. In our event list only a few clearly desirable events had been included, principally such events as promotion, engagement, marriage. A much larger group of events was clearly undesirable, such as demotion, being fired, death of a close family member, major financial problems.

Findings are shown in Table 2. Undesirable events were reported in both groups of subjects more frequently than desirable events, but this may merely reflect the item content of our list. When depressives were compared with controls, undesirable events were reported much more frequently by the depressives. By contrast, there were no significant differences between the two groups regarding desirable events. Indeed, although not significant, the pattern was reversed, with controls reporting more events than depressives.

A third and more specific categorization referred to 10 events which involved changes in the immediate social field of the subject. Two classes of events were defined. Entrances referred to those events that involved the introduction of a new person into the social field, and exits those events that clearly involved a departure from the social field. The findings are presented in Table 3. Exits were reported much more frequently by depressives than controls. Entrances, although reported with almost equal frequency overall, were equally distributed between the two groups. Exits from the social field, of course, correspond to the familiar psychiatric concept of loss, which has been particularly linked with depression.

These findings do give some indication of specific relationships. Only certain kinds of event precede depression. It is not just a question of magnitude of life

Table 2. Desirable and Undesirable Events: Number of Individuals Reporting at Least One Event in Category

Category	Depressed Patients	Controls	Significance [1]	Events Included in Category
Desirable	6	10	N.S.	Engagement Marriage Promotion
Undesirable	82	31	<.01	Death of family member Separation Demotion Serious illness of family member Jail Major financial problems Unemployment Court appearance Son drafted Divorce Business failure Fired Stillbirth

[1] X^2 (with Yates correction).

Modified from E. S. Paykel, J. K. Myers, M. N. Dienelt, G. L. Klerman, J. J. Lindenthal, and M. P. Pepper, Life events and depression: A controlled study, *Archives of General Psychiatry,* 1969, 21, 753–760. Copyright 1969, American Medical Association.

change; the direction of the change and its desirability are also important. However, the link between event and disorder is far from exact.

Findings based on a patient group must be put into context. Most of the events reported by the depressives were in the range of everyday experience rather than catastrophic, and most often are negotiated without clinical depression. It is easy in retrospective studies to lose sight of the importance of base rates for the population. I attempted to transpose these retrospective findings into an epidemiological frame in a rough calculation (Paykel, 1973). Assuming a 4% annual incidence of depression, and the event frequencies we found for depressives and the general population, it was easy to show that only a small proportion of exits, less than 10%, appear to be followed by clinical depression. It was clear that most of the variance in determining development of depression was due not to the occurrence of the event itself but to its interaction with predisposing factors of vulnerability. However, in this somewhat hypothetical example the effect of the event was important; it increased the risk of depression approximately sixfold.

Table 3. Entrances and Exits from Social Field: Number of Individuals Reporting at Least One Event in Category

Category	Depressed Patients	Controls	Significance [1]	Events Included in Category
Entrance	21	18	N.S.	Engagement Marriage Birth of child New person in home
Exit	46	9	$< .01$	Death of close family member Separation Divorce Family member leaves home Child married Son drafted

[1] X^2 (with Yates correction).

Modified from E. S. Paykel, J. K. Myers, M. N. Dienelt, G. L. Klerman, J. J. Lindenthal, and M. P. Pepper, Life events and depression: A controlled study, *Archives of General Psychiatry,* 1969, 21, 753–760. Copyright 1969, American Medical Association.

FOLLOW-UP

The previous findings used general population controls. Another kind of control which has been little exploited is the within-patient control provided by follow-up study. This would enable us to deal with the criticism that, whatever the precaution, experience of psychiatric treatment may render the subject more willing than a nonpsychiatric control to recall and report unpleasant events. It also deals with a different and potentially valid criticism—the possibility that events reported at onset by depressives are primarily reflections of personality disturbance and habitual unstable life patterns, and might be reported just as frequently at any other time.

Such a follow-up is not without its own methodological problems. In our comparison with general population controls, we chose a time period prior to onset for which to record events, so as to avoid those which were consequences rather than causes of depression. For a follow-up, at least in the short term, it is not easy to do this. Many events occurring soon after recovery, such as return to work and job changes, may be consequences of the recovery itself.

We did carry out a short-term nine-month follow-up study on the depressives. As part of this, life-event information was collected on a randomly selected 70 of the subjects (Paykel, in press). To obtain a comparable time period to that for onset, and to reduce effects of persistent illness, analyses were confined to the last six months of the nine-month follow-up period, and to

Table 4. Onset and Recovery: Percentages of Subjects Reporting at Least One Event from Each Category

	Depressives (onset) (N = 185)	Depressives (recovered) (N = 30)	Normal Controls (N = 185)
Entrances	12	16	10
Desirable events	3	3	5
Exits	25	10	5
Undesirable events	45	23	16

Modified from E. S. Paykel, Recent life events and clinical depression. In E. K. Gunderson and R. H. Rahe (Eds.), *Life Stress and Illness*. Charles C. Thomas, Springfield, Ill.

30 subjects who had recovered within three months and remained well for the subsequent six months under consideration. The numbers in this crucial follow-up sample were therefore low.

Table 4 shows the proportion of these subjects reporting the main categories of events, and includes, for comparison, figures from the onset study for patients when ill and for the controls. Frequencies of entrances and desirable events remained low and showed no convincing change. Those for exits and undesirable events fell considerably to about half the frequency at onset, from 25 to 10% for exits, 45 to 23% for undesirable events. They still remained a little higher than control values—10 versus 5% for exits, 23 versus 16% for undesirable events. In some other respects the changes appeared to involve patterns of events more than the total number of events. Some events, particularly those related to employment, increased in frequency. On close scrutiny many of these were changes consequent upon the recent illness and recovery. It would require a longer follow-up to establish a clear period of freedom from illness and its effects, and any findings from this small study are clearly only tentative.

Within these limits, this follow-up study does confirm the relationship between depression and the major classes of exits and undesirable events. The failure of these event groups to fall in frequency all the way to control levels probably reflects a mixture of illness residue, reporting bias, and the element in event occurrence which is due to habitual maladaptive patterns tending to produce events.

PERCEPTIONS OF EVENTS

Some supporting evidence that there is a more general difference between exit and entrance events came from perceptions of life events. This approach was utilized in a study carried out with Dr. E. H. Uhlenhuth (Paykel, Prusoff, & Uhlenhuth, 1971; Paykel & Uhlenhuth, 1972). We asked 373 subjects to scale, on a 0–20 equal interval scale, the degree to which each of 61 events was perceived as upsetting. The general findings were similar to those obtained by Holmes and Rahe (1967), using a different scaling technique. The scaling proved readily feasible, and there was remarkably high agreement across different sociodemographic groups. Mean scores covered almost all the available scale range of 0–20.

Among the 61 events included in this study, 6 were entrances to the social field and 13 were exits. Differences between these two groups of events on mean scaling scores were examined (Paykel & Uhlenhuth, 1972). Findings were striking. Almost all the exits were scaled high and all the entrances low. There was scarcely any overlap; only 3 exits scored lower than the highest entrances. It appeared that exits and entrances are perceived as very different in stressful implications by most individuals, and in a way which coincides with their relation to depression. Similar findings have also been obtained recently in an English sample in a study we are carrying out at St. George's Hospital.

SUICIDE ATTEMPTS

Since the original studies of depression, findings have been extended to other patient groups. The patterns show some similarities and some differences from those for depression.

One such study involved suicide attempters (Paykel, Prusoff, & Myers, unpublished). Although patients who make unsuccessful suicide attempts might seem at first thought merely a group of more severe depressives, the relationship is not straightforward. Suicide attempters tend to be a special group, younger than most depressives, with a background of disturbed social relations and personality disorder.

We sought in this case to study the relationship of life events to the attempt. Subjects were 53 patients, aged 18–65, comprising an approximately 1:4 sample of those fitting the age criteria who arrived after a suicide attempt at the Emergency Room of the Yale New Haven Hospital. Life-event information was obtained within a week after presentation in the same way as before. The time period under consideration in this study was the six months prior to the attempt. For control purposes, these patients were matched on age, sex, marital status, social class, and race with two groups: depressives from the depression study, and general population controls from the general population survey. The 61 events were reduced to 33 as before for analysis.

Some of the findings are summarized in Table 5. Suicide attempters (mean number of events = 3.3) reported four times as many events as did the general

Table 5. Life Events Reported by Suicide Attempters, Matched Depressives, and General Population Controls (Number of Subjects Reporting One or More Event in Each Category)

	Suicide Attempters ($N = 53$)	Depressives ($N = 53$)	General Population ($N = 53$)	Significance: Attempters versus General Population	Significance: Attempters versus Depressives
Entrances	18	7	6	<.05	<.05
Exits	11	13	2	<.05	N.S.
Desirable	8	2	6	N.S.	N.S.
Undesirable	32	21	11	<.001	<.05
Employment	10	18	12	N.S.	N. S.
Health	26	15	7	<.001	<.05
Family	12	6	0	<.001	N.S.
Marital	22	18	3	<.001	N.S.
Legal	15	5	3	<.001	<.05
Mean number of events	3.3	2.0	0.8	<.001	<.01

population controls (mean = 0.8 events), and 50% more than the depressives. When event categories were examined the excess over general population controls was distributed over almost all types of events; the excess over depressives was a little more selective. The table shows the findings for the three sets of categories of greatest interest. For area of activity, suicide attempters reported more events than the general population controls in all categories but employment. They also reported more events than the depressives in all but this category, although not all differences reached significance. For the classification of greatest interest, the exit-entrance dichotomy, attempters reported more entrances than depressives but no more exits. Instead of the specific relationship to exits found for depression, entrances were just as strongly related to suicide attempts. For the desirable-undesirable dichotomy the pattern was different; suicide attempters showed an excess of undesirable, but not of desirable events, over both groups. The pattern for attempters was an exaggeration of that for depressives, although attempters did in fact tend weakly to report more desirable events than did depressives.

Table 6 presents findings for two other groups of events. For the first, we divided events into three groups, minor, intermediate, and major, by their scaling scores in terms of perceived upset in the previous scaling study (Paykel, Prusoff, & Uhlenhuth, 1971). Depressives showed more events than general

Table 6. Events Classified by Intensity and by Degree of Control

	Suicide Attempters ($N = 53$)	Depressives ($N = 53$)	General Population ($N = 53$)	Significance: Attempters versus General Population	Significance: Attempters versus Depressives
Minor	26	24	13	<.05	N.S.
Intermediate	28	14	2	<.001	<.01
Major	36	24	12	<.001	<.05
Controlled	18	17	9	N.S.	N.S.
Uncontrolled	35	21	11	<.001	<.05

population controls in all three categories; attempters showed a further excess for major and intermediate, but not minor events. The second categorization was by the degree of control or choice the respondent might exert over the initiation of the event. Some events, like serious illness of a family member, are likely to be outside his control; other events, such as marriage, may be within it. In both these categories depressives tended to report more events than the general population subjects. Attempters reported more uncontrolled events than either group, but no more controlled events than did depressives.

To summarize these findings, suicide attempters report more events than general population subjects in almost every category except that of desirable events. When they are compared with depressives the excess is more selective: it particularly involves the more threatening categories of undesirable events, events scaled as major or intermediate in terms of upset, and events outside the respondent's control. One categorization departs from this pattern. Exits and entrances precede suicide attempts equally, in contrast to their relationship to depression.

In this study we also recorded the month of occurrence of each event. We returned to the original data to obtain this information, which had been recorded but not previously analyzed, for the depressives and general population subjects. Figure 1 shows the mean number of events reported in each of the six months. For general population subjects there was a fairly even spread of events over the entire six months. For depressives there was a mild peaking in the month before onset. The excess of events they reported compared with general population subjects was, however, spread over most of the six months and might have extended even earlier. These findings are consistent with those reported by Brown, Sklair, Harris, and Birley (1973). For suicide attempters, there was a marked peaking of events in the month before the attempt. Detailed analysis showed this was particularly marked in the week immediately preced-

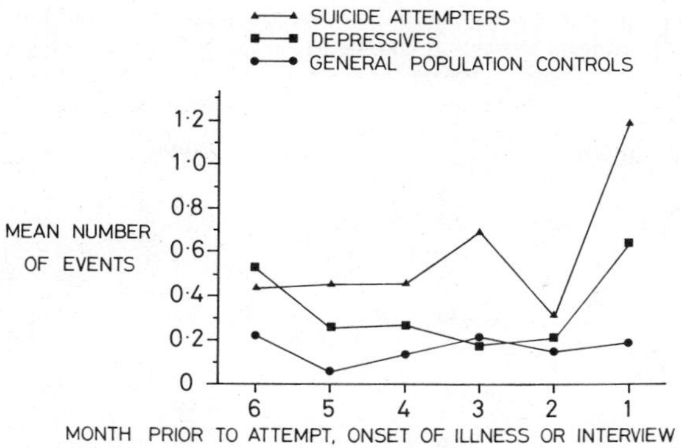

Figure 1. Suicide attempters, depressives, and general population: mean number of events per month.

ing the attempt. Six months before the attempt the event rate was similar to that reported by the depressives and still above control values. It should be kept in mind that suicide attempters were interviewed respecting the period six months before the attempt, whereas for the depressives it was the six months before onset that was studied. Some of the attempters had had symptoms for some time before the attempt, so that some of the earlier excess may reflect consequences of illness. It is, however, clear that the temporal pattern in relation to suicide attempters is different from that for mixed depressives. The link between event and suicide attempt is much more immediate than is that for depression in general.

SCHIZOPHRENIA

More recently, Selby Jacobs at Yale has been extending these findings to schizophrenics. He studied 62 first-admission schizophrenics obtained by screening several facilities. Patients were interviewed two or more weeks after admission, when the acute disturbance had subsided. Events were recorded for the year before onset, divided into two six-month periods.

In Jacobs' data analyses schizophrenics will be matched both with depressives and with general population controls. In a first analysis 50 schizophrenics, all those who could be matched on age, sex, marital status, social class, and race, were compared with 50 depressives from the earlier study regarding events in the six months before onset. The full 61 events of the original list were available for comparison, rather than the 33 used in studies with the general population controls. Findings are shown in Table 7.

Overall the schizophrenics (mean number of events = 2.5) reported about

Table 7. Events Reported by Schizophrenics and Depressives in Six Months before Onset (Number of Subjects Reporting One or More Event in Each Category)

	Schizophrenics ($N = 50$)	Depressives ($N = 50$)	Significance of Difference
Entrances	8	4	N.S.
Exits	12	23	<.05
Desirable	5	3	N.S.
Undesirable	34	44	<.05
Work	19	19	N.S.
Educational	8	6	N.S.
Financial	6	15	<.05
Health	10	25	<.01
Deaths	4	4	N.S.
Relocation	10	11	N.S.
Marital	5	10	N.S.
Children	13	21	N.S.
Dating	6	13	N.S.
Legal	5	12	N.S.
Mean number of events	2.5	3.6	< .05

one-third fewer events than did the depressives (mean = 3.6 events). The table shows some categories examined so far. Schizophrenics reported fewer exits and undesirable events than the depressives, but about the same low number of entrances and desirable events. In an expanded categorization by area of activity, the reduction in event rates was more marked among events related to health and finance, although there were similar trends in a number of other categories. Pending comparisons with general population subjects, conclusions must be tentative. Inspection suggests that the overall event rate and the rates for exits and undesirable events are higher for schizophrenics than for the general population. Life events appear to bear some relationship to the onset of schizophrenia, but the relationship is weaker than that for depression or suicide attempts.

NEUROTIC SYNDROMES

These differences between diagnostic groups in event patterns are by no means universal, however. In collaboration with Dr. E. H. Uhlenhuth event experience was examined in 213 mixed psychiatric patients, the majority of them outpatients with various neurotic disorders (Uhlenhuth & Paykel, 1973a; 1973b). Information was also obtained on 160 relatives of psychiatric patients. Techniques were rather different. Information on the occurrence of the 61 life events was obtained by self-report questionnaire, and it referred to the year immediately preceding. Information as to symptom patterns was also obtained by a self-report symptom checklist. Data were analyzed by Uhlenhuth in a special multivariate covariance analysis procedure he has developed (Uhlenhuth, Duncan, & Park, 1969).

Using this procedure we found no relationship between symptom profile on five factor scores developed from the symptom checklist and intensity of previous stress. Two small groups, one of 22 patients with predominant anxiety and another of 15 patients with predominant depression, showed no differences in types of event categorized, as in previous studies. The relatively small *N*s in these two groups reflect the fact that, as is common in neurotic patients, most of these subjects displayed a mixture of symptoms of anxiety, depression, and other neurotic symptoms. Within this narrower range of mixed neurotic disorders there do not appear important differences in the types of event preceding development of different symptom patterns.

There were, however, some other significant findings. Psychiatric patients reported more life events than well relatives. We also looked at the relationship between overall symptom severity and intensity of previous stress measured by an additive score employing scaling weights derived for each event. Regressions were examined separately for 147 outpatients, 21 day patients, 45 inpatients. In both outpatients and day patients severity of symptoms increased as did severity of preceding stress. This relationship was absent for inpatients.

This relationship between symptom intensity and preceding stress in neurotic outpatients and day patients conforms to expectation. A possible explanation for its absence in inpatients might be that their illnesses, which are more likely to be severe and psychotic, bear less relation to stress. We have other evidence that the relationship does not extend to all groups. In the first study in this series, using purely depressed patients, the amount of stress in the six months before onset was in fact unrelated to overall symptom severity, although it did relate weakly to symptom patterns said to characterize reactive rather than endogenous depression (Paykel, Prusoff, & Klerman, 1971).

CONCLUSIONS

What can be concluded from these studies? I have summarized here the relevant findings from a series of retrospective studies in different patient and control groups. It is clear from these studies that life events tend to occur to an extent greater than chance expectation before a variety of psychiatric disorders.

The amount of preceding stress, its time relationship to onset, and, to a limited extent, the types of event involved, vary from disorder to disorder. Further information is needed to specify these patterns more precisely. The most marked differences appear to be in amount of stress, presumably reflecting, in a retrospective frame, the degree to which life events are implicated in the onset of the disorder. Suicide attempters report the most events, depressives the next highest number, then schizophrenics. Among mixed neurotic outpatients there is a linear relationship between amount of stress and severity of symptoms; this relationship may not apply within other disorders. In time relationships the link with suicide attempts seems to be the most immediate one; there is a marked peak in event occurrence just prior to the attempt. The differences in types of event are less marked. There are meaningful distinctions overall between different classes of event. For instance, events that can be regarded as desirable do not appear to occur excessively before any of the psychiatric disorders examined, but undesirable events do. An additional distinction, that between exits and entrances, appears particularly relevant to clinical depression; exits precede depression but entrances do not. The more threatening classes of events are particularly implicated in suicide attempts.

These patterns support the validity of the retrospective approach; they would be hard to attribute merely to reporting bias. They suggest some specific relationships between events and disorders. Such links are clearly very far from precise. The same life events may be followed by a range of disorders or, perhaps most often, by no disorder at all. In these circumstances it is not only the event that is important, but the kind of soil on which it falls. Interactions with predisposing factors of personal vulnerability, and with incipient or borderline disease processes, must be of great importance in determining whether the disorder will develop and what its type will be. Presumably the patterns found in these studies reflect the ways in which these interactions occur. These patterns do, however, indicate that the qualities of the event play some part in determining whether a psychiatric disorder will develop, and that there are at least partly specific relationships between events and the kinds of illness that may follow them.

REFERENCES

Brown, G. W., Sklair, F., Harris, T. O., & Birley, J. L. T. Life events and psychiatric disorders: Part I. Some methodological issues. *Psychological Medicine,* 1973, **3,** 74–87.

Holmes, T. H., & Rahe, R. H. The Social Readjustment Rating Scale. *Journal of Psychosomatic Research,* 1967, **11,** 213–218.

Myers, J. K., Lindenthal, J. J., & Pepper, M. P. Life events and psychiatric impairment. *Journal of Nervous and Mental Disease,* 1971, **152,** 149–157.

Paykel, E. S. Life events and acute depression. In J. P. Scott & E. C. Senay (Eds.), *Separation and Depression: Clinical and Research Aspects.* Washington, D.C.: American Association for the Advancement of Science, 1973. Pp. 215–236.

Paykel, E. S. Recent life events and clinical depression. In E. K. Gunderson & R. H. Rahe (Eds.), *Life Stress and Illness.* Springfield, Ill.: Charles C Thomas, in press. Chapter 5.

Paykel, E. S., Myers, J. K., Dienelt, M. N., Klerman, G. L., Lindenthal, J. J., & Pepper, M. P. Life events and depression: A controlled study. *Archives of General Psychiatry,* 1969, **21,** 753–760.

Paykel, E. S., Prusoff, B. A., & Klerman, G. L. The endogenous-neurotic continuum: Rater independence and factor distributions. *Journal of Psychiatric Research,* 1971, **8,** 73–90.

Paykel, E. S., Prusoff, B. A., & Myers, J. K. Suicide attempts and recent life events: A controlled comparison. Unpublished.

Paykel, E. S., Prusoff, B. A., & Uhlenhuth, E. H. Scaling of life events. *Archives of General Psychiatry,* 1971, **25,** 340–347.

Paykel, E. S., & Uhlenhuth, E. H. Rating the magnitude of life stress. *Canadian Psychiatric Association Journal,* 1972, **17,** SS93–SS100.

Uhlenhuth, E. H., Duncan, D. B., & Park, C. C. Some nonpharmacologic modifiers of the response to imipramine in depressed psychoneurotic outpatients: A confirmatory study. In P. R. A. May & J. R. Wittenborn (Eds.), *Psychotropic Drug Response: Advances in Prediction.* Springfield, Ill.: Charles C Thomas, 1969. Pp. 155–197.

Uhlenhuth, E. H., & Paykel, E. S. Symptom intensity and life events. *Archives of General Psychiatry,* 1973, **28,** 473–477. (a)

Uhlenhuth, E. H., & Paykel, E. S. Symptom configuration and life events. *Archives of General Psychiatry,* 1973, **28,** 744–748. (b)

CHAPTER 9

A Model for Life Events and Their Consequences

SIDNEY COBB

INTRODUCTION

The purpose of this discussion is twofold. I begin with some comments on the three preceding chapters and then present a metatheoretical model that may eventually lead us to a more basic understanding of the phenomena with which we are concerned in this book.

Theorell discusses possible mechanisms that might be involved in the relationships with which we are concerned. He writes about ways in which elevated catecholamine levels may contribute to coronary artery disease and presents data to suggest that catecholamine excretion, particularly epinephrine, may be elevated in proportion to life events. I have data from a study which I presented at the annual meeting of the American Psychosomatic Society in 1973, that norepinephrine excretion is similarly elevated in proportion to the frequency of life events (Cobb, Kasl, Roth, & Brooks, 1974). Theorell also points out that the subjective evaluation of these events is more predictive than just the average evaluation. I think this is a particularly important point to understand. He spoke of the ambitious, aggressive personality type A (Friedman & Rosenman, 1959) and I wonder if he's looked at it as a conditioning variable rather than as a correlate. In the work of French and Caplan (1973), my colleagues at The Institute for Social Research, it seems that those who are of the type A disposition are more likely to experience strain when they are put under certain kinds of stresses, particularly heavy work loads.

I was fascinated by Hudgens' list of difficulties in these retrospective studies. I agree with him very much, but, as an epidemiologist, I must point out that there are ways to get around many or even most of these problems and I hope in studies to come sounder epidemiologic techniques will be used. There is one thing he did not mention which interferes with almost any study: the bias of denial. We have evidence from our studies that those who are high on the measure of denial do, in fact, report fewer life events in the last year than those who are low on denial. The same thing is true with respect to symptoms, with respect to depression, with respect to going to the dispensary, and with other such phenomena, so there is the possibility of a built-in correlation between these which is purely spurious and is based on the degree of denial. Therefore one of the things we have to do in future studies is to see if we can control for this factor or at the very least discover how important a variable it may be.

Hudgens presented us with some interesting clinical observations; but I am a little hesitant about accepting some of his cases. Many people become depressed as a consequence of viral infections, and I am not convinced we should think of this in terms of life events. This is particularly true of infectious hepatitis, but it is noted also in the course of infectious mononucleosis and in the course of influenza. The depression in some of these cases may be only a physsiological consequence of the disease. It is known that rheumatoid arthritis is associated with depression. However, the probability of depression is not a function of the severity of the illness (Kasl & Cobb, 1969). Furthermore, I know of one case in which the depression began before the arthritis. The same may be true of lupus erythematosus (Otto & Mackay, 1967) and ulcerative colitis (Engle, 1958). Thus, although accepting the realities of serious illness is clearly stressful, there are other important considerations here.

I was very intrigued by Paykel's chapter and grateful to him for again emphasizing the issue of susceptibility. I wonder, however, whether entrance events could be associated with increased social support, and if therefore the change aspects of their effects may be ameliorated by the supportive aspects of their quality as entrances.

THE METATHEORETICAL MODEL

I turn now to the construction of a metatheoretical model which will I hope help us develop proper theories about the nature of the relationship between life events and illness. The model considered here is not new. Its first presentation was in 1962 (French & Kahn, 1962) and since then it has appeared in various forms (Cobb, Brooks, Kasl, & Connelly, 1966; Kahn, 1973), but the basic concepts of intervening and interacting variables have persisted. This model (Figure 1) is intended to clarify some of the complex relationships among the intervening and interacting variables that need to be considered.

There are several panels with arrows between them, implying causation moving from left to right. Let us start with Life Event and note that I have omitted the "s" because I firmly believe that one should study individual events by themselves singly. For the last seven years I have been working at this in a study of people whose jobs have been abolished. Employment termination is a

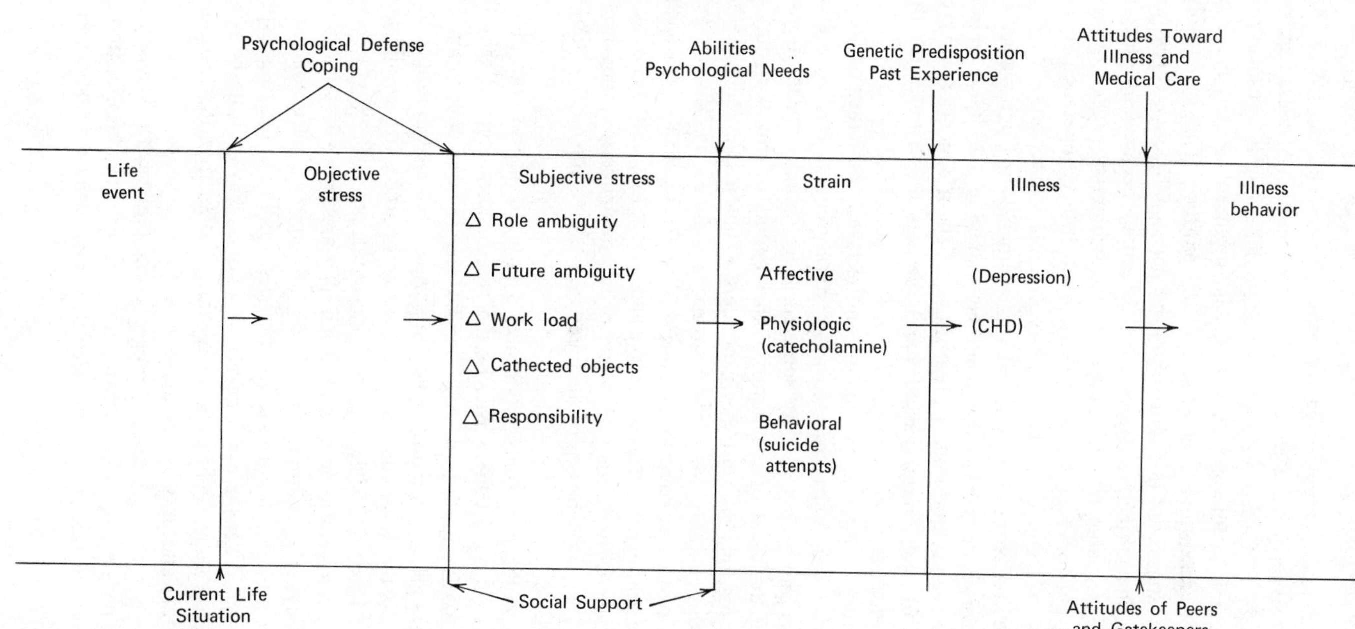

Figure 1. An oversimplified diagram to help clarify the relationship of life events to illness (items in parentheses were presented in the papers under discussion).

single life event and one can trace its consequences. Parkes (1972) has been working on the issue of bereavement and Ostfeld and Kasl at Yale are now carrying out a study of forced residential change. I believe it is useful to be this specific in research in this area, because it is important to start breaking these events down into the dimensions of stress they produce. This is not only possible but actually suggested in Figure 1 by the panels Objective Stress and Subjective Stress. The Objective Stress panel is empty because the data we deal with generally are subjective in nature. These subjective reports surely represent objective phenomena, but as yet there is little competence in objective measurement so we are forced to deal largely with self-reports.

Under Subjective Stress I have listed some dimensions I believe are relevant. Primary emphasis is on workload or a similar change in workload. Although it is not true of all events, certainly a great many of them engender work overload that may last for substantial periods; and there is much evidence that work overload can produce strain.

Role ambiguity is induced by changes in the family structure or the structure of the work situation; future ambiguity is certainly engendered by a great many of these events and object loss by some of them. Finally, promotions, demotions, death of the head of the family, other events of this sort may substantially alter the responsibility of the respondent. Thus it is evident that there are a number of dimensions along which stress is induced by life-change events. Among these, particular attention should be directed to work overload, role ambiguity, future ambiguity, responsibility, and object loss. The refinement of the first four of these dimensions plus some of the evidence that they are stressful was recently presented by my colleagues and me (Kahn, 1973; Cobb, 1973; French, 1973).

Moving on to the panel labeled Strain, it is gratifying to note that we have had serious attention given to two of the three dimensions. Theorell has reported some additional information on the physiologic consequences of life changes. Although the literature in this important area is still a bit thin, it seems probable that in the long run the relationship between life events and illness will be clarified by understanding the intervening physiologic variables.

Reports of behavioral evidence of strain also are scarce in the life-events literature, so Paykel's chapter on suicide attempts is particularly welcome. Though it is not uncommon to view completed suicide as the fatal aspect of the disease depression, I believe it is correct to classify Paykel's study as a study of behavior because there seem to be many things other than depression that contribute to suicide attempts or gestures.

Turning to the Illness panel, I agree completely with Mechanic that we should focus on single illnesses from now on. Holmes, Rahe, and their colleagues have presented ample evidence that interesting results can be obtained by summing across illnesses, but if we want to understand the mechanisms involved we must become disease specific in our studies. Specific diseases that have been discussed in this book are listed in parentheses in the panel. As mentioned earlier, Theorell's chapter on the possible mechanisms involved in the association of increased catecholamine output and coronary heart disease is particularly gratifying. In my view it is only when we understand mechanism that we can be sure that observed associations are not spurious.

The final panel is labeled Illness Behavior to remind us that in many of the earlier studies it is not clear whether the consequence of life events was an increase in illness or merely an increase in illness behavior. It should be clear that complaining and seeking medical advice, which increase the probability of a given case being identified, are parts of what is called illness behavior (Kasl & Cobb, 1966).

Let us now turn to the remaining areas of Figure 1, Personal Characteristics above and Social Situation below. These areas are particularly important for it is in contemplating them that we are able to focus on the variables that contribute to immunity versus susceptibility. These variables are control variables. That means that they produce what the statistician calls interaction effects. For example, it seems clear that psychological defenses may intervene between objective stress and subjective stress. As mentioned previously my colleagues and I have found that those with a high tendency to denial report fewer life events than those who are low on our measure of denial. Similarly, it is obvious that susceptibility to certain diseases may be enhanced by genetic factors. There is reason to believe that genetic factors operate to some extent in both of the diseases listed in the Illness panel. Past experience also can condition responses to stressful events. In perhaps oversimplified terms, an anxiety neurosis can be looked on as conditioned overresponse of anxiety that is severe enough to be maladaptive.

Turning to the lowest panel, Social Situation, we should note that an event which led to an increase in workload for a man who was underloaded and bored could be a beneficient event whereas the same change could be destructive for one who was already overloaded. Social support can substantially moderate the effects of job loss (Gore, 1973). Similarly, the attitudes about medical attendance can dramatically influence the frequency of dispensary visits and the time between first symptom and first relevant visit to a physician (Kasl & Cobb, 1966).

In closing I want to emphasize that the utility of this metatheoretical diagram is in its blank spaces. We can each fill in variables to suit our own hypotheses. The great advantage of the framework provided in the diagram is that it reminds us to be complex in our thinking as we seek to explain the mechanisms by which life events influence health.

REFERENCES

Cobb, S. Role responsibility: The differentiation of a concept. *Occupational Mental Health,* 1973, **3,** 10–14.

Cobb, S., Brooks, G. W., Kasl, S. V., & Connelly, W. E. The health of people changing jobs: A description of a longitudinal study. *American Journal of Public Health,* 1966, **56,** 1476–1481.

Cobb, S., Kasl, S. V., Roth, T. L, & Brooks, G. W. Urinary nor-epinephrine in men whose jobs are abolished. *Psychosomatic Medicine,* 1974, in press.

Engel, G. L. Studies of ulcerative colitis. V. Psychological aspects and their implications for treatment. *American Journal of Digestive Disorders,* 1958, **3,** 315–337.

French, J. R. P., Jr. Person role fit. *Occupational Mental Health,* 1973, **3,** 15–20.

French, J. R. P., Jr., & Caplan, R. D. Organizational stress and individual strain. In Alfred J. Morrow (Ed.), *The Failure of Success.* New York: AMACOM, 1973. Pp. 30–66.

French, J. R. P., Jr., & Kahn, R. L. A programmatic approach to studying the industrial environment and mental health. *Journal of Social Issues,* 1962, **18,** 1–47.

Friedman, M., & Rosenman, R. Association of specific overt behavior pattern with blood and cardiovascular findings. *Journal of the American Medical Association,* 1959, **169,** 1286–1296.

Gore, S. The influence of social support and related variables in ameliorating the consequences of job loss. Doctoral dissertation, Department of Sociology, University of Pennsylvania, 1973.

Kahn, R. L. Conflict, ambiguity, and overload: Three elements in job stress. *Occupational Mental Health,* 1973, **3,** 2–9.

Kasl, S. V., & Cobb, S. Health behavior, illness behavior, and sick role behavior. *Archives of Environmental Medicine,* 1966, **12,** 246–266; 531–541.

Kasl, S. V., & Cobb, S. The intrafamilial transmission of rheumatoid arthritis. V. Differences between rheumatoid arthritis and controls on selected personality variables. *Journal of Chronic Diseases,* 1969, **22,** 239–258.

Otto, R., & Mackay, I. R. Psychosocial and emotional disturbance in systemic lupus erythematosus. *Medical Journal of Austrialia,* 1967, **2,** 488–493.

Parkes, C. M. *Bereavement—Studies of Grief in Adult Life.* New York: International Universities Press, 1972.

PART 3

Community Research on Relations Between Stressful Life Events and Psychiatric Symptomatology

Although there is no program of research on life events and psychiatric symptoms that is analogous to those reported for episodes of physical illness in Part 1, there is a growing body of individual studies. All are offshoots of research programs in psychiatric epidemiology and focus on community populations.

Each of the first three chapters in Part 3 describes an investigation that makes a unique contribution to the study of life events in relation to psychiatric symptoms: Joanne C. Gersten, Thomas S. Langner, Jeanne G. Eisenberg, and Lida Orzeck focus on children sampled from the general population, whereas the next two chapters are concerned with adults. Robert E. Markush and Rachel V. Favero provide comparisons of samples from a large city and a relatively rural area where the same standardized procedures were used. Jerome K. Myers, Jacob J. Lindenthal, and Max P. Pepper present longitudinal analyses of data collected from a general population sample over time. In the fourth chapter Sheppard Kellam presents both kudos and cautions in his review of the work presented in the preceding three chapters.

CHAPTER 10

Child Behavior and Life Events:

Undesirable Change or Change Per Se? *

JOANNE C. GERSTEN

THOMAS S. LANGNER †

JEANNE G. EISENBERG

LIDA ORZECK

INTRODUCTION

A crucial issue in the investigation of life events is the characteristic of a life event which makes that event a stressor, that is, makes it likely to produce a stress reaction or strain (Langner & Michael, 1963), which, for the purposes of this chapter, is conceptualized as symptoms of psychological distress. For most people a stressful event is thought of as something undesirable or threatening. A typical psychological definition of stress is "a state where the well-being (or integrity) of an individual is endangered and he must devote all of his energies to its protection" (Cofer & Appley, 1964, p. 463). However, mainly because of the work of Holmes and Rahe (1967) and others (Dohrenwend & Dohrenwend, 1970; Fröberg, Karlsson, Levi, & Lidberg, 1971), change became the critical element in the assessment of stress. In other words, the key component in making a life event stressful was conceptualized as its ability to *change* an individual's usual activities, and not its desirability or undesirability. Holmes and Rahe (1967) then scaled the change introduced by a life event in terms of the

* This investigation has been supported by Public Health Service Project Grants MH 11545 and MH 18260 of the National Institute of Mental Health, Center for Epidemiologic Studies.

† Support for the Principal Investigator has been given by Career Scientist Grants I-338 and I-640 of the Health Research Council of the City of New York. The Principal Investigator is currently supported through Research Scientist Award K5-MH-20868 of the National Institute of Mental Health.

readjustment required by the individual.

Dohrenwend (1973) compared the relationships of four different measures of stressful life events to symptoms of psychological impairment. The latter was assessed by the Langner (1962) 22-item screening score. Her four measures were what she termed an "undesirability score," a simple total of life events or changes, and weighted versions of each of these scores. The simple total score was simply the sum of all events, each with a weight of 1; the weighted scores were the sums of the appropriate events, each being weighted by the social adjustment rating developed by Holmes and Rahe (1967). The undesirability score was not a sum of all undesirable events, as its name implied, but instead was a difference score between undesirable and desirable events. In other words, it was a total in which undesirable events were weighted +1, desirable events −1, and ambiguous events 0. Examination of the pattern of correlations of these four measures to the psychological distress measure led Dohrenwend to conclude that "change rather than undesirability is the characteristic of life events that should be measured for the more accurate assessment of their stressfulness."

A number of problems arise, however, in the acceptance of this conclusion. First, whereas the *weighted* total change score did show higher correlations with the distress scores in both dichotomous and continuous form (.40 and .35, respectively) than did the undesirability measure (.28 and .29, respectively), it was not ascertained whether the two sets of correlations were significantly different. In fact, it is very likely that they were not. Since the author did not report the intercorrelation of the two life-event measures, we determined what would be the necessary intercorrelation for the correlations with the distress measures to significantly differ at the .05 level using the t-test for difference in nonindependent correlations (McNemar, 1969, p. 158). In the case of the correlations with the continuous scale of the distress scores, they would not significantly differ if the intercorrelation ranged from 0 to .90. The correlations with the dichotomy would differ only if the intercorrelation was at least .75. It can be seen then that one comparison was definitely insignificant and the other was likely to be because of the high level of intercorrelation required.

Moreover, it may be argued that undesirability of events should be looked at separately from the balance in one's life among undesirable and desirable events. The difference notion implies that every positive event perfectly cancels out a negative event or that the two classes of events are related to distress with nearly equal strength but in opposite directions. The tenability of this assumption should be examined empirically.

Finally, the nature of the dependent variable raises many questions. Many studies have relied on such measures of psychological impairment as the Langner 22-item scale (1962) or the Gurin, Veroff, and Feld (1960) items. Both of these scales are characterized by a preponderance of items dealing with psychological and physiological expressions of anxiety. Gurin, Veroff, and Feld's (1960) factor analysis of the 20 items in their inventory resulted in four factors, with only two items each: Psychological Anxiety, Physical Anxiety, Physical Health, and Immobilization. A greater proportion of people had pathological scores on each of the two anxiety scales than the other two factors (16 and 11% versus 6 and 9%, respectively). In like manner, those items on the Langner scale which were most likely to receive an affirmative pathological response were mainly anxiety items ("being a worrying type"; "bothered by nervousness"; "personal worries get me down physically"; etc.). Thus, although the factorial compositions of these overall measures are far from clear, there is little question that the anxiety items show the highest probability of entering into each of the final scores.

It is hypothesized that the superiority of change over undesirability measures of the stressfulness of life events stems from the use of dependent measures which mainly reflect anxiety. Anxiety, like arousal, is likely to be the first result of any change, whether it is positive or negative (Hebb, 1958; Cofer & Appley, 1963; Levi, 1972). In other words, anxiety is probably the basic or initial preparatory response to environmental changes or stimuli. The appearance of other forms of disturbed behavior, however, such as aggression, antisocial behavior, or withdrawn behavior, may depend on the quality of the life event and not the fact that it introduces *change* per se. Therefore the dependent variable, psychological impairment, should be assessed using a variety of dimensions tapping different types of impairment.

This preliminary investigation, then, proposed to study the relationships of different measures of the stressfulness of life events to a number of dimensions reflecting different types of impairment in children and young adults from the age of 11 to 23.

METHOD

The subjects of this study were 674 Manhattan children and young adults. They constituted the families contacted up to the point of this investigation in a five-year follow-up of an original cross section sample of Manhattan families from Houston Street to 125th Street. As such, they comprised 90% of the follow-up sample when completed. Although this makes the study preliminary in nature, it is expected that the small number of additional cases will have minimal impact on the findings since they are already based on such a large number of subjects.

The original sample was collected according to a stratified systematic cluster sampling plan in which clusters were designated within each New York City health area in that geographical section of the city. A cluster of eight dwelling units in a health area was randomly selected and every thirtieth cluster thereafter was considered. The final sample was 56% White, 14% Black, 29% Spanish-speaking, and 1% other. Each mother was questioned at both times about various aspects of her child's behavior, and a computer summary of the 654 items was used by two psychiatrists to rate the level of a child's psychological impairment on a 5-point rating scale (total impairment rating). The reliability of the average of two raters for this rating was 0.84. Those items that had adequate frequencies and were not highly contingent upon age or sex were factor analyzed at time 1 and formed 18 dimensions of child behavior, which contained a total of 221 items. On the basis of the correlation of each of the factors at time 1 with the psychiatric total impairment rating, seven of the factors were selected to form a short screening inventory for children.

Each factor was represented by its five highest loaded items. The alpha coefficient or internal-consistency reliability of the total score was 0.76. An additional five items were added to enhance the inventory's screening ability with welfare-assisted children. (For further information about the inventory see Langner, Gersten, Eisenberg, McCarthy, Greene, Herson, Jameson, & Temkin, in press.) Each child's behavior at time 2 was then scored on these eight subscales (Regressive Anxiety, Self-Destructive Tendencies, Conflict with Parents, Mentation Problems, Fighting, Delinquency, Isolation, and Miscellaneous) and two total scores were obtained, a 35-item and a 40-item total. In addition, each mother was asked if there had been changes in her child's moods, family behavior, behavior with peers, and so on, for better or worse over the past five years. These nine items were used to form a Behavior Change Score in which each item was scored in the following manner: much worse = +2; worse = +1; no change = 0; better = −1; much better = −2.

In the development of independent variables, three researchers on the staff evaluated whether the 25 events or changes which occurred within the intervening five years were desirable, undesirable, or ambiguous in their quality. There was complete agreement among the three researchers on the categories to which the events were assigned. Sixteen events were considered undesirable, five desirable, and four ambiguous. Four scores were then developed in which each event was given a weight of 1: Undesirable Event Score = sum of 16 events; Desirable Event Score = sum of 5 events; Total Change Score = sum of 25 events; and Difference Score = Undesirable Event Score minus Desirable Event Score. In addition, weighted versions of the total change score and the difference score were developed in which each event was weighted by the amount of social readjustment it required. The social readjustment weights used were an average of the two ratings assigned by professionals (131 teachers, 25 pediatricians, and 87 mental health workers) to events experienced by junior high school students and senior high students in Coddington's work (1972).

Table 1 lists the events and gives the desirability rating and social readjustment weight of each. Inspection of the Table indicates that most of the events listed can be considered outside the child's control. The means, standard deviations, and Pearson intercorrelations of the 11 dependent variables and the 6 independent variables were then obtained. Significant differences between correlations were determined using the *t*-test for nonindependent correlations.

Table 1. Life Event List with the Desirability Rating and Social Readjustment Rating Weight of Each

Event (Occurred within past five years —between two interviews)	Desirability Rating [1]	Weight
1. Mother had severe illness or accident	U	54
2. Father had severe illness or accident	U	54
3. Family had serious financial troubles	U	42
4. Parents were divorced	U	80
5. Parents were separated	U	73
6. Mother remarried	U	63
7. Father remarried	U	63
8. Death(s) occurred in family	U	80
9. Child had a severe illness or accident	U	58
10. Child lost a close friend	U	68
11. Child didn't get along with a new teacher	U	50
12. Other incident or event occurred that affected child badly,	U	50
13. made him sad, angry, unable to study or work, see friends	U	50
14. or otherwise interfered with his life	U	50
15. Mother's mood or feelings about life have become worse or much worse	U	50
16. Father's mood or feelings about life have become worse or much worse	U	50
17. Child made a new friend	D	68
18. Some incident or event occurred that made child very happy, proud, or excited	D	46
19. Child got along very well with a new teacher	D	50
20. Mother's mood or feelings about life have become better or much better	D	50
21. Father's mood or feelings about life have become better or much better	D	50
22. Family had to move	A	54
23. New birth(s) in family	A	50
24. Any brother or sister left household	A	35
25. Child changed schools	A	44

[1] U = Undesirable; D = Desirable; A = Ambiguous.

RESULTS

The first striking finding was that a higher average ($\bar{X} = 2.4$) of desirable events was reported than undesirable events ($\bar{X} = 2.2$), even though the undesirable event list was three times as great as the desirable list. A question this immediately raises is whether an increase in the desirable event list to the length of the undesirable event list would yield the same proportion of affirmative responses (50%) as opposed to only 14% of the negative events.

The correlations of the life event measures with the child behavior dependent variables are presented in Table 2. Focusing attention first on the correlations of the simple life event score, it was noted that the Total Change Score was significantly correlated ($p \leq .05$) with every dependent variable. More important, however, only in the case of the anxiety measure was the Total Change Score more highly correlated than the Difference Score. This difference was significant ($p \leq .01$) and the desirable and undesirable events measures had nearly equal correlations with anxiety. For every other dependent variable, the Difference Score showed a higher correlation than the Total Change Score. The

Table 2. Correlations of the Six Life-Event Measures [1] with the Measures of Psychological Impairment and Behavior Change

	Simple (Unit-one Weight) Score				Social Readjustment Weighted Scores	
Dependent Measure	U [2]	D [3]	Total Change	U–D	Total Change	U–D
Regressive anxiety	.16	.14	.17 ***	.08	.17	.10
Mentation problems	.17	−.07	.10	.20 **	.10	.18
Self-destructive tendency	.21 **	−.02	.14	.21	.14	.20
Conflict with parents	.25 **	.01	.18	.23	.18	.22
Fighting	.22	.05	.18	.19	.18	.18
Delinquency	.20	−.14	.09	.27 **	.10	.24
Isolation	.14 *	−.03	.09	.15	.08	.14
35-Item total	.32 **	−.01	.23	.31	.23	.30
Miscellaneous	.19 *	−.03	.14	.20	.14	.17
40-Item total	.33 **	−.01	.24	.32	.24	.30
Behavior change	.03	−.28 **	−.11	.18 **	−.11	.17

[1] Any $r \geq .10, p \leq .01$.
[2] Undesirable event.
[3] Desirable event.
* Difference from simple total change significant .05 level.
** Difference from simple total change significant .01 level.
*** Difference from simple U–D significant .01 level.

correlation was substantially and significantly higher when the Undesirable Event Score and the Desirable Event Score were correlated with a dependent variable in *opposite* directions and when each of the correlations was significant when tested by a one-tailed t-test. (A one-tailed significance test was appropriate since the use of a difference measure implicitly hypothesizes that undesirable and desirable events have opposing influences on distress.) Thus when this assumption underlying the use of a difference score was supported, this measure showed a significantly greater correlation with a dependent variable than the total change measure. This significant differential pattern between the two measures was evidenced by the subscales Mentation Problems (e.g., "mind drifts"; "slow thinking"; "trouble remembering"; "poor grades") and Delinquency (e.g., "does rash and dangerous things"; "trouble with police"; "ran away from home four or more times"). In each case desirable events were associated with lower levels of such impairment.

Every other impairment scale, except for Fighting, and including the two total scores, showed significantly higher correlations with the Undesirable Event score than with the Total Change Score. In addition, there was little difference between the correlations of the Undesirable Event Score and the Difference Score on these measures.

Since Regressive Anxiety items constituted only one-seventh or less of the total possible scores and this subscale had the lowest correlation with the total score of the seven factor-analytically derived subscales, it was not surprising that the total impairment scores had higher correlations with the Undesirable Event Score and Difference Score than the Total Change Score. This was the pattern shown by all the subscales, save one (Anxiety), which entered into those total scores.

Turning attention now to the social readjustment weighted scores, in no case did the weighted versions of the total change and difference scores show a higher correlation with a dependent variable than the simple unit-one weight versions of those scores. In fact, the correlations of the social readjustment weighted total change score were nearly always equal to those of the simple total change score. This was understandable when the intercorrelations among the measures, which are listed in Table 3, were examined. As can be seen, the intercorrelation of the simple and weighted versions of the total change score was .99. Since the intercorrelation between the two versions of the difference score was lower but still very high ($r = .92$), the weighted score showed correlations which were equal to or less than those of the simple score. These intercorrelations suggested that the weighted and simple scores were practically interchangeable, with considerations of economy and the actual findings definitely favoring the simple scores. In contrast, the undesirable and desirable scores had a low intercorrelation ($r = .19$), indicating there was wide latitude in the extent to which the two qualities of events occurred together. A question

Table 3. Intercorrelations of the Life-Event Measures

	Simple Scores				Weighted Scores	
Event Measures	U	D	Total Change	U–D	Total Change	U–D
Simple undesirable (U)		.19	.84	.84	.86	.82
Simple desirable (D)			.57	−.37	.57	−.27
Simple total change				.49	.99	.39
Simple difference (U–D)					.50	.92
Weighted total change						.43

for future research is whether the two classes of events show differential levels of relationships by social class, race, sex, and so forth.

The findings with respect to the Behavior Change Score, in which a mother evaluated and reported on changes in her child's behavior, were equally striking. Admittedly this is a crude measure, but it has importance in that a mother's evaluation of the trends for better or worse in her child's behavior is probably one of the factors involved in treatment initiation and labeling of the child within the family. On the average, these mothers reported that their children's behavior had improved or changed for the better over the past five years in one or more of the nine areas ($\overline{X} = 3.07$). When the mean total score for these children at time 2 was compared to the mean total score for the original sample at time 1, this also showed a substantial drop (1.8 versus 3.0, respectively). Those subscales which showed substantial drops (time 2 score was about one-half the time 1 score) were Regressive Anxiety, Mentation Problems, Fighting, and Isolation. Self-Destructive Tendencies and Conflict with Parents evidenced only minimal decreases and Delinquency showed a slight increase. All subscales, with the important exception of Regressive Anxiety, were positively related to Behavior Change Scores: the higher the score, the more likely an evaluation of change for the worse. Higher Anxiety scores, however, were associated with evaluations of change for the better. Although the relationship was not significant, it was nonetheless striking not only for its deviation from the pattern of the other subscales but also since it was congruent with many conceptions for a necessary condition for successful change in therapeutic situations—the presence of anxiety or a state of acute distress. Those subscales which had significant positive correlations with the evaluation of behavior change were, in rank order, Delinquency, Conflict with Parents, Self-Destructive Tendencies, Fighting, and Isolation.

The relationships of the various life-event measures to the Behavior Change Score showed substantial differences. Only the score reflecting the differential between undesirable and desirable events was significantly associated with evaluation of change for the worse. Contrary to expectation, the total change score was significantly related to evaluations of *improvement*. In other words, it showed the same relationship to evaluations of behavior change as did the Desirable Event Score. The latter measure, however, accounted for six times more variance in the behavior change measure than did the former. Once again the weighted versions of scores showed correlations equal to or less than those of their simple score counterparts.

DISCUSSION

First and foremost, this research dramatically demonstrates the importance of using multiple measures of the very broad universe called psychological or behavioral impairment. The use of an instrument which was composed of a number of factorially defined, homogeneous subscales, with known contributions to the total scale, made it possible to determine to what extent different conceptions of the stressfulness of life events contributed to different types of behavioral impairment.

As hypothesized, the finding for anxiety was the only instance which substantiated Dohrenwend's (1973) contention that life change rather than undesirability (difference) was the more useful conception in the assessment of the stressor potential of life events. As theorized and shown by innumerable workers in the area of personality and abnormal psychology, anxiety is often the first response to any sudden stimulus change, facing a new and unknown situation, being confronted with a very complex task, and so on. This occurs whether the circumstances are positive or negative—all stimulus change having both an arousal and a cue function (Hebb, 1958). In fact, the arousal is necessary for the maintenance of efficient behavior; the well-documented inverse U-shaped function between arousal and behavior efficiency attests to this (Cofer & Appley, 1963). The arousal theory itself plus work in many diverse areas such as perception (novelty, complexity, pacers) and motivation (exploration, manipulation, tension-induction theories, competence, mastery, stimulus deprivation) suggests that a certain optimal level of *change* is necessary for adaptive, integrated behavior. Accordingly, maladaptive behavior would occur either at levels of extremely low arousal (change) or extremely high arousal (change).

To leave that topic for a moment, the findings with respect to all the other types of behavior strongly support the conclusion that undesirability, whether conceived in pure terms or as a balance notion, was the more productive operational measure of stress than amount of change. The difference or balance measure of undesirability played a central role since it related to Delinquency. Antisocial or delinquent behavior is particularly important since on the basis of research done to the present time (Robins, 1966; Kohlberg, LaCrosse, & Ricks,

1972) it is one of the few childhood behavior domains demonstrating predictive power for future or adult impairment of a similar nature (sociopathy and character disorders) and for all other nonneurotic forms of adult maladjustment. Thus Delinquency can be seen as a serious disorder in contrast to symptoms such as anxiety which are more likely to be transient.

The other subscale which showed its strongest relationship to the undesirability-difference score was Mentation Problems, the subscale most closely related on a face content basis to the concept of general intellectual ability. If this is the case, it is probably the other subscale which has the greatest potential for long-term predictive power of adult maladjustment and thus is an index of more serious disorders. Hence the data would suggest at least that the undesirability of life events, especially the balance between undesirable and desirable events, is the criticial dimension and not pure undesirability and certainly not change per se in symptoms or disordered behaviors which are serious and have long-term implications between childhood and adulthood. This contention is further strengthened or supported by the fact that only this measure was related to evaluations that behavior worsened or did not improve over time, whereas the change measure was related to evaluations of improvement.

Perhaps the difference concept of undesirability would have been significantly different from total change for the other subscales and more strongly correlated with all subscales if the universe of desirable events was more adequately sampled. A common failing of the research in this area, certainly in this case, is that we accentuate the negative. Given the high response rate for positive events with such a small sample of these events and the association of desirable events with evaluations of behavioral improvement and nondelinquency, this area deserves further and more extensive work.

In contrast to the work on adults, the results of this study with children to young adults (age 11 to 23) definitely indicated that weighting change or the undesirability difference score by the social readjustment ratings which were obtained from Coddington (1972) produced no benefits. Coddington's rating sample included no Spanish-speaking persons and no young adults, as did our sample. The extent to which such sample differences account for the poor results with the weighted scores is a function of the extent to which rating weights differ across Spanish-speaking and other samples.

Rahe (1969) found that very similar rating weights were given by different national groups. Divergent results were found, however, when one group of Spanish-speaking Americans (Mexican-Americans) were compared to White Americans (Komaroff, Masuda, & Holmes, 1968). No research to this time, however, has ascertained if there are rating differences between mainly Puerto Rican Spanish-speaking Americans and White or Black Americans. Thus all that can be definitely said at this point is that use of the weights given in Table

1 with samples like the present one results in no advantages over a simple score.

Finally, before we attempt to offer a suggestion for the long-term thrust of research in this area, our immediate concern is with the problems inherent in this preliminary work. First, as the methodological chapter written by Bruce Dohrenwend eloquently points out, attention should be addressed to the locus of control or responsibility for the events. Although the majority of events on the list used were outside the child's control, not all were. Thus one goal will be to determine if the same pattern of relationship is found when the events are limited to those beyond the control of the subject. Second, although the results with regard to the evaluations of behavior change were interesting, it must be pointed out that there are drawbacks to considering them anything but tentative. A problem in this research was that the same respondent reported on the events, the behavior, and the evaluation of change—the mother with respect to her child. It is possible that the occurrence of an undesirable or desirable event will color the mother's perception of her child's current behavior as better or worse than formerly. Alternatively, a change in her child's behavior for better or worse may impel her to search for explanations in certain types of past event. To disentangle such possible mutual influences, it would be necessary to have the reports of events and behavior change made by different respondents. A random subsample of the older children and young adults reported on in this chapter were interviewed directly and thus their life-event reports and behavior reports can be compared in the near future with the opposite measure obtained from their mother.

In concluding this chapter, let us return to the earlier point about the implication of arousal theory concerning the maladaptive potential of either excessive change or no change and attempt to integrate that with the information gained here about the central importance of undesirability. Perhaps we should include as an event on an event list a nonevent. A nonevent simply is an event that is desired or anticipated and does not occur; thus nonevents could be either desirable or undesirable. Alternatively, a nonevent could be seen as something desirable which does not occur when its occurrence is normative for people of a certain group. In other words, a stressful situation could be a general deprivation of events. Although such nonevents (e.g., not getting job applied for, not having a girlfriend, not being laid off when funds are cut) could easily be integrated into an undesirability scale, they would present major problems for a total change score and certainly for a change score based on social *readjustment* ratings. Considerable energy and effort has been expended in developing sophisticated, refined systems to gradate change. Perhaps time should now be invested in quantifying the negativity and positivity of events that represent changes and nonchanges.

REFERENCES

Coddington, R. D. The significance of life events as etiologic factors in the diseases of children. II. A study of a normal population. *Journal of Psychosomatic Research,* 1972, **16,** 205–213.

Cofer, C. N., & Appley, M. H. *Motivation: Theory and Research.* New York: John Wiley & Sons, 1964.

Dohrenwend, B. S. Life events as stressors: A methodological inquiry. *Journal of Health and Social Behavior,* 1973, **14,** 167–175.

Dohrenwend, B. S., & Dohrenwend, B. P. Class and race as status related sources of stress. In S. Levine & N.A. Scotch (Eds.), *Social Stress.* Chicago: Aldine Publishing Company, 1970. Pp. 111–140.

Fröberg, J., Karlsson, C. G., Levi, L., & Lidberg, L. Physiological and biochemical stress reactions induced by psychosocial stimuli. In L. Levi (Ed.), *Society, Stress and Disease: The Psychosocial Environment and Psychosomatic Diseases.* New York: Oxford University Press, 1971. Pp. 280–295.

Gurin, G., Veroff, J., & Feld, S. *Americans View Their Mental Health.* New York: Basic Books, 1960.

Hebb, D. O. *A Textbook of Psychology.* Philadelphia: W. B. Saunders, 1958.

Holmes, T. H., & Rahe, R. H. The social readjustment rating scale. *Journal of Psychosomatic Research,* 1967, **11,** 213–218.

Kohlberg, L., LaCrosse, J., & Ricks, D. The predictability of adult mental health from childhood behavior. In B. B. Wolman (Ed.), *Manual of Child Psychopathology.* New York: McGraw-Hill Book Company, 1972. Pp. 1217–1284.

Komaroff, A. L., Masuda, M., & Holmes, T. H. The social readjustment rating scale: A comparative study of Negro, Mexican and White Americans. *Journal of Psychosomatic Research,* 1968, **12,** 121–128.

Langner, T. S. A twenty-two item screening score of psychiatric symptoms indicating impairment. *Journal of Health and Human Behavior,* 1962, **3,** 269–276.

Langner, T. S., Gersten, J., Eisenberg, J. G., McCarthy, E. D., Greene, E. L., Herson, J. H., Jameson, J. D., & Temkin, S. M. A screening score for assessing psychiatric impairment in children six to eighteen. In R. Prince & H. B. M. Murphy (Eds.), *Brief Psychosocial Stress Measures for Community Studies.* Baltimore, Md.: National Education Consultants, in press.

Langner, T. S., & Michael, S. T. *Life Stress and Mental Health.* New York: Free Press of Glencoe, 1963.

Levi, L. *Stress and Distress in Response to Psychosocial Stimuli.* Stockholm: Almqvist and Wiksell Periodical Company, 1972.

McNemar, Q. *Psychological Statistics,* Fourth Edition. New York: John Wiley & Sons, 1969.

Rahe, R. H. Multi-cultural correlations of life change scaling: America, Japan, Denmark and Sweden. *Journal of Psychosomatic Research,* 1969, **13,** 191–195.

Robins, L. N. *Deviant Children Grown Up.* Baltimore, Md.: The Williams and Wilkins Company, 1966.

CHAPTER 11

Epidemiologic Assessment of Stressful Life Events, Depressed Mood, and Psychophysiological Symptoms –A Preliminary Report *

ROBERT E. MARKUSH

RACHEL V. FAVERO

INTRODUCTION

This chapter presents preliminary analyses of the relationship of life change unit scores to depressed mood and psychophysiological symptom scores. The data are from the Community Mental Health Assessment (CMHA) project, a series of studies initiated by the Center for Epidemiologic Studies in 1971 to develop epidemiologic techniques for continuous measurement of community mental health. The primary concern at the present stage of CMHA is to evaluate validity and develop methods for data reduction. The analyses that follow have particular relevance to the use of life change unit (LCU) scores to measure the stress of life events, and to the hypothesis proposed by Dohrenwend and Dohrenwend (1969) that stressful life events account for the excess of psychological symptoms in low social strata.

METHOD

The Community Mental Health Assessment project is a collaboration between two contract-supported field stations, one in Kansas City, Missouri, and the

* From the Community Mental Health Epidemiology Program, Center for Epidemiologic Studies, Division of Extramural Research Programs, National Institute of Mental Health. The authors gratefully acknowledge the assistance of the following staff of the Center for Epidemiologic Studies: Helen Barbano, M.S.P.H.; Bertram Brenner, Ph.D.; Lenore Radloff and Sarah Turner, M.P.H.

other in Washington County, Maryland. The project's main emphasis is development of procedures for production of descriptive epidemiologic data, but the analysis of its data is a critical part of the evaluation of the project's progress. For dependent variables, the focus of the project during its first year has been on depressed mood, although other related variables have also been measured. Questions on stressful life events in the previous year were included in the study because of their hypothesized influence on mood and psychological symptoms.

A sample of randomly selected adults 18 years old and over was selected from probability samples of households in each community (see Appendix). Data were collected in both communities from continuous weekly samples throughout 1972. Response rates for the year were 74.8% in Kansas City and 80.5% in Washington County.

The interview consisted primarily of structured questions on demographic, psychological, and health variables. The three sets of scales analyzed in this report are a mood scale developed by the Center for Epidemiologic Studies (CES), designated the CES depression (CES-D) scale, a version of the 22-item symptom scale (Langner, 1962), and a list of life changes developed by Dohrenwend (1971). The CES-D scale came early in the interview, followed soon after by the 22-item scale. The list of life events came near the end of the interview.

The CES-D scale presented in Table 1 consists of 20 items taken from five previously developed scales: the depression scale developed by Zung (1965a, 1965b, 1967); a depression inventory developed by Beck (1961, 1967); a self-report rating of depression developed by Raskin (1969); the depression scale of the MMPI (Minnesota Multiphasic Inventory) (Dahlstrom & Welsh, 1960); and a scale developed by Gardner (1968) and pretested on clinical populations in Philadelphia. Of these, so far as we know, only the MMPI-D scale has been used in general populations. The scales by Zung and Beck have been validated in clinical populations. Because CMHA is concerned with assessment of change across time, the CES-D scale asked for feelings during the week preceding the interview.

The 22-item screening score was included in CMHA to help judge whether psychological patterns in the two populations under study conformed to those reported in other studies; to help interpret findings on new scales included in the interview; and, since probes were included which asked additional information on each item, to help interpret the findings of other studies. The original item on troubled sleep was split into two items, and several other items underwent minor changes in wording and response set. In both communities the interview asked only for 22-item symptoms experienced during the past year; this time limitation was repeated with each question only in Kansas City. When a respondent gave a positive answer to any item, the interviewer asked at least

Table 1. Center for Epidemiologic Studies Depression (CES-D) Scale (CMHA, 1972)

INSTRUCTIONS FOR QUESTIONS: Below is a list of the way you might have felt or behaved. Please indicate how often you have felt this way during the last week. Interviewer used the following response set card for each question:

Rarely or None of the Time (less than 1 day)	Some or a Little of the Time (1–2 days)	Occasionally or a Moderate Amount of Time (3–4 days)	Most or All of the Time (5–7 days)

During the last week

1. I was bothered by things that usually don't bother me.
2. I did not feel like eating; my appetite was poor.
3. I felt that I could not shake off the blues even with help from my family or friends.
4. I felt that I was just as good as other people.
5. I had trouble keeping my mind on what I was doing.
6. I felt depressed.
7. I felt that everything I did was an effort.
8. I felt hopeful about the future.
9. I thought my life had been a failure.
10. I felt fearful.
11. My sleep was restless.
12. I was happy.
13. It seemed that I talked less than usual.
    I talked less than usual.
14. I felt lonely.
15. People were unfriendly.
16. I enjoyed life.
17. I had crying spells.
18. I felt sad.
19. I felt that people disliked me.
20. I could not get "going."

two probes to determine the seriousness of the symptom and its cause.

The list of 40 life events used in the CMHA surveys was similar to that used by Dohrenwend in the Washington Heights study (in press). It included 20 items which Dohrenwend judged equivalent to items for which Holmes and Rahe (1967) obtained readjustment ratings. The weights used were the geometric means of those ratings (Masuda & Holmes, 1967). These 20 items were used to calculate life change unit (LCU) scores in this report. The respondents were asked first whether each event had occurred during the previous year. If they gave a positive response, the month of occurrence was also recorded. If the event occurred more than once during the year, the months of occurrence were recorded. An open-ended question for other major events, plus the identical list for events occurring to any other person "important" to the respondent, were also asked but are not used in this report.

Table 2. Life-Event Scale

Event	Life-Change Score
1. Married	500
2. Widowed	771
3. Divorced	593
4. Separated	516
5. Pregnancy	284
6. Birth of first child	337
7. Birth of child other than first	337
8. Illness or injury	416
9. Death of a loved one or other important person	469
10. Started school or training, etc.	191
11. Graduated from school or training, etc.	191
12. Job or own business improved in responsibility, type, location, or other ways	243
13. Job or own business downgraded in responsibility, type, location, or other work	308
14. Retired from work	361
15. Laid off, fired from job, or own business failed	378
16. Changed residence for better	140
17. Changed residence for worse	140
18. Started new hobby or recreational activity	127
19. Dropped hobby or recreational activity	127
20. Took a vacation	74

Events derived from Bruce and Barbara Dohrenwend (mimeographed, 1971); life-change scores derived from Masuda and Holmes (1967).

Table 3. Proportions of Kansas City and Washington County Samples in LCU, CES-D, and 22-Item Midtown Categories

		1972 CMHA Sample (%)	
Category	Score	Kansas City	Washington County
LCU			
Low	335 or less	46.1	52.8
Middle	336–642	28.8	26.0
High	643 and over	25.1	21.2
CES-D			
Low	0–5	41.0	41.3
Middle	6–15	37.4	40.2
High	16–60	21.2	18.5
22-Item			
Low	0	49.3	54.7
Middle	1–3	38.3	34.1
High	4–6	7.7	7.7
	7–22	4.7	3.4

In this report we used the same cutoff scores for categories of life-change units (LCU) as those used by Dohrenwend (in press). These categories, based on the weights in Table 2, and the proportion of the total CMHA 1972 sample in each of them are shown in Table 3.

CES-D scores were also put into three categories, defining the highest to include about 20% of the sample, and dividing the remainder roughly into two equal groups. Each response was weighted 0 to 3, so that the possible range for the 20-item scale was 0 to 60. The categories of scores and the proportion of the total CMHA 1972 population in each are shown in Table 3.

The 22-item scores were based on a simple count of positive responses which were divided into the four categories in Table 3 for analyses in this report. For presentation of data in all but Table 4 we have combined the two higher categories. The range of the possible values is 0 to 22.

RESULTS

All Demographic Groups Combined: Association of LCU with Symptom Scales

Table 4 combines data from both communities and presents the overall relationship of LCU (life-change units) to the two scales under consideration. For each scale there is a clear relationship between LCU and symptoms: the higher

Table 4. Association of Depressed Mood (CES-D) and Psychophysiological (22-Item Midtown) Scales with Life Change Units (CMHA, 1972)

Scale	Life Change Units							
	Low		Mid.		High		Total	
Score	*N*	%	*N*	%	*N*	%	*N*	%
A. Depressed Mood (CES-D) [1]								
Low	512	47.3	226	38.4	154	31.1	892	41.2
Mid	411	38.0	235	39.9	200	40.4	846	39.0
High	160	14.8	128	21.7	141	28.5	429	19.8
Total	1083	100.0	589	100.0	495	100.0	2167	100.0
B. Psychophysiological Symptoms (22-Item Midtown)								
0	635	58.6	290	49.2	213	43.0	1138	52.5
1–3	361	33.3	216	36.7	201	40.6	778	35.9
4–6	60	5.5	55	9.3	52	10.5	167	7.7
7 and over	28	2.6	28	4.8	29	5.9	85	3.9
Total	1084	100.0	589	100.0	495	100.0	2168	100.0

Note: For Part A, Gamma = .22, $p < .001$; for Part B, Gamma = .21, $p < .001$.

[1] One subject who did not complete CES-D scale omitted.

the LCU score, the higher the depressed mood score and the higher the psychophysiological symptom score. There is a fairly consistent increase in depressed mood symptoms as LCU scores progress into the middle and high categories. For psychophysiological symptoms, however, there is more of an increase in moving from low to middle levels of LCU scores than in moving from middle to high levels.

Table 5. Number of Subjects, Distribution of Subjects by Age, Sex, Color, Education, and Community (CMHA, 1972)

	Washington County			Kansas City					
	White Only			White			Black		
Age (years)	Men	Women	Total	Men	Women	Total	Men	Women	Total
Less than High School Education									
Under 35	30	70	100	9	22	31	11	19	30
35–54	80	123	203	29	37	66	21	22	43
55 and over	105 [1]	159	264 [1]	34	62	96	23	28	51
Total	215 [1]	352	567 [1]	72	123	195	55	69	124
High School Education									
Under 35	85	99	184	36	60	96	14	24	38
35–54	70	88	158	22	59	81	11	10	21
55 and over	25	33	58	14	36	50	2	5	7
Total	180	220	400	72	156	228	27	39	66
More than High School Education									
Under 35	47	52	99	47	69	116	6	11	17
35–54	45	49	94	36	26	62	6	4	10
55 and over	25	52	77	23	40	63	0	2	2
Total	117	153	270	106	136	242	12	17	29
Total Education									
Under 35	162	221	383	92	151	243	31	54	85
35–54	195	260	455	87	122	209	38	36	74
55 and over	156 [1]	246	402 [1]	71	142	213	25	35	60
Total	513 [1]	727	1240 [1]	250	420	670	94	125	219

Note: Small inconsistencies in subtotals result from subjects with partially missing demographic data.

[1] One of these subjects did not complete CES-D scale.

Numbers of Subjects

Table 5 presents the demographic distribution of the study populations, indicating the denominators for the proportions in subsequent tables. There was a greater number of interviews completed in Washington County than Kansas City, a greater number of interviews of women than men, of white than black, and of less educated than well educated. Although age group categories were defined in this analysis to split the frequencies into roughly equal groups, the interviews in Kansas City included greater proportions of younger adults than in Washington County. The blacks in Washington County are a small, heterogeneous group and are therefore not included in this report. Educational levels in Kansas City were higher than in Washington County.

There are several demographic subgroups from Kansas City for which the number of subjects interviewed is so small that estimates based on them in subsequent tables are subject to large sampling errors. This is particularly true for the higher educational categories of older blacks.

Distributions of Variables among Demographic Groups

Table 6 indicates the demographic distribution of high LCU scores in the two CMHA communities. The only fairly consistent pattern is the higher scores among the under-35-year age groups. There was no major difference between the whites in the two communities, nor between the blacks and the whites within Kansas City. The proportions with high scores tend to be lower in the low-education groups, but there are several inconsistencies in this pattern among the different age, sex, and community categories.

The pattern of high depressed mood scores (Table 7) is somewhat less complex. Scores tend to be about the same among the whites in Kansas City and in Washington County. Wherever demographic categories were large enough for comparisons, blacks in Kansas City have scores that are similar to the Kansas City whites' scores. Proportions with high scores generally decreased with increasing education, decreased with increasing age, and were higher in women than men. Of those demographic subgroups consisting of at least 20 subjects, the highest proportion with high scores was in blacks under age 35. The lowest proportion was for white, high-education men, age 55 or over in Washington County and white, high-education men, age 35–54 in Kansas City, where none of the subjects had a high score.

There were no appreciable differences in proportions with high scores on the 22-Item scale between the two communities. Where numbers permit comparisons, the Kansas City blacks tended to have lower proportions than the Kansas City whites. Except for Kansas City blacks, the proportion tended to decrease with increasing education. The pattern with age was mixed, with no consistent

Table 6. Proportion with High Life Change Unit Scores by Age, Sex, Color, Education, and Community (CMHA, 1972)

	Washington County			Kansas City					
	White Only			White			Black		
Age (years)	Men	Women	Total	Men	Women	Total	Men	Women	Total
Less than High School Education									
Under 35	.30	.29	.29	(.56)	.18	.29	(.64)	(.37)	.47
35–54	.15	.14	.14	.24	.14	.18	.19	.23	.21
55 and over	.16	.17	.17	.03	.23	.16	.09	.11	.10
Total	.18	.18	.18	.18	.19	.18	.24	.22	.23
High School Education									
Under 35	.29	.30	.30	.39	.48	.45	(.29)	.13	.18
35–54	.19	.19	.19	.14	.17	.16	(.09)	(.00)	.05
55 and over	.24	.12	.17	(.07)	.19	.16	(.00)	(.00)	(.00)
Total	.24	.23	.24	.25	.29	.28	.19	.08	.12
More than High School Education									
Under 35	.30	.40	.35	.55	.38	.45	(.33)	(.45)	(.41)
35–54	.22	.16	.19	.19	.27	.23	(.50)	(.00)	(.30)
55 and over	.08	.21	.17	.09	.13	.11	N.S.	(.50)	(.50)
Total	.22	.26	.24	.33	.28	.30	(.42)	(.35)	.38
Total Education									
Under 35	.30	.32	.31	.49	.39	.43	.42	.28	.33
35–54	.18	.16	.17	.20	.18	.19	.21	.14	.18
55 and over	.16	.17	.17	.06	.18	.14	.08	.11	.10
Total	.21	.21	.21	.26	.25	.26	.24	.19	.21

Note: Parentheses indicate less than 20 subjects in denominator.

differences. Women generally had higher proportions than men, but this was not true for the Kansas City blacks. The demographic subgroup with the highest proportion was the Kansas City white, low-education women, age 55 and over, with 29% having high scores. The lowest proportion was again present in Washington County white, high-education men, age 55 and over, where none out of 25 subjects reported a high score.

Table 7. Proportions with High Scores on Depressed Mood (CES-D) Scale (CMHA, 1972)

	Washington County			Kansas City					
	White Only			White			Black		
Age (years)	Men	Women	Total	Men	Women	Total	Men	Women	Total
				Less than High School Education					
Under 35	.17	.39	.32	(.22)	.23	.23	(.36)	(.37)	.37
35–54	.11	.31	.23	.17	.43	.32	.19	.45	.33
55 and over	.14	.18	.16	.21	.29	.26	.17	.25	.22
Total	.14	.26	.22	.19	.33	.28	.22	.35	.29
				High School Education					
Under 35	.15	.28	.22	.22	.30	.27	(.43)	.29	.34
35–54	.11	.17	.15	.14	.15	.15	(.09)	(.20)	.14
55 and over	.12	.12	.12	(.07)	.17	.14	(.00)	(.00)	(.00)
Total	.13	.21	.18	.17	.21	.20	.26	.23	.24
				More than High School Education					
Under 35	.11	.19	.15	.15	.17	.16	(.00)	(.18)	(.12)
35–54	.18	.14	.16	.00	.19	.08	(.17)	(.25)	(.20)
55 and over	.00	.15	.10	.17	.15	.16	N.S.	(.50)	(.50)
Total	.11	.16	.14	.10	.17	.14	(.08)	(.24)	.17
				Total Education					
Under 35	.14	.29	.23	.18	.23	.21	.32	.30	.31
35–54	.13	.23	.19	.09	.25	.18	.16	.36	.26
55 and over	.12	.17	.15	.17	.21	.20	.16	.23	.20
Total	.13	.23	.19	.15	.23	.20	.21	.30	.26

Note: Parentheses indicate less than 20 subjects in denominator.

Associations of LCU with Symptoms

We used Goodman and Kruskal's (1954) gamma to measure the degree of association between each scale and LCU scores. Those for the relationship between LCU and CES-D are presented in Table 9. Significant gammas are scattered among the different demographic subgroups in no clear pattern. Significant gammas occur in both communities, in both color groups, in each education

Table 8. Proportions with High Scores On Psychophysiological (22-Item Midtown) Scale (CMHA, 1972)

	Washington County			Kansas City					
	White Only			White			Black		
Age (years)	Men	Women	Total	Men	Women	Total	Men	Women	Total
Less than High School Education									
Under 35	.03	.24	.18	(.11)	.27	.23	(.18)	(.11)	.13
35–54	.05	.24	.16	.14	.19	.17	.10	.09	.09
55 and over	.15	.14	.15	.09	.29	.22	.13	.11	.12
Total	.10	.20	.16	.11	.26	.21	.13	.10	.11
High School Education									
Under 35	.05	.09	.07	.08	.15	.12	(.14)	.13	.13
35–54	.07	.11	.09	.09	.14	.12	(.00)	(.10)	.05
55 and over	.04	.12	.09	.07	.11	.10	(.00)	(.00)	(.00)
Total	.06	.10	.08	.08	.13	.12	.07	.10	.09
More than High School Education									
Under 35	.02	.06	.04	.06	.07	.07	(.00)	(.18)	(.12)
35–54	.02	.10	.06	.03	.15	.08	(.17)	(.00)	(.10)
55 and over	.00	.08	.05	.13	.10	.11	N.S.	(.00)	(.00)
Total	.02	.08	.05	.07	.10	.08	(.08)	(.12)	.10
Total Education									
Under 35	.04	.13	.09	.08	.13	.11	.13	.13	.13
35–54	.05	.17	.12	.08	.16	.12	.08	.08	.08
55 and over	.11	.13	.12	.10	.18	.15	.12	.09	.10
Total	.06	.14	.11	.08	.16	.13	.11	.10	.11

Note: Parentheses indicate less than 20 subjects in denominator.

group, and in each age group and in both sex groups. The strongest association occurred in the Kansas City black, low-education, 35–54-year-old men, where the gamma was .92 and was significant at the .05 level. A few associations were negative, but for none of these was gamma significant.

Gammas for the association between LCU and 22-Item Midtown scales are presented in Table 10. As in Table 9, the pattern of high and low gammas and their degrees of significance is complex. Gammas range from .87 to −.33, but none of the negative ones is significant.

For neither depressed mood nor psychophysiological symptoms is there any

Table 9. Gamma for Association Between Life-Change Units (LCU) and Depressed Mood (CES-D) Scales, by Age, Sex, Color, Education, and Community (CMHA, 1972)

	Washington County			Kansas City					
	White Only			White			Black		
Age (years)	Men	Women	Total	Men	Women	Total	Men	Women	Total
				Less than High School Education					
Under 35	.22	.43 [1]	.34	(.88)	−.40	−.07	(.50)	(.19)	.29
35–54	.03	.21	.13	.12	.45	.21	.92 [1]	−.08	.43
55 and over	.23	.09	.14	−.28	.44 [1]	.26 [1]	.11	−.01	.00
Total	.19	.20	.19 [1]	.09	.29 [1]	.20	.54 [2]	.06	.26
				High School Education					
Under 35	.34	.21	.25	.28	.34	.33	(.26)	(.40)	.35
35–54	.26	.29	.28	−.52	.14	−.03	(.56)	(−.60)	.13
55 and over	.53	.28	.36	.41	.41	.43 [1]	(−.01)	(.01)	(.33)
Total	.34	.28 [1]	.30 [3]	.17	.35 [1]	.30 [2]	.33	.30	.31
				More than High School Education					
Under 35	−.06	.00	−.02	−.05	.28	.14	(.67)	(.11)	(.29)
35–54	.01	.43	.21	.42	.48	.44 [1]	(.33)	(.00)	(.18)
55 and over	.59	−.09	.12 [1]	.39	.54	.49	N.S.	(.01)	(.01)
Total	.14	.10	.12	.34 [1]	.43 [2]	.38 [3]	(.38)	(.18)	.25
				Total Education					
Under 35	.21	.19	.19	.17	.24	.20	.29	.20	.23
35–54	.10	.27	.20	.09	.28	.19	.75 [2]	−.06	.38
55 and over	.33 [1]	.06	.17	.08	.46 [3]	.37 [3]	.01	.23	.11
Total	.23 [2]	.19 [2]	.20 [3]	.21	.34 [3]	.28 [3]	.42 [2]	.13	.25 [2]

[1] $p < .05$.
[2] $p < .01$.
[3] $p < .001$.

suggestion that the association with LCU is stronger in those with low education than in the other educational groups.

Life-Change Units and Number of Reported Events

To learn more about LCU scores in the different education groups we have analyzed our data specifically for the number of events reported. This analysis

Table 10. Gamma for Association Between Life-Change Units and Psychopathological (22-Item Midtown) Scales, by Age, Sex, Color, Education, and Community (CMHA, 1972)

	Washington County			Kansas City					
	White Only			White			Black		
Age (years)	Men	Women	Total	Men	Women	Total	Men	Women	Total
				Less than High School Education					
Under 35	.51 [1]	.16	.23 [1]	(.69)	.18	.12	(.38)	(.55)	.40
35–54	.36	.08	.15	−.24	.87 [2]	.38	.63	.13	.37
55 and over	.30	.14	.20	.31 [1]	.34 [1]	.39	−.29	−.19	−.25
Total	.36 [2]	.11	.19	.11	.47 [1]	.33	.30	.18	.20
				High School Education					
Under 35	.06	.13	.10	.29	.50	.42	(.55)	(−.13)	.10
35–54	.10	.37 [1]	.27 [1]	.37	−.09	.04	(.64)	(−.01)	−.03
55 and over	.66	.04	.27	(.41)	.53 [2]	.51 [2]	(—) [4]	(−.33)	(−.33)
Total	.15	.21	.18	.40	.33 [2]	.35 [2]	.61	−.20	.09 [1]
				More than High School Education					
Under 35	.50	.39	.43	.13	.34	.24	(—) [4]	(.42)	(.41)
35–54	−.17	.39	.11	.58	.46	.53	(−.14)	(−.01)	(−.26)
55 and over	−.06	−.27	−.07	.65	.13	.34	N.S.	(−.01)	(−.01)
Total	.21	.14	.16	.30	.27	.28	(−.26)	(−.01)	−.10
				Total Education					
Under 35	.27	.17	.20 [1]	.21	.32	.26	.45	.25	.26
35–54	.14	.21	.18	.28 [1]	.32	.29	.53	.01	.27
55 and over	.36	.03	.16	.44 [3]	.39 [1]	.41 [3]	−.26	−.30	−.30
Total	.25 [1]	.13	.17 [2]	.27	.33 [3]	.30 [3]	.33 [1]	.07	.14 [1]

[1] $p < .05$.
[2] $p < .01$.
[3] $p < .001$.
[4] (—) = degenerate table.

Table 11. Life Change Units (LCU) Related to Number of Events Reported by Education, Kansas City and Washington County (CMHA, 1972)

	Distribution of Subjects				Percentage with High LCU Scores	
	Kansas City		Washington County			
Number of Events Reported	*N*	%	*N*	%	Kansas City	Washington County
Less than High School						
None	91	28.1	190	32.8	—	—
1–2	184	56.8	320	55.2	10.9	14.1
3 or more	49	15.1	70	12.1	85.7	81.4
Total	324	100.0	580	100.0	20.1	18.1
High School						
None	74	25.0	72	17.7	—	—
1–2	147	49.7	244	60.1	6.8	8.6
3 or more	75	25.3	90	22.2	82.7	81.1
Total	296	100.0	406	100.0	25.0	23.6
More than High School						
None	36	13.1	43	15.5	—	—
1–2	133	48.4	157	56.7	5.3	3.2
3 or more	106	38.5	77	27.8	74.5	79.2
Total	275	100.0	277	100.0	31.6	24.2

indicates that the increase in scores with education results from an increase in the number of events reported as level of education increases. Given the same number of events, however, the scores for the well educated are lower than those for the poorly educated. It appears that the well educated are reporting a greater number of events, but that these events tend to have lower LCU scores.

DISCUSSION

The findings of this preliminary analysis can be summarized as: (1) a significant overall association of LCU scores with both depressed mood and psychophysiological symptom scores; (2) no differences between the two communities, controlling for subgroups, on any of the scales or associations examined; (3) no major differences between demographically comparable blacks and whites, with the exception of lower proportions of blacks having high 22-item symptom scores; (4) an association of low education with lower LCU scores, with higher depressed mood scores, and with higher 22-item symptom scores;

the high LCU scores in the low-education group, however, are derived from a smaller number of events than in the higher education groups; (5) higher LCU scores and higher depressed mood scores in the younger age group; (6) higher depressed mood scores and higher psychophysiological symptom scores in women than men; and (7) considerable variability in the strength of the association of LCU and symptom scores across demographic subgroups, so that no demographic variable had a consistent effect across the remaining demographic variables.

These findings agree only partially with those found by Dohrenwend in a sample of Washington Heights, New York, household heads (Dohrenwend, 1973). This study, which used a slightly shorter list of life events but the same scores for each event as used in this chapter, also found a positive association between LCU scores and psychophysiological symptoms measured with the 22-item scale. The studies also agree in finding an inverse relationship between social class, as measured by education, and psychophysiological symptoms. Dohrenwend, however, found social class, measured by education, to be inversely related to LCU score, whereas we have found the relationship to be a direct one. She found, furthermore, that the association between symptom scores and LCU scores was strong only in the lower class, whereas there is no indication in the data from either of our communities that the classes (i.e., educational groups) differed appreciably in the strength of the event-symptom relationship.

Dohrenwend also examined the relationship of sex to life change and symptom scores. In agreement with several other reports (Gove & Tudor, 1973), and with our results, she found higher symptom scores among women than among men. Her findings, however, differed from ours in that she found that women tended to have higher LCU scores than men; in the CMHA communities, women's LCU scores were similar to men's (despite the fact that only women could answer the pregnancy item on the events list).

A third demographic factor investigated by Dohrenwend was ethnicity. Her findings again only partially agree with ours. Both the Washington Heights and the CMHA communities provide no evidence of higher symptom levels among blacks than among whites. In fact, for the 22-item scale, the CMHA data suggest that blacks may have lower scores; the data from Washington Heights also go in this direction. The two studies differ, however, in their findings regarding LCU scores since Dohrenwend found significantly higher scores for the black, whereas CMHA shows no difference.

Dohrenwend applies her results to test the hypothesis that persons in low social status are disproportionately exposed to stressful life events, and that this exposure can explain the higher symptom levels in those with low social status. From her data she found support for her hypothesis with regard to social class (i.e., education) and low status defined by sex, but not for low status defined ethnically. From our data, however, the hypothesis obtains no support at all.

Analytic techniques differed, although this seems unlikely to explain the differences. Dohrenwend used product-moment correlation and partial correlation coefficients. We have used the Goodman-Kruskal gamma, and instead of partial correlations we have in this chapter relied on direct comparisons of subgroups specific for whatever demographic factors were being controlled. Dohrenwend excluded from her analysis subjects who reported no events, which we have not done. In Washington Heights a large proportion (49%) of blacks reported no events, whereas no events was reported by 28% of white respondents. In the CMHA samples the proportions reporting no events were smaller: for the white, they were 13% in Kansas City and 24% in Washington County, whereas for nonwhites (mostly blacks) they were 35 and 21%, respectively. Reporting no events may be a sign of underreporting, yet underreporting may also exist even when one or more events are reported. In Table 11, even when those reporting no events are excluded, the proportion reporting 3 or more events increases with education (e.g., from 49/233 = 21% to 106/239 = 44% in Kansas City). But the nonreporting problem goes beyond that of reporting the true number of events. Clinical studies demonstrating differential reporting of stressful events suggest that less educated groups may have a greater tendency to underreport less heavily weighted events, so that biases may exist both in numbers and in characteristics of events reported (Lipman, Hammer, Bernades, Park, & Cole, 1965; Alarcon & Covi, 1972).

Although we hope eventually to validate life-event reporting at least for some selected events, such as those reported in routine vital statistics, we have had to assume in this report that life-event differentials are not due to selective underreporting. It is possible that our different treatment of reporters of no events may explain some of the difference between the CMHA and Washington Heights results.

A review of the differences between results from the two studies indicates that they are exclusively in relationships involving the LCU measure; the differences we have noted involve the relation of social class (education) to LCU, the relation of symptoms to LCU across social class, the relation of sex to LCU, and the relation of ethnicity to LCU. We are therefore suspicious that something about the LCU measure may be amiss.

There were differences between the two studies in how both the 22-item and the LCU scales were administered. The 22-item scale in CMHA, for example, included probes after each item, which lengthened considerably the time taken to complete the scale whenever there were positive responses. The CMHA life-events list was somewhat longer than that in Washington Heights. But it also seems likely that the list of events that is psychologically significant for one geographic area or demographic subgroup is different from that appropriate for another. The trauma of job change, for example, may be different in Washington Heights from that in the CMHA communities.

The complex demographic pattern of associations between symptoms and LCU seen in Tables 9 and 10 may in a similar manner result from differential impacts of the same life events in different demographic subgroups. The impact of having a child, for example, may be different for a 25-year-old than for a 45-year-old. The complexity of the patterns, in fact, suggests that the LCU score we used may not be appropriate for epidemiologic studies of general populations.

Whereas the lack of reports on the use of a comparable LCU score in general population studies does not permit further comparison of the CMHA results for the score as we have calculated it, for the symptom scales some comparable data do exist.

Depressed Mood

Data from the two CMHA communities, for example, suggest that the proportion with high depressed mood scores is larger in the younger than in the older groups. In a 1957 national sample, the proportion ''happy'' decreased with age, and the proportion ''not too happy'' increased with age (Gurin, Veroff, & Feld, 1960). Although this is not necessarily inversely equivalent to our depression scores, it suggests an opposite age relationship for depressed mood to that which we have found in our two communities. Leighton et al. found in 1952 in Nova Scotia that psychoneurotic depression increased with age until peaks at ages 50–59 and 70 and over, with little change with age in women. (Leighton, Harding, Macklin, Macmillan, & Leighton, 1963). Patients with clinically diagnosed depression appear to have their greatest frequency in the middle years (Silverman, 1968). A population survey in 1970 of Alachua County, Florida, found depression scores determined by an 18-item scale generally increased with age except for higher rates under 20 years of age (Warheit, Holzer, & Schwab, 1972). The finding in the CMHA communities that CES-D scores decrease with age suggests that there has been a recent change, that our two communities are unusual, or that depressed mood measured by the CES-D scale is different from the other measures of affect to which we have referred.

Women had consistently larger proportions with high depressed mood scores than men in the two sites. This conforms with many observations reported in the literature. Silverman, for example, states that ''There appear to be no exceptions to the generalization that depression is more common in women than in men, whether it is the feeling of depression, neurotic depression, or depressive psychosis'' (Silverman, 1968, p. 73).

Our finding that the proportion with high scores for depressed mood decreases with education conforms with data from Gurin, Veroff, and Feld's 1957 national sample, in which the proportion ''very happy'' went from 43%

in their college group to 23% in the grade school group, and the proportions "not too happy" in the same two groups went from 5 to 20% (Gurin et al., 1960). It also agrees with 1970 data reported for Alachua County (Warheit et al., 1972).

Psychophysiologic Symptoms

The increase with age in 22-item scale scores conforms with results from the original Midtown study (Srole, Langner, Michael, Opler, & Rennie, 1962), and our finding that women had more symptoms than men agrees with data in the literature on mental illness in general (Gove & Tudor, 1973). The decrease in symptoms with education conforms to data from the Midtown study (Srole et al., 1962) and from the Washington Heights study (Dohrenwend & Dohrenwend, 1969).

Depressed Mood and Psychophysiological Scales Compared

The CES-D and 22-item scales agreed in their distributions across sex and education but had opposite relationships to age and color. On the basis of data collected during the first six months of the study we found the product-moment correlation coefficient between the two scales was .54 in Kansas City and .58 in Washington County. The emphasis in the 22-item scale is on psychophysiologic symptoms and in the CES-D is on depressed affect, which could account for their differences by age and color. Presumably the correlation between the two scales would be higher if we held age and color constant, but we have not yet examined this.

Although we feel that the LCU score may be inappropriate for use in epidemiologic community studies, we have found it to be significantly associated with both symptom scales in both communities. Although the LCU scale may not be adequate to compare the strength of associations across demographic subgroups, we nevertheless feel that there is some real underlying relationship. The relationship has also been found for the 22-item scale in the Washington Heights study and for total life-event counts and the Gurin scale of psychophysiological symptoms in New Haven, Connecticut (Myers, Lindenthal, & Pepper, 1971; Meyers, Lindenthal, Pepper & Ostrander, 1972). We therefore conclude that there is a relationship between life events and psychological symptoms and that this relationship should be pursued with a more refined measure of the stress of life events than the LCU score.

Finally, the CMHA study may already be demonstrating its intended value in furthering the epidemiologic measurement of mental health variables. Simultaneous replication of studies in multiple sites can provide unique clues to the meaning of mental health measures. It may also act as a rapid and powerful test of hypotheses suggested by other research.

SUMMARY

Survey data collected continuously during 1972 in Kansas City, Missouri, and Washington County, Maryland, suggest a significant association between proportions with high LCU scores and proportions with high depressed mood and psychophysiological symptom scores.

Since we found smaller proportions with high LCU in the low-education group, no difference in proportions with high LCU scores between men and women, no difference between white and black, and no indication that education groups differed in the strength of the association between LCU scores and symptoms, the data do not support the hypothesis that stressful life events may account for the excess of psychological symptoms in the lower social strata.

These preliminary analyses verify the findings in other studies of higher rates of depression and psychophysiological symptoms in women and in the less educated. They suggest, however, that depressed mood may be more common under age 35 than at older ages, which does not conform with previous research. The proportions with high symptom and LCU scores, and their relationships, found in Kansas City are similar to those in Washington County if one controls for differences in the demographic composition of the two communities.

The data suggest that the LCU scores as used in these analyses may be inappropriate measures of the stress of life events for use in epidemiologic studies.

APPENDIX

To select households in Kansas City, the Sampling Section of the Survey Research Center, Ann Arbor, Michigan, provided an area sampling design. By using data published by the U.S. Census Bureau for 1960 and 1970, each block in Kansas City was put into one of 56 strata defined by racial composition, whether or not a model neighborhood, economic level, and geography.

The intent of the sampling was to select an independent random sample of 28 households for each week of the year. The 56 strata were therefore grouped into 14 subgroups of 4, with each set of 4 as homogeneous as possible within and as different as possible from each other. Each of the homogeneous strata was assigned, in order, to every first, second, third, and fourth week of the year.

From each of the 56 strata, two blocks were selected with probability proportionate to size, yielding 112 sample blocks. One-fourth of these, or 28, would be assigned to any given week of the year with the same 28 recurring every four weeks. One household was selected at random each week from each of these 28 blocks.

The result was a clustered sample of households, 13 or 14 in each cluster, representing all Kansas City households, evenly distributed across each week of the year.

In Washington County a representative sample of households was simpler to obtain because of the availability of a complete household roster, derived from a private census conducted in the community in 1963 and updated. From this roster, 33 households were randomly selected, without replacement, for each week of the year.

A random adult 18 years or older was then selected from each household in each community. Since households vary in size, each individual should receive a sampling weight according to the size of the household, with those from larger households receiving larger weights, since they represent more people. Although these weights must be applied to household data before the sample can be said to represent the community, they have not been applied to the data in this report.

Lay interviewers tried to complete assigned interviews on the week of assignment, since one of the goals of the sampling design was to represent a given week in order to examine changes in the community across time. If interviews were not completed on the week assigned, however, three further weeks were permitted for completion.

The Kansas City survey began in October, and the Washington County survey in December 1971.

REFERENCES

Alarcon, R. D., & Covi, L. The precipitating event in depression. *The Journal of Nervous and Mental Disease*. 1972, **155,** 379–391.

Beck, A. T. *Depression: Clinical, Experimental and Theoretical Aspects*. New York: Harper and Row, 1967.

Beck, A. T., Ward, C. H., Mendelson, M., Mock, J., & Erbaugh, J. An inventory for measuring depression. *Archives of General Psychiatry,* 1961, **4,** 561–571.

Dahlstrom, W. G., & Welsh, G. S. *An MMPI Handbook*. Minneapolis: University of Minnesota Press, 1960.

Dohrenwend, B. P., & Dohrenwend, B. S. *Social Status and Psychological Disorder: A Causal Inquiry*. New York: John Wiley & Sons, 1969.

Dohrenwend, B. S. Social status and stressful life events. *Journal of Personality and Social Psychology,* 1973, **28,** 225–235.

Dohrenwend, B. S. Stressful events and psychological symptoms. In R. Prince & H. B. M. Murphy (Eds.), *Psychosocial Stress Measures*. Baltimore, Md: National Educational Consultants, in press.

Gardner, E. A. Development of a symptom check list for the measurement of depression in a population. Unpublished data. November 1, 1968.

Goodman, L. A., & Kruskal, W. H. Measures of association for cross classifications. *Journal of the American Statistical Association,* 1954, **48,** 732–764.

Gove, W. R., & Tudor, G. F. Adult sex roles and mental illness. *American Journal of Sociology.* 1973, **78,** 812–835.

Gurin, G., Veroff, I., & Feld, S. *Americans View Their Mental Health.* New York: Basic Books, 1960.

Holmes, T. H., & Rahe, R. H. The social readjustment rating scale. *Journal of Psychosomatic Research,* 1967, **11,** 213–218.

Langner, T. S. A twenty-two item screening score of psychiatric symptoms indicating impairment. *Journal of Health and Human Behaviour,* 1962, **3,** 269–276.

Leighton, D. C., Harding, J. S., Macklin, D. B., Macmillan, A. M. & Leighton, A. H. *The Character of Danger.* New York: Basic Books, 1963.

Lipman, R. S., Hammer, H. M., Bernades, J. F., Park, L. E., & Cole, J. O. Patient report of significant life situation events. *Diseases of the Nervous System,* 1965, **26,** 586–590.

Masuda, M., & Holmes, T. H. Magnitude estimations of social readjustments. *Journal of Psychosomatic Research,* 1967, **11,** 219–225.

Myers, J. K., Lindenthal, J. J., & Pepper, M. P. Life events and psychiatric impairment. *The Journal of Nervous and Mental Diseases.* 1971, **152,** 149–157.

Myers, J. K., Lindenthal, J. J., Pepper, M. P., & Ostrander, D. R. Life events and mental status: A longitudinal study. *Journal of Health and Social Behavior,* 1972, **13,** 398–406.

Raskin, A., Schulterbrandt, J., Reating, N., & McKeon, J. Replication of factors of psychopathology in interview, ward behavior and self-report ratings of hospitalized depressives. *Journal of Nervous and Mental Disease,* 1969, **198,** 87–96.

Silverman, C. *The Epidemiology of Depression.* Baltimore, Md.: The Johns Hopkins Press, 1968.

Srole, L., Langner, T. S., Michael, S. T., Opler, M. K., & Rennie, T. A. C. *Mental Health in the Metropolis: The Midtown Study,* Volume 1. New York: McGraw-Hill Book Company, 1962.

Warheit, G. J., Holzer, C. E., & Schwab, J. J. An analysis of social class and racial differences in depressive symptomatology: A community study. Presented at the annual meeting of the American Sociological Association, August 28–31, 1972, New Orleans, La.

CHAPTER 12

Social Class, Life Events, and Psychiatric Symptoms:

*A Longitudinal Study **

JEROME K. MYERS

JACOB J. LINDENTHAL

MAX P. PEPPER

This is a report on relationships between social class, life events, and psychiatric symptomatology in a community sample of 720 adults in New Haven, Connecticut. It is part of a longitudinal study of the population of a community mental health center catchment area (Lindenthal, Myers, Pepper, & Stern, 1970; Lindenthal, Thomas, & Myers, 1971; Myers, Lindenthal, & Pepper, 1971; Myers, Lindenthal, Pepper, & Ostrander, 1972; Paykel, Myers, Dienelt, Klerman, Lindenthal, & Pepper, 1969).

The study grew out of two bodies of sociomedical research: epidemiological field studies of mental illness and stress research. Epidemiological studies of the relationships between sociodemographic variables and judged psychopathology in the community generally have yielded inconsistent results with one exception: low socioeconomic status within a community is found consistently to be associated with high overall rates of judged disorder (Dohrenwend & Dohrenwend, 1969, pp. 9–31). For example, Srole et al. report nearly four times as much impairment in the lowest as the highest socioeconomic stratum in New York City: 47% contrasted to 13% (Srole, Langner, Michael, Opler, & Rennie, 1962, p. 230), and Phillips in his New England study found about

* The research upon which this paper is based was supported by Public Health Service Contract 43-67-743 and Research Grant MH 15522 from the National Institute of Mental Health, Department of Health, Education and Welfare. At the time of the research all of the authors were affiliated with Yale University.

twice as much in the lowest as highest class: 32% compared to 18% (Phillips, 1966).

In investigations of stress, many researchers have demonstrated a positive relationship between the occurrence of "stress," "life crises," or "life events" and the onset of physical illness and/or the presence of psychiatric symptomatology (Brown & Birley, 1968; Fischer, Dlin, & Winters, 1962; Graham & Stevenson, 1963; Greene, 1954; Greene, Young, & Swisher, 1956; Greene & Miller, 1958; Hawkins, Davies, & Holmes, 1957; Hinkle & Wolff, 1957; Kissen, 1958; Rahe & Holmes, 1965; Rahe, 1969; Rahe, Myer, Smith, Kjaer, & Holmes, 1964; Weiss, Dlin, & Rollin, 1957). In four recent studies, for example, significant relationships were found between life events and illness in such diverse groups as naval personnel aboard ship, male college students, patients in a university hospital, and depressed patients under treatment (Rahe, Mahan, Arthur, & Gunderson, 1970; Spilken & Jacobs, 1971; Wyler, Masuda, & Holmes, 1971; Paykel et al., 1969).

In research related to social class differences in stressful living conditions, there is much evidence that persons in the lower social classes live under generally more unfavorable life conditions than those higher in the social status system (Caplovitz, 1963; Hollingshead & Redlich, 1958). More specifically, Dohrenwend has found that lower-class persons experience more life events that can be described as social losses (an event or change that other people would generally think undesirable) than do higher status individuals (Dohrenwend, 1970).

The question, then, is to determine to what extent the relationship between social class and psychiatric symptoms found in community studies may be due to the uneven distribution of life events in the various classes. The current report addresses itself to this issue, using data from our investigation of life events and psychological distress.

METHODOLOGY

Most research in stress and mental illness, although provocative theoretically, has been handicapped methodologically in at least four respects. First, such investigations have been restricted to very specific populations, such as schizophrenics, college students, and alcoholics. Next, the number of respondents has been relatively small. Third, the range and number of life events examined have been limited. Finally, most studies were made at only one time; two exceptions, the Dohrenwend (1969) and Haberman (1965) panels, had small numbers. Thus it has been impossible to determine the stability of the relationships between life events, sociodemographic factors, and mental status.

The current study, in contrast, allows for the first time a detailed examination of relationships between life events, social class, and mental status in a large community sample over time.

The sample consists of one adult selected at random from each of 720 households in a systematic sample of a mental health catchment area of approximately 72,000 population in metropolitan New Haven. The area includes a changing inner-city section of 22,000 and a more stable industrial town of 50,000. It represents a cross section of the community's population and includes all ethnic, racial, and socioeconomic groups. Interviews were conducted in person with each respondent between July 1967 and January 1968. A total of 1095 individuals was contacted. Of these, 12% refused to be interviewed, 2% could not be reached at home to be contacted, and 86% (938) were interviewed.

Two years later the same population was reinterviewed. Of the original 938, 8% refused to be reinterviewed, 11% had moved out of the area, 4% had died, and 77% were reinterviewed. It is these 720 persons who provided the data on which this chapter is based. With one exception, the reinterviewed sample did not differ significantly from the original cohort within any of the major categories of the following variables: social class, race, sex, religion, marital status, mental status, and age. The exception cited above was the under-30 age group, which dropped from 25% in 1967 to 19% in 1969.

Information was gathered for each respondent on the following dimensions: (1) basic demographic variables; (2) physical health status; (3) mental health status (as measured by items which have been found to discriminate between psychiatrically sick and healthy populations); (4) social and instrumental role performances; (5) help-seeking behavior and use of community health and social agency facilities; and (6) life crises that occurred during the past year. We defined such crises or events as experiences involving a role transformation, changes in status or environment, or impositions of pain (Antonovsky & Kats, 1967). The respondent was asked whether any of 62 such events had occurred to him in the year previous to our interview. This list of events was based on selected items developed by Antonovsky and Kats (1967), Holmes and Rahe (Hawkins et al., 1957; Rahe et al., 1964), and an array of other items developed by ourselves. These events ranged from change in residence, a child starting school, marriage, and loss of job to divorce, serious illness, and the death of a loved one. In addition, there were open-end questions to elicit information about events we may not have covered in our list. The events can be analyzed individually or in terms of larger conceptual categories.

Psychopathology is measured by an index of mental status. Although a comprehensive evaluation of mental status requires an extensive clinical examination in which a composite assessment is made of the individual's behavior, thought, and emotional processes, recent studies have employed short screening devices as an alternative to this clinical evaluation (Langner, 1965; Leighton,

Harding, Macklin, Macmillan, & Leighton, 1963; Phillips, 1966; Rogler & Hollingshead, 1965).

We have adopted the instrument developed by Macmillan (1957) and further modified by Gurin and his associates (Gurin, Veroff, & Feld, 1960). It utilizes a list of 20 psychiatric symptoms which are scored and developed into an index of mental status. Examples of the questions are: Do you ever feel that you are bothered by all sorts of pains or ailments in different parts of your body? Do you ever have trouble in getting to sleep or staying asleep? Are you ever bothered by nervousness (feeling fidgety, irritable, tense)? A response of Often is scored 1; Sometimes, 2; Hardly ever, 3; Never, 4. Scores range from 20 (maximum impairment) to 80 (total absence of symptoms). Previous research indicates that relatively low scores identify individuals with major psychological problems and that the individual scores may be grouped into larger categories (Jackson, 1962; Leighton et al., 1963; Srole et al., 1962). We have examined our data both in terms of individual scores and by categories. When dealing with categories we have classified those scoring 66 and lower as "high symptom level," those scoring between 67 and 76 as "moderate symptom level," and those scoring 77 and above as "low symptom level" (Jackson, 1962).

Social class is measured by Hollingshead's Two Factor Index of Social Position, which utilizes occupation and education to rank the study population into five classes where I is the highest and V the lowest.*

In our statistical analyses we employed correlation and tests of significance. Significance is defined at the .05 level. Statistical tests were made utilizing both actual scores and categories for the Gurin and various life events indices. Chi-square, gamma, Somers' D-YX, and product moment correlation (zero-order and multiple) were used. The various methods produced similar results.

RESULTS

Findings at One Time

As in other studies, we found a significant relationship between social class and psychiatric symptomatology. In 1967 proportionately twice as many persons in the lowest class (V) as in the highest (I-II) had Gurin scores in the highest symptom category: 25% contrasted to 12% (see Table 1). Two years later the relationship between social class and symptoms was found to be very similar.

We also found a strong relationship between life events and psychological distress. Our first measure of life events was in terms of the total numbers of

* See A. B. Hollingshead, 1957. For a detailed description of the five social classes see Hollingshead & Redlich, 1958.

Table 1. Social Class and Psychiatric Symptons

Social Class	Gurin Category (%) High Symptom	Moderate Symptom	Low Symptom	*N*
I–II	12	48	40	67
III	12	45	43	100
IV	18	46	36	337
V	25	46	29	216
				720

Note: Gamma = − .17; $p<.001$.

events experienced by the respondent during the year before the interview. As reported in a previous paper, using our 1967 data, we found a strong association between the number of events experienced by individuals and their mental status: the greater the number of events experienced, the greater the individual's symptomatology (Myers et al., 1971). In 1969 we found the same relationship. However, we found no relationship between social class and the number of events an individual had experienced. Moreoever, in both years, when we controlled for class the relationship between events and symptoms remained significant; but when we controlled for number of events the relationship between class and symptoms disappeared.

Because of their demonstrated utility, we next turned to the "social readjustment ratings" of Holmes and Rahe for events which they found to be associated with illness onset (Holmes & Masuda, this volume; Holmes & Rahe, 1967). These "life-change" events were obtained by asking judges to rate a series of 43 life events in terms of the relative degree of necessary readjustment (Holmes & Rahe, 1967, p. 213). For our analyses, we used the geometric mean of ratings reported by Masuda and Holmes (1967).

We employed three versions of this change index in our analyses. First we limited the analysis to only those persons who had experienced at least 1 of the 30 events listed in the Holmes-Rahe instrument and for which we have information. This index is the traditional one, in which the weighted scores for events are summed. Second we included everyone in our sample by assigning a score of zero to those persons who had not experienced an event on their list. Third we examined the total number of events on the list that each respondent had experienced. This analysis was undertaken to determine whether the relationships between number of events, symptomatology, and social class would be the same for the 30 events on the Holmes-Rahe list as we found for the 62 events on our list.

When we analyzed our data using these three indices we again discovered a

Table 2. Desirability of Events

Desirable events
Started to school or training program, etc.
Graduated from school or training program
Moved to better neighborhood
Built a new house
Major remodeling of house
Engaged
Married
Birth of first child
Adoption of child
Started to work for the first time
Promoted or moved to more responsible job
Expanded business
Significant success at work
Major improvement in financial status (i.e., a lot better off than usual)
Undesirable events
Failed school or training program, etc.
Problems in school
Moved to worse neighborhood
Widowed
Divorced
Separated
Troubles with in-laws
Serious physical illness
Serious injury or accident
Death of a loved one (family or close friend)
Stillbirth
Frequent minor illness
Mental illness
Death of a pet
Demoted or changed to less responsible job

strong relationship between a high score on the life-change index and a high symptom score, and no significant relationship between social class and the life-events score.*

Since many studies have shown the adverse conditions under which lower-class persons live, we next examined events in terms of desirability. That is, we classified events in terms of an evaluated dimension corresponding to social desirability. In terms of the currently shared values of society one group of events which was clearly *desirable* includes events such as graduation from school, moved to a better neighborhood, engagement, marriage, promotion in job, success at work, and improvement in financial status. The second group of

* In both years, when we controlled for social class the relationship between events and symptoms remained significant; but when we controlled for life-change events score, the relationship between social class and symptoms disappeared.

Undesirable events (continued)
- **Laid off (temporarily)**
- **Business failed**
- **Trouble with boss**
- **Out of work over a month**
- **Fired**
- **Financial status a lot worse than usual (e.g., loss of large amount of money, unusually heavy debts or expenses)**
- **Foreclosure of mortgage or loan (e.g., car, house, furniture)**
- **Been in court**
- **Detention in jail or other correctional institution**
- **Been arrested**
- **Law suit or legal action**
- **Loss of driver's license**
- **Major catastrophes or crises in neighborhood or community (e.g., fire, major crime, demolition of home, changes in neighborhood)**

Ambiguous events
- **Changed school or training program, etc.**
- **If moved, to same type of neighborhood**
- **Major changes in relationship with spouse**
- **Family member entered the Armed Forces or other service**
- **Birth of child (other than first)**
- **Member of family or household left home**
- **New person moved into family or household**
- **Change in number of family get-togethers**
- **Pregnancy**
- **If change in job, changed to same type job**
- **Changes at work (i.e., changes in hours or conditions, changes in responsibilities, changes to a different kind of work, transfer to a different department)**
- **Any big reorganization at work**
- **Retirement**
- **Change in relations with neighbor, friend, or relative**

---

events was *undesirable* for most persons, such as failure in school, a move to a less desirable neighborhood, divorce, trouble with in-laws, serious injury or accident, death of a loved one, business failure, and detention in jail. Finally, we classified as *ambiguous* those events for which there is probably disagreement such as pregnancy, entered armed forces, and retired from work. Table 2 lists events according to this classification. Thus the direction of an event is defined in objective terms rather than in terms of the respondent's assessment of his experience. Some people might characterize their divorce as a change for the better (or desirable), for example, although we classify the event as undesirable. This classification system follows that of Dohrenwend (1973), who uses the terms social gain and social loss.

The results of this analysis are similar to those for total events: the more psychologically distressed the individual, the more likely he was to have experienced undesirable or social loss life events prior to being interviewed, but there was no relationship between social class and undesirable events.*

At first glance these results do not seem to support those of the Dohrenwends, who found relationships between social class and social loss events as well as between events and psychiatric symptoms (Dohrenwend & Dohrenwend, 1969; Dohrenwend, 1970). However, upon further analysis they are not as contradictory as they first seem. When we devised a slightly different "desirability" index—the ratio of undesirable to desirable events—we found, as before, a strong relationship with symptomatology: the larger the ratio of undesirable events, the higher the proportion of persons who exhibited severe symptoms. In 1967 this index was related to social class as well: the lower the class, the higher the proportion of undesirable events. However, the relationship was not significant in 1969.

With this lead we combined the Holmes-Rahe idea of life change or social readjustment with the concept of desirability into a single index. Following Dohrenwend's (1973) technique, each undesirable event was assigned the appropriate rating with a negative sign and each desirable one the appropriate rating with a positive sign. The individual's total score therefore consists of the algebraic sum of the positive and negative readjustment ratings of events reported for the last year.

We employed this index in two ways. First we included only those persons who had experienced desirable and/or undesirable events on the Holmes-Rahe list. Second we included everyone by assigning individuals with ambiguous events a zero score (between a negative and a positive score) and those who experienced no events whatsoever to a category above the highest positive score.†

When we examined the relationship between our new combined Desirability-Change Index and Gurin scores we again found very significant relationships in both 1967 and in 1969 for both indices (i.e., only those persons who had experienced an event and everyone). As examples, see Tables 3 and 4 for 1969 data. In contrast to previous indices, however, these Desirability-Change indices were related to social class in both 1967 and 1969. As examples, see Tables 5 and 6 for 1969 data. Thus we find that social class is related to both Gurin score and Desirability-Change Life-Events score.

Since both social class and life events are related to Gurin score, the question arises as to which of the foregoing independent variables explains more of the variation in symptomatology. To answer this question we first examined the

* When we cross-controlled for social class, the relationship between undesirable events and symptoms remained significant in both years; when we controlled for number of undesirable events, the relationship between social class and symptoms disappeared.

† B. S. Dohrenwend (1973) also assigned ambiguous events a score of zero. The assignment of "no events" was made on the basis of previous evidence of the impact of sheer numbers alone, regardless of type of event, upon symptomatology.

Table 3. Desirability-Change Life Events and Psychiatric Symptomatology, 1969

Desirability-Change Life Events Index Score [1]	Gurin Category (%)			
	High Symptoms	Moderate Symptoms	Low Symptoms	*N*
− 1187 to − 483	39	48	13	54
− 482 to − 297	18	49	33	116
− 296 to + 48	17	52	31	112
+ 49 to + 895	13	42	45	94
				376

Note: Gamma = .22; $p < .001$.
[1] A minus score represents high readjustment and high undesirability. Only persons with an event are reported here.

Table 4. Desirability-Change Life Events and Symptomatology, 1969

Desirability-Change Life Events Index Score [1]	Gurin Category (%)			
	High Symptoms	Moderate Symptoms	Low Symptoms	*N*
− 1187 to − 378	28	50	22	107
− 377 to − 1	17	51	32	167
Ambiguous	21	39	40	131
+ 1 to + 895	14	42	44	102
None	8	45	47	213
				720

Note: Gamma = .24; $p < .001$.
[1] A minus score represents high readjustment and high undesirability.

relationship between social class and symptom score controlling for Desirability-Change Index scores. The results of this procedure demonstrate that the relationship between social class and symptom score disappears in both years. On the other hand, the relationship between life-event scores, as measured by desirability-change, and symptom scores continues to be significant within each class in both 1967 and 1969.* Thus it is clear that the relationship between life events and psychiatric symptoms is an independent psychosocial phenomenon and not primarily a reflection of underlying social class differences.

In turn, the relationship between social class and psychiatric symptoms is a

* In class III the level of significance for chi-square and all correlations was at the .10 level in 1969.

Table 5. Social Class and Desirability-Change Life Events, 1969

Social Class	Desirability-Change Life Events Index Score (%) [1]			N
	– 1187 to – 378	– 377 to – 270	– 269 to + 895	
I–II	17	28	55	36
III	20	28	52	54
IV	25	38	37	175
V	41	37	22	111
				376

Note: Gamma = – .27; $p < .001$.

[1] A minus score represents high readjustment and high undesirability. Only persons with an event are reported here.

Table 6. Social Class and Desirability-Change Life Events, 1969

Social Class	Desirability-Change Life Events Index Score (%) [1]					N
	– 1187 to – 378	– 377 to – 1	Ambiguous	1 to 895	None	
I–II	9	20	13	25	33	67
III	11	21	13	22	33	100
IV	13	26	21	13	27	337
V	21	21	19	9	30	216
						720

Note: Gamma = – .12; $p < .005$.

[1] A minus score represents high readjustment and high undesirability.

reflection of social class differences in the distribution of Desirability-Change Life Events in the community. Lower-class people do not experience more events than persons of higher status, do not experience more undesirable events, and do not score higher on the Holmes-Rahe Life-Change index. However, when we combine life change and desirability into a single index, we find that lower-class persons are subject to more high-impact events of an undesirable nature.

Change over time

So far our analyses have been limited to one time. We now address ourselves to the findings over two points in time. When we examine changes in life events and changes in symptoms between 1967 and 1969, we find a pattern similar to that found at each time for all the life-events indices presented in this chapter: the greater the number of changes in life events or in index scores, the more likely there is to be a substantial change in the individual's symptoms. The data for Desirability-Change events are listed in Tables 7 and 8. More specifically, a relative increase in the readjustment-undesirability of events is associated with a worsening of symptomatology; a relative decrease with an improvement.

In turn, social class is unrelated to change in events for any of the indices or to change in Gurin score. When we control for social class, the relationship be-

Table 7. Desirability-Change Life Events and Change in Symptomatology, 1967–1969

	Gurin Category Change in Symptoms (%)			
Change in Desirability-Change Life Events Index Score [1]	Worse	No Change	Better	*N*
– 1266 to – 336	33	48	19	88
– 335 to – 187	23	50	27	118
– 186 to + 80	21	62	17	110
+ 81 to + 334	18	59	23	101
+ 335 to + 1414	16	45	39	109
				526

Note: Gamma = .18; $p < .001$.

[1] A minus score represents a relative increase in readjustment—undesirability over time; a positive score, a relative decrease. Only persons with an event are reported here.

Table 8. Desirability-Change Life Events and Change in Symptomatology, 1967–1969

	Gurin Category Change in Symptoms (%)			
Change in Desirability-Change Life Events Index Score [1]	Worse	No Change	Better	N
– 1266 to – 336	33	48	19	88
– 335 to – 187	23	50	27	118
– 186 to + 80 [2]	19	59	22	304
+ 81 to + 334	18	59	23	101
+ 335 to + 1414	16	45	39	109
				720

Note: Gamma = .16; $p < .002$.

[1] A minute score represents a relative increase in readjustment—undesirability over time; a positive score, a relative decrease.

[2] Includes persons with no events in either year.

tween change in events and change in symptoms remains significant for all event indices.* When we control for change in event score, there continues to be no significant relationship between social class and change in Gurin score. Thus there is a clear relationship between changes in the occurrence of life events (as measured by any index we use) in a two-year period and changes in psychiatric symptomatology.

DISCUSSION

The data presented in this chapter suggest that the greater amount of psychiatric distress found in the lower class in community studies is due to the uneven distribution of life events measured by a scale of Desirability-Change. Lower-class individuals experience more unpleasant events which have a high readjustment or change impact than persons higher in the social status system. Such events, in turn, are related to psychiatric symptomatology. These relationships between social class, events, and symptoms were found in both 1967 and 1969 in New Haven and may be characteristic of many American communities today. Over time, however, there is no relationship between social class and changes in symptoms or changes in events. A strong relationship does exist, however, between changes in events and changes in symptoms.

Thus the data shed light on the tenuous balance between the individual's psychic economy and the social milieu within which he is forced to adapt. They demonstrate the importance of social and interpersonal forces frequently external to the individual in influencing psychological status. The readjustment impact of events combined with their desirability seems to have a striking effect upon one's capacity to maintain a state of mental health. On a more theoretical level, the findings advance our knowledge of the relationship between an individual's overall well-being and the challenges of everyday living. Apparently events requiring attention and/or some form of behavioral adaptation or coping which have a high readjustment impact and which are undesirable are more common in the lower classes and deleterious to mental health.

Thus the lower-class person, confronted with a certain quantum of disturbance and living in relative economic and cultural poverty, exhibits symptoms because of the increased strain imposed upon him. Interpersonal relationships at this social level tend to be fragile and provide relatively minimal social support to the individual facing an undesirable crisis which requires considerable coping. His symptoms therefore may very well be a cry for the needed support which he is otherwise not getting.

* In class III the level of significance for chi-square and all correlations was at the .10 level in 1969.

Changes in the occurrence of such events over time are closely related to changes in symptomatology. This highlights the tenuous balance between the individual's psychological status and social environment. Since such changes occur with about equal frequency at all social levels, the unequal distribution of these events by social class remains rather constant at any point in time. Thus lower-class persons, as shown by the New Haven data of 1967 and 1969, experienced more frequently events associated with a higher degree of psychiatric symptomatology. These findings perhaps help to explain the consistent relationship found between social class and psychiatric symptomatology in community studies.*

REFERENCES

Antonovsky, A., & Kats, R. The life crisis history as a tool in epidemiological research. *Journal of Health and Social Behavior,* 1967, **8,** 15–21.

Brown, G. W., & Birley, J. L. T. Crisis and life changes and the onset of schizophrenia. *Journal of Health and Social Behavior,* 1968,**9,** 203–214.

Caplovitz, D. *The Poor Pay More.* New York: The Free Press of Glencoe, 1963.

Dohrenwend, B. P., & Dohrenwend, B. S. *Social Status and Psychological Disorder: A Causal Inquiry.* New York: John Wiley & Sons, 1969.

Dohrenwend, B. S. Life events as stressors: A methodological inquiry. *Journal of Health and Social Behavior,* 1973, **14,** 167–175.

Dohrenwend, B. S. Social class and stressful events. In E. H. Hare & J. K. Wing (Eds.), *Psychiatric Epidemiology: Proceedings of the International Symposium Held at Aberdeen University, July 22–25, 1969.* New York: Oxford University Press, 1970. Pp. 313–319.

Fischer, H. K., Dlin, B., & Winters, W. Time patterns and emotional factors related to the onset of coronary occlusion. *Psychosomatic Medicine,* 1962, **24,** 516.

Graham, D. T., & Stevenson, I. Disease as response to life stress. In H. I. Lief, V. F. Lief, & N. R. Lief (Eds.), *Psychological Basis of Medical Practice.* New York: Harper and Row, 1963. Pp. 115–136.

Greene, W. A. Psychological factors and reticuloendothelial disease. I. Preliminary observations on a group of males with lymphomas and leukemias. *Psychosomatic Medicine,* 1954, **16,** 220–230.

* In interpreting these findings, we must note the possibility that the more impaired an individual, the more likely he is to report events because he feels they are stressful. However, the events we list are generally discrete and of such a factual nature that they are not likely to go unreported. For example, when the one-year period is broken into two successive six-month periods, there is no significant difference in the number of events reported. Furthermore, what was recorded initially was the occurrence of an event, not the individual's perception of its stressfulness.

Greene, W. A., & Miller, G. Psychological factors and reticuloendothelial disease. IV. Observations on a group of chhildren and adolescents with leukemia: An interpretation of disease development in terms of the mother-child unit. *Psychosomatic Medicine,* 1958, **20,** 124–144.

Greene, W. A., Young, L. E., & Swisher, S. N. Psychological factors and reticuloendothelial disease. II. Observations on a group of women with lymphomas and leukemias. *Psychosomatic Medicine,* 1956, **18,** 284–303.

Gurin, G., Veroff, J., & Feld, S. *Americans View Their Mental Health: A Nationwide Survey*. New York: Basic Books, 1960.

Haberman, P. W. An analysis of retest scores for an index of psychophysiological disturbance. *Journal of Health and Human Behavior,* 1965, **6,** 257–260.

Hawkins, N. G., Davies, R., & Holmes, T. H. Evidence of psychosocial factors in the development of pulmonary tuberculosis. *American Review of Tuberculosis and Pulmonary Diseases,* 1957, **75,** 768–780.

Hinkle, L. E., Jr., & Wolff, H. G. Health and the social environment: Experimental investigations. In A. H. Leighton, J. A. Clausen, & R. N. Wilson (Eds.), *Explorations in Social Psychiatry*. New York: Basic Books, 1957. Pp. 105–137.

Hollingshead, A. B. Two factor index of social position. 1965 Yale Station, New Haven, Conn. Mimeographed, 1957.

Hollingshead, A. B., & Redlich, F. C. *Social Class and Mental Illness*. New York: John Wiley & Sons, 1958.

Holmes, T. H., & Rahe, R. H. The Social Readjustment Rating Scale. *Journal of Psychosomatic Research,* 1967, **11,** 213–218.

Jackson, E. F. Status consistency and symptoms of stress. *American Sociological Review,* 1962, **27,** 469–480.

Kissen, D. K. Some psychosocial aspects of pulmonary tuberculosis. *International Journal of Social Psychiatry,* 1958, **3,** 252–259.

Langner, T. S. Psychophysiological symptoms and women's status in Mexico. In J. M. Murphy & A. H. Leighton (Eds.), *Approaches in Cross-Cultural Psychiatry*. Ithaca, N.Y.: Cornell University Press, 1965.

Leighton, D. C., Harding, J. S., Macklin, D. B., Macmillan, A. M., & Leighton, A. H. *The Character of Danger*. New York: Basic Books, 1963.

Lindenthal, J. J., Myers, J. K., Pepper, M. P., & Stern, M. S. Mental status and religious behavior. *Journal for the Scientific Study of Religion,* 1970, **9,** 143–149.

Lindenthal, J. J., Thomas, C. S., & Myers, J. K. Psychological status and the perception of primary and secondary support from the social milieu in time of crisis. *The Journal of Nervous and Mental Disease,* 1971, **153,** 92–98.

Macmillan, A. M. The health opinion survey: Technique for estimating prevalence of psychoneurotic and related types of disorder in communities. *Psychological Reports,* 1957, **3,** 325–329.

Masuda, M., & Holmes, T. The Social Readjustment Rating Scale. *Journal of Psychosomatic Research,* 1967, **11,** 219–225.

Myers, J. K., Lindenthal, J. J., & Pepper, M. P. Life events and psychiatric impairment. *The Journal of Nervous and Mental Disease,* 1971, **152,** 149–157.

Myers, J. K., Lindenthal, J. J., Pepper, M. P., & Ostrander, D. R. Life events and mental status: A longitudinal study. *Journal of Health and Social Behavior,* 1972, **13,** 398–406.

Paykel, E. S., Myers, J. K., Dienelt, M. N., Klerman, G. L., Lindenthal, J. J., & Pepper, M. P. Life events and depression: A controlled study. *Archives of General Psychiatry,* 1969, **21,** 753–760.

Phillips, D. L. The "true prevalence" of mental illness in a New England state. *Community Mental Health Journal,* 1966, **2,** 35–40.

Rahe, R. H. Life crisis and health change. In P. R. A. May & J. R. Wittenborn (Eds.), *Psychotropic Drug Response: Advances in Prediction.* Springfield, Ill.: Charles C Thomas, 1969. P. 92.

Rahe, R. H. & Holmes, T. H. Social, psychologic and psychophysiologic aspects of inguinal hernia. *Journal of Psychosomatic Research,* 1965, **8,** 487–491.

Rahe, R. H., Mahan, J. L. Jr., Arthur, R. J., & Gunderson, E. K. E. The epidemiology of illness in naval environments. I. Illness types, distribution, severities, and relationship to life change. *Military Medicine,* 1970, **135,** 443–452.

Rahe R. H., Myer, M., Smith, M., Kjaer, G., & Holmes, T. H. Social stress and illness onset. *Journal of Psychosomatic Research,* 1964, **8,** 35–44.

Rogler, L. H., & Hollingshead, A. B. *Trapped: Families and Schizophrenia.* New York: John Wiley, & Sons, 1965.

Spilken, A. Z., & Jacobs, M. A. Prediction of illness behavior from measures of life crisis, manifest distress and maladaptive coping. *Psychosomatic Medicine,* 1971, **33,** 251–264.

Srole, L., Langner, T. S., Michael, S. T., Opler, M. K., & Rennie, T. A. C. *Mental Health in the Metropolis.* New York: McGraw-Hill Book Company, 1962.

Weiss, E., Dlin, B., & Rollin, H. R. Emotional factors in coronary occlusion. *Archives of Internal Medicine,* 1957, **99,** 628–641.

Wyler, A. R., Masuda, M., & Holmes, T. H. Magnitude of life events and seriousness of illness. *Psychosomatic Medicine,* 1971, **33,** 115–122.

CHAPTER 13

Stressful Life Events and Illness:

A Research Area in Need of Conceptual Development

SHEPPARD G. KELLAM

INTRODUCTION

Isaiah Berlin (1953) once made the distinction between people called hedgehogs—who are temperamentally disposed to look for connections between things, and are content only with a unified theory explaining reality—and people called foxes—who are content to examine in detail individual aspects of life and have no need to search for the interrelationships among such aspects. Investigators in the broad domain called mental health can be spread along a dimension extending from those concerned with rich (some would say florid) theoretical frameworks tying everything into a comprehensive theory to those who prefer to remain strict empiricists, cautiously using only minimal theoretical development in an effort to avoid drawing inferences prematurely and erroneously. The latter might be said to be a somewhat exaggerated characterization of many investigators in the field of stressful life events and illness.

Recent years have seen a renewed interest in studying the relationship between life stress and health and illness. For the most part the work in this area has been based on simple, relatively atheoretical inventories of life events thought to be stressful—events which are hypothesized to lead to a higher risk of physical and/or mental illness. I would suggest that the four preceding chapters in this section are examples of good work and perhaps represent the most sophisticated level of research one can attain in this first stage of developing investigation in this area. Until now we have been concerned mainly with the correlation between supposedly stressful events and illness, and we have been only minimally concerned with the theoretical basis for selecting any particular life events as stressful or for predicting differences among categories of life events in relation to illness. It is now time to move on to Stage Two in this research, and this will require the elaboration of the concept of stressful life events.

In this discussion, I would like to concentrate on what approaches further conceptual development might take—for example, categories of life events by stages of life, by levels of social organization, and by issues such as fateful events in contrast to personal failure events. In addition, I would like to explore the usefulness of a conceptual scheme developed by my colleagues and me called *The Life Course-Social Field Concept*. The purpose is to set out sufficient conceptual development so that different kinds of life event can be compared in terms of their stressfulness. ''Kinds of life event'' refers to categories with important theoretical meaningfulness in terms of the processes of causality operating in any correlations between life events and health and illness.

Returning to Isaiah Berlin's dichotomy, it is useful to note James Thurber's further elaboration of Berlin's original concept of hedgehogs and foxes. Thurber subdivided hedgehogs and foxes into Alices and Mables, and—if my memory is correct—Alices were those hedgehogs and foxes who needed to do something about the world however they saw it; Mables were those, either hedgehogs or foxes, who were content to observe the world but do nothing about it.

I suppose that this discussion puts me in the category of an Alice tending toward hedgehoginess. We can predict that the foxes among us will not understand or think very highly of the comments I will make, while the hedgehogs will understand and, if they are Alices, will cheer wildly.

In opening the conference on which this book is based Barbara Dohrenwend asked three questions: What is a stressful life event? What makes it stressful? What are the consequences of its stressfulness? These questions are the business of Stage Two of this area of investigation and to answer them we must look more closely at the concept of stressful life events.

I am raising the issue of measuring the concept of stressful life events. The inventories used in the research we have heard consist of lists of many different kinds of events—some ''good,'' some ''bad,'' some indifferent—numbering anywhere from 20 to 100 with few or no subdivisions. What domain do these events sample? The term *life event* could refer to any event imaginable, however microscopic or macrosociological. If the word *stressful* is used in our definition of the domain these inventories purport to measure, the boundaries of the universe being measured are narrowed considerably, but still the area of concern is enormous. It is impressive that measurement of such a vaguely defined universe as *stressful life events* yielded correlations with health variables both concurrently and over time; but these correlations cannot help us understand the relationship between the stress stimulus and the stress response unless the *concept* of stressful life events receives considerable conceptual development.

Before moving into some examples of conceptual development, however, let us pause for a moment to comment on several specific aspects of the four chapters that provided the basis of this discussion. Markush and Favero reported a correlation between stressful event scores and age. The fact that correlation with age did not occur in the Washington County area but did occur in urban Kansas City raises the question of whether there are important distinctions in what constitute stressful life events in rural versus urban areas. Washington County, you may recall, is the area in which Clausen and Kohn (1959) attempted to replicate Faris and Dunham's classic study (1939) of the relation of urban areas to the frequencies of hospitalization for psychosis, particularly schizophrenia. The inference drawn by some investigators is that certain aspects of urban life are stressful and are associated with hospitalization—either because of what has been termed the drift of patients toward lower class, or because the characteristics of urban life in those types of neighborhood are more stressful and cause more schizophrenia or both. The absence of similar correlations in rural areas such as Washington County tends to narrow these hypotheses to urban life in contrast to rural life. Markush and Favero's results again point toward differences in stressful events in rural versus urban settings.

Basically, their results indicate that the inventory produced higher stressful event scores for one stage of life than it did for others. Perhaps the inventory samples all stages of life adequately and different stages of life have higher levels of stress. Alternatively, the inventory might not sample each stage of life adequately, so that the scores are higher in those stages of life that are oversampled as compared to those that are underrepresented. Since there was little or no theoretical reason for choosing particular life events of one type or another, it is very difficult to interpret how meaningful the stage of life differences is—a conclusion which supports the idea that there is a serious need for further conceptual development on which to base the design of instruments for measuring stressful life events.

This chapter also demonstrates another problem we must face. Although we are concerned with the conceptual development of stressful life events, we cannot forget that our dependent variables may be in equally bad condition and may also require careful scrutiny. There are problems with the methods for measuring depression such as the issues of reliability and validity and how much depression measures may be confounded by age and social class. Multiple measures of depression and holding the study population constant—at least in regard to social class, stage of life, rural/urban, and major cultural characteristics—can help minimize these problems.

The chapter by Gersten, Langner, Eisenberg, and Orzeck made an important step toward elaborating the concept of stressful life events. The questions raised by these investigators concerned the relationship between "good" events and "bad" events: whether these two categories tend to cancel each other out, whether they are additive in their stressfulness, whether one is important and the other not. The answers they obtained were suggestive but were restricted by the instrument used to measure stressful life events. Whether good events and bad events were both adequately sampled was not really addressed.

Again, given a simple inventory of life events, it is of interest that inferences could be drawn concerning the possible relationships between good events and bad events. The problem of instrument design, particularly in regard to content validity, leads one to think that the next stage of instrument development should be concerned with proper studies of the samples of good and bad events.

One added comment about this chapter concerns the interpretation of anxiety as an adaptive behavior. Although it is true that there is some evidence that mild anxiety is associated with better performance on such tasks as IQ test performance, it is also clear that anxiety can be an overwhelmingly debilitating symptom, one associated with major morbidity. Again, the problem lies in the conceptual development. The concept of anxiety as "signal anxiety" or "anxiety in the service of mobilizing the individual" is different from the concept of anxiety as psychopathology entailing considerable morbidity. They may or may not be on the same continuum, but they should not be confused either conceptually or in terms of their measurement.

I mentioned that one solution to the problem of measuring psychopathology is to use multiple measures, while holding constant the population of people about whom one is concerned. It should be added that the use of multiple measures is a solution only if the concept being measured by each of the instruments is explicit and clear. In much of the measurement of psychopathology the concept being measured is not clear; in fact, psychiatric symptomatology is badly in need of conceptual development and empirical work. The various dimensions of psychopathology which have been conceptualized and measured in previous research have been reasonably well analyzed by Blum (1962) and by Scott (1958).

The Myers, Lindenthal, and Pepper report was an aesthetically pleasing example of how it is possible to take simple measures of vague concepts and, through careful analysis, arrive at useful information which helps us think about the next stage of research. One of the problems that this chapter reflects, which all of us including the authors recognize, is the possibility of confounding reports of life events with reports of illness by the same individuals. We need to keep this methodological problem in mind.

THE RELATIVE STRENGTH OF THREE RESEARCH MODELS

In both the Gersten chapter and the Myers chapter, there is an opportunity to consider causality which does not exist in concurrent correlation between independent and dependent variables. In these two chapters, for example, we can hypothesize from time 1 how illness will be distributed in the study populations at time 2. The Dohrenwends (1969) have pointed out the advantage of longitudinal study for drawing causal inferences. One can outline a hierarchy of research designs based on three levels of strength. The first and weakest level is concurrent correlation, which provides hints of possible causal relations but does not itself determine direction of causation or even whether third variables could be the cause of the correlation between the two variables under study. The second level of strength is longitudinal correlation, which provides a basis for predicting over time what will happen differentially between two populations.

The third and most powerful level is that of experimentation over time. In such a study, one can hypothesize different outcomes from time 1 to time 2 based on a causal hypothesis concerning different conditions at time 1, and one can manipulate conditions at time 1 such that the hypothesized differences in effect of condition A compared to condition B can be predicted to be either enhanced or eliminated in respect to condition B. None of these papers involves such experimentation and indeed such experimentation would entail the use of interventions aimed, for example, at reducing stressful conditions hypothesized to relate to a higher risk of illness for a randomly drawn portion of the *hypothesized high risk* group. Such interventions might be in the form of treatment programs and/or social programs aimed at alleviating stressful conditions.

EVALUATION RESEARCH AND THE EXPERIMENTAL DESIGN

It is a parenthetical note to our main purpose to call attention to the fact that there is growing pressure in our society for social and bahavioral sciences to do evaluation research into the effectiveness of various human services. This could be a major opportunity to do longitudinal experiments into the causality of illness. If done properly, evaluation research must involve longitudinal experimentation. Since research into stressful life events in relation to illness involves studying individuals under conditions hypothetically stressful to them compared to individuals who are not experiencing such conditions, the experimental alleviation of stressful conditions or stress responses provides an opportunity to study in the most powerful way the causal effect of the hypothetically stressful condition on inducing illness.

Evaluation research then is not only immediately useful to society but, in my view, will be a vitally important part of the transition of many of the behavioral and social scientific efforts from correlational sciences to experimental sciences. I see this as a major asset in the development of theory regarding causation of illness, and it bodes well for those who are wise enough to use the evaluation research opportunity as a tool of basic research rather than just a lower-status research activity for money-making private corporations.

I began this chapter by suggesting that a lack of conceptual development has characterized the stressful life events inventories used thus far. My complaint is not that there should have been better conceptual development from the beginning, but rather that the first stage should now give way to the second stage in which we begin to develop life stress inventories that take into account more theoretically meaningful categories of stressful life events. By *events,* I suggest we mean *events* or *conditions* and allow specific theoretical considerations to determine brevity or longevity. We may then move toward a better understanding of causal relations, which may lie somewhere in the numerous correlations observed thus far. What kinds of concept within the general domain of stressful life events would be most useful to take into account in designing instruments in the next stage of research? The following simple concepts might be useful as a basis for selecting events or conditions which could be vitally important.

Stage of Life

First, we need to take into account the stage of life of the individuals being assessed. The events chosen to represent stressful *events or conditions* during adolescence would be quite different from those at middle age, which in turn would be different from those at old age. Inventories of stressful life events must be carefully constructed for each stage of life; we cannot assume that stage of life is irrelevant to the measurement of stressful life events.

Fate versus Failure

Another conceptual frame that may be important is fateful events versus personal failure events. In our work in Woodlawn we found that the impact of events such as the family moving and causing the child to change schools between kindergarten and first grade had a very different impact on the child's later adaptive capacity than did events such as academic failure in first grade. The fateful event—changing schools between kindergarten and first grade—tended to increase adaptive capacity later on when the child was faced with the potentially stressful event of losing his teacher during the course of a later school year. However, the prior personal failure event—failing first grade—was associated with decreased adaptive capacity. This conceptual distinction is probably important to study. The next stage of instrumentation might include adequate samples of these two categories of events.

Good versus Bad Events

Several investigators have attempted to take such a difference into account; the Gersten chapter presented here dealt with the issue of good and bad events. The next stage of instrument development, then, should follow their lead and address the problem of sampling good events and bad events sufficiently and coequally in inventories of stressful life events.

Social Organizational Hierarchy

In designing a study one should organize the conceptual frame so that it includes the measure of stressful life events. Such issues as social class and national, state, city, neighborhood, and family events and characteristics are all categories from which stressful life events may be sampled, but confusing all of these in one polyglot and calling it an inventory of stressful life events seems overly simple. Certainly being of lower social class has been hypothesized by many investigators to be associated with greater risk of schizophrenia. Within that area of research, some investigators have even suggested a causal relationship between "lower classness" and this major psychosis. Living in certain national conditions such as war or peace has been hypothesized to be stressful. In many minority neighborhoods in the last several years the quest for political power has been successful, whereas in other minority neighborhoods this quest has been unsuccessful. I had the good fortune to be associated with Saul Alinsky in the Woodlawn community in Chicago. He suggested a study of the impact of neighborhood community powerlessness on issues of health and illness, particularly in the area of mental health. Events of segregation, conflict, and confrontation can be considered to be stressful and reflect a condition of local community. These can be measured. Characteristics of family life are certainly distinguishable from community events and from larger social class characteristics. All of these classes of events can be kept distinct and events or conditions sampled within each of them in a newer stage of instrument development.

Overall, then, we need to go back and elaborate our concept of stressful life events, then develop instruments based on meaningful and theoretically related categories of stressful life events. I have suggested that the stage of life of the individual, the social organizational hierarchy from broad societal to familial, the question of good and bad events, the question of fateful versus personal failure events should all be taken into account in a more sophisticated measurement of the concept. These are but a few basic, simple conceptual elaborations.

In our work in Woodlawn my colleagues and I developed a concept called the *life course-social field concept* (Kellam, Branch, Agrawal, & Grabill, 1972; Kellam, Branch, Agrawal, & Ensminger, in press). It suggests that at each stage of life the individual is immersed in one or more major social fields. In each of these social fields there is a natural rater who defines the social tasks expected in that social field. Over time, the social adaptational status of the individuals in that field is determined following interaction between the individual and the "natural rater," who defines the tasks and ultimately judges the individual's social adaptational status in that particular field. Examples of natural raters and social fields are parents in the family, teachers in the classroom, significant others in the peer group, and foremen in the work social field. In our view the social adaptational process is a very fundamental one which constitutes an interface between the individual and society.

One can measure the social adaptational status of individuals within social fields at particular stages of life by going into those fields, determining from the natural raters the social tasks expected of individuals, coding these tasks, standardizing measures of social adaptational status within these fields, and thus obtaining what we have termed SAS (social adaptational status) measures of the individual in the specific social field. This conceptual framework is another example of parsimonious elaboration of the overly simple stressful life-event inventories. It is a further example of how modest conceptual development can lead to more specification concerning kinds of stressful life event. One can ask whether, for example, maladapting in a specific social field is stressful in the sense of being associated over time with increased risk of psychiatric symptoms or of physical illness. Such studies are within the domain of stressful life events but represent the kind of elaboration which I suggest is vitally important if this area of research is to move toward understanding causal relations between stressful life events and health or illness.

REFERENCES

Berlin, I. *The Hedgehog and the Fox: An Essay on Tolstoy's View of History.* New York: Simon and Schuster, 1953.

Blum, R. H. Case identification in psychiatric epidemiology: Methods and problems. *Milbank Memorial Fund Quarterly,* 1962, **40,** 253–88.

Clausen, J. A., & Kohn, M. L. Relation of schizophrenia to the social structure of a small city. In B. Pasamanick (Ed.), *Epidemiology of Mental Disorder.* Washington, D.C.: American Association for the Advancement of Science, 1959.

Dohrenwend, B. P., & Dohrenwend, B. S. *Social Status and Psychological Disorder: A Causal Inquiry.* New York: John Wiley & Sons, 1969.

Faris, R. E., & Dunham, H. W. *Mental Disorders in Urban Areas.* Chicago: University of Chicago Press, 1939.

Kellam, S. G., Branch, J. D., Agrawal, K. C., & Ensminger, M. E. *Mental Health and Going to School: The Woodlawn Child Mental Health Program of Assessment, Early Intervention and Evaluation.* Chicago: University of Chicago Press, in press.

Kellam, S. G., Branch, J. D., Agrawal, K. C., & Grabill, M. E. Woodlawn Mental Health Center: An evolving strategy for planning in community mental health. In S. G. Golann & C. Eisdorfer (Eds.), *Handbook of Community Mental Health.* New York: Appleton-Century-Crofts, 1972. Pp. 711–727.

Scott, W. A. Research definitions of mental health and mental illness. *Psychological Bulletin,* 1958, **55,** 29–45.

PART 4

Methodological Research on Stressful Life Events

When investigators from different disciplines and with different purposes converge on a set of phenomena such as life events, a certain number of collisions can be expected. One investigator, for example, may develop an approach to conceptualizing and measuring life events that, he finds, differs from that developed by another investigator. Questions arise as to the whys and wherefores of the differences. Still another investigator may attempt to use an approach developed by others and find it incomplete for his purposes; questions arise as to why. Still a third investigator becomes concerned with the adequacy of measures of life events for the particular group he is interested in studying and raises questions about the generality of the measurement procedures; more questions arise. Each chapter in Part 4 is by a researcher or researchers who have found themselves in such circumstances, raised such questions, and, more important, devoted major research effort to answering them.

The first paper by George Brown presents a detailed methodological critique of the procedures developed by Holmes and Rahe and their colleagues and a description of Brown's own approach in his studies of the role of life events in the precipitation of depressive disorder and schizophrenia.

Aaron Antonovsky returns to a venerable question that is raised and reraised throughout the book: Why do substantial portions of subjects experiencing disasters or "crisis" scores on life events not become ill? This question, tangential in other chapters, becomes central to his inquiry into "resistance resources."

F. T. Miller, K. W. Bentz, Joseph Aponte, and D. R. Brogan present data testing the generalizability to different populations of the Holmes and Rahe procedures for scaling life events.

Bruce P. Dohrenwend examines differences in lists of life events and differences in ways of categorizing the events: in terms of LCU scores; in terms of gain versus loss; as objective versus subjective; as within versus outside the control of the individual. He raises the question of how to delimit and sample the population of stressful life events, and pursues this question with data on life events from his ongoing research into relations between social factors and psychopathology.

CHAPTER 14

Meaning, Measurement, and Stress of Life Events *

GEORGE W. BROWN

In this chapter I assume that we wish to do more than predict illness rates from life events, however useful this may be. I also assume that we have aspirations to understand, and to argue causally—to say whether life events do or do not influence chances of becoming ill.

It is possible to predict what will happen without understanding; and I believe that this is the situation of much research on life events and illness. Prediction may be successful, but failure to understand can come about in two ways. Ideas about what is going on may simply be wrong. The public health movement in nineteenth-century England claimed a link between noxious vapors arising from rubbish in our cities and the spread of typhoid. But success that followed clearing the streets was not, of course, based on understanding; and in any case predictions in the long run were accurate only when rubbish happened to be dumped downstream from water supplies. Noxious vapors had nothing to do with typhoid.

Such outright failure of understanding is to be expected where there have been only halfhearted attempts to develop theoretical ideas. But prediction may run ahead of understanding simply because measures are just not up to the job. Measurement of a selected variable can easily be contaminated by the very causal process the investigator wishes to study. Where this occurs it is not that understanding is necessarily wrong; it is that measurement is not sufficiently free from contamination for theory to be convincing.

Since these points run through my chapter, I begin with a brief account of three major sources of invalidity. The first two concern measurement and the last the theoretical activity itself.

* The work on depression reported in this chapter has been supported by the Foundations' Fund for Research in Psychiatry, the Medical Research Council, and the Social Science Research Council.

THREE SOURCES OF INVALIDITY

Direct Contamination

Consider the simple situation of two variables, the independent *X* and the dependent *Y*. These may be life event *X* and subsequent illness *Y*, but the argument has general applicability. To study the influence of *X* on *Y* (or merely to predict *Y* from *X*) the investigator does not have to rely on prospective research. Events that have already occurred such as loss of a job can be established retrospectively once a person has become ill. But if such material is used, there is the possibility of *direct contamination:* that is, through the measurement procedure itself the independent variable and the dependent variable influence each other. Perhaps most likely is the situation where measurement of the independent variable *X* is influenced by knowledge of the predicted variable *Y*. This must occur through the agency of the subject or the investigator *M*. The situation is shown in Figure 1 where, since *X* occurs at time 1 but is not measured until later, at time 2, its measurement can be affected by *M*'s knowledge of the illness *Y*. The time of occurrence is shown separately (the top line) from the time of measurement (the bottom line).

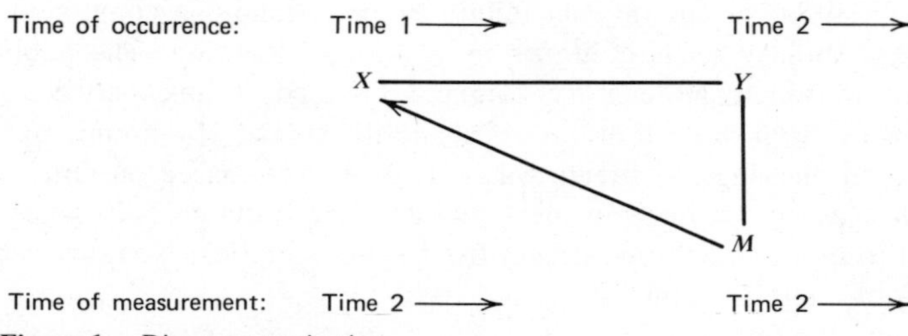

Figure 1. Direct contamination.

Such contamination means that an investigator cannot claim that a correlation between *X* and *Y* represents a causal link—that life events influence illness rates. But, in addition, the lesser claim of being able to predict *Y* from *X* is invalid. In a prospective study the correlation between *X* and *Y* would disappear because *M* would no longer have knowledge of *Y* when measuring *X*.

The arrow on the line from *M* to *X* represents a causal link: that *M*'s knowledge of *Y* brings about *X*. This convention can be confusing if it is not realized that it is merely a way of representing the fact of contamination. Of course, *M* cannot really influence *X* as such (which has already happened); but it can bring about *X* as *measured* and this is the critical point since in a particular study we know of factors such as life events only insofar as they are measured. Contamination can therefore be seen as linking two causal systems: that of the "real" world and that of the measurement process itself.

Empirical prediction need only worry about such direct contamination and an obvious way to deal with it is to carry out a prospective study. However, the requirements of explanatory research are far more stringent. There is also the need to deal with the possibility that X and Y are the result of a common factor influencing them both. This is the well-recognized issue of the spurious relationship, which can take two forms. The first is an indirect form of measurement contamination.

Indirect Contamination

For explanatory research it is also essential that the measurement of X should not be influenced by *any* factor that influences Y. Such *indirect contamination* is seen in Figure 2. As an example, X (life event) is measured by investigator

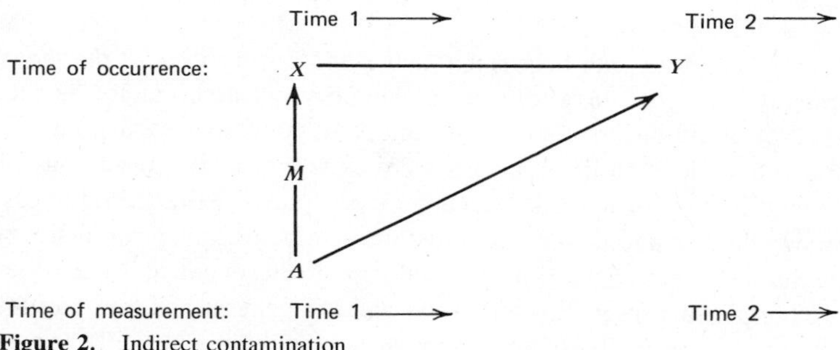

Figure 2. Indirect contamination.

M before Y (illness) and direct contamination must therefore be ruled out. But the measurement of X in the figure is influenced by knowledge of whether or not the subject is anxious A and it is, in fact, A and not X that is causally linked with Y. It follows that without M's awareness of A the correlation between X and Y would disappear. Contamination is therefore still present.

There are various ways in which this could come about. The investigator, for example, may tend to record more life events when respondents show signs of anxiety during the interview. The important point is that X and Y appear to be causally linked only because A is "causing" both of them. However, since X is measured at some time before Y, X can be used validly to predict Y. In this sense empirical prediction is far less demanding than explanatory research. It is only necessary to establish that prediction can be made from a given point in time. It does not matter that *M* is really using signs of anxiety *A* to predict illness *Y*—at least as long as the procedure is repeatable.

Spuriousness

The sources of invalidity discussed so far concern the measurement process itself; the final source deals with the validity of inferences drawn from correlations between measures. The principle just discussed still applies: the investigator must take account of the possibility that the correlation between *X* and *Y* does not represent a causal link but merely the influence of a third variable (*A*) on them both, as in Figure 3.

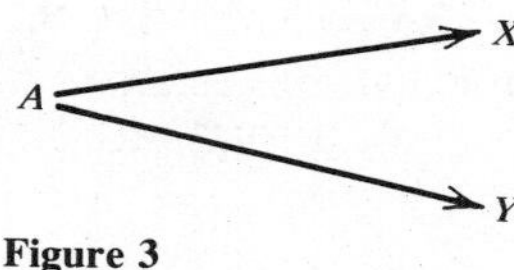

Figure 3

This kind of spurious link between *X* and *Y* may occur even if *the measures are completely accurate*. Invalidity in explanatory research cannot be reduced to the issue of avoiding error in measurement. Erroneous conclusions, for instance, may be made even if life events were experienced as "upsetting" in the way described by the respondent. Accurate description of the stressfulness of a life event would not avoid false conclusions if a third and prior factor influenced the subject's *experience* of stressfulness of the event and the illness itself. For example, a personality trait such as high general anxiety may lead to both a greater chance of illness and a greater tendency to experience life events as markedly stressful. In such a case a conclusion about the existence of a causal link between events and illness would be wrong. The correlation between *X* and *Y* is not causal since it has been produced by the prior factor *A;* and the only way to sort this out would be to control for the component of the life-event measure that was due to the personality trait. In this way deliberately introduced error can lead to valid conclusions about the role of life events.

THE SCHEDULE OF RECENT LIFE EXPERIENCES

I have gone to some length to spell out these distinctions because I believe that they are at the heart of the problems that must be faced in arguing for a causal link between life events and illness.

I will illustrate this with the Schedule of Recent Experiences (SRE) developed by Holmes and Rahe (1967) and described in this book in the chapter by Holmes and Masuda. I have chosen the measure not least because the work has important accomplishments. Perhaps most impressive has been the use of the SRE in prospective research (Rahe, 1969) (Although not all work has been so successful; see Rahe, Gunderson, & Pugh, 1972). I leave to one side the troublesome issue of illness behavior—my points hold equally whether the dependent variable is the illness itself, or illness that has been perceived as worthy of taking to a treatment setting. Using either criterion, I do not believe the work has provided convincing evidence for a causal link between life events and illness.*

In their chapter Holmes and Masuda report that during the early developmental phase of the instrument an interview was used to assess the meaning of the events for the individual and, "As expected, the psychological significance and emotions varied widely with patient (p. 46)." This suggests that the investigators were discouraged by the wide range of meanings and emotions that could be associated with the same description. The descriptions used to rate degree of readjustment made necessary by the event are brief. A person simply "begins or stops work"; we do not know whether the change is forced or voluntary, whether due to the birth of a baby, a husband's antagonism, or winning money in the lottery, whether it means losing important ties or the need to make new ones, or whether the change is the first or had occurred many times before. Raters to some degree have to call on their own experience. Psychological significance and emotion are not avoided. Moreover, because the descriptions are so elliptic there is little control over the way experience is drawn upon. Variability of scores obtained for each life event is then conveniently lost by using the average of the dispersion. The high correlations usually obtained when comparing results from different calibration studies are irrelevant for this point (e.g., Masuda & Holmes, 1967; Komaroff, Masuda, & Holmes, 1968; Mendels & Weinstein, 1972); these high correlations are based on comparing *averages* and therefore again ignore the considerable variation in scores obtained for most items *within* each study.

I am not in principle against trying to obtain average scores. Sociologists by the nature of their discipline attempt to do just this, using an *average building block approach* to the analysis of meaning (Douglas, 1967, p. 238). I can see nothing wrong with this tradition. My criticism of the SRE is that it is far too vague in specifying the situation to be rated. The way in which each subject understands the brief account of each life event must vary; and we can have little

* I do not attempt a comprehensive review of other instruments: as far as I am aware other methods developed for use in the general population are open to the same broad objections (e.g., Myers et al., 1971; Paykel et al., 1971; Dohrenwend, 1970; Antonovsky & Kats, 1967). Most have been heavily influenced by the Holmes and Rahe schedule. Some research can be criticized on other grounds (see Brown et al., 1972a).

idea of how to interpret results which show associations between life-event scores and illness.

This vagueness is made worse in a mystifying way in the next stage of the work, when SRE questionnaires asking about the occurrence of the life events are filled out, and weights from the calibration study are then used to obtain a total life-change score for each respondent. ''Change in health in family member'' is, for instance, always given a score of 44. (This is relatively high: marital separation has a score of 65.) And yet items in the calibration study and the SRE items in the questionnaire are not always the same. To take one example, in the calibration study raters are asked to rate the severity of major changes in family health, but in the final questionnaire the word ''major'' is omitted. This is a startling discrepancy for it now leaves completely open just how the item is to be interpreted. Just *what* is a ''change in health'' and just *who* is a ''family member''? There is bound to be variability in interpretation; but the same score of 44 is given to anyone ticking the item. Instead of avoiding the issue of personal meaning the investigators have come full circle and have little control over the way meaning influences their scores.

Such an approach can lead to two kinds of error. The first is essentially random; since the investigator in his measurement procedure is not placing like with like the whole quality of research will suffer. This is a matter of sound data collection methods and one which I do not deal with directly in this essay.* I am concerned with the systematic biases that might well stem from the kind of procedures employed in the SRE.

To return to the argument, because of the open-endedness of the items there is a considerable risk that the illness, or factors involved in bringing it about, will influence the filling up of the SRE questionnaire. I have described this as direct and indirect contamination. It may work by raising or lowering the threshold of either (1) what is considered worthwhile to report, or (2) the range of persons borne in mind when reporting a particular event. Under certain circumstances a person may be more likely to report a trivial illness; or, leaving aside severity, one may be more likely to report illnesses occurring to a wider range of kin than he would usually consider in answering such a question.

One way contamination can occur concerns the *emergence* of meaning. The past, present, and future are not distinct in their influence on behavior. Past experience can influence the definition of the present, but inferences about the future can have a similar effect; perhaps most important, the present and the future can influence an understanding of past events—new meanings may emerge (McHugh, 1968). A well-known example is Freud's early conclusion about the effects of sexual trauma in infancy. It was some years before he realized that such experience had not occurred to his patients. The error was partly due to

* See Brown and Rutter, 1966; Rutter and Brown, 1966; and Brown et al., 1973a.

his reluctance to recognize childhood sexuality, but his patients provided him with the life events on which to base his trauma theory (Wollheim, 1971). Bartlett studied more common manifestations when he coined the phrase "effort after meaning." Such processes can also influence the reporting of central life experiences and play havoc with research efforts.

I have quoted a particular example before—but I think it is apt enough to bear repeating. Research published in 1958 by Stott which suggested the importance of psychosomatic factors in the production of mongoloid children is particularly interesting because subsequent findings concerning chromosomal abnormalities indicate that the conclusions were almost certainly wrong (Polani, Briggs, Ford, Clarke, & Berg, 1960). The mothers of mongoloid children not only reported more "shocks" during pregnancy (22% in mongoloid, 17% in nonmongoloid defectives, and 6% in the normal controls) but also stated that more of the shocks occurred in the early part of the pregnancy compared with the other two groups. The most likely explanation is that the mothers had been searching for reasons to explain their defective child and therefore recalled more "shocks" when interviewed; thus the accumulation of reported shocks in the *early* part of pregnancy for the mongoloid group (where they would be expected on scientific grounds) is due to some influence on the part of the investigator. We now know a good deal about the way in which expectations can be conveyed to subjects in experiments and the same process can certainly occur in interview situations.

Much of the research with the SRE is retrospective and because of the very general nature of its questions about events is particularly open to such direct contamination through, for example, "effort after meaning" on the part of the respondents. However, there have been a number of prospective studies; although direct contamination in these is no longer possible because of the nature of the questions, indirect contamination is unfortunately still likely. For example, it is possible that a high general level of anxiety leads *both* to illness and a greater tendency to report life events. It is well established that generally worded questionnaire items are particularly subject to response-sets (e.g., Berg, 1967). That is, items systematically pick up some characteristic of the respondent other than that which it is hoped to study. It is not at all far-fetched to suggest that in the use of the SRE, factors such as anxiety level influence reporting of events and illness experience (leaving aside the issue of illness behavior). Indeed, the items of the SRE are so general that it may well function as a measure of mood or personality.

We have already seen there is a third possible source of invalidity—spuriousness. Even if life-event scores are not subject to either type of contamination, conclusions may still be invalid because the *experience* of life events as stressful is influenced by a third factor such as anxiety, which also influences the rate of illness. Again because of the general nature of its questions, the SRE schedule is particularly open to this criticism.

A recent account of its use in a prospective study of 4463 naval personnel does nothing to allay suspicion about these possibilities. Life changes and anxiety both have small associations with subsequent illness (.07 and .15, respectively); but the correlation between anxiety and life events is a good deal greater (.32) (Rahe et al., 1972). There are several possible interpretations. Life events may be of causal significance and anxiety merely an intervening variable linking life event to illness. But equally life events may be causally irrelevant. A high life-change score may simply be the result of anxiety (this in turn might be due to an environmental factor such as job stress, which in fact had the largest association with illness, .20). Although it is not worth speculating on such possibilities without additional data, the results do underline the argument that the SRE has such serious flaws that it cannot provide a plausible case for a causal link between life events and illness.*

MEANING AND MEASUREMENT OF LIFE EVENTS

I believe the issue of meaning is at the root of all three sources of invalidity that I have discussed.† Let us consider an example from the past. Henry VIII's fifth wife committed adultery (or at least was sufficiently indiscreet to make it easy to appear that she had). The King, according to contemporary accounts, at the disclosure of Katheryn's blemish was "pierced with pensiveness" and moved to tears before the assembled Council. The French ambassador wrote in a letter to his own King: "The King has wonderfully felt the case of the Queen his wife and has certainly shown greater sorrows at her loss than at the faults, loss

* I have criticized the SRE largely on logical grounds. This I believe is sufficient; it is enough to make a case that contamination and spuriousness are likely. However, measures of concurrent validity (in the sense of agreement by independent respondents about the occurrence of life events) would be a relevant consideration. Reliability is not directly pertinent to the issues I have raised; high or low reliability is consistent with my argument, although low reliability seems more likely. Blair et al. (1972) report test-retest reliability for total scores over two 12-month periods of .61 and .52; and Casey et al. (1967) report correlations of .67, .64, and .74 for three 6-months recall periods. These figures may be too high since a correlation coefficient is not a suitable index of agreement if the life-change scores compared differ in overall means. Also, agreement about individual items is presented in terms of overall percentages (Figure 3 in Casey et al., 1967). This is unsatisfactory and misleading if items are relatively uncommon. For instance, if on both occasions 5% report an item, but with no one reporting the item on *both* occasions, overall agreement would still be 90%. Nevertheless, on the data provided differences about the overall score in the year before the first interview are apparently substantial.

† It seems almost reckless to offer a definition of such a complex term; but I believe Fried's definition (in a similar position) is sufficiently broad to serve as a starting point. He refers "to the subjective sense of the relationship between any given situation or experience and the individual's conscious and unconscious goals and objectives" (1965, p. 124).

or divorce of his preceding wives. It is like the case of the woman who cried more bitterly at the loss of her tenth husband than at the deaths of all the others together, though they had all been good men, but it was because she had never buried one of them before without being sure of the next; and as yet this King has formed neither a plan nor a preference.''

At this distance the interpretation rings true—and touches poignantly on the meaning of the news for the King. Perhaps for the first time one of his wives *had* been unfaithful. The ambassador relates the event to the King's plans and preferences (or rather in the present case his lack of them). McCall and Simmons (1966) remind us that until we have determined the identity and meaning of a thing *vis-à-vis our plans,* we have no bearings—we cannot proceed. An essential element of meaning therefore concerns a person's plans of action. I believe that this offers hope in our methodological dilemma. The ambassador's report rings true because he relates the incident to what he knew of the present and past *behavior* of the King and the way of life at his Court. It is unnecessary to see the measurement of meaning as inevitably tied to the respondent's account of feelings or his account of his reasons for feelings and actions. Clearly these are desirable—but if, as in our present case, they are suspect, a description of circumstance and behavior will enable us to make a reasonable estimate of the meaning of an event. I use the term reasonable in the sociologist's sense that the aggregate results of such a procedure when carried out for many individuals will approximate to the truth and be free of the kind of systematic bias that vitiates hope of explanatory enquiry.

It seems to me that Alfred Schutz takes a similar position to this when he writes of the use of commonsense experience of the world:

> ''But the world of everyday life is from the outset also a social cultural world in which I am inter-related in manifold ways of interaction with fellow-men known to me in varying degrees of intimacy and anonymity. To a certain extent, sufficient for many practical purposes, I understand their behaviour, if I understand their motives, goals, choices and plans originating in *their* biographically determined circumstances. Yet only in particular situations, and then only fragmentarily, can I experience the Others' motives, goals etc.—briefly, the subjective meaning they bestow upon their actions, in their uniqueness. I can, however, experience them in their typicality. In order to do so I construct typical patterns of actors' motives and ends, even of their attitudes and personalities, of which their actual conduct is just an instance or example'' (Schütz, 1971, p. 496).

Rather than a more conventional figure, I have quoted Schutz in support because his work is closely linked with various schools of ''phenomenological'' sociology that emerged in the 1960s. A good deal of this work can be construed as an attack on the position I take over the measurement of meaning. Criticism has surrounded the way researchers unthinkingly draw on a vast array of commonsense meanings and understandings to categorize social phenomena. But one can accept that many have been unduly complacent without going along with the view that, since meanings are never directly given by the situation or appearances, one cannot make general statements about situations.

I see the issue as a good deal less fundamental. It hinges on the point at which one is willing as an investigator to begin constructing "typical patterns of motives and ends." Schutz makes it clear that the investigator must build on knowledge of typical patterns created by individuals in their day-to-day life. The investigator, of course, cannot be in the subject's position in the same *practical* sense. Like the ambassador we must understand events by taking account of as much of the "biographically determined circumstances" as possible. Yet the constructs are by no means arbitrary. They can be checked in two ways: first by whether they make sense to individuals in the real world; and second, and most important, we can use the measures to check formulations derived from theory. It is by the successful exposure of ideas to empirical test that we can claim some validity for particular measures. However, such tests must be more than confirmation of simple hypotheses that life events correlate with illness. They should include tests of the measurement procedure itself (e.g., the convergent and discriminant validity discussed by Campbell and Fiske, 1959); and they should include the testing of derivations deduced from the theory (e.g., that it is a certain type of life event that is important for a particular condition). Both kinds of check are needed. For example, in the study by Stott the fact that "shocks" occurred in the early part of pregnancy for the mothers of mongoloid children, although making theoretical sense, is almost certainly due to some form of direct contamination. Bias, if not controlled, is likely to produce findings that are theoretically sensible. We have come therefore full circle. We can check theoretical derivations with confidence only if our results do not rest on contamination or faulty logic. How then is it possible to construct useful measures of life events that take account of biographical circumstances and yet are not open to the three sources of invalidity I have discussed?

THE LONDON STUDIES OF SCHIZOPHRENIA AND DEPRESSION

In 1965 my colleagues and I attempted a very radical solution. In our work on the role of life events in the onset of acute schizophrenic conditions we attempted to define life events and obtain reports about them without relying on what the respondent said about his reaction to or experience of the event. We also strictly controlled what the investigator could include as a life event (Brown & Birley, 1968). The approach controls contamination by both the respondent and the interviewer and in this way attempts to combat all three sources of invalidity. We avoid any attempt to obtain reports of stressful events as such. Instead we define classes of event which on commonsense grounds are more likely than most to produce marked emotional arousal. We were much influenced by Basowitz and his colleagues, who noted:

". . . any stimulus may in principle arouse an anxiety response because of the particular meaning of threat it may have acquired for the particular individual. However, we distinguish a class of stimuli which are more likely to produce disturbance in most individuals. The term stress has been applied to this class of conditions. Thus we can conceive a continuum of stimuli differing in meaning to the organism and in their anxiety-producing consequences. At one end are such stimuli or cues, often highly symbolic, which have meaning only to single or limited numbers of persons and which to the observer may appear as innocuous or trivial. At the other end are such stimuli, here called stress, which by their explicit threat to vital functioning and their intensity are likely to overload the capacity of most organisms' coping mechanisms.

". . . Ultimately we can truly speak of a stress situation only when a given response occurs, but for schematic purposes as well as consistency with common usage, we may use the term stress to designate certain kinds of stimulating conditions without regard for response. Such stimuli are called stress because of their assumed or potential effect, although we well know that in any given case the organisms' adaptive capacity, threshold, or previous learning may preclude any disturbance of behavior" (Basowitz et al., 1955, p. 7).

Following through this notion means that life events which seem likely to be innocuous to most people are automatically excluded, although they might be markedly disturbing to a few for idiosyncratic reasons. We avoid the sources of contamination outlined in relation to the SRE by defining before any of the main interviews are carried out (1) the classes of event and (2) the person to be covered. That is, only standard questions about the occurrence of certain events to certain categories of individuals are asked and questions about reaction to events are avoided. We set out to establish whether phenomena had occurred quite irrespective of how the person felt about them.

Although in most instances the exact details of events to be included were well defined for the interviewer before the main study began, for a few classes of event we could not avoid taking account of features that could not be specified in advance. For example, one man after his regular job played in a small musical group several evenings a week; the unexpected news that their manager had settled a contract involving a considerably increased income was included as an event. It would have been quite impossible to list before the study began the full details of such events. (I emphasize again that our inclusion of the event did not depend on the subject's reported reaction to it.)

Luckily, this is rare. Almost all events included in the schizophrenic study were in fact defined in detail before data collection began.

In this way we established the causal importance of life events in the onset of schizophrenic attacks; * also, I believe, we went some way to meet the sources of invalidity involved in open-ended questioning approaches to the measurement of stressful experience. In essence it is not up to the individual to decide *what* event or *what* person to include; possible influence from the investigator is similarly controlled by detailed instructions about rating set out before data collection begins. This obviously helps to control direct contamination; and since actual experience of the event is ignored, we can hope to rule out the possibility that some unknown factor is influencing both onset and the reporting or experience of events (i.e., to rule out indirect contamination and spuriousness). But there is a cost: A very wide range of events are treated alike and in effect given the same weight. At this stage of our research it was obvious that if work was to progress, we had to do more about incorporating some notion of personal meaning into the measurement of events. In work on depression begun in 1967 we attempt to do just this.†

Research has kept to the same overall design. Patients are seen, onset is dated, and events occurring before onset are dated and described. A random sample from the general population provides comparison material about the expected rate of events. Life events are asked about and recorded in the same way as in the schizophrenic project. However, the approach then changes. Once events have been established the interviewer covers in as freely flowing a way as possible a lengthy list of enquiries about the circumstances surrounding each event. She asks in detail about what led up to and what followed the event, and the feelings and attitudes surrounding the event and the associated circumstances. We are now interested not only in what happened but the meaning of what had happened for the subject—in the sense of the social implications and the thoughts and feelings she had before the event, at the time, and since. The questioning is standardized only in the sense that there is a list of fairly detailed topics to be covered. For example, we question about worry before the event itself occurred; the following probes are suggested: After you knew it was going to happen, but before it happened, did you worry at all? What about? When did you start? How much did you worry? Did you talk it over with anyone? When? Did it affect your sleep? Did it make you restless, want to smoke a lot? The interviewer encourages the subject to talk spontaneously and in the light of the picture that emerges questions may be omitted and others added as she thinks fit.

* See Brown and Birley (1968) and Birley and Brown (1970) for substantive findings.

† Brown, Sklair, Harris, and Birley (1973) give a general account of methods and some preliminary results; Brown, Harris, and Peto (1973) deal with the kind of causality involved in the link between life events in schizophrenia and depression.

The interview is tape recorded and the interviewer completes 30 rating scales dealing with *each* event. There are three main areas: (1) prior experience and preparation; (2) immediate reaction; and (3) the consequences and implications of the event. Although the scales are designed to take account of any relevant experience or plans, most emphasis is placed on obtaining a full account of the current situation. It is the interviewer who carries out the actual job of measurement. For example, two of the scales concern the length of two types of warning of the event. A *specific warning* is defined by cues which predicted its definite occurrence regardless of whether this allows the timing of it to be anticipated by the person. A *general warning* is one that gives the person some idea that the event will occur, without definitely predicting its occurrence. In rating the scales the investigator should not be content with vague statements but go on to seek supporting evidence—that the subject's son had *said* he was considering emigrating and so on.

Material is not necessarily obtained in response to set questions; much is brought up spontaneously in general talk about what happened. It is then filtered in various ways. The interviewer has established categories to work with. She knows, for instance, that to rate the presence of a specific warning, the timing of the event does not have to be known by the subject, only its definite occurrence at some time. Where the reverse is true (e.g., for someone waiting to hear an examination result) a general and not specific warning is rated. Now these are theoretical categories in the sense that they order everyday experience in a way that, we believe, will prove useful for understanding how people deal with new situations. The categories may go beyond the kind of distinction made by the subject himself. It is possible that we may rate a general warning where he did not see one; and we may, of course, find that our distinction between general and specific warnings is of no significance in understanding how people prepare for life changes and crises. But since the ratings are based on the subject's account there is no obvious reason why they should not prove of some relevance for our inquiry.

We decided to make some allowance for misreporting on the subject's part insofar as this could be sensed by the interviewer. One patient, for example, answered to a direct question that her father's death had been completely unexpected and yet earlier in the interview had spontaneously described the doctor's warning about her father's likely death. Such discrepancies seemed more likely in accounts of feelings than descriptions of what actually happened and of circumstances surrounding the event. However, in practice the interviewer so rarely was able to sense them that we gave up making a separate set of ratings to deal with them.*

* There is also high degree of agreement between ratings based on the independent reports of a patient and a close relative interviewed separately by different interviewers. Relatives mentioned few events in the 12 months not reported by the patient (10% of the total) and there was an overall

CONTEXTUAL MEASURES OF THREAT

When I discussed the Ambassador's letter I argued that it is important to consider the configuration of factors surrounding a life event. The 30 additional ratings made for each event in the depressive study are designed to do just this. In developing them we started with the general notion that we should look for the reasons for different responses to life changes not so much in the meaning that is given by men and women, young and old, low- and middle-class, and so on, to an event as such, but in the particular circumstances surrounding it; and we should then go on to correlate social positions such as class status with these circumstances. Perhaps it is not so much that two women react with different meaning in the sense of emotions and understanding to, say, the fact that they have been told their husband has inoperable cancer; both may react with equal amounts of distress and be equally aware of the consequences. But it may be critical to know that one has no close tie other than her husband, has no security of tenure on her house, and was for a long period led to believe the symptoms were of minor significance, whereas the other has had the reverse experiences. In this sense we can talk of *contextual* meaning, which takes account of the biographical circumstances surrounding an event but, for the methodological reasons I have outlined, excluded consideration of the person's reaction to it.

Although most of the additional descriptive scales place no reliance on the subject's account of his reactions, we can still be accused of opening ourselves to some form of measurement contamination since the interviewer is aware of *all* the interview material when making ratings. We have therefore developed special ratings of threat, which exclude any consideration of the person's account of his reaction to the event. Following my argument about biographical circumstances surrounding events, we call these *contextual* measures of threat and it is on them that we have placed most weight in our analysis. We hope in this way to retain an important element of meaning while ignoring the actual self-report of threat and unpleasantness.

The contextual contrasts with the self-reported measures of threat. Four measures in all are involved, since contextual and self-reported threat are each rated on two scales according to the time perspective involved. The consequences of events such as unexpectedly having to deliver a neighbor's baby at night are usually largely resolved within a week. Others such as discovery of a

agreement of 76%. For marked and moderately threatening events (those important in the onset of depression) agreement is 92%. The amount of agreement about various scales describing the *same* event ranges from .74 for degree of threat said to have been experienced by the patient, .89 for the expectancy of the event occurring at the time it did, to almost total agreement for measures dealing with more objective aspects such as amount of change it involved in routine and face-to-face contact with others. (See Brown, Sklair, et al., 1973, for a fuller discussion.)

daughter's thefts at home have longer term implications. *Short-term* threat is that implied on the day it occurred and *long-term* threat is that implied by the event about one week after its occurrence. This, as will be seen, turned out to be a critical distinction.

There are therefore four ratings of threat for each event, as indicated in Figure 4. Each is rated on a 4-point scale of "marked," "moderate," "some," and "little or no" threat. The category *severe* used in this chapter contains all marked events and moderate events which were focused on the subject.

The contextual ratings are made by the interviewer reading to other members of the research team (usually four) an account of the event and its surrounding circumstances but leaving out any mention of the person's reaction. It should be emphasized that this account was based on the extensive material collected to rate the 30 descriptive scales. The interviewer's description is then rated independently by all who are present in terms of how threatening the event would be to most people.

The interviewers had three aids in rating the contextual scales:

1. There was a series of anchoring examples to illustrate the four points on each scale.

2. Although ratings were made independently, they were followed by a discussion about any discrepancy, and a final rating was agreed upon. Interrater agreement was high, and these discussions undoubtedly helped to establish and maintain this.

3. Fairly standard ratings were applied to events such as death and childbirth. These were not subtle, and we usually required quite major events to change a standard rating. For example, we had a convention that childbirths were not rated high on long-term threat unless they occurred in markedly overcrowded or otherwise poor housing or in an obviously difficult social situation (for instance, to a woman who had not long separated from her husband or was unmarried). All deaths of close relatives were rated on the highest scale

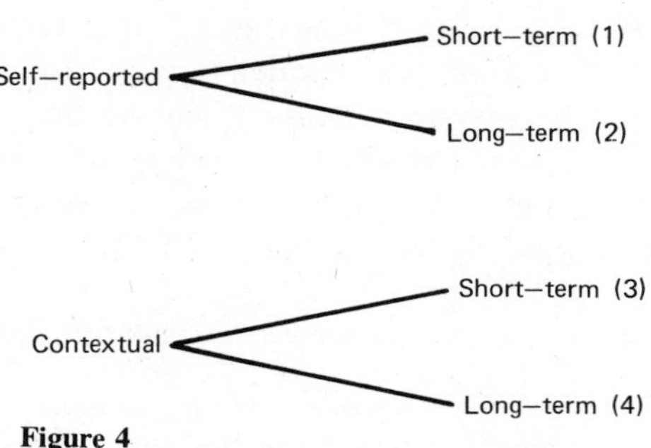

Figure 4

point (except for one mother who was 80 and who lived in South America and who had not been seen for 20 years).

To convey some of the quality of the ratings I have selected at *random* 5 of the 70 patients with severe events and given brief descriptions of each severe event in an appendix.

The contextual measures of threat are therefore made in three stages. First, the event is obtained by a method which ignores the respondent's judgment of its impact on her (as in the schizophrenic study). Second, the interviewer goes on to collect extensive background material about it. Third, a rating of threat is made by persons not involved in the interview taking into account circumstances surrounding the event but without information about the subject's reaction. It is based on how the rater thinks most people would be expected to react in the circumstances. Since self-reports and definition of threat and unpleasantness are controlled both at the stage of establishing the occurrence of the event itself and also at the stage of rating threat, we believe we reduce both the risk of contamination and of arriving at invalid conclusions because of the effect of unknown third factors (i.e., spuriousness). Since most of my discussion concerns the rating of *contextual threat,* if I talk of threat without further elaboration I will be referring to this scale.

A random sample of 220 women from the same local population as the 114 patients provided comparison data about the rate of events. Long-term, severely threatening events were uncommon among ordinary women. Of the women in the general population 21% had at least one severe long-term threat event in a nine-month period. This contrasted with 61% of patients who had at least one in a nine-month period before onset. The distinction between short- and long-term threat is crucial. It is only severe long-term threat events that play a role in onset of depression. Although severe short-term threat events occur twice as often, when long-term threat is controlled, they show no association at all with onset.

Therefore in spite of an element of crudeness, the contextual scales are highly successful. We estimate that at least half of the patients had a severe long-term threat event of etiological importance.* It is therefore important to ask how these scales relate to the self-reported threat scales and the many other descriptive measures. The answer is clear-cut and, at first, perhaps puzzling. Other scales add nothing to our ability to ''predict'' depression. I should add that the additional descriptive scales had taken several years to prepare and we had some reason to believe in their validity. I will first deal with the self-reported threat scales.

There was in fact a good deal of agreement between the self-reported and

* The figure is 48%. It is a corrected percentage allowing for chance association of a severe event and onset (see Brown, Harris, & Peto, 1973, for the correction formula).

contextual measures of threat for both patients and general population. Results for long-term threat are presented in Table 1. Agreement is somewhat lower for the patients than for the general population; agreement coefficients, taking account of chance association, are 68 and 85%, respectively.*

Using the self-report measures of long-term threat does not, in fact, provide a greater level of association between events and onset of depression; the result is almost the same as for the contextual measure. The use of the self-reported scale *in addition* to the contextual one improves the association only to a negligible extent. (The percentage with a severe event of causal importance

Table 1

	Patient (%)		General Population (%)	
Severe on both	34	(114)	14	(76)
Severe self-report only	8	(26)	2	(13)
Severe contextual only	5	(16)	2	(8)
Nonsevere on both	53	(176)	82	(429)
	100	(332)	100	(526)

increases from 48 to 54%.) We therefore arrive at a surprising conclusion: taking account of the self-report measures of threat does not add to our power to "predict" depression.

Equally notable is the failure of the other 26 descriptive scales to increase the association between events and onset. What seems to have happened is that the intuitive contextual assessment of long-term threat coincides with a factor of critical etiological importance, experience of loss. We use this term in a broad sense to include: (1) separation or threat of it, such as death of a parent or a husband saying he is going to leave home; (2) an unpleasant revelation about someone close, forcing a major reassessment of the person and the relationship,

* Patients are more likely than women in the general population to report severe threat when the contextual rating is less (8 compared with 2%). However, reading through the interview protocols does not suggest any tendency to exaggerate on the part of patients; the result appears to be almost entirely explained (1) by the raters being somewhat more cautious in rating severe threat for patients, and (2) by the fact that for several women where the depression followed the event within a few days the illness itself seems to have been the reason for the high rating on self-reported threat. One woman, for example, reported great distress and unhappiness that her second child was not a girl; but she also become very depressed and disturbed within a few days of the birth. There is little doubt that she did experience these feelings about the child but there was no reason for the contextual scale to be rated severe. Such instances were, however, comparatively rare. Another result confirms that patients had no particular tendency to exaggerate the threat experienced from the events: there is a high agreement between what the patient's self-report and what a relative quite independently described the patient felt. (Agreement is 71% when corrected for chance association.)

such as finding out about a husband's unfaithfulness; (3) a life-threatening illness to someone close; (4) a major material loss or disappointment or threat of this, such as a couple living in poor housing learning that their chances of being rehoused were minimal; (5) an enforced change of residence or the threat of it; and finally (6) a miscellaneous group of crises involving some element of loss, such as being made redundant in a job held for some time, or obtaining a legal separation. Of those patients with a severe event 77% had at least one of these forms of loss; and loss is therefore much the most important component of long-term threat.*

Our long-term contextual threat scale accounts for the relevant variance in the other descriptive scales—at least as far as understanding the onset of depression is concerned. It is not that these additional scales do not relate to onset of depression; the majority are correlated. However, none show an association when long-term threat is controlled. For example, the rate of totally unexpected life events is almost 50% more in the patient group than the general population; but there is no difference at all within the various severity categories of long-term threat.

I will discuss just three of the issues these results raise.

1. Does the fact that the self-reports add so little to contextual ratings of threat suggest that the SRE is valid? The result is not incompatible with the argument I have made against "open-ended" measures of life events. The contextual and self-report measures of threat in the London study are based on measuring procedures different from the SRE ratings. The argument need not be repeated. It does not follow therefore that SRE measures would agree at all closely with more "objective" measures. Second, the question suggests a basic misunderstanding of the argument. It is not that such open-ended measures are necessarily invalid—simply that it is at present difficult to believe they are not. In any case the need for valid measurement is partly political. There is a widespread reluctance among the medical profession to take seriously the case that life events play an important etiological role in psychiatric or physical illness. This is perhaps understandable given their training and professional interests. In such a situation valid measurement may serve as much to refute criticism as to increase the actual association between life events and illness. Methodological demands are bound to be greatest in areas of research that threaten vested professional, scientific, or political interests.

* Such loss rarely or never occurs among events rated severe only on *short-term* threat. Of these events half involved an illness or accident whose threatening implications had largely cleared up within a week; a further 11% concerned some contact with police or courts, 11% births, 7% witness of an accident away from home, and a few incidents such as witnessing an acquaintance getting hurt in a fight in a pub or during a weekend spent staying with a friend and her husband, being told by the friend that she planned to leave her husband.

2. *Does it matter that ratings of long-term threat parallel so closely the fact of loss?* I do not think that this indicates bias. It surely means no more than that our intuitive ideas about long-term threat coincide with the fact of loss in its various forms. Perhaps all that is surprising is that we did not fully realize this until we began to analyze our material.

It is possible that any useful conception of long-term threat will involve instances of loss or disappointment—at least in an industrialized urban population. It just happens to be these events that play a major role in the onset of depressive disorder (but not in schizophrenia; see Brown, Sklair, et al., 1973). It is possible to imagine other times and places where long-term threatening events have a somewhat different basis, perhaps reflecting more often the quality of threat involved in what happened when one of our patients was seriously attacked in the street in which she lived (a rare event in London). Whether *such* severe events would play a role in the onset of depressive disorder is, of course, another matter. At present our substantive findings concerning life events and depression remain time and culture bound.*

3. *Are simpler measures of life events possible?* The contextual measures of threat used in the London depression project are complex and we have found it easy to make mistakes when thinking about the material. For example, we have carried out a good deal of analysis on the issue of the additivity of stress phenomena. Can event and event, or event and ongoing difficulty, add in some manner to make onset of depression more likely? (I will not describe our measurement of *difficulties* which concern phenomena such as overcrowding and chronic ill health. They are defined in such a way that none stem from long-term, severely threatening life events in the year of study. We have shown that marked difficulties can independently lead to depression as long as they have lasted more than two years.) Additivity in the year before onset may involve the following:

1. Events that are not severe. Can many minor events add to bring about depression on their own?
2. Can more than one severe event increase the chance of depression beyond the probability associated with just one severe event?
3. Do marked difficulties increase the chance of a severe event leading to onset?

Additivity itself can take two forms. First, it may simply involve adding the independent probabilities of separate factors influencing onset. Thus far we have found little evidence of this. Minor events, however frequent, do not on their own appear to be capable of producing depression. Moreover, the chance

* But they are not treatment bound. Our findings have been almost exactly duplicated on a series of women with untreated affective disorders in the general community.

of depression occurring is largely accounted for by *one* severe event. Multiple severe events increase only slightly the probability of depression. Second, additivity may involve genuine interaction. The occurrence of factor *A* may increase the chance of depression following factor *B* in excess of the sum of their independent probabilities of leading to onset. We have evidence that a severe event and a marked difficulty when occurring together do increase the chances of depression in proportion to the addition of their independent probabilities of producing depression, but there is so far little convincing evidence that they *interact;* that a marked difficulty increases the chance of a severe event leading to onset over and above their joint probability.

We believe these general conclusions are broadly valid, but it has proved surprisingly easy to forget the constraints provided by our methods of measurement. For example, we may forget that the rating of long-term contextual threat takes into account any obviously relevant background difficulties. Birth of a baby is rated severe only on long-term contextual threat in the setting of bad housing and the like. Under these circumstances we must be cautious about concluding that event and difficulty do not interact. How can event and difficulty interact if the difficulty has been taken account of in the measurement of event? It has proved particularly easy to fall into such error in pursuing more complex theoretical arguments.

To some extent we are prisoners of our measurement procedures. For tackling certain problems it would be good to have simpler measures of events. But how reasonable is it to try to ignore contextual factors? For events such as birth and death it is certainly possible to use the event as such as a basis for classification and later cross-tabulate with factors such as overcrowding, marital happiness, and loneliness. However, it is extraordinarily difficult to do this if the broad sweep of life events is taken. They vary so widely that where one basic unit ends and another begins is continually open to question. Should a brother leaving home to get married be placed with the classification of a daughter leaving home? Does it matter that there are other brothers and daughters at home? These practical problems of creating a simple basic classification are so great that I have come to doubt whether a simple *general* measure is possible. At any rate, our approach at present is to try to develop a greater awareness of the nature of our contextual threat measures rather than to simplify them.

FINAL THOUGHTS

It is time to sum up. There is little doubt that the existence of a causal link between life events and illness makes theoretical sense only when considered in terms of the meaning of life events for particular individuals. But this does not mean that we naively accept the respondent's account—either in answer to general questions or in terms of a structured questionnaire.

The issue of error is central. In this chapter I have left to one side a general discussion and concentrated on one form—the likelihood of certain measuring procedures leading to systematic error. This turns on whether the life event is contaminated or influenced by possible third factors linking both illness and event. I have discussed this in terms of three possible sources of invalidity which can lead to totally erroneous conclusions about etiology. It is the meaningful element of the life event that is the central element of all three kinds of invalidity. In direct contamination, for instance, the respondent may report more disturbing life events to make sense of his illness; in indirect contamination, anxiety of the person or some other such trait may lead both to a greater reporting of life events and to subsequent illness. And in spuriousness the account of life events may be accurate, but the association of events with illness may be due to another factor such as general anxiety, which leads both to a greater tendency to experience distress in response to life events and also a greater illness rate. It is therefore not necessarily a matter of whether the person actually experienced what he reports. Totally accurate accounts can still lead to invalid conclusions. The anxious person may not only report more life events, but his account of distress in regard to them may be quite accurate. But this would still hopelessly confound our measures and make conclusions about causal processes unconvincing. We are faced in the measurement of life events with controlling meaning—something that is an essential component of the phenomena we wish to measure.

This paradox cannot be met by ignoring it, as I believe most have done in studying life events and illness. Nor is the radical step taken in the London schizophrenic study likely to have general applicability. Here the effect of personal meaning was controlled, but at the cost of treating all events as alike. I have discussed the general outline of the solution developed in the London depressive study building on the schizophrenic study. It is present, at least by implication, in much sociological writing; for instance, in Weber's discussion of motivational understanding (*erklärendes Verstehen*). It lies essentially in the convention of dealing with the meaningfulness of events in commonsense terms. Given knowledge of behavior, experiences, and circumstances, how would it be reasonable to expect an individual to react? In this way we developed contextual measures of threat based on wide knowledge of everything surrounding the event as such but excluding any knowledge of the person's account of his feelings and reaction to it. Interpretation and classification can only approximate to what actually happens, and there will be error. But it is a certain kind of error. First, it avoids the risk of invalidity that must be present when personal meaning is allowed full play. Second, resulting estimates of the role of life events are bound to be conservative, since events that proved stressful for idiosyncratic reasons will be missed.

This approach can, on brief acquaintance, be equated with some form of crude positivism. This would be wrong. Meaning is not ignored; it is dealt with in a certain way. The hope is that the contextual ratings of threat, although not taking account of a person's feelings and reactions, will approximate to them. There is reason to believe we managed to do this. Of course in rating events interviewers must depend greatly on their experience in the same society, if not subculture, as the respondent. In this sense raters are not really trained to rate threat on the contextual scales—it is probably more accurate to say that they largely learn to discipline their intuitive assessment. My criticism of the SRE approach is not that it uses commonsense judgments, but that they are used too timidly, too inconsistently, and with too little regard to the full social and personal context of the life event.

The approach in the London depression study assumes that detailed knowledge of the particular biographical circumstances of a life event for a person are needed, and that self-reports of feelings can be ignored. Justification for the approach in the end, I believe, can only come from forging links between analysis and theory. We have found, for example, there is no causal link between depression and events severe only on short-term threat. And yet short- and long-term threat are similar in conception and methods of measurement. The sole difference is that the long-term rating is based on consideration of the event's implications one week rather than one day after it occurred. The clear-cut result does make theoretical sense in terms of the nature of depression—and is difficult to square with the notion that the association is due to some measuring artifact. If this were so, why should results differ so dramatically when the straightforward distinction is made between perspective on the day of the event and that one week later? Why should bias be restricted to just one of the two measures? Of course, the plausibility of our findings rests on far more than this particular argument, but it is an example of the kind of support to be found in theoretical considerations.

I have, in fact, not attempted to support my case for the use of contextual meaning with much more than a general argument, but we have already a good deal of evidence in its favor. For example, events associated with pregnancy or birth are related to the onset of depression only if they are also defined as severely threatening on the contextual threat measure. Patients had 4.4 births per 100 rated nonsevere on long-term threat, and the normal women had 4.9; but patients had 5.3 births per 100 rated severe with none among normal women ($p < .05$). It is only birth directly tied up with a major social problem that leads to depression. Leaving aside the substantive issue, such results indicate how much would be lost if events were not weighted in terms of the particular biographical context in which they occurred.

Here the argument devolves into a number of practical issues. Is it subject or interviewer who *does* the measurement? I have no doubt that it must be the interviewer, although this may add greatly to the cost of our research (or in the short-term appear to do so). Measurement carried out by the interviewer not only allows much greater control over sources of error (e.g., the procedure for rating contextual threat is possible only in this way), it greatly increases flexibility in data collection. If this is accepted, we must settle at what point in the collection of material about the biographical circumstances of the person do we impose commonsense judgments of contextual threat and the like? The SRE approach chooses to do this very early (e.g., by providing little content for rating life events in the calibration study); the London study does it much later. But is has to be done at some stage. Just how much material should be collected is best settled by experience. In one sense we can never be said to have enough. It is a matter of establishing how much must be collected to make our analysis reasonably convincing. There is here another practical issue. It is unreasonable to expect to cram into the event rating all the contextual material. We have evidence, for example, that the existence of alternative sources of social support are important for understanding whether or not a woman will go on to develop depression after a major loss. But such material seems best dealt with independently of the contextual threat rating, and its role is best explored in analysis. The life-event measure itself should not be asked to do too much. Just how much is again a practical matter. It is clear that very many kinds of contextual phenomena help to determine the significance of events. There are so many that it does not seem to me to be practical merely to classify the formal characteristics of the event *as such* (e.g., birth, change of house) and later take account of the myriad other possible factors by some form of statistical analysis. We must rely on human judgment to make this synthesis. Just how much of the biographical material should be kept apart in making such ratings is something I suggest is best left to emerge from the research process itself.

I have argued therefore that studies that link life events and illness and are based on the SRE or derivations of it are unconvincing because of basic theoretical and measurement problems. Nor do I think the approach can be improved without fundamental changes. I have described an alternative approach developed in the London schizophrenic and depressive studies. If I were to sum up my theme, it is that it is unwise to neglect the detailed study of the biographical context of life events: the measurement of a person's environment using commonsense judgments of investigators. The personal, self-reported meanings associated with events may well be subject to distorted reporting and radical changes in time—and if not, the meaning element can still confound causal analysis even if measurement is accurate. It seems therefore foolhardy in the measurement of life stress to neglect the fact that behavior and circumstances can be reasonably accurately described. Since such descriptions are still open to marked bias unless great effort is taken, there is still plenty to challenge us. But my reasons are not simply methodological. I believe that a contextual approach is far more flexible and more able to deal with a much wider range of phenomena. In short, it is likely to prove theoretically more rewarding.

APPENDIX: BRIEF DESCRIPTIONS OF LIFE EVENTS RATED SEVERE ON THE LONG-TERM CONTEXTUAL MEASURE OF THREAT FOR FIVE RANDOMLY SELECTED PATIENTS

	Weeks Event Occurred before Onset	Description	Degree of Contextual Threat
Case 1	27	In overcrowded and very poor housing; three children. Old acquaintance told patient's husband that he could get them a flat (and also a job for her husband). They had been planning for the move (i.e., did not go on holiday) but found out nothing in it.	Marked
	23	Second baby born.	Marked
	21	A woman came round from the Council about their application for rehousing; said they would not get a house for 10 years unless they went to a new town.	Marked
	1	Landlady left letter giving two weeks notice "for personal reasons"; no warning.	Marked
Case 2	32	Aunt (did not have father and this aunt looked after patient and mother in childhood) in very bad condition in hospital. Patient had not realized she was so ill—blind and paralyzed.	Moderate
	9	Disappointment over housing; very overcrowded: eight people three rooms. On housing list. Despite letter from doctor about daughter's tuberculosis, "housing man" told them could not move for three years.	Moderate
	1	Realized husband had slept with her friend; husband did not admit it but she said she saw guilt on their faces and they did not deny it (confirmed later). Told him to go.	Marked
Case 3	(29)	(Mother-in-law [living in household and confidant] in hospital for 5/52.)	(Not rated severe)
	21	Mother-in-law died; had been very ill since discharge from hospital.	Marked

REFERENCES

Antonovsky, A., & Kats, R. The life crisis history. *Journal of Health and Social Behavior,* 1967, **8,** 15–21.

Bartlett, F. C. *Remembering: A Study of Experimental and Social Psychology.* Oxford: Cambridge University Press, 1932.

Basowitz, H., Persky, H., Korchin, S. J., & Grinker, R. R. *Anxiety and Stress.* New York: McGraw-Hill Book Company, 1955.

	Weeks Event Occurred before Onset	Description	Degree of Contextual Threat
	16	Patient and husband received letter from solicitor saying that if they did not pay the increased rent they would receive notice of eviction (landlord had put rent up after mother-in-law died).	Moderate
	2	Son unexpectedly announced he was going to emigrate to Canada.	Moderate
Case 4	44	Patient about 60 and married. Youngest sister admitted to hospital with stroke and died. Patient saw her every month or so.	Marked
	32	Brother died—ill four weeks, hemorrhaged, then died; patient saw him every few weeks.	Marked
	7	Second elder sister had stroke—lost use of leg. Would not go into hospital while looking after other sister with cancer. Patient saw her every month or so.	Marked
Case 5	41	Left husband, taking daughter with her. Husband going with other woman. Financial difficulties—friends looked after her daughter.	Marked
	38	Back to husband.	Moderate
	29	Left husband for second time: found herself a room—left baby with friends.	Marked
	27	Fostered her child because she could not manage while working nights (a nurse).	Marked
	26	Went to solicitor about a separation.	Marked
	17	Court for legal separation. Husband friendly—said she should not have done it.	Moderate
	(17)	(Started new job—moved house.)	(Not rated severe)
	(3)	(Husband tried to get maintenance reduced; S went to Court to give information about earnings, etc.)	(Not rated severe)

Berg, I. A. (Ed.) *Response Set in Personality Assessment*. Chicago: Aldine Press, 1967.

Birley, J. L. T., & Brown, G. W. Crises and life changes preceding the onset or relapse of acute schizophrenia: Clinical aspects. *British Journal of Psychiatry*, 1970, **116,** 327–333.

Brown, G. W., & Birley, J. L. T. Crises and life changes and the onset of schizophrenia. *Journal of Health and Social Behavior*, 1968, **9,** 203–214.

Brown, G. W., & Rutter, M. The measurement of family activities and relationships: A methodological study. *Human Relations*, 1966, **19,** 241.

Brown, G. W., Sklair, F., Harris, T. O., & Birley, J. L. T. Life-events and psychiatric disorders. Part 1: Some methodological issues. *Psychological Medicine,* 1973, **3,** 74–87. (a)

Brown, G. W., Harris, T. O., & Peto, J. Life-events and psychiatric disorders. Part 2: Nature of causal link. *Psychological Medicine,* 1973, **3.** (b)

Campbell, D. T., & Fiske, D. W. Convergent and discriminant validation by the multitrait-multimethod matrix. *Psychological Bulletin,* 1959, **56,** 81–105.

Casey, R. L., Masuda, M., & Holmes, T. H. Quantitative study of recall of life events. *Journal of Psychosomatic Research,* 1967, **11,** 239–247.

Dohrenwend, B. S. Social class and stressful events. In E. H. Hare & J. K. Wing (Eds.), *Psychiatric Epidemiology.* London: Oxford University Press, 1970, Chapter 9.

Douglas, J. D. *The Social Meanings of Suicide.* Princeton, N.J.: Princeton University Press, 1967.

Fried, M. A. Transitional functions of working-class communities: Implications for forced relocation. In Mildred B. Kantor (Ed.), *Mobility and Mental Health.* Springfield, Ill.: Charles C. Thomas, 1965. Pp. 123–165.

Holmes, T. H., & Rahe, R. H. The social readjustment rating scale. *Journal of Psychosomatic Research,* 1967, **11,** 213–218.

Kamaroff, A. L., Masuda, M., & Holmes, T. H. The social readjustment rating scale: A comparative study of Negro, Mexican, and White Americans. *Journal of Psychosomatic Research,* 1968, **12,** 121–128.

Masuda, M., & Holmes, T. H. The social readjustment rating scale: A cross-cultural study of Japanese and Americans. *Journal of Psychosomatic Research,* 1967, **11,** 227–237.

McCall, G. J., & Simmons, J. L. *Identities and Interactions.* New York: The Free Press; London: Collier-Macmillan, 1966.

McDonald, B. W., Pugh, W. M., Gunderson, E. K. E., & Rahe, R. H. Reliability of life change cluster scores. *British Journal of Social and Clinical Psychology,* 1972, **11,** 407–409.

McHugh, P. *Defining the Situation. The Organization of Meaning in Social Interaction.* Indianapolis and New York: The Bobbs-Merrill Co., 1968.

Mendels, J., & Weinstein, N. The schedule of recent experiences: A reliability study. *Psychosomatic Medicine,* 1972, **34,** 527–531.

Myers, J. K., Lindenthal, J. J., & Pepper, M. P. Life events and psychiatric impairment. *The Journal of Nervous and Mental Disease,* 1971, **152,** 149–157.

Paykel, E. J., Myers, J. K., Dienelt, M. N., Klerman, C. L., Lindenthal, J. J., & Pepper, M. P. Life events and depression: A controlled study. *Archives of General Psychiatry,* 1969, **21,** 753–60.

Polani, P. E., Briggs, J. N., Ford, C. E., Clarke, C. M., & Berg, J. M. A mongol girl with 46 chromosomes. *Lancet,* 1960, **1,** 721–724.

Paykel, E. S., Prusoff, B. A., & Uhlenhuth, E. H. Scaling of life events. *Archives of General Psychiatry,* 1971, **25,** 340–347.

Rahe, R. H. Life crisis and health change. In P. R. A. May & J. R. Wittenborn, *Psychotropic Drug Response: Advances in Prediction.* Springfield, Ill.: Charles C Thomas, 1969.

Rahe, R. H., Gunderson, E. K. E., & Pugh, W. M. Illness prediction studies. *Archives of Environmental Health,* 1972, **25,** 192–197.

Rutter, M., & Brown, G. W. The reliability and validity of measures of family life and relationships in families containing a psychiatric patient. *Social Psychiatry,* 1966, **1,** 38.

Schutz, A. In Kenneth Thompson & Jeremy Tunstall (Eds.), *Sociological Perspectives.* Baltimore, Md.: Penguin Books. Part 5, p. 38.

Stott, D. H. Some psychosomatic aspects of casualty in reproduction. *Journal of Psychosomatic Research,* 1958, **3,** 42–55.

Wollheim, R. *Freud.* London: Fontana, Wm. Collins Sons & Co., 1971.

CHAPTER 15

Conceptual and Methodological Problems in the Study of Resistance Resources and Stressful Life Events

AARON ANTONOVSKY

All our lives long, every day and every hour, we are engaged in the process of accommodating our changed and unchanged selves to changed and unchanged surroundings; living, in fact, is nothing else than this process of accommodation; when we fail in it a little we are stupid, when we fail flagrantly we are mad, when we suspend it temporarily we sleep, when we give up the attempt altogether, we die.

Samuel Butler

SOME RELEVANT PERSONAL INTELLECTUAL HISTORY

Exactly six years ago I experienced, as an Israeli, the culmination of what was probably the most stressful life event I have ever faced. On Monday, June 5, 1967, what later came to be known as the Six Day War broke out. As an American Jew I had been fortunate in not being touched directly by the Holocaust of World War II, though there were unpleasant moments for me as a soldier in the American Army in those years. But in 1967 we had gone through months of knowing a war was inevitable; through weeks of a sense of its imminence, each of us (with the exception of a few highly placed Israelis) having an acute sense of the possibility that not only individuals, but that all of us, family and friends, might be driven into the sea, literally. Once again the world seemed to be looking on with indifference. I was not particularly relaxed as I ran through the streets of Jerusalem in the early afternoon to reach my family, not knowing how one dodges shells and rifle fire peppering Jewish Jerusalem at random. It was not until 2 AM the next morning that we learned that there had been no objective basis for having perceived the situation of the past weeks as a stressful life event. But if anything has been learned in the study of stressful life events, it is that what is important for their consequences is the subjective perception of the meaning of the event rather than its objective character.

I had even earlier than 1967 begun to become aware of the fact that those of us who were working in the study of the relationship of life crises to health had been giving inadequate attention to a complex set of variables which, it seems reasonable to think, mediated this relationship. In early 1967 I had written, "Moreover, we know . . . that the impact of a given external situation upon a person is mediated by the psychological, social and cultural resources at his disposal" (Antonovsky & Kats, 1967). But this was essentially a remark made in passing.

Having been a participant-observer, as well as a researcher, of the experience of the Israeli population in May–June 1967, I looked again at the disaster literature. This brief review, and particularly discussions with a colleague writing his doctoral dissertation on the survey material we had collected in June (Kamen, 1971), made me aware of an interesting phenomenon. There seems to be no evidence that the life crises undoubtedly posed by disaster situations had either an immediate or even a delayed deleterious impact on health. If anything, the contrary might even be true. There must be something, then, in the experience of disaster which may hold in check the development of pathological responses.

Preparing a theoretical paper in 1968 (Antonovsky, 1972), I pinned a label on this something, this mediating set of variables between life crises and health. I called it "resistance resources," defined as the "power which can be applied (by an individual) to resolve the tension" expressive of a state of disturbed homeostasis. In this paper I made a preliminary attempt at spelling out the types of resistance resource that might be relevant in coping with disturbed homeostasis.

Subsequently, in writing about stress and coronary heart disease, I developed a model at the core of which was the phrase "the centrality of tension management" (Antonovsky, 1971). The model rests on four concepts: (1) problem-confrontation, or, in the language of this book, stressful life events; (2) tension, or the inner response to problem-confrontation; (3) tension-management, defined as the rapidity and completeness with which problems are resolved and tension dissipated; and (4) stress, defined as a state of the organism in which energy is utilized in continuously dealing with problems over and above the energy that would have been demanded had the problem been resolved. Stress, in other words, was seen as a consequence of poor tension management, and it, rather than tension, is what should be hypothesized as contributing to pathology. Given this model, it became clear to me that one's resistance resources, as the set of variables determinant of the adequacy of tension management, are the most exciting things to be studied.

Before I had the opportunity to engage in a study which allowed me to go into this question even partially, one further experience sensitized me even more to its importance, if I may be permitted to report just one more stage in my intellectual development over these years. In the context of a study on ethnic patterns in the adaptation of women to menopause, I became involved in the question of the long-range impact of the concentration camp experience (Antonovsky, Maoz, Dowty, & Wijsenbeek, 1971). Within the study population one subgroup contained all women then aged 45 to 54 in an Israeli city who had been born in central Europe. Of these, 77 had been in a concentration camp during World War II, and 210 had not been in a camp. The finding that the latter, on a large variety of measures of adaptation, were more often well adapted than the camp survivors may have been a contribution to the surprisingly scarce solid empirical literature, but it was much less exciting to me than the fact that a not inconsiderable number of concentration camp survivors were found to be well adapted. These women, it should be noted, had not only been in the concentration camps. Their subsequent lives in DP camps and in an Israel which had been through three wars had not exactly been devoid of stressful life events. Yet something had given them the strength not only to survive, but to be well adapted.*

THE PRESENT STUDY

Given this intellectual background, then, it is hardly surprising that I took advantage of the first opportunity to engage in a study of resistance resources. In 1970–1971, the Department of Social Medicine of the Hebrew University-Hadassah Medical School undertook a total Community Health Study in the area of Jerusalem which serves as its practice base. The entire population (circa 10,000 persons) was divided into 10 random samples. Each wave was interviewed, using a general health screening questionnaire, and then invited to a medical examination. The completion rate approximated 85%. The subpopulation which receives total preventive and curative care in the Department-run center is called the "family practice." After the medical examinations had been completed, all adults from the family practice who had been interviewed and examined in the last five waves of the study were again visited by an interviewer. It is the questionnaire used in this last series of interviews, of which

* In citing only my own papers here, I certainly do not wish to pretend that others have not done valuable work which has influenced me. In each of the papers cited, I refer to those papers that have had an important impact on my thinking. Reference to Levine and Scotch (1970) will indicate that the concept of resistance resources is very far from being personal property. But it will also indicate the limited extent to which the concept has been clarified, much less the subject of empirical work. Further evidence of the lack of relevant empirical work is found in Coelho's bibliography (1970) on *Coping and Adaptation*.

391 were completed, which is the subject of the following discussion. Within the constraints of an interview that had to be limited to 25–30 minutes, I sought to develop an instrument that would measure both life crises and resistance resources.*

Life Crisis History

My initial impulse was to use the Holmes-Rahe Schedule of Recent Experiences as a measure of life crises. This was, however, rejected for a variety of reasons, most pertinent of which was the fact that our interest was in the total life span. Further, it was thought that application to the Israeli context would require revision sufficient to prevent the possibility of comparison.

Our first objection raises a fundamental theoretical issue. Rahe and Holmes (1966) have demonstrated that life change in a two-year period is predictive of illness. Myers and his colleagues (1972) have also produced evidence to this effect. But the very argument of the former, in which they indicate that their own data support Hinkle's argument (1958) that "more illness occurs in a small percentage of a given population" would suggest the value of obtaining data over a substantially longer period of time. In any case, I do not propose a substitution of consideration of the life span for a focus on a more recent period, but rather think that at this stage of our knowledge, work should go on in both directions.

Having made the decision to cover the life span, the next question faced was that of the items to be included. Our population, though all adult Jewish Israelis and residents of one urban area, was very heterogeneous with respect to country of origin, socioeconomic status, age, and so on, as well as inclusive of men and women. We required a series of items that would make sense and be of possible applicability to all respondents. Further, we did not wish to take the chance that items be differentially evaluated as critical by different individuals. This led us to the decision to use a series of items which were all characterized by an assumption that all human beings would regard them as life crises, or which were so phrased as to make it difficult to make light of such an experience. Thus, although doubtless there would be some individual variation in evaluating the seriousness of the 20 items about which we asked, I was confident that all would be rated by all respondents as substantially serious experiences. Limiting oneself to such serious items, incidentally, helps to cope with the serious problem of the validity of recall.

The third issue faced was the selection of specific items. Any set of questions

* At the time of writing, only limited data runs were available to me; these include none of the health variables. I will therefore, at appropriate places, refer to such data as I believe may be of interest to the reader.

is a nonrandom sample from the universe of possible questions, and I know of no rules which would assure one of a representative sample. The best that one can do, I think, is, on the basis of familiarity with the culture and history of one's population, select items that cover a variety of life areas. Actually, of the 20 items we ended up using, only 3 (items 1, 2, and 20) would be particular to the specific population and not universally applicable, although the frequency of experience would vary considerably in different populations.

The items we used were distributed as follows (the individual items are given in the Appendix):

1. Life in danger (4 items).
2. Economic crises (3 items).
3. Separation from or death of someone close (5 items).
4. Interpersonal relations (3 items).
5. Major role activity (4 items for men, 4 parallel items for women).
6. Migration (1 item).

In several cases, where our pretest had indicated that multiple recurrence of the crisis was not infrequent, the questionnaire had room for recording such recurrences. For each item the respondent was asked whether he had ever had the experience; if so, each was asked at what age it had occurred and, if the nature of the experience was such, how long the experience had lasted.

As the pretest had indicated, this selection of 20 life crisis items proved capable of eliciting from the study population a set of data sufficiently rich for analysis. The members of this Israeli sample have indeed not lived uneventful lives. A total of 2240 "life crises" were recorded, or an average of 5.73 crises per respondent. The proportion of the total sample responding positively to each of the 20 items is given in the Appendix. The positive responses go up to 71% of the sample on the migration item and fall below 10% on only 3 items. Nor is there a concentration in any one of the several substantive areas; in each, at least an average of 20% of the sample replied that they had experienced each of the items in that area. In the area of major role activity, an average of 35% answered each item positively.

Our life crisis history scoring system is undoubtedly crude, but I could see no alternative. For each reported experience, a respondent received a score of 1 if the experience was by its nature a specific event, or if it had lasted for less than two years. For each additional year of events of the latter type, a point was added. Having been in Europe during World War II, however, was scored 25. Being an area of extreme sensitivity, we did not wish to probe experiences during 1939–1945. It was assumed that anyone who had been in Europe then had been exposed to experiences which "merited" such a weighting. This scoring system thus provided us with a total life crisis history score, a total score for each of four age periods, and subscores for each of the areas covered. We might note that more than half the population (53%) received total life crisis scores of 10 or more; half of these are accounted for by those who were in Europe during World War II.

Current Tensions

This approach, it is true, allows the calculation of a recent life crisis score, since age was always recorded. But given the seriousness of the experiences asked about, it was not likely that more than a few individuals would have had more than one or two of these experiences in a short span of time. Instead, we sought some measure which would provide an overall direct picture of the current tension levels of respondents, without going into a detailed exploration of specific experiences. Our answer is based on the concept of frustration, both statistically and dynamically.

The technique used was the Self-Anchoring Striving Scale developed by Cantril (1965; cf. Antonovsky & Arian, 1972). Respondents are shown a 10-rung ladder. The top rung is defined as the most ideal and the bottom rung as the worst possible situation he can imagine. He is then asked to locate himself on the ladder at the present and five years ago. The ladder device was used with reference to four general areas of life:

1. Material things (whatever can be bought with money).
2. Nonmaterial aspirations (respect, freedom to do what one wants to, security).
3. Family life (number of children, relations with spouse and relatives).
4. Personal characteristics (honest, respect-worthy, attractive).

The ladder was then used again to obtain a summary evaluation, "taking everything into account."

This approach rests upon two assumptions: first, that what matters about life crises is that they create tensions; second, that tensions are best measured by the gap between aspirations and perceived reality (cf. Syme & Reeder, 1967, where an analogous concept of incongruity lies at the heart of the consensus arrived at in the symposium). Further, we reasoned that it was important to obtain ladder ratings at two different times. The present rating does indeed give a measure of the current degree of frustration. This degree, however, is tempered by the sense of movement from the past. At any given level of present frustration, we would expect the individual who perceives upward movement from the past to feel less tension than one who feels he has remained at the same level or moved down.

The mean scores of the total population on the present ladder ratings range from 6.04 on material things to 7.83 on personal characteristics, the overall mean ladder rating being 6.99, the variance being sufficiently large to allow meaningful comparisons among subgroups. More significantly, we find that in each case, small groups report that, compared to the situation five years ago, their present situation has gotten worse (from 4 to 13% on the different ladders). On the other hand, from 4 to 37% report improvements in the past five years.

Past Resistance Resources

Our purview being the entire life span, we sought for some simple way to measure the resistance resources available to people throughout their lives which would have mediated, in terms of our theoretical approach, the impact of the reported life crises. We could think of no way to do so which would not have required a complex, detailed investigation, manifestly out of the question. Our crude solution tried to cut to the heart of the matter. Given our interest in predicting to current and future health states, what seemed to us to matter most was the *impact* of the life crises of the past. For each life crisis question to which the response was positive, then, we posed an additional question: Would you say that . . .

1. you still suffer from this experience?
2. you suffered from it for a long time, but time has healed?
3. you suffered from it afterward, but not for very long?
4. once it was over, it was over, and left no marks?

Clearly, this is not a measure of resistance resources in any substantive sense. It tells nothing about why one was or was not able to cope with the life crisis. But it at least gives us some measure of the residual effects, as perceived by the respondent, of his life crisis history. As will be seen below, the capacity for what I call homeostatic flexibility, or resilience, or, if you will, rolling with the punches and coming to livable terms with suffering, is an important component of resistance resources. It is this component, I believe, that our measure of past resistance resources expresses.

To arrive at an overall past resistance resource score, we summed the sheer number of life crises experienced (without weighting) by an individual and divided this number into the total raw score of the residual effect responses, as numbered above. Thus if a person had experienced six life crises and had said that in each case he "still suffers from this experience," thus obtaining a total raw impact score of 6, his overall past resistance resource score would be 1.0. The higher the score (the maximum, of course, being 4.0), the fewer the residual effects, or the greater the resilience. The distribution of scores derived in this manner is normal: 28% had scores of 1.0–2.1; 45%, scores of 2.2–3.1; and 27%, scores of 3.2–4.0.

Current Resistance Resources

If the concept of resistance resources is to be a powerful explanatory device, it must not be limited to specific defensive measures against specific threats. This approach, of course, is consistent with Selye's (1956) concept of the general adaptation syndrome. Our search must be concerned with those generalized resources which can be brought to bear upon any state of tension, irrespective of its specific source.

Second, I would make it clear that the study of resistance resources must be a multidisciplinary effort. My geneticist friends tell me that there is considerable interest in the possibility of a genetic basis for plasticity (cf. Dobzhansky, 1962). Engels and his colleagues (Schmale, 1972), in developing the concept of "psychic giving up," have stressed the "genetic, constitutional and early life experiences" as important determinants of "the psychological and physiological predisposition" in response to tension. In the present study I made no attempt to go very far from my own competence, and concentrated on social-psychological variables.

Our measures of generalized resistance resources expressed, in essence, three such resources: (1) homeostatic flexibility; (2) ties to concrete others; and (3) ties to the total community.

Homeostatic Flexibility

By homeostatic flexibility I mean the ability to accept alternatives and not, in simple language, banging one's head against the wall, and the perception of the availability of such alternatives. (I am, of course, reminded of Merton's famous declension of flexibility: I am firm, thou art stubborn, he is pig-headed, suggesting that it is not the easiest thing in the world to objectively measure flexibility. But this is no reason for not trying.) Our empirical measures sought to refer to social role, value, and personal behavior aspects of flexibility.

1. Social roles. The underlying idea here is that the more one's self-image is rich and complex in terms of the roles one sees onself as occupying, in actuality or potentiality, the more can one be flexible. Frustration in one role is not necessarily paralyzing. To measure this, respondents were asked to give as many responses as they could, in the space of 2 minutes, to the question Who are you? Responses were coded first in terms of sheer number, whether or not a social role was mentioned, second in terms of social roles or institutionalized social interactions, and third in terms of the number of different social settings or institutions mentioned (e.g., husband, father, grandfather were counted as three roles but one setting).

In all three cases the distributions of responses make analysis possible. On the first scoring, 30% gave three or fewer responses, 38% gave four responses, and 32% gave five or more responses. More significant for our purposes was the distribution of institutionalized social roles: 18% failed to mention a single role; 19% cited one role; 25%, two roles; 20%, three roles; and 18% four or more roles. Third, 20% do not have an image of themselves in a single social institution, while 40% mention one institution (overwhelmingly, a family role); another third referred to two institutions; and 7% to three or more.

2. Values. Here we followed Lerner's (1958) concept of empathy, defined as the capacity to accept alternative values as legitimate. The ethnocentric limitation to one's own norms, being upset, angry, revolted at others who conform to different norms, particularly in a heterogeneous, changing world, is an expression of inflexibility. This was measured by three multiple choice items describing emotional reactions to various situations (e.g., "It happens very frequently that you see people behaving in a way that you cannot stand"). (Distribution as yet unavailable.)

3. Personal behavior. Here we most directly made an attempt to get at the self-perceived behavioral response to situations which, on their face, presumably would knock most of us off balance. The capacity to recover one's balance quickly, to go about one's affairs—though without necessarily being blunted emotionally—would seem to be a meaningful resistance resource. Operationally, we described two situations which would have widespread application (learning that a young man close to one had to undergo a serious operation; having had a serious quarrel the day before with someone close), and asked people to estimate to what extent they would function normally the following day.

The four-category multiple choice answers to these items elicited a spread of answers: 22 and 12%, respectively, on the operation and quarrel questions said they would not be able to do much that day; at the other extreme, 9 and 31% said they would function normally.

Ties to Others

Profound ties to concrete others, I would suggest, are a second significant generalized resistance resource. As I wrote elsewhere (Antonovsky, 1972), "On the simplest level, a person who has someone who cares for him is likely to more adequately resolve tension than one who does not. Even without employing the resources of others, simply knowing that these are available to one increases one's strength." Studies of institutionalized children, no less than epidemiologic data on isolate adults, provide abundant evidence for this contention (Gove, 1973). Our measures of this variable were on two levels. First, we asked for the first names of and frequency of interaction with people close to one, outside of one's immediate family. Second, we asked for degree of agreement with three items which have been widely used in alienation scales (no dependable ties between people today, at times feel all alone, and today can't know for certain on whom one can count). (Distribution as yet unavailable.)

Community Ties

Ties to the total community constitute the third type of resistance resource measured. In a study of commitment in a kibbutz which was just completed (Antonovsky & Antonovsky, 1973), we sought to distinguish between ties to concrete others and ties to the total community in which one lived. The two concepts are not necessarily correlated, and both, I suggest, are significant in determining one's capacity to resolve tension. At the time the present study was designed, I had not yet fully grasped the need for making the distinction, and followed the alienation literature in posing the concrete questions to measure ties to the total community. For each of the three concepts involved—normlessness, meaninglessness, and powerlessness—three traditional multiple choice items were asked. (Distribution as yet unavailable.)

SOME FURTHER PROBLEMS

I have now described each component of the instrument used to study life crisis history and resistance resources, discussing briefly the theoretical problems involved. I have also presented those data which were available at the time of writing, the point of this being to examine the possibility, in terms of distribution, of subsequently analyzing the relationship of these variables to the measures of health status used in the study. In closing, I raise three further problems that relate to the concept of resistance resources.

First, I note that the question of the structure of the interrelationships of the various components of resistance resources is not at all clear. As mentioned earlier, ties to immediate others and to the community are not necessarily correlated. Further, there may well be a negative correlation between the capacity for empathy and the degree of normative commitment to one's society. The true believer may have profound ties to others, yet by definition he cannot see alternative ways of living. The answer to the question of structure depends, in the first instance, on far more adequate theoretical clarification and, of no less importance, far more empirical work than is available today.

Second, I have been troubled, in the course of seeking to operationalize the concept, by the difficulty of assigning a given variable to the life crisis (or stressor) category or to the resistance resource category. Is poor health, or status inconsistency, or alienation one or the other? Insofar as such experiences or states produce tension, they may legitimately be regarded as stressors. But at the same time they clearly may affect one's capacity to cope with the tension produced by other stressors. This too, then, is a problem to which I have no adequate answer.

Finally, I call attention to the absence, both in my study and in others, of properties of the social environment for people. Thus, for example, the institutionalized social value that the society is responsible for helping the individual deal with threat, concretized in a national health service, will make a substantial difference in the capacity of people to cope successfully with life crises. At the same time, however, one must see such properties only as providing a potential, which does not necessarily mean that there is no differential access or differential exploitation of the potential.

APPENDIX

Items used to elicit life crisis history	Percentage with specified life crisis ($N = 391$)
Life in danger	
1. Where were you in the years of World War II (1939–1945)? (If reply is under Nazi rule or in Soviet Union at any time, no experiences during this period are recorded subsequently.)	26
2. Were you ever in a situation where your life was in danger because you are Jewish, such as in a concentration camp (not in 1939–1945)?	7
3. Were you ever in a war situation or something similar where people around you were killed?	27
4. Were you ever so ill that your life was in danger?	24
Economic crises	
5. Were you or the head of your family ever in a situation of looking for work and being unable to find it for at least several months?	33
6. Was there ever a time when you literally didn't have enough to eat for several months?	18
7. Was your family ever in so much financial debt that you just didn't know how to get out of it?	17
Separation from or death of someone close	
8. When you were 15 years old, were you living with both your parents? (Crisis defined separately for mother and father.)	20
9. Up till the time you were 18 years old, did a brother or sister of yours die?	15
10. For ever-married respondents: Were you ever divorced or widowed? (Up to two events recorded as crises.)	12
11. For ever-married respondents: Did it ever happen, God forbid, that a child of yours died? (Separate crisis recorded for each death.)	9
12. In the past three years, has someone who was very close to you died (other than the above)?	42
Interpersonal relations	
13. Did you ever quarrel so badly with someone close to you that you never wished to see him again?	23
14. Did it ever happen that someone you truly had faith in betrayed you?	28

Items used to elicit life crisis history	Percentage with specified life crisis ($N = 391$)
Interpersonal relations	
15. Did anyone who truly had faith in you ever feel, justly or not, that you betrayed him?	9
Major role activity	
Men ($N = 177$)	
16. Did you ever lose your place of work, for any reason at all?	27
17. Were you ever denied a promotion you strongly felt you had coming to you?	47
18. Were your relations with another person at work ever so bad that you literally hated to come into contact with him?	29
19. From the time you started to work, did you ever make a major change in the type of work, such as manual to office work, work in a kibbutz to work in the city, employed to self-employed?	49
Women ($N = 214$)	
16. Did you ever feel, over a goodly period of time (months), that conditions at home were so bad that you just weren't able to do what you had to do at home?	28
17. Did you ever work at the same time that you had responsibilities at home (or studies and housework, or studies and work) and felt that you just couldn't do both things successfully?	25
18. Did you ever have the feeling, for a goodly period of time (months) that you just couldn't give your children what they needed?	31
19. Has it happened that after a long time of being a housewife only you went out to work (at least half-time)?	41
Other	
20. Were you born in Israel? (One crisis recorded for each migration from one country to another.)	71
21. Other than the things you've told me in answer to the above questions, was there anything else that happened to you in your life that at the time caused you to suffer a great deal or put you under a great deal of tension?	39

REFERENCES

Antonovsky, A. Breakdown: A needed fourth step in the conceptual armamentarium of modern medicine. *Social Science and Medicine,* 1972, **6,** 537–544.

Antonovsky, A. Social and cultural factors in coronary heart disease. An Israel-North American sibling study. *Israel Journal of Medical Sciences,* 1971, **7,** 1578–1583.

Antonovsky, A., & Arian, A. *Hopes and Fears of Israelis*. Jerusalem: Jerusalem Academic Press, 1972.

Antonovsky, A., & Kats, R. The life crisis history as a tool in epidemiologic research. *Journal of Health and Social Behavior,* 1967, **8,** 15–20.

Antonovsky, A., Maoz, B., Dowty, N., & Wijsenbeek, H. Twenty-five years later: A limited study of the sequelae of the concentration camp experience. *Social Psychiatry,* 1971, **6,** 186–193.

Antonovsky, H. F., & A. Antonovsky. Commitment in an Israeli kibbutz. *Human Relations* (in press).

Cantril, H. *The Pattern of Human Concerns*. New Brunswick, N.J.: Rutgers University Press, 1965.

Coelho, G. V., et al. (Eds.) *Coping and Adaptation: A Behavioral Sciences Bibliography*. Washington, D.C.: U.S. Public Health Service, 1970.

Dobzhansky, T. *Mankind Evolving*. New Haven, Conn.: Yale University Press, 1962.

Gove, W. R. Sex, marital status and mortality. *American Journal of Sociology,* 1973, **79,** 45–67.

Hinkle, L. E., Jr., et al. An investigation of the relation between life experience, personality characteristics, and general susceptibility to illness. *Psychosomatic Medicine,* 1958, **20,** 278.

Kamen, C. S. *Crisis, Stress and Social Integration. The Case of Israel and the Six Day War*. Unpublished doctoral dissertation, University of Chicago, 1971.

Lerner, D. *The Passing of Traditional Society*. New York: Free Press, 1958.

Levine, S., & Scotch, N. A. (Eds.) *Social Stress*. Chicago: Aldine Publishing Company, 1970.

Myers, J. K., Lindenthal, J. J., & Pepper, M. P. Life events and mental status: A longitudinal study. *Journal of Health and Social Behavior,* 1972, **13,** 398–406.

Rahe, R. H., & Holmes, T. H. Life crisis and disease onset. Department of Psychiatry, University of Washington School of Medicine, Seattle, 1966. (Mimeographed)

Schmale, A. H. Giving up as a final common pathway to changes in health. *Advances in Psychosomatic Medicine,* 1972, **8,** 20–40.

Selye, H. *The Stress of Life*. New York: McGraw-Hill Book Company, 1956.

Syme, S. L., & Reeder, L. G. (Eds.) Social stress and cardiovascular disease. *Milbank Memorial Fund Quarterly,* April 1967, **45,** no. 2, part 2.

CHAPTER 16

Perception of Life Crisis Events:

A Comparative Study of Rural and Urban Samples *

F. T. Miller

W. K. Bentz

J. F. Aponte

D. R. Brogan †

In recent years much research attention has been focused on potential sources of stressors or stress events. The family (Croog, 1970), work and organizational situations (Gross, 1970), and class-race-status (Dohrenwend & Dohrenwend, 1970) have been studied. Such potential sources of stress events have been sampled and combined into an objective test instrument amenable to administration to large groups. This instrument is the Social Readjustment Rating Scale or SRRS (Holmes & Rahe, 1967). The instrument contains 43 items weighted according to the amount of readjustment or getting used to each requires. Subjects receive cumulative weighted scores which reflect the amount of change occurring in their life space in the recent past.

The SRRS has been standardized on white (Holmes & Rahe, 1967), black, and Mexican-Americans (Komaroff, Masuda, & Holmes, 1968) in the United States. Standardizations have also been effected on samples drawn from Japan (Masuda & Holmes, 1967) and Europe (Harmon, Masuda, & Holmes, 1969). These studies have shown that samples from different populations tend to give similar intensity rankings to life crisis events. Correlations of each to the original middle-class urban sample have ranged from .74 to .94. Hence the SRRS appears to be stable both across subculture groups in the United States and

* This investigation was partly supported by NIMH Grant 5 R01 MH16515. A version of this chapter was presented at the SEPA meeting in Miami, on April 29, 1971.

† The authors wish to express their thanks to Dr. Herbert Eber for his advice concerning research design and statistical analysis.

cross-culturally. However, all scale standardizations to date have focused on urban populations. This chapter reports the results of a standardization of the SRRS items on a sample drawn from rural North Carolina and seeks to compare this sample to other United States standardization samples.*

METHOD

Instrument

The SRRS is made up of 43 life crisis events likely to occur in the life of any adult in most cultures. It contains a sampling of life situations drawn from the areas of family constellation, marriage, occupation, economics, residence, group and peer relationships, education, religion, recreation, and health. Each event is assumed to require some readjustment by the experiencing individual. Interpersonal and/or social events such as having troubles with the boss or changing residences make up the list. Some events may be viewed as desirable. For example, getting married, getting a job promotion, or taking a vacation may be events to be sought for. Others, such as serious illness in the family, having a mortgage foreclosed, or being fired from a job, may be viewed as events to be avoided.

Some SRRS items are worded so that one does not know if an event is positive or negative. For example, ''major change in living conditions'' may be good or bad for an individual. Holmes assumes that change rather than valence is of primary concern. Nevertheless, three such items were subdivided into positive and negative statements for the rural standardization. Therefore the scale we administered contained 46 items. The subdivided items are not directly comparable to those of the other studies. They are therefore deleted from this report.

Administration

The SRRS was administered verbally by interviewers trained by one of the authors. Subjects were asked to rate each event on a scale from 0 to 1000 in terms of the amount of ''change'' or ''getting used to'' or ''readjustment'' required by the event. As a reference item, ''getting married'' was assigned a rating of 500. Subjects were asked if each item would require more or less readjustment than getting married. Then they were asked how much. A histogram scaled in units of 50 from 0 to 1000 was presented with each item as a visual aid for

* To facilitate this effort, Dr. Holmes was kind enough to make available the raw data from his original standardization.

judgment-making. Many judgments were made simply by pointing to the appropriate point on the histogram.

Subjects

Subjects for this study were a random sample of 96 citizens selected from a rural county in North Carolina through an area sampling technique. The sample is representative of various racial and socioeconomic groups in approximately the same proportion as shown in the 1970 census. The sample is 89% rural and 11% urban; 64% white and 36% nonwhite; and 51% male and 49% female. It includes 11% aged 20–29; 24% aged 30–39; 27% aged 40–49; 21% aged 50–59; and 17% of age 60 and older. In the sample 12% attended college; 33% finished high school; 39% had some high school training; and 16% had less than a seventh-grade education. Reflecting the underemployment in the area, 23% of the sample families had incomes of less than $3000; 34% made between $3000 and $5999; 28% fell within the range of $6000 to $8999; and 15% were from families with an income of greater than $9000. Thus the rural sample was high school and less than high school educated, poor, and of lower socioeconomic status.

RESULTS

Ordering of Events

Ratings pooled across subjects and averaged constitute community or social consensus values for the events. The arithmetic mean was computed for each event. Also, for general scale use in the field, the geometric mean (antilogarithm of the mean of the log of the scores) (Stevens, 1966) was computed. The geometric mean is less influenced by extreme judgments than the arithmetic mean.

The 40 items presented both to the rural North Carolinians and to the original predominantly white (7% nonwhite) middle-class standardization sample drawn from the urban Pacific Northwest are listed in Table 1 along with both their rank ordering and mean values. Visual examination of the events shows similarity between the two populations. Both Pearson and Spearman coefficients of correlation were computed to show order relationships between the two samples. The arithmetic mean comparisons yielded $r = .86$ and rho = .85. Comparisons based on the geometric means yielded $r = .85$ and rho = .82. Rural and white-urban individuals tend to impose a similar ordering on the 40 items on a scale of readjustment or stress.

Similar results were found in comparing the rural North Carolina sample to

Table 1. Means and Ranks for Two Standardization Groups

	Geometric Mean				Arithmetic Mean			
	West Coast White American		Rural North Carolina		West Coast White American		Rural North Carolina	
	Rank	Score	Rank	Score	Rank	Score	Rank	Score
Death of spouse	1	771	1	843	1	1,020	1	883
Divorce	2	593	3	730	2	727	3	787
Marital separation	3	516	2	780	3	652	2	820
Marriage	4	500	21	500	7	500	29	500
Death of a close family member	5	469	11	580	5	626	7	667
Detention in jail	6	439	5	636	4	631	6	697
Major personal injury or illness	7	416	4	673	6	528	4	746
Fired from work	8	378	15	537	8	466	13	633
Marital reconciliation	9	366	13	568	10	451	12	644
Retirement from work	10	361	16	534	9	455	17	594
Gain of a new family member	11	337	10	595	14	391	14	629
Change in health of family member	12	335	8	613	11	438	10	657
Sexual difficulties	13	316	20	508	13	392	20	581
Business readjustment	14.5	308	7	619	15	385	8	665
Change in financial state	14.5	308	9	605	16	377	9	658
Change to different work	16	287	29	443	18	363	27	513
Change in arguments with spouse	17	286	33	395	19	345	32	474
Pregnancy	18	284	12	576	12	403	11	645
Death of close friend	19	270	18	528	17	369	18.5	592
Foreclosure of mortgage	20	231	19	522	21	304	18.5	592
Trouble with inlaws	21	213	26	447	22	286	24	532
Mortgage greater than $10,000	22	210	6	629	20	311	5	706
Outstanding personal achievement	23	192	22	484	23	277	22	555

Begin or end of formal schooling	24	191	17	532	24	259	15	600
Change in living conditions	25	186	14	542	25	246	16	597
Trouble with the boss	26	178	28	438	27	227	28	505
Major revision of personal habits	27	149	31	407	26	239	33	470
Change in work conditions	28	148	30	425	28	202	30	498
Change in residence	29	140	27	444	29	201	25	532
Change in schools	30	135	23	483	30	196	21	565
Change in recreation	31	127	34	378	31	189	35	435
Change in social activities	32	125	38	350	33	177	38	409
Change in church activities	33	112	24	461	32	188	26	520
Mortgage loan less than $10,000	34.5	105	36	364	34	173	34	442
Change in sleeping habits	34.5	105	37	359	35	156	37	423
Change in family get-togethers	36	103	32	397	36	151	31	483
Change in eating habits	37	98	35	368	37	147	36	431
Vacation	38	74	40	305	38	130	40	398
Christmas	39	59	39	306	39	119	39	402
Minor violations of the law	40	54	25	455	40	106	23	542

samples drawn from ghetto areas in Los Angeles. Using geometric mean data, a comparison of the racially mixed rural sample to one of black urbanites yielded $r = .77$, rho = .78, whereas a comparison with Mexican-Americans resulted in $r = .60$, rho = .70. Thus the rural and urban samples tend to order the 40 life crisis events similarly.

Event Values

Across the standardization groups, however, the amount of readjustment attributed to the life crisis events is different. This difference is illustrated in Figure 1 where the numbers of events in different geometric mean ranges are plotted for each United States standardization sample. This difference is also reflected in Table 1 where, with the exception of the reference-standard item, each mean value given by the rural sample is higher than that given by the original Holmes and Rahe sample for the same item.

The distributions of the mean ratings for the urban and rural samples, as

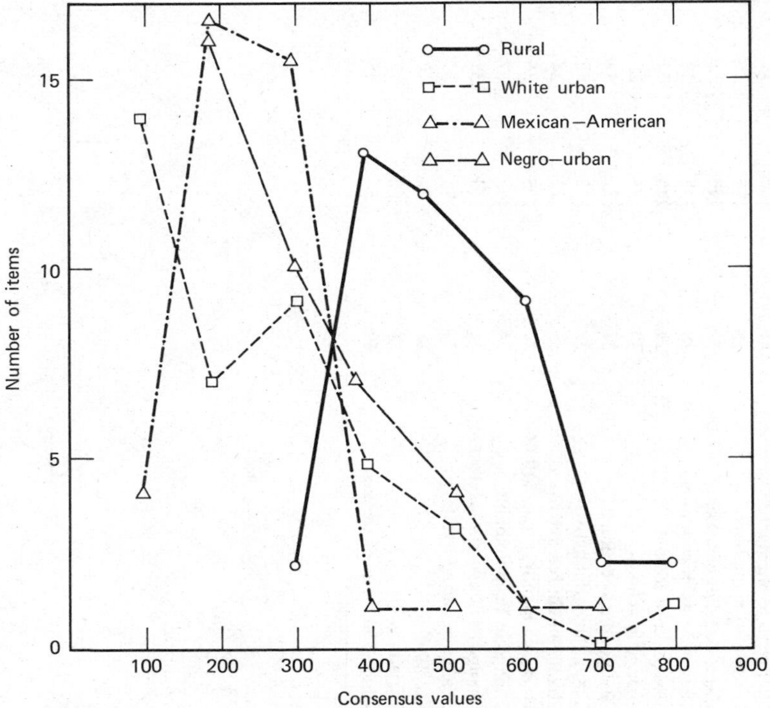

Figure 1. Distribution of geometric means by population groups.

illustrated in Figure 1, are so different that the question was raised whether the urban and rural samples can be considered as deriving from the same population of responders. The average consensus rating (over the 40 items) for the rural sample was compared to that for each of the three urban samples, and the urban samples were compared with each other. Table 2 presents the result of

Table 2. *t*-Test Comparisons of Averages of Geometric Mean Distributions of Ratings of Events by Rural and Urban Samples

	1	2	3	4
Washington state urban	—	− 17.90 *	0.76	3.66 *
North Carolina rural		—	16.38 *	14.23 *
Mexican-Americans			—	5.94 *
Blacks				—

* $p < .001$; $df = 78$.

these comparisons. A comparison of Washington State white-urban sample and the group of Mexican-Americans does not yield a significant t value. The averages of the geometric mean score distributions for all other groups differ significantly at a P value less than the .001 level of confidence.

The rural sample presents ratings that are significantly different from those evoked from all the urban groups reported above. However, the t value is smaller when the rural sample is compared to the blacks than when the comparison is with the other two groups.

Factor Patterns

To further explore rural-urban similarities and differences, ratings by the original Holmes-Rahe sample and by the one drawn from North Carolina were normalized through logarithmic transformations and subjected to a principal components factor analysis. The resulting structures were rotated for an orthogonal solution by varimax. A four-factor solution was considered optimal. Factor structures from the two data sets were similar. Events with loadings greater than .45 were arbitrarily selected for factor description.

Factor 1 contains a clustering of events that relate to alterations in the smooth flow of events occurring around the individual. They are primarily family-and job-related events. The factors from the two sets of ratings share nine events. The rural sample, as seen in Table 3, adds three unique items to the cluster and the urban group adds four. The common items relate to changes related to work or a family member beginning or retiring from work. Associated with these items are recreation and Christmas, each of which might be easily affected by the other mentioned areas of change. In the rural area job and life-space

Table 3. Factor Analysis of Rural and Urban Responses

Events in Common		Events in Contrast
Factor 1: Life-Space Change		
Wife beginning or ceasing work outside the home	Rural:	In-law problems
Change in working hours or conditions		Change in arguments with spouse
Change in usual type and/or amount of recreation		Change in family get-togethers
Change in living conditions	Urban:	Change in residence
Vacation		Change in social activities
Change in responsibilities at work		Changing to a new school
Change to a different kind of work		Beginning or ceasing formal schooling
Retirement		
Christmas		
Factor 2: Personal Life Style Change		
Personal achievement	Rural:	Death of a friend
Personal habits		Pregnancy
Minor violations of the law		Change in health of a family member
		Financial change
		Gaining a new family member
	Urban:	Eating habits
		Sleeping habits
		Change in family get-togethers
		Changes in recreation
Factor 3: Dissolution of Relationships		
Being fired from work	Rural:	Change in residence
Marital separation		Major personal injury or illness
Divorce	Urban:	Marital reconciliation
		Detention in jail
Factor 4: Relationship Termination		
Death of spouse	Rural:	In-law problems
Death of close family member		Having purchase repossessed
Death of close friend		Being put in jail
Major change in health or behavior of a family member	Urban:	Personal injury or illness
		Change in personal health

changes are associated with changes in arguments with one's spouse and in-laws and with family get togethers. The clustering derived from the urban ratings place change in residence, in social activities, and in schooling along with the work and life style items. For the rural group this cluster of changes appears to affect the interpersonal climate of the family. For the urbanite the unique items appear to be associated with relationships with the community.

Factor 2 appears to be related to change in personal life style. The two samples have three events in common: personal achievement, change in personal habits, and minor violations of the law. In the rural group the unique events focus on interpersonal relationships and include change in health of a family member, pregnancy, gaining a new family member, death of a friend, and financial change. The unique events added by the urbanite, which tend to be more self-oriented, are change in recreation, in eating habits, in sleeping habits, and in family get-togethers. The event elements for the two samples are different. However, the theme of the clusters is strikingly similar.

The third factor contains change items which bear on the dissolution or interruption of relationships on the job, in the family, or in the neighborhood. Associated with this cluster are detention in jail and major personal illness or injury. Three items are held in common by the two groups: marital separation, divorce, and being fired from work. Added to the cluster by the rural sample is change in residence. The urban sample adds detention in jail and reconciliation.

Factor 4 has to do with loss or with exits from the life space of the individual. It contains items having to do with death or major changes in the health or behavior of family members. This factor yields four events in common and only five unique ones, each of which is related to loss or exits from the personal social field.

The factor analysis underscores areas of common concern, change, or stress. Change in life space, life style, and in the stability of relationships are clearly to be experienced by individuals in all locales. The factor structures are of interest because the number of common items suggests a cultural communality whereas the unique items indicate cultural differences between the urban Northwesterner and the rural Southeasterner.

DISCUSSION

General Conclusions

Normal stress events tend to be ordered similarly by samples drawn from demographically different populations. In this chapter we have pointed out the high correlations, significant at well beyond the .001 level, obtained when rural and urban subsamples are compared. The similarity in response is also reflected in Table 3 by the close agreement of the factor structures derived from rural and urban responses. These conclusions are in general agreement with previous findings (Komaroff et al., 1968; Masuda & Holmes, 1967; and Harmon et al., 1969).

Similarities in the ranking of events and similarities in factor structures do not necessarily mean that different populations view events with the same gravity. Significant differences between the urban white and rural samples were obtained for all the stress event items. These findings parallel those of Rahe, Lundberg, Bennett, and Theorell (1971), who found significant differences between American and Swedish samples on 30 of the 43 events (70%) with the Swedish sample rating all but one event item higher than the ratings of the American comparison group.

One might hesitate to use SRRS weightings standardized on one population group with another without first testing for similarity in the amount of stress potential attributed to the events. The need for such caution is underscored in Table 2, where distributions of the mean values are compared, and in Figure 1, where the frequency distributions of mean values for urban and rural samples differ so greatly. For example, the geometric mean value for the distribution of the 40 consensus ratings by the white-urban group is 261.9 (arithmetic mean = 346), whereas that for the rural group is 508.7 (arithmetic mean=570). The differences in weightings may be due to differences in perception of the stressfulness of events, differences in the perception of the amount of readjustment required by getting married, or, in the case of the North Carolina sample, differences in methodology.

Presentation Method

Differences in procedure may account for some of the differences in weights obtained from the Holmes-Rahe and the North Carolina sample. The Holmes-Rahe procedure involved questionnaire presentation of events with a request that each be evaluated against the reference-standard item on a scale from zero to infinity. The North Carolina procedure involved an arbitrary cutoff at 1000 and a verbal presentation of items. The verbal presentation was accompanied by a visual presentation of a histogram in units of 50 with the reference-standard event and its weight clearly delineated. The visual aid was presented for each event and the subject was asked if the item required more or less readjustment than getting married and how much.

The arbitrary truncating of the rural ratings at a value of 1000 might be expected to affect mean values. However, it would seem reasonable to expect the mean values for the rural sample to be lower than those obtained from a sample free to give ratings as large as they chose. This did not happen. The arithmetic mean values for the North Carolina sample were higher than those obtained from the urban sample for all but the event "death of spouse."

It is also possible that the method of item presentation with the accompanying visual aid may have encouraged subjects to distribute their scores around the reference standard in a somewhat normal distribution. The North Carolina sample had 28 events greater than 500 and 11 below. There is obvious skewness in the North Carolina as well as the urban distribution of means, although not as much.

The method of presentation may have contributed to the differences obtained from rural North Carolina and the West Coast urban samples. Which, if either, was affected adversely is not clear. However, the fact that significant differences in weightings were found between urban groups examined with more similar methodology made the authors of this study unwilling to attribute all of the consensus rating differences between the white-urban and rural North Carolina samples to methodological artifact.

The Reference Standard

It is possible that differences in the distributions of the event means might be attributable to differences in the perception of the reference standard. Getting married might well have a meaning in an urban environment different from that in a rural area with low mobility. People tend to remain resident in the rural county and their rate of divorce is lower than the national average. This study provides no direct test of the hypothesis of different meanings being attributed to the reference standard. The same is not true for all the existing literature. Komaroff, Masuda, & Holmes (1968) found that different ethnic groups (white, black, and Mexican-American) made similar ratings of the standard item—marriage—on a scale of 0 to 1000. These ethnic groups, however were all urbanites residing in the West Coast region of the country. Each group considered marriage at or near the top of their ranking of stressful events. Other work has been done on the reference standard by Rahe and his colleagues (1971), who demonstrated that using different reference-standard items (marriage and adding a new family member) still yields highly correlated rankings of items. Even the manipulation of the reference standard does not seriously affect the ordering. Therefore where there are major differences in ordering one can assume that there is a major difference in the meaning attributed to the event. When the rural and urban data are examined from that point of view differences in the reference standard appear to stand out. The white-middle-class urbanite group reported only three events as requiring greater readjustment than getting married. Blacks reported four and Mexican-Americans reported no events as requiring more readjustment than getting married (Komaroff et al., 1968). The rural North Carolina sample, in contrast, rated 20 events as requiring greater readjustment than marriage. Only one other sample reported thus far shows a marked difference in the ordering of the reference standard. That sample which is drawn from Sweden reports 14 life events as requiring more readjustment than marriage (Rahe, 1969).

An alternate hypothesis is also tenable. It may well be that different population groups perceive the amount of readjustment required by change events to be different. The North Carolina sample yielded means for all but two events which were higher than those obtained from the white-urban standardization group. Supporting evidence can also be derived from reported results on Swedish (Rahe et al., 1971) and student samples (Mendels & Weinstein, 1972). The sample from Sweden rated all but one event higher (30 of the 43 events significantly higher) than the original Washington state sample. In contrast, the student group rated all but three events lower than the Holmes-Rahe standardization sample.

Differences in the amount of readjustment attributed to events have also been noted in the weighting scores obtained from the ratings of other groups. For example, Komaroff, Masuda, and Holmes (1968) found 29 of the 43 items rated significantly different by whites, blacks and Mexican-Americans. Whites and Mexican-Americans had 20 items different by the Mann-Whitney U-test and whites and blacks had 26 events rated differently. French, Belgian, and Swiss samples (Harmon et al., 1969) rated 18 events differently from the United States urban group and Japanese samples rated 17 items significantly different. These differences are such that one might be quite intrigued by the instrument as a tool for cross-cultural research. At the same time, one would hesitate to apply norms derived from one group to another without first checking the appropriateness of the weightings.

Rural-Urban Differentiating Events

Two methods are immediately available for teasing out the most striking differences in the perception of events by rural and urban subjects. Both are relatively free of differences that might be imposed by methodological variance. One can identify events with the greatest rank difference in the ratings of the comparison samples. This method seems reasonable in view of the high correlation in the data obtained from the different samples. The second method is to study event differences that were demonstrated in the factors derived from analyzing the sets of rural and urban data.

Rank Differences

Rank differences were studied by examining Table 1 and selecting the four most disparate events between the two samples. Selected were marriage, change in number of arguments with spouse, minor violations of the law, and taking out a mortgage of greater than $10,000.

Getting married is the event with the greatest rank difference. For the urban sample it is rank 4 and for the rural sample it is rank 21. This may be explained in terms of the relative mobility of the two samples. In rural North Carolina when one marries the expectation is to move only a few miles and to stay where you move—or at least to stay in the locale. In an urban area marriage may mean the uprooting of one or the other of the couple, a change in living abode for more space, and a change in recreation because of a change in expenses.

Taking out a mortgage of greater than $10,000 is almost antithetical for the rural North Carolinian, whereas such a loan might be assumed with relative ease by the city dweller. In the rural South, a general pay-as-you-go philosophy still prevails. This is particularly true for families where the money base is small. It is not at all unusual to find all or most members of a family doing "public work," investing their weekly income in building materials, and spending weekends and spare time building their own home. Such a house might take years to build but would be completed, financially as well as materially, as soon as it was finished.

The third most disparate ranking applies to a change in argument with spouse. Predictably, this event is viewed as more severe by the urbanite, who ranks it 17, than by the rural dweller, who ranks it 33. This difference may result from the fact that divorce occurs much less frequently in a rural place than an urban one. The wife tends to be tied to the home and does not have as many options open. Under such conditions, family tensions might be viewed as more of a transitory phenomenon than in a setting where the dissolution of a marriage can occur with relative ease.

The fourth most disparate event involves minor violations of the law. This event is seen as much more severe by the rural dweller (rank 25) than the urbanite, who places it at the bottom of his list of events (rank 40) to be concerned about. In a rural area law violations have high visibility and are viewed negatively. In contrast, in an urban place the law is encountered as an impersonal entity that hands out tickets. Only the receiver of a summons and his or her insurance company are likely to know of a violation.

Factor Pattern Differences

The second approach to rural-urban differences involves an examination of Table 3 and an assumption that the same factors or dimensions apply to both populations even though specific items may be different. This assumption is based on the similarities in the event clusters in the two sets of data. Events that are shared represent the communality in the dimensions. Events that are different for the two groups represent the unique additions of each to the definition of the factors. Similarities and differences are easier to explain for some factors than for others. For example, Factor 1 appears to involve changes in life space. To the common events the rural sample adds three events: change in arguments with spouse; in-law problems; and change in family get-togethers. The urban group also adds three events: change to a new school; beginning or ceasing formal schooling; and change in residence. The set of unique events might be viewed as extensions of the dimension of stressfulness represented by the factor. Family and job changes show up in family and extended family relationship change in a geographically stable rural area. In a more mobile urban grouping the unique elements of the stress or change dimensions would move to include changes in schooling and residence, both of which are more vulnerable in an urban than in a rural area.

Factor 2 has three items in common with a loading of $>.45$, but the events added to the cluster by each sample reflect changes in personal life style. The rural group appears to look to interpersonal relationships for such changes. To the common pool of events they add pregnancy, gaining a new family member, health change in a family member, death of a friend, and change in amount of money. In contrast, the urban group tends to look inward and focus on events such as change in sleeping habits, change in eating habits, change in amount or type of recreation, and change in family get-togethers. The differences in the unique events again may be associated with the stronger extended family relationships that still exist in rural areas where extended family changes can very much affect individual life style.

Factor 3 has in common events having to do with dissolution of relationships. The urban group adds to that dimension detention in jail or some other institution and marital reconciliation. The rural group adds change in residence and major personal injury or illness. Any of the four can be associated with relationship change. The association of the four unique events is not uniformly clear.

The fourth factor involves termination of relationships, loss or exits from an individual's life space. The urban group adds to the basic cluster items having to do with changes in health status which might affect job, residence, activities, and so on. The rural sample adds loss items such as having items repossessed for nonpayment and being put in jail, both of which contain some element of termination of relationships.

SUMMARY

In summary, data drawn from rural and urban samples, even when there are differences in methodology, are ordered in similar ways when pooled averages are compared. Factor analysis of transformed individual responses yields similar structures and suggests that the urbanite from a Northwestern city and his rural counterpart may live in matrices of similar stresses, but with the dimensions of stress slightly involving some events unique to the subculture. Differences in the events located on the same dimensions were examined. Also, the events marriage, change in arguments with spouse, taking out a mortgage of greater than $10,000, and minor violations of the law were examined as most differentiating the two standardization groups.

Finally, differences in the distributions of means were examined through t-tests and found to be significant. Both methodological and perceptual explanations were explored. Because of ordering differences and because of mean differences, it is suggested that caution be exercised in using norms derived from one group on another without first checking the consensus values appropriate for the particular population under consideration.

REFERENCES

Croog, S. H. The family as a source of stress. In S. Levine and N. A. Scotch (Eds.), *Social Stress*. Chicago: Aldine Press, 1970.

Dohrenwend, B. S., & Dohrenwend, B. P. Class and race as status-related sources of stress. In S. Levine and N. A. Scotch (Eds.), *Social Stress*. Chicago: Aldine Press, 1970.

Gross, E. Work, organization, and stress. In S. Levine and N. A. Scotch (Ed.), *Social Stress*. Chicago: Aldine Press, 1970.

Harmon, D. K., Masuda, M., & Holmes, T. H. The social readjustment rating scale: A cross-cultural study of Western Europeans and Americans. Paper presented at the meeting of the American Psychiatric Association, Bal Harbour, Florida, May 1969.

Holmes, T. H., & Rahe, R. H. The social readjustment rating scale. *Journal of Psychosomatic Research,* 1967, **11,** 213–218.

Komaroff, A. L., Masuda, M. & Holmes, T. H. The social readjustment rating scale: A comparative study of Negro, Mexican, and White Americans. *Journal of Psychosomatic Research,* 1968, **12,** 121–128.

Masuda, M., & Holmes, T. H. The social readjustment rating scale: A cross-cultural study of Japanese and Americans. *Journal of Psychosomatic Research,* 1967, **11,** 227–237.

Mendels, J., & Weinstein, N. Schedule of recent experience. *Psychosomatic Medicine,* 1972, **34** (6), 527–531.

Rahe, R. H. Multi-cultural correlations of life change scaling: America, Japan, Denmark, and Sweden. *Journal of Psychosomatic Research,* 1969, **13,** 191–195.

Rahe, R. H., Lundberg, U., Bennett, L., & Theorell, T. The social readjustment rating scale: A comparative study of Swedes and Americans. *Journal of Psychosomatic Research,* 1971, **15,** 241–249.

Siegel, S. *Nonparametric Statistics for the Behavioral Sciences*. New York: McGraw-Hill Book Company, 1956.

Stevens, S. S. A metric for the social consensus. *Science,* 1966, **151**(3710), 530–541.

CHAPTER 17

Problems in Defining and Sampling the Relevant Population of Stressful Life Events *

BRUCE P. DOHRENWEND

A growing number of investigators are using lists of stressful life events. Some are studying the relation of the events to episodes of physical illness in general (e.g., Rahe, McKean, & Arthur, 1967; Thurlow, 1971), some to specific types of physical illness (e.g., Antonovsky & Kats, 1967; Theorell, 1970), some to various types of psychiatric disorder (e.g., Brown & Birley, 1968; Hudgens, Morrison, & Barchha, 1967), and some to various types of psychological symptoms (e.g., Dohrenwend, 1973b; Coates, Moyer, & Wellman, 1969; Myers, Lindenthal, Pepper, & Ostrander, 1972). Whether the investigator has provided his own list (Holmes & Rahe, 1967; Brown & Birley, 1968; Murphy, Robins, Kuhn, & Christensen, 1962; Antonovsky & Kats, 1967), used a list provided by others (Thurlow, 1971; Coates et al., 1969), or some combination of these (Myers et al., 1972; Cochrane & Robertson, 1973), there have been two main bases for arguing on a priori grounds that a particular list is a good one. One basis consists of an appeal to ''common sense''; that is, the assumption is made that most people would agree that the events chosen are stressful (cf. Holmes & Rahe, 1967; Brown & Birley, 1968; Antonovsky & Kats, 1967). The other basis is that patient histories taken in the hospitals or clinics in which the investigators have worked contain retrospective reports by the patients that the kinds of occurrence included on the lists preceded their admission to treatment (e.g., Holmes & Rahe, 1967; Cochrane & Robertson, 1973).

* This study was supported by Research Grant MH 10328 and by Research Scientist Award K5-MH-14,663 from the National Institute of Mental Health, U.S. Public Health Service. I would like to express my appreciation to Gerald Adler for his assistance in the statistical analyses and for his very helpful comments.

THE PROBLEM

Although the event lists compiled by the different investigators always overlap—the events of marriage, birth of a first child, loss of a job, and death of a loved one, for example, are common to most—the lists are by no means identical. Rather, they vary in number of items; for example, 27 on the list used by Murphy, Robins, Kuhn, and Christensen (1962); 43 on the list developed by Holmes, Rahe, and their colleagues (1967), 62 on the list used by Myers and his co-workers (1972). They also vary in content; for example, court martial is specific to lists used to investigate military personnel (Rahe et al., 1967); experience in Nazi concentration camps is included in research done in Israel (Antonovsky & Kats, 1967). In sum, the dictates of "commonsense" definitions vary with the subjects being studied, the setting in which the research takes place, and the types of illness or disorder being investigated.

Some of the differences are, it seems to me, straightforward in the sense that there are important events that are specific and meaningful to some groups of subjects and not to others. Other differences, however, reflect underlying issues of first theoretical and methodological importance. I am referring here to differences among investigators over how important it is to distinguish between objective events and subjective events (Thurlow, 1971), gain events and loss events (Dohrenwend 1973a), and between events that the individual is responsible for bringing about and events over which he has no control (Brown, Sklair, Harris, & Birley, 1973; Dohrenwend, 1973b). Finally, I have in mind major questions about the relation of psychopathology to physical illness that seem to me to be obscured in most of the research by investigators concerned with using life events lists in attempts at predicting or explaining psychopathology. In such research, physical illness is one type of event among many; the contribution of physical illness to psychopathology is obscured in reductions of the life events reported to total LCU scores (Masuda & Holmes, 1967; Rahe & Arthur, 1968), total events, or summary qualitative distinctions such as "gain" versus "loss" (Dohrenwend, 1973a) or, a close cousin, "desirable" versus "undesirable" (Myers et al., 1972).

Before getting further into such matters, it will be useful to have some data to talk about with reference to them. I mentioned that the defense of the event lists used by different investigators has been based on appeals to common sense and reference to retrospective reports of the types of event or crisis included by patients under treatment for various disorders or illnesses. Please note that I am speaking now of the items on the lists, not the ratings of these items for the purpose of obtaining LCU scores. As far as I know, there are no accounts in the literature of nominations, made independently of the researcher-constructed lists themselves, by samples of subjects drawn from the general population. Can such respondents, unselected for particular types of disorder or illness experience, help us to assess the adequacy with which various investigators relying on patient accounts and common sense have defined the population of stressful life events?

For example, when respondents sampled from the general population are asked to tell us what events have been important to them, do they nominate the same events or events different from those that we have put on our checklists without consulting them? Are they more likely to report subjective or objective events? Gain or loss events? Events for which they are responsible or events over which they have no control? Do they give a prominent place to physical illness? To emotional crises? And, most important, do they differ from groups of patients in these regards? If so, what are the consequences of these differences for research on relations between stressful life events and various types of psychiatric disorder and physical illness in general populations?

METHOD OF PROCEDURE

The data for the present investigation of these questions come from a larger methodological study concerned with the measurement of psychopathology and related role functioning over time and in the context of changing situations in contrasting class and ethnic groups (e.g., Dohrenwend, Chin-Shong, Egri, Mendelsohn, & Stokes, 1970). Our focus here is on the approach that we have used to elicit stressful life events as a key aspect of such situational contexts.

Research Setting and Subjects

The more than 500 subjects interviewed were drawn mainly from the Washington Heights section of New York City. These consist of 67 community leaders including, for example, state assemblymen, school principals, clergymen, and businessmen; a community sample consisting of 257 adult heads of families (both men and women, married and single) drawn on a probability basis from the general population of Washington Heights; 118 outpatients from various psychiatric clinics in or adjacent to Washington Heights; 62 inpatients admitted to either of two mental hospitals; and 24 convicts at city prisons. These represent completion rates of 79% of the leaders we set out to interview; 67% of the cross-sectional sample; 76% of the patients; and all of the convicts. All subjects were between 21 and 64 years of age. Most of the patients were not recent first admissions. The announced criterion for including convicts was repeated recidivism, although some first offenders were mistakenly selected for us by the prison authorities when these authorities suspected that they were suffering from severe emotional disturbances. In sum, the patients and convicts were selected in terms of the likely presence, often of long standing, of impairing psychopathology. In this regard, they were expected to contrast markedly with the leaders, who were selected in terms of the likelihood of superior functioning.

The Psychiatrist-Interviewers

The leader, outpatient, and community sample respondents were divided among 15 psychiatrists who conducted interviews with them, for the most part in the homes of the respondents. All but one of the psychiatrists had completed residency training. The initial interview assignments were randomized, and the large majority of the interviews were tape recorded. The inpatients and prisoners were interviewed in institutional settings in separate operations.

The Interview Instruments

The respondents were also divided at random between two different types of interview instrument—one called the Structured Interview Schedule (Dohrenwend et al., 1970) and the other the Psychiatric Status Schedule (Spitzer, Endicott, Fleiss, & Cohen, 1970). Both questionnaires were designed to elicit evidence of psychiatric symptomatology and attendant impairment of functioning in work, marital and sexual relations, and leisure activities. Each type of interview also contained an identical section designed to elicit reports of stressful life events in ways that will be described later.

The Clinical Judgments by Interviewers

Toward the end of the interview, but before questions were asked about stressful life events, the psychiatrist-interviewer made a series of global clinical assessments. These included psychiatric judgments using the main rating scales developed in the Midtown (Srole, Langner, Michael, Opler, & Rennie, 1962) and Stirling County studies (Leighton, Harding, Macklin, Macmillan, & Leighton, 1963).

The four categories of the Stirling County study ''caseness'' scale are designated A, B, C, and D in the order of greatest to least likelihood that the subject is suffering from one of the psychiatric disorders described in the 1952 *Diagnostic and Statistical Manual* of the American Psychiatric Association. The Midtown impairment rating, by contrast, ranges respondents on a scale from Well through five degrees of severity of symptomatology: Mild, Moderate, Marked, Severe, and Incapacitated (Srole et al., 1962, p. 399).* Independent

* These global ''caseness'' and ''impairment'' ratings are not appropriate for many epidemiological purposes that require distinctions among nosological types of psychiatric disorder. They are appropriate and even elegant for present purposes, however, since taken together they permit us to

reratings from tape recordings of 69 of the interviews by a second psychiatrist indicate satisfactory reliability for these ratings, as made by our psychiatrists.*

Since we get highly similar results on these interviewer ratings regardless of which type of interview was used so far as gross comparisons of patient and nonpatient groups are concerned (e.g., Dohrenwend, Egri, & Mendelsohn, 1971, p. 1307), we will combine respondents across the two types of interview in such comparisons for this chapter.† Moreover, since the two types of clinical rating show a strong positive correlation with each other, we will combine them into the following typology of disorder:

1. Well are those respondents rated D on the Stirling caseness scale.
2. Some symptoms but probably no psychiatric disorder equals C on the Stirling scale.
3. Mild psychiatric disorder equals A or B on the Stirling scale but Moderate or less on the Midtown scale.

test the contrasts in functioning that the leaders, community sample, and psychiatric patient respondents were selected to show.

* These independent reratings by a second psychiatrist were made as a check on the quality of the training of the psychiatrist-interviewers as well as a formal check on reliability in the rating procedures. The majority of the reratings were therefore concentrated in the first few interviews each psychiatrist did so that unreliable trends could be corrected at the outset. In brief summary: for the Stirling "caseness" rating, there was complete agreement 69.6% of the time and one-step disagreement 21.7% of the time by contrast with 65 and 31%, respectively reported by the Stirling County researchers for their own reliability study. However, the agreement in our Washington Heights study for patients and leaders was greater than for the 35 community sample respondents in the spot check who are really more comparable to respondents in the Midtown and Stirling County samples. For the community sample, complete agreement was 60.0% and one-step disagreement was 28.6% in the Washington Heights study. On the Midtown impariment rating, complete agreement in the Washington Heights check was achieved 52.2% of the time and one-step disagreements 37.7% of the time by contrast with respective figures of 47.2 and 44.7% reported in the Midtown study. Again, however, the reliability was less good for the Washington Heights community sample where complete agreement was 42.9% and one-step disagreement 43.8%. Nevertheless, the degree of reliability seems comparable to that achieved in the Midtown and Stirling County studies, especially when it is realized that the Washington Heights situations of the original rating (on the basis of the actual interview) and review rating (on the basis of a tape recording) are not as comparable as when both sets of ratings are made from the same written record as in the Midtown and Stirling County investigations where lay interviewers rather than psychiatrists conducted the interviews on the basis of which the psychiatrists made their ratings. This supposition of adequate reliability for these ratings in our study was supported when we calculated the statistic "weighted kappa," interpretable as an intraclass correlation coefficient, to summarize the amount of agreement (e.g., Fleiss, Spitzer, Endicott, & Cohen, 1972). Weighted kappa for agreement between the interviewing and reviewing psychiatrists in our study on the "caseness" rating is .73 and for the impairment rating .71, both appreciable.

† As a check, the analyses of these ratings contained in the remainder of the paper have been run separately for respondents interviewed with each type of interview. The relationships investigated are substantially the same regardless of which interview provided the basis for the psychiatrists' ratings.

4. Marked psychiatric disorder equals A or B on the Stirling scale and Marked on the Midtown scale.

5. Severe psychiatric disorder equals A or B on the Stirling scale and Severe or Incapacitated on the Midtown scale.

Table 5 Types of Last Major Event Reported by Respondents in Patient and Nonpatient Groups (%)

	Respondent Groups				
Severity of Psychiatric Disorder	**Leader**	**Community Sample**	**Psychiatric Outpatient**	**Psychiatric Hospital Patient**	**Convict**
Well	55.2	33.9	3.4	—	—
Some symptoms but probably no disorder	25.4	35.0	12.0	—	8.7
Mild disorder	10.4	9.0	3.4	—	—
Marked disorder	6.0	12.8	19.7	3.2	13.0
Severe disorder	3.0	9.3	61.5	96.8	78.3
Total	100.0	100.0	100.0	100.0	100.0
Total respondents (minus 2 unrated respondents)	(67)	(257)	(117)	(62)	(23)

Note: Gamma = .79; $p < .001$. Calculated with psychiatric patient and convict groups combined.

Table 1 shows, as expected, that our patient and nonpatient groups differ greatly in amount and severity of psychiatric disorder according to this index. Substantial majorities of the patient groups and the convicts were judged by our psychiatrists to show severe psychiatric disorder. The majority of the leaders, by contrast, were judged Well; community sample respondents were intermediate between these extremes, although considerably more similar to the leaders than to the patients and convicts.

Procedures for Eliciting Events

Consider some of the general descriptions of stressful life events or life crises provided in previous publications by researchers contributing to this book. For Holmes and Rahe, stressful life events are those "whose advent is either indicative of or requires a significant change in the ongoing life pattern of the individual" (1967, p. 217). For Myers and his colleagues, "crises" or "events" are defined as "experiences involving a role transformation, changes in status or environment, or impositions of pain'' (1972, p. 399). Brown and Birley focus on ''events which on common sense grounds are likely to produce emotional disturbance in many people . . . [and usually involve] either danger; significant changes in health, status or way of life; the promise of these; or important fulfillments or disappointments'' (1968, p. 204). And Antonovsky and Kats refer to ''life crises'' consisting of ''objective situations which, on the face of it, would seem to be universally stressful'' and involving ''an experience which either imposed pain or necessitated a role transformation'' (1967, p. 16).

The common denominators of all these definitions as well as our own is change in the individual's usual activities. Accordingly, the question that we put to the subjects of our research to get their own nominations of stressful life events was this simple one:

''What was the last major event in your life that, for better or for worse, interrupted or changed your usual activities?''

If no response was forthcoming, the interviewer used the following standard probe:

''For example, events affecting your occupation, your physical health, your living arrangements, your relations with other family members, your friends, or your personal values or beliefs.''

If a ''major event'' was recalled, the respondent was asked:

''When did this occur?'' Date(s)——————————————

''What happened?''

Several other questions were asked about additional events since then, but our main focus here is on the last major event.

After the preceding open-ended questions were asked and the responses recorded, we presented the respondents with a checklist and introduced it with the following question:

''Some things happen to most people at one time or another. Other things happen to only a few people. Which of these events have you experienced during the last 12 months?''

The events they were given on the checklist are as follows:

Started to school, training program, etc.
Graduated from school, training program, etc.
Failed school, training program, etc.
Moved to better neighborhood
Moved to worse neighborhood

Engaged
Married
Widowed
Divorced
Separated
Other broken love relationship—Explain
Birth of first child
Birth of child other than first
Serious physical illness to self
Serious injury to self
Serious injury to loved one—Who?
Serious physical illness to loved one—Who?
Death of a loved one—Who?
Started to work on a job for the first time
Expanded business
Promoted or moved to more responsible job
Changed to more secure job
Business failed
Demoted or changed to less responsible job
Laid off
Fired

Each of the items on this checklist is an objective event in the sense that its existence theoretically and often practically can be verified independently of the respondent's report of its occurrence and independently of the changes in usual activities that it is likely to bring about. These are relatively public, either/or occurrences. Specifically excluded from the list are some of the types of item that are included, along with objective events like those above, on other lists such as the one developed by Holmes and Rahe (1967). One of the types of item that we excluded describes events that both theoretically and practically are difficult or impossible to verify independently of the respondent's reports of their occurrence (e.g., trouble with in-laws, arguments with spouse and boss, sexual difficulties).

The other class of excluded items are those describing changes in the usual activities of the respondent (e.g., changes in eating or sleeping habits) that could be reactions to any or all of the objective and subjective events included on most lists. Unlike the objective events, these subjective events and subjective reactions are relatively private and their presence or absence frequently turns on somewhat arbitrary judgments about matters of degree. Finally, all occurrences—be they objective events, subjective events, or subjective reactions—that involve descriptions of a subject's psychiatric disturbance or treatment for such disturbances have been excluded.

The Plan of Analysis

Our procedure is to examine the events reported in response to the open-ended questioning and to the checklist by the leaders and by the psychiatric patients and convicts to see how both contrast with events reported by the community sample respondents. Our aim in these comparisons is to see what we can learn about the relevant population of life events to be defined and sampled for purposes of investigating the etiology of psychopathology in general populations. Although our main focus is on psychopathology, our expectation is that the analysis will have implications for further research on life events and physical illness as well.

RESULTS

The Last Major Event in Their Lives as Defined by Respondents

Let us start where the respondents started: with their own definition of the last major event in their lives that, for better or worse, interrupted or changed their usual activities. As Table 2 shows, large majorities of the respondents in all of the patient and nonpatient groups that we studied reported a last major event.

Table 2. Extent to Which Checklist Categories Describe Last Major Events Reported in Response to Open-Ended Question in Patient and Nonpatient Groups (%)

	Respondent Groups				
Categorization of Event	Leader	Community Sample	Psychiatric Outpatient	Psychiatric Hospital Patient	Convict
No major event	7.6	16.5	21.1	18.9	10.5
Checklist category	54.5	56.3	38.6	26.4	15.8
Nonchecklist category	37.9	27.2	40.3	54.7	73.7
Total percentage	100.0	100.0	100.0	100.0	100.0
Base for percentage equals total respondents minus "no answers"	(66)	(254)	(114)	(53)	(19)

Note: With the psychiatric patient and convict groups combined, X^2 for the overall results = 11.40, $df = 2$, $p < .01$. Moreover, 2 x $2X^2$'s show that the difference in proportions of events in nonchecklist categories between the community sample and the combined patients and convicts is significant at the .01 level ($X^2 = 19.07$). The difference between the leaders and community sample respondents in this regard is just short of significance at the .10 level ($X^2 = 2.40$).

There are, however, sharp contrasts among the groups in the proportions of these events that corresponded to the categories of objective events that we included on our list. Leaders and community sample respondents were considerably more likely to report such events than were the groups of psychiatric patients or convicts. Nevertheless, especially in the leader but also in the community sample, substantial minorities reported last major events that were not included on our checklist. What kinds of "new" events were involved in these reports by respondents from our patient and nonpatient groups?

The first thing to note in Table 3 is that, by contrast with the leaders and the community sample respondents, the "new" events reported by the psychiatric patients tend to describe either episodes of psychiatric disturbance or entrance into treatment for such disturbance—types of subjective and objective events that we explicitly excluded from our checklist of objective events. For convicts, description of their legal plight takes the place of the patients' description of their psychiatric treatment.

By contrast with the patients and prisoners, the "new" or nonchecklist events reported by leader and community sample respondents tend to be objective events that we might well have included on our checklist. Some of these are specific to the circumstances of a portion of the leaders who held elective offices; not infrequently such respondents reported that the last major event in their lives was an important election that they had won. In addition, some respondents reported objective events that could happen to most people but that we simply overlooked—such as accidents in which they themselves were not hurt, a child getting married, or a child leaving for school.

Smaller proportions of the patients and prisoners than of the leaders and the community sample respondents, it will be recalled, reported types of event in response to the open-ended question that could be classified in the categories included in our checklist. Did these types of event for patients and convicts also differ from those in the checklist categories reported by leaders and community sample respondents?

For the relatively few patients and convicts who did nominate events that could be classified in checklist categories, Table 4 shows that the concentrations are in marriage, its breakup by death or other causes, physical illnesses and injuries, births of children, and death of loved ones—also the types of event in checklist categories that were most frequently nominated by leaders and community sample respondents. However, for the most part the patients and convicts simply did not nominate events in most of the checklist categories, as Table 2 showed.

One way in which the events in Tables 3 and 4 differ from each other is in terms of whether they are likely to represent gains or losses to most people who experience them. We think that this distinction is relatively clear cut, and you can check your judgments against a portion of mine and Barbara Dohrenwend's

Table 3. Other than Checklist Events Reported in Response to the Open-Ended Question about Last Major Event by Respondents in Patient and Nonpatient Groups (%)

Type of Other than Checklist Event	Respondent Groups				
	Leader	Community Sample	Psychiatric Outpatient	Psychiatric Hospital Patient	Convict
Events which are subdivisions or add detail to existing checklist categories	12.0	11.6	10.9	13.8	—
Events which could be added to checklist categories if more information were available	12.0	10.2	6.5	—	7.1
Events which apply primarily to children of respondents	8.0	17.4	6.5	—	—
Major objective events of types new to the checklist	60.0	34.8	19.5	6.9	—
Insignificant-seeming objective events	—	8.7	2.2	13.8	—
Interpersonal conflicts with a strong subjective component, not referable to objective events	—	5.8	2.2	10.3	—
Episode of psychiatric or emotional disturbance to family member other than self	—	2.9	2.2	—	—
Episode of psychiatric or emotional disturbance to self—no mention of treatment	—	4.3	23.9	24.2	50.0
Entrance into psychiatric treatment	—	4.3	23.9	20.7	—
Severe legal difficulties, especially being imprisoned	—	—	2.2	—	42.9
Other, e.g., faith gained or lost	8.0	—	—	10.3	—
Total percentage	100.0	100.0	100.0	100.0	100.0
Base for percentage equals total respondents reporting other than checklist events	(25)	(69)	(46)	(29)	(14)

Table 4. Checklist Events Reported in Response to Open-Ended Question about Last Major Event by Respondents in Patient and Nonpatient Groups (* = gain; ** = mix; no * = loss; + = occurrence, other than physical illness or injury to self, outside subject's control; numbers in parentheses are Masuda and Holmes, 1967, LCU scores (%))

	Respondent Groups				
Checklist Event	Leader	Community Sample	Psychiatric Outpatient	Psychiatric Hospital Patient	Convict
* Started to school, training program, etc. (191)	—	—	2.3	—	—
* Graduated from school, training program, etc. (191)	—	—	—	—	—
Failed school, training program, etc. (378)	—	—	—	—	—
* Moved to better neighborhood (140)	5.5	4.9	—	—	—
Moved to worse neighborhood (140)	—	—	2.3	7.1	—
* Engaged (500)	—	0.7	—	—	—
* Married (500)	19.5	10.5	20.4	35.7	66.7
+ Widowed (771)	8.3	9.1	—	14.3	—
Divorced (593)	—	3.5	6.8	—	—
Separated (516)	—	7.0	9.1	14.3	—
Other broken love relationship (286)	2.8	1.4	13.6	—	—
* Birth of first child (337)	—	6.3	9.1	7.1	—
** Birth of child other than first (337)	5.5	2.1	2.3	—	—
Serious physical illness to self (416)	22.2	15.3	4.5	21.4	—
Serious injury to self (416)	2.8	6.3	4.5	—	—

by looking at the asterisked events in Table 4.

A second way in which they differ is in the control the respondent is likely to have had over their occurrence. This question of control is a more difficult one since matters of degree are more crucially involved than in differentiating gain from loss. At the extreme, however, the judgment is not too difficult to make, we think, if you are willing to rely on two considerations: first, whether the respondent is unlikely to have intended or planned the event; second, regardless of his intent or plan, whether the subject is unlikely to be in a position to bring about or prevent its occurrence. Events clearly meeting both of these considerations in our judgment are noted by a plus sign in Table 4 as events whose occurrence are likely to be beyond the control of the respondent by contrast with events for which he is more likely, in the above sense, to be responsible. Again,

Checklist Event	Respondent Groups				
	Leader	Community Sample	Psychiatric Outpatient	Psychiatric Hospital Patient	Convict
+ Serious injury to loved one (not spouse) (335)	—	—	—	—	—
+ Serious physical illness to loved one (not spouse) (335)	—	2.8	2.3	—	—
+ Death of a loved one (not spouse) (469)	2.8	11.9	11.4	—	33.3
+ Death, illness, or injury to significant other (e.g., boss) (287)	—	0.7	2.3	—	—
+ Injury to spouse (335)	2.8	0.7	—	—	—
+ Illness to spouse (335)	2.8	4.2	—	—	—
* Started to work on a job for the first time (308)	5.5	0.7	—	—	—
* Expanded business (308)	—	0.7	—	—	—
* Promoted or moved to more responsible job (243)	16.7	3.5	2.3	—	—
* Changed to more secure job (243)	—	—	—	—	—
Business failed (308)	2.8	2.8	—	—	—
Demoted or changed to less responsible job (243)	—	—	—	—	—
+ Laid off (308)	—	3.5	—	—	—
Fired (378)	—	1.4	6.8	—	—
Total percentage	100.0	100.0	100.0	100.0	100.0
Base for percentage equals total respondents reporting checklist type of event	(36)	(143)	(44)	(14)	(3)

you can check your own judgments against Barbara Dohrenwend's and mine by examining the events noted in Table 4.

With these distinctions in mind along with the earlier distinctions between objective and subjective events and between events that are direct manifestations or consequences of psychopathology and those that are not, we have classified the events reported into broader types in order to summarize the similarities and contrasts among our patient and nonpatient groups. From most likely to be consequences of psychiatric disorder to most likely to be consequences of superior functioning, the types of event are as follows:

1. The respondent's subjective crises that are direct manifestations of psychiatric or emotional disturbance (e.g., a "nervous breakdown") and/or objective

events such as hospitalization or imprisonment that are direct consequences of such disturbance.

2. The respondent's interpersonal conflicts.

3. Miscellaneous insignificant-seeming objective events and rare or unusual subjective events that are not clear in their relation to the respondent's psychiatric condition.

4. Objective loss events for whose occurrence the respondent is likely to share significant responsibility (e.g., divorce, separation).

5. Serious physical illness or injury to the respondent.

6. Objective loss events—other than serious physical illness or injury to the respondent—that are likely to be outside the respondent's control (e.g., being widowed, husband's loss of job, spouse's physical or psychiatric illness).

7. Objective events that our own disagreeing judgments suggested to us that most people would see as representing mixtures of gains and losses in roughly equal portions or mainly gains to some respondents and mainly losses to equal numbers of other respondents (e.g., birth of a child other than first).

8. Objective gain events (e.g., promotion, birth of a first child).

The first four types of event listed above are ordered in terms of likelihood of being consequences of the individual's psychopathology (cf. Langner & Michael, 1963, pp. 117–146). By contrast, the last two types of event are ordered in terms of likelihood of being consequences of generally superior functioning on the part of the individual. The two remaining types—serious physical illness and injury to the respondent and other objective loss events that are likely to be outside the person's control—are intermediate in the ordering. Especially in the case of the latter type of objective loss, there is little reason to believe that such events are consequences of either the individual's psychopathology or of his superior functioning. Moreover, such types of objective loss and also physical illness and injury can be operationally defined independently of the individual's psychiatric condition. Thus they are meant to occupy a neutral midpoint in the ordering of types of events from most likely to be confounded with psychopathology to most likely to be confounded with superior functioning.*

As Table 5 shows, there are sharp differences in these types of last major event reported by the patient and nonpatient groups. The leaders are more likely than either community sample respondents or outpatients to have reported gain events. Moreover, closer inspection than our categories in Table 5 afford reveals that these gains for the leaders are likely to be consistent with their plans and to some extent within their power to bring about—such as the

* This ordering lacks precision. For example, some types of physical illness and injury are more likely to be comsequences of psychopathology than others. Also, some of the gain events that occur to children of the respondents may reflect only very indirectly on the psychiatric condition of the respondents themselves (e.g., having children of whom they can obviously be proud).

Table 5. Types of Last Major Event Reported by Respondents in Patient and Nonpatient Groups (%)

	Respondent Groups				
Type of Last Major Event	Leader	Community Sample	Psychiatric Outpatients	Psychiatric Hospital	Convicts
No last major event	7.6	16.5	21.1	18.9	10.5
Objective gain event	36.4	20.5	17.6	18.9	10.5
Objective event that may mix gain and loss	9.1	7.1	3.5	1.9	5.3
Objective loss event other than physical illness or injury—outside *R*'s control	18.2	24.8	13.2	7.5	5.3
Loss event involving physical illness or injury to respondent	13.6	12.2	3.5	5.7	—
Objective loss event less likely to be outside respondent's control	12.1	12.6	19.3	3.7	—
Miscellaneous event, insignificant objective event, or rare subjective event	3.0	2.4	0.9	13.2	—
Largely subjective events in the form of interpersonal conflicts involving respondent	—	1.5	0.9	5.7	—
Events which are direct manifestations of psychopathology or sociopathy and/or their dispositions	—	2.4	20.2	24.5	68.4
Total Percentage	100.0	100.0	100.0	100.0	100.0
Base for percentage equals total respondents minus no answers	(66)	(254)	(114)	(53)	(19)

Note: With "no last major event" excluded and psychiatric outpatients, hospital patients and convicts combined, gamma = .37, $p < .001$.

elections they have won and the promotions they have received. The patients and convicts, by contrast, are far more likely than leaders or community sample respondents to report events that are direct manifestations or consequences of their psychopathology.

Note also that there is a tendency for leaders and community sample respondents to report more last major events involving physical illness and injury and other objective losses over which they have no control than the patients and convicts. These differences are probably due to the overriding importance that the patients and convicts place on events intrinsic to their psychopathology. As will be seen later, they appear to experience physical illness or injury and other objective events whose occurrence is outside their control as frequently as do leaders and community sample respondents.

The marked differences in types of last major event reported are not, however, simply a function, for example, of a recent legal or psychiatric crisis for the convicts or patients by contrast with recent successes of the leaders. Table 6 shows that the large majority of the leaders, community sample respondents, and psychiatric outpatients reported last major events that occurred a year or more before the interview. Moreover, not shown in Table 6 is the fact that only 13% of the psychiatric outpatients whose last major event was a manifestation or disposition of psychiatric disorder said that it occurred within the preceding 12 months whereas 22% said that it occurred over 10 years ago with the remainder evenly distributed over the intervening time intervals shown in Table 6. Nor were the leaders focusing on recent gain events; only 20% of those who reported gains as their last major event said that the gain occurred in the 12 months prior to the interview, with the remainder distributed evenly over more remote time intervals. That the psychiatric hospital patients and prisoners reported last major events within the past year is probably a function of where and how we selected them for our interview: in jails and hospitals on the basis of their recent admission.

The differences in the last major events reported by our patient and nonpatient groups, then, appear to stem from the differing life histories of typical respondents in these groups. For the typical patients and prisoners, the factors that have brought about major changes in their lives are not independent of their impairing psychopathology. And for typical leaders, the major events as they define them are not independent of their generally superior functioning.

As a group, our community sample respondents contrast with the leaders and with the patient and convict groups with regard to the last major events that they report and with regard to their psychiatric condition. Some community sample respondents appear to resemble typical leaders, some typical patients on these counts. It seems reasonable therefore to expect that those community respondents who report last major events resembling those of the leaders will tend to have life histories and hence psychiatric conditions more in common

Table 6. Recency of Last Major Event Reported by Respondents in Patient and Nonpatient Groups (%)

Recency of last major event	Leaders	Community Sample	Psychiatric Outpatients	Psychiatric Hospital Patients	Convicts
	Respondent Groups				
0–7 days	—	1.4	—	4.9	—
8–14 days	3.3	1.4	—	12.2	—
15 days through 1 month	—	2.4	—	4.9	—
Over 1 month through 2 months	—	0.5	2.2	7.3	—
Over 2 months through 6 months	13.1	8.6	8.9	7.3	37.5
Over 6 months through 1 year	9.8	13.8	10.0	9.8	12.5
Over 1 year through 2 years	9.8	12.8	15.6	12.2	6.3
Over 2 years through 5 years	21.3	24.8	22.2	14.6	31.3
Over 5 years through 10 years	21.3	15.7	16.7	12.2	12.5
Over 10 years	21.3	18.6	24.4	14.6	—
Total percentage	99.9	100.0	100.0	100.0	100.1
Base for percentage equals respondents reporting last major event and time of last major event	(61)	(210)	(90)	(41)	(16)

Note: X^2 for overall results with psychiatric patient and convict groups combined = 15.4, 18 *df*, n.s.

with the leaders. By contrast, we would expect those community respondents who report last major events more nearly resembling those reported by the patients and the prisoners to have life histories and hence psychiatric conditions more like those of the patients and prisoners.

The results in Table 7 are consistent with these expectations. Community sample respondents who report gain or mixed gain and loss events contrast sharply with respondents who report events that are directly related to their psychiatric disturbance. Moreover, respondents who report objective loss events for which they may be responsible are intermediate between these extremes in severity of psychiatric disorder. Note, however, the surprising difference between respondents reporting physical illness or injury and those reporting some other objective loss for which they were not likely to be responsible. Those reporting a serious physical illness or injury are far more likely to show marked

Table 7. Severity of Psychiatric Disorder According to Type of Last Major Event in Community Sample (%)

Severity of Disorder	Type of Last Major Event								
	No Last Major Event	Gain	Mixed	Loss: Not Responsible	Physical Illness or Injury	Loss: Own Responsibility	Miscellaneous	Interpersonal Conflict	Direct manifestations or Consequences of Psychiatric Disturbance
Well	45.2	40.4	55.6	34.9	16.1	25.0	16.7	—	—
Some symptoms but probably no disorder	26.2	30.8	27.8	44.5	51.6	31.3	33.3	25.0	16.7
Mild disorder	11.9	9.6	11.1	11.1	3.3	6.2	16.7	—	—
Marked disorder	4.8	11.5	5.5	7.9	16.1	25.0	—	50.0	50.0
Severe disorder	11.9	7.7	—	1.6	12.9	12.5	33.3	25.0	33.3
Total	100.0	100.0	100.0	100.0	100.0	100.0	100.0	100.0	100.0
Total respondents (excluding no answers)	(42)	(52)	(18)	(63)	(31)	(32)	(6)	(4)	(6)

Note: With "no last major event" excluded, gamma = .29; $p < .001$. For "Severity of disorder" by "loss: not responsible" versus "Loss: physical illness or injury," $X^2 = 10.61$, 4 *df*, $p < .05$.

or severe psychiatric disorder. Those reporting loss events whose occurrence is outside their control, by contrast, differ little in severity of psychiatric disorder from those reporting gain events.

Is it possible that this difference is a function of greater change associated with physical illness and injury than with other objective events over which the individual has no control? In fact, is it possible that we could account for the entire set of results in Table 7 on the basis of differences in the LCU scores associated with the events in each of the types?

Unfortunately, we can investigate this possibility only for the last major events that were classified in checklist categories since only such events were near enough to events on the Holmes and Rahe list for us to be able to make use of the LCU scores developed by Masuda and Holmes (1967). These are presented in Table 4 and some arithmetic with the results for the community sample respondents in Table 4 will show you that the differences in LCU scores are unlikely to be able to explain the results in Table 7. Thus whereas the respondents in the "gain" and "mixed" categories have low average LCU scores of 355.0 and 337.0, respectively, the respondents with the highest LCU scores—those experiencing a last major event involving loss over which they had no control—are from a group very like the respondents in the "gain" or "mixed" categories in severity of psychopathology. The respondents with a loss over which they had no control had a mean LCU score of 500.2 by contrast with 416.0 for those reporting a serious injury or illness to themselves and 464.6 for those reporting an objective loss event for which they may have been responsible.

Events Reported in Response to the Checklist for the Preceding Year

There are two sharp differences in the conditions for reporting events in response to the checklist by contrast with the open-ended question about last major events. The checklist provides the respondent with a definition of events that he is to report on, all of them objective; moreover, the time period for his report is limited to events that occurred during the preceding year. The open-ended approach to eliciting last major events, by contrast, does not restrict the respondent to a particular time period nor does it define for him the events he is to report on. Hence a question arises as to how great the overlap is in the events reported in response to the two approaches: To what extent were the checklist events reported for the preceding year also defined by respondents as the last major events that occurred for them in the preceding year?

Table 8 contains the answer: Surprisingly few of the events reported in response to the checklist were previously nominated by the respondents themselves as last major events in their lives occurring in the preceding year. With the exception of events such as marriage, birth of a first child, being widowed,

Table 8. Events Reported in Checklist Together With Percentage of Overlap with Last Major Events in Preceding 12 Months According to Group Membership of Respondents (In upper left corner of each cell is percentage of respondents reporting the checklist event. In lower right corner is percentage of these respondents who also reported the event as the last major event in the preceding year.)

	Respondent Groups				
Type of Event (checklist categories only)	Leader	Community Sample	Psychiatric Outpatients	Psychiatric Hospital Patients	Convicts
* Started to school, training program, etc. (191)	7.6 0.0	5.9 0.0	8.8 0.0	9.4 0.0	5.3 0.0
* Graduated from school, training program, etc. (191)	1.5 0.0	2.0 0.0	— —	1.9 0.0	— —
Failed school, training program, etc. (378)	— —	0.8 0.0	2.6 0.0	— —	5.3 0.0
* Moved to better neighborhood (140)	2.1 0.0	9.4 12.5	10.5 0.0	22.6 0.0	10.5 0.0
Moved to worse neighborhood (140)	— —	1.2 0.0	6.1 14.3	13.2 0.0	42.1 0.0
* Engaged (500)	— —	0.4 0.0	1.8 0.0	9.4 20.0	— —
* Married (500)	3.0 50.0	0.8 50.0	1.8 50.0	3.8 0.0	— —
+ Widowed (771)	— —	3.1 50.0	— —	1.9 0.0	— —
Divorced (593)	— —	0.8 0.0	— —	1.9 0.0	10.5 0.0
Separated (516)	1.5 0.0	0.8 0.0	8.8 10.0	11.3 0.0	15.8 0.0
Other broken love relationship (286)	3.0 50.0	0.8 0.0	10.5 16.7	11.3 0.0	21.1 0.0
* Birth of first child (337)	— —	1.2 66.7	3.5 50.0	1.9 0.0	5.3 0.0
** Birth of child other than first (337)	— —	3.1 0.0	4.4 0.0	— —	5.3 0.0
Serious physical illness to self (416)	16.7 36.4	14.6 24.3	16.7 0.0	13.2 28.6	5.3 0.0
Serious injury to self (416)	1.5 0.0	2.0 60.0	4.4 20.0	3.8 0.0	15.8 0.0

Type of Event (checklist categories only)	Respondent Groups Leader	Community Sample	Psychiatric Outpatients	Psychiatric Hospital Patients	Convicts
+ Serious injury to loved one (not spouse) (335)	4.5 0.0	2.4 0.0	0.9 0.0	— —	— —
+ Serious physical illness to loved one (not spouse) (335)	13.6 0.0	8.3 14.3	10.5 8.3	3.8 0.0	5.3 0.0
+ Death of a loved one (not spouse) (469)	16.7 0.0	15.7 5.0	16.7 10.5	17.0 0.0	21.1 25.0
+ Death, illness, or injury to significant other (e.g., boss) (287)	— —	0.8 0.0	— —	5.7 0.0	— —
+ Injury to spouse (335)	1.5 100.0	0.8 0.0	1.8 0.0	— —	— —
+ Illness to spouse (335)	1.5 0.0	4.7 16.7	2.6 0.0	— —	— —
* Started to work on a job for the first time (308)	10.6 0.0	6.3 0.0	15.8 0.0	7.5 0.0	10.5 0.0
* Expanded business (308)	7.6 0.0	3.1 12.5	1.8 0.0	1.9 0.0	— —
* Promoted or moved to more responsible job (243)	22.7 6.7	8.7 9.1	6.1 14.3	3.8 0.0	— —
* Changed to more secure job (243)	3.0 0.0	2.4 0.0	5.3 0.0	5.7 0.0	— —
Business failed (308)	— —	1.6 25.0	0.9 0.0	— —	— —
Demoted or changed to less responsible job (243)	1.5 0.0	2.0 0.0	0.9 0.0	5.7 0.0	— —
+ Laid off (308)	— —	3.9 20.0	6.1 0.0	5.7 0.0	15.8 0.0
Fired (378)	— —	2.4 33.3	2.6 33.3	7.5 0.0	5.3 0.0
Total respondents minus no answers	66	254	114	53	19

Note: * = gain; ** = mix; no * = loss; + = occurrence, other than physical illness or injury to self, that is outside subject's control; numbers in parentheses are Masuda and Holmes (1967) LCU scores.

perhaps being fired, and, possibly, physical illness and injury for leaders and community sample respondents, most of the events on our one-year checklist are not "major" by the definitions of even a substantial minority of the respondents who experienced them. With regard to our earlier observation about the infrequency of physical illness to self and injury to self among the last major events reported by patients and convicts, note that they report these events at least as frequently on the one-year checklist as do leaders and community sample respondents—although, as we could anticipate from the earlier results, proportionally fewer patients and convicts define them as last major events.

A one-year checklist of the kind that we have used is not, apparently, a very good way to elicit events that the respondents define as major. Nor is an open-ended question about last major events a very good way to elicit the types of objective event that actually occur in a given year and that we defined as major. A main reason, we believe, is that what are "major" events for leaders on the one hand and patients and convicts on the other are defined to a considerable extent in terms of the successes of the leaders and the psychopathology of the patients and prisoners; the checklist simply does not include many events that are direct indications of either. By extension, we believe that it also excludes many events that are most likely to be "major" for community sample respondents whose psychiatric conditions closely resemble those of either the leaders or the patients or convicts.

If it is true that some of the broad types of event that we have been considering are more likely than other types to occur as a function of the individual's enduring psychiatric condition, we would expect to find similar differences in types of event reported on the checklist to those we found earlier in the last major events reported by our patient and nonpatient respondents—even though the checklist covers a narrower range of events. In addition, we would expect to be able to predict to some extent the reports of types of event in the past year in response to the checklist from reports of types of more remote last major event in response to the open-ended question. Confirmation of such a relationship would be especially compelling in the community sample. Moreover, we should be able to at least partially replicate with the checklist results on these broad types of event some of the major findings on relations between psychiatric condition and the broad types of last major event.

Accordingly, let us first compare our patient and nonpatient groups in terms of the gain, loss, and responsibility characteristics of the checklist events they reported. Since, unlike the last major event reported, respondents could report more than one checklist event, it was necessary to combine such multiple events in the analyses that follow. For the results in Tables 9, 10, and 11, we decided to give greatest weight to the types that showed the strongest relationship with psychopathology in our previous analysis of reports of last major events. Thus of the checklist types of events, highest priority in the combina-

Table 9. Types of Event Reported in Response to Checklist by Respondents in Patient and Nonpatient Groups (%)

	Respondent Groups				
Type of Checklist Event	Leaders	Community Sample	Psychiatric Outpatients	Psychiatric Hospital Patients	Convicts
No checklist event	31.8	40.5	27.2	22.6	10.5
Gain events only or gain events plus mixed events only	30.3	17.7	21.1	18.9	5.3
Event that may mix gain and loss	—	1.6	—	—	—
Loss: not responsible and no other types of loss event	24.3	21.3	18.4	17.0	10.5
Loss: physical illness and injury and no loss: own responsibility	10.6	11.4	14.0	7.5	5.3
Loss: own responsibility and any other types of events	3.0	7.5	19.3	34.0	68.4
Total Percentage	100.0	100.0	100.0	100.0	100.0
Total respondents (minus no answers)	(66)	(254)	(114)	(53)	(19)

Note: With "no checklist events" excluded and psychiatric outpatients, hospital patients, and convicts combined, gamma = .34; $p < .001$.

tions was given to loss events for which the respondent may have been responsible; next to physical illness or injury; next to other loss events likely to be outside the respondents' control; least to gain and to ambiguous events, though more to gain events when they occurred together with ambiguous events for the same respondents.

Table 9 shows that there are, as in the case of the results with differing types of last major events, contrasts between the leaders on the one hand and the psychiatric patient and prisoner groups on the other, with the community sample again intermediate. Consistent with the previous results, moreover, the type characterized by gain is more frequent among the leaders; the type characterized by loss for which the respondent is likely to be responsible is more frequent among the patients and convicts.

Let us turn to the question of whether we can predict the types of more current checklist event in the community sample from the types of more remote last major event—excluding, of course, respondents whose "last major event"

Table 10. Relation of Types of Event Reported on Checklist for Past 12 Months to Reports of Last Major Events Occurring over 12 Months Ago by Community Sample Respondents

Type of Checklist Event	Type of Last Major Event (over 1 year)							
	Gain	Mixes of Gain and Loss	Loss: Not Responsible	Loss: Physical Illness or Injury	Loss: Own Responsi-bility	Miscellaneous	Interpersonal Conflict	Direct Consequence of Psychiatric Disturbance
No checklist event	44.4	20.0	40.4	47.4	48.2	66.7	—	50.0
Gain events only or gain events plus events that mix gain and loss	27.8	40.0	14.9	10.5	11.1	—	—	—
Mixes of gain and loss	8.3	—	—	5.3	—	—	—	—
Loss: not responsible and no other types of loss events	13.9	26.6	17.0	21.0	33.3	—	50.0	50.0
Loss: physical illness and injury and no loss: own responsibility	2.8	6.7	21.3	15.8	3.7	—	—	—
Loss: own responsibility and any other types of events	2.8	6.7	6.4	—	3.7	33.3	50.0	—
Total percentage	100.0	100.0	100.0	100.0	100.0	100.0	100.0	100.0
Base for percentage equals total respondents reporting last major event over 12 months ago	(36)	(15)	(47)	(19)	(27)	(3)	(2)	(2)

Note: With "no checklist event" excluded, gamma = .29; $p < .05$, two-tailed test.

occurred during the previous 12 months. Table 10 shows that there does appear to be some relation between the types of more remote last major event and the types of more recent checklist event that were reported by community sample respondents. Note, however, that in the last three columns of Table 10, which show the greatest contrast with the first two, the number of respondents is very small. It is rare that such events are reported as "major" by community respondents when they occurred more than a year ago.

Our final question about the relation of the reports of last major events to the reports in response to the checklist centers on whether we can replicate the earlier relationship shown in Table 7 substituting the types of checklist event for the types of last major event. Table 11 shows that, to a considerable extent, we can. The type characterized by loss for which the subject may have been responsible and the type characterized by physical illness and injury are associated with the more severe psychopathology.

We saw earlier that the types of last major event that could be categorized in checklist categories differed in mean LCU scores for those reporting them. The differences did not, however, account for the differences in psychopathology among the community sample respondents reporting the different types of last major event. We can also calculate mean LCU scores for the different types of checklist event reported by community sample respondents on the basis of the results reported in Table 8. Accordingly, the mean LCU scores for the gain events reported on the checklist by community sample respondents is 232.2; for the mixed events, 337.0; for the physical illness and injury events, 416; for the other loss events for which the subject was not responsible, 406.5; and for loss events for which the subject may have been responsible, 331.2. These mean scores for the types of event reported in response to the checklist tend to be lower than for the last major events of the same general type reported in response to the open-ended questioning. This difference suggests that, by and large, the last major events tended to be objectively as well as subjectively more important for community sample respondents. Nevertheless, the checklist results are similar to the last major event results in that differences in LCU scores for the different types *qua types* do not account for differences in psychopathology.

Recall, however, that unlike last major events, more than one type of event could be reported by a subject in response to the checklist. Note, moreover, that the way we have combined reports of multiple types of event in order to investigate their relation to psychopathology in Table 11 is highly likely to confound the number of events reported by a respondent with the gain, loss, and responsibility characteristics that are the basis for ordering the types in terms of least to greatest likelihood of being consequences of psychiatric disorder. That is, by giving highest priority in combinations of more than one type of event to loss events for which the respondent may be responsible, we singled out re-

Table 11. Severity of Psychiatric Disorder According to Type of Event Reported in Response to the Checklist by Community Sample Respondents ("Loss: own responsibility" given first priority in combination) (%)

Severity of Psychiatric Disorder	Type of Event on Checklist					
	No Checklist Event	Gain Events Only or Gain Events Plus Mixed Events Only	Events That May Mix Gain and Loss	Loss: Not Responsible and No Other Types Of Loss Event	Loss: Physical Illness or Injury and No Loss: Own Responsibility	Loss: Own Responsibility and Any Other Types of Event
Well	39.8	42.2	—	40.7	6.9	10.5
Some symptoms but probably no disorder	30.1	26.7	75.0	33.3	62.1	42.1
Mild disorder	10.7	8.9	—	9.3	6.9	5.2
Marked disorder	12.6	13.3	25.0	7.4	13.8	21.1
Severe disorder	6.8	8.9	—	9.3	10.3	21.1
Total percentage	100.0	100.0	100.0	100.0	100.0	100.0
Total respondents	(103)	(45)	(4)	(54)	(29)	(19)

Note: With "no checklist event" excluded, gamma = .24; $p < .01$, two-tailed test.

Table 12. Severity of Psychiatric Disorder According to Type of Event Reported in Response to Checklist by Community Sample Respondents ("Loss: not responsible" given first priority in combination) (%)

Severity of Psychiatric Disorder	Type of Event on Checklist					
	No Checklist Event	Gain Events Only or Gain Events Plus Mixed Events Only	Events That May Mix Gain and Loss	Loss: Not Responsible and Any Other Type of Event	Loss: Physical Illness or Injury and No Loss: Not Responsible	Loss: Own Responsibility and No Other Types of Event
Well	39.8	42.2	—	33.3	5.3	9.1
Some symptoms but probably no disorder	30.1	26.7	75.0	38.9	57.9	45.4
Mild disorder	10.7	8.9	—	7.0	10.6	9.1
Marked disorder	12.6	13.3	25.0	8.3	21.0	18.2
Severe disorder	6.8	8.9	—	12.5	5.3	18.2
Total percentage	100.0	100.0	100.0	100.0	100.1	100.0
Total respondents	(103)	(45)	(4)	(72)	(19)	(11)

Note: With "no checklist event" excluded, gamma = .21; $p < .05$, two-tailed test.

spondents whose events may be contaminated with psychiatric disorder, which was our intention. We also loaded the dice, however, since such respondents can have experienced the other types of loss event as well. Other things constant, such respondents would have more events and hence higher LCU scores than, for example, respondents typed as having only a loss event for which they are unlikely to be responsible according to the weighting procedure that we used. Thus it is possible that the most striking contrast in Table 11—more severe psychiatric disorder among respondents reporting serious physical illness or injury and losses for which they may be responsible than for respondents reporting losses for which they are unlikely to be responsible—might be an artifact of our procedure for combining the types.

To test this, let us reverse the priorities for the loss events, giving highest priority in the combinations to loss events over which the respondent has no control and lowest priority to loss events that he may be responsible for bringing about. As Table 12 shows, the essential relationship remains unaltered. Thus the results in Table 11 are not simply an artifact of the weighting procedure that we used in combining the types of checklist event when more than one type of checklist event was reported.

The analysis with the checklist events thus tends to replicate our findings with last major events. Most important is the fact that among the objective events we have studied that are not direct consequences of psychopathology, it is again the type of loss event involving physical illness and injury and the type involving losses for which the individual may be responsible that are most likely to be accompanied by psychiatric disorder in the community sample. The strength of the relation between psychopathology and the type of loss event for which the individual may be responsible poses a major methodological problem of contamination between the supposedly stressful events and psychopathology. By contrast, the strength of the relation between psychopathology and the type of loss event involving physical illness or injury poses a major substantive issue of the nature of the relationship between the two broad categories of disorder.

SUMMARY OF THE FINDINGS AND DISCUSSION OF THEIR IMPLICATIONS

Let me try to summarize the results briefly and spell out what I take to be their implications for further research. This investigation has focused on contrasts among several groups of subjects: leaders, community sample, psychiatric outpatients, psychiatric hospital patients, and convicts. The leaders on the one hand and the psychiatric patients and convicts on the other were selected on the basis of their likely contrasts in psychiatric condition: superior functioning in the case of the leaders; impairing psychopathology in the cases of the psychiatric patients and prisoners. That these contrasts actually existed was confirmed by the clinical assessments made by the psychiatrists who conducted the interviews in this study. By contrast with the leaders and with the patients and convicts, the community sample respondents were unselected with regard to psychiatric condition. As would be expected, they were found to be intermediate in amount of psychiatric disorder when compared with the leaders on the one hand and the psychiatric patients and convicts on the other.

We found sharp differences among the leaders by contrast with the patient and convict groups in the types of event that they themselves nominated as the last major event in their lives that, for better or worse, interrupted or changed their usual activities. The leaders tended to report objective gain events that they were likely to have had some responsibility for bringing about. By contrast, the patients and prisoners tended to report either subjective or objective events that were direct manifestations or consequences of their psychiatric disorder or objective loss events for which they were likely to be at least partly responsible. Moreover, community sample respondents who resembled the leaders in reporting last major events involving gain also resembled them in showing low rates of psychiatric disorder. By contrast, community respondents who reported last major events involving objective losses for which they are likely to be responsible or events that are direct manifestations of or consequences of psychiatric disorder tended to show high rates of psychiatric disorder, as did the patients and convicts. These relationships, although somewhat reduced in strength, were replicated when we substituted objective events in the preceding year only as reported on our checklist. This replication held despite the fact that most of the events reported on the checklist were not also defined as last major events occurring in the preceding year and despite the fact that fewer events are involved on the checklist, which excludes, for example, all events of a subjective variety and all events that are direct manifestations or consequences of psychopathology.

Two types of loss event did not consistently differentiate leaders from the patient and convict respondents. One consists of objective events involving losses that are likely to be outside the respondent's control such as death of a loved one or physical illness of a spouse. The other is serious physical illness or injury to the respondent himself. There were thus no grounds on the basis of leader versus patient and convict differences for predicting which of these two types of event, if either, would be associated with more severe psychiatric disorder in the community sample. Nor, as the results turned out, did differences in their LCU scores predict different relationships with psychopathology for these two types of objective loss event or for either one of them by contrast with other objective loss events for which subjects in the community sample may have been responsible. Rather, the outcome was that those respondents reporting physical illness or injury were considerably more likely to show psychiatric disorder than those respondents reporting other objective loss events whose occurrence was outside their control. They were exceeded in amount of psychiatric disorder only by respondents reporting events that seemed on the face of it more likely to be confounded with psychopathology. Perhaps this is not as surprising as it first seems in view of the number of previous studies that have found a strong positive correlation between psychiatric disturbance and episodes of physical illness (e.g., Hinkle & Wolff, 1957; Shepherd, Cooper, Brown, & Kalton, 1966; Eastwood & Trevelyan, 1972).

If our analysis is correct, then, it is not whether they represent gain or loss, the number involved, or the amount of change associated with them that is likely to tell us most about the role of stressful life events in the etiology of psychopathology. Some types of gain and loss events are too hopelessly confounded with superior functioning on the one hand and impairing psychopathology on the other to be useful in investigating the causation of either. Moreover, the number of events involved and the amount of change as measured by LCU scores does not appear to be related to differences in psychopathology among respondents reporting different types of objective loss event. Rather, what appears to be crucial to the differences in psychopathology among those reporting different types of objective loss event is whether the events involve physical illness or injury to the respondent and whether or not their occurrence is outside the subject's control. Moreover, it is these distinctions that are involved in the two types of objective loss event that not only contrast in the rates of psychopathology associated with them but also can be defined independently of the subject's psychiatric condition—physical illness or injury on the one hand and other objective loss events whose occurrence is outside the control of the individual on the other. In my opinion therefore the main clues to our understanding of the role of stressful life events in the causation of psychopathology are to be found in how individuals react to these two types of objective loss event. It is here that LCU scores may be important if they can be developed to provide an indication of the relative magnitude of events, singly and in combination, within these two types.

What are the implications of these findings and conclusions for further research? It seems to me that there are several major implications, and that they differ according to whether your interest is in pure actuarial prediction of disorders or in investigating the possible significance of stressful life events in the etiology of the disorders. There are also differences according to whether your main focus is on physical illnesses of various kinds or on various kinds of psychopathology.

If you are interested mainly in the actuarial prediction of impairing psychiatric disorder, then you should infest your list of life events with loss events for which the individual is responsible, trivial seeming objective events that the respondent defines as "major," interpersonal conflicts and changes in eating and sleeping habits, subjective events that are manifestations of psychological distress, and episodes of treatment for psychiatric disorder. After all, there is nothing that predicts the symptomatology that defines disorder like a portion of that very same symptomatology. To increase the precision of the discrimination, you should add a separate list of gain events whose occurrences are under the respondent's control since these are highly likely to be confounded with superior functioning. Needless to say, such research will tell you little about etiology. In fact, if you try to make more than an actuarial interpretation of your results, you are likely to be misled.

You will also probably do fairly well with such a procedure in the actuarial prediction of at least some kinds of physical illness and injury. In his study of brewery workers, for example, Thurlow (1971) found, despite the fact that events on the Holmes and Rahe list that he classified as subjective had lower LCU scores than the more objective events, that only the subjective events showed statistically significant positive relationships with number of illnesses and number of days off. The reason for this finding may well be a strong positive correlation between physical illness and psychopathology on the one hand, and between the psychiatric condition of his subjects and the more subjective events they reported on the other. Again, however, a purely actuarial approach would tell you little about the role of stressful life events in the etiology of physical illness. Rather, it would re-pose for more theoretically oriented researchers the fascinating problem of the nature of relations between physical illness and psychiatric disorder.

If your interest is in etiology rather than in actuarial prediction per se, the implications of our results are more far reaching, more complicated, and, I think, more interesting. Let me try to spell out how and why.

Most current measures of stressful life events are based on the implicit assumption by the researchers who develop and use them that there is only one population of stressful life events or, if there are more than one, that there is great overlap among them where many of the most commonly occurring events are concerned. Some support for these assumptions might be seen in the fact that seemingly dissimilar events—for example, objective by contrast with subjective events—both entail changes in a person's activities; or in the fact that the individual may be more or less responsible for events such as divorce or separation depending on the circumstances in each instance. In this general view it is quite legitimate to measure severity of stress in terms of the number of events an individual experiences or, more powerfully, in terms of the LCU scores of these events. Other investigators, by contrast, imply that there are several very different event populations by making distinctions, for example, between objective and subjective events, gain and loss events, and events for which the individual may or may not be responsible. I share this latter general view. Moreover, I think that the present results demonstrate that there are at least three vastly different populations of events that it is vitally important to keep analytically distinct if the investigation is focused on problems of etiology. These three are:

1. A population of events that are confounded with the psychiatric condition of the subject.
2. A population of events consisting of physical illness and injury to the subject.
3. A population of events whose occurrences are independent of either the subject's physical health or his psychiatric condition.

As a general principle, the more the sample of items in a particular measure of stressful life events represents a mixture from these three event populations, the more difficult it will be to assess the implications of a relationship between such a measure and either various types of psychopathology or various types of physical illness.

In current measures of stressful life events, including our own, the samples of events from each are, indeed, to a greater or lesser extent intermixed. There are two main reasons for this and each suggests the types of solution required.

One reason for the mixtures is the imprecision with which the items are defined. Thus, for example, a subject may indicate that he had a serious physical illness based on his own diagnosis which would prove on clinical examination to be a psychiatric problem; and with more information on the intent of a respondent and the circumstances, it is likely that events such as divorce or separation, classified as a rule as objective losses for which the respondent was likely to bear responsibility, would prove in some instances to be objective losses for which the respondent was not responsible. A major problem for future research, it seems to me, is how to reduce this imprecision. Its solution lies in securing more information about the events.

The second reason for the mixture lies in the ways that the individual events from the three event populations are combined to measure the magnitude of stress. The greatest mixture, for example, is produced by summary counts of the number of events an individual experiences or by the procedure of calculating the total LCU score attached to his events regardless of which of the three event populations they come from. Lesser but nevertheless seriously confounding mixtures are produced, for example, by combinations distinguishing between gain and loss, but not between physical illness and other losses or between events within or outside the individual's control. One step toward a solution is simply to take apart what has been put together. Once this has been done, however, we face the problem of how to put the events sampled from the three populations back together again in a more meaningful way for measurement purposes. How do we proceed?

Consider, for example, that you are concerned with investigating the possible etiological significance of stressful life events in the occurrence of various types of psychopathology. The important life events to be investigated then are those drawn from event populations 2 and 3 above—that is, those events involving physical illness and injury and those involving other objective losses whose occurrence is outside the control of the respondent. Possibly some gain events that are outside the control of the respondent should also be included, though these were rarely defined as major events by respondents in any of our groups. The key problem is how to sample these events in such a way that their interrelations with each other and their possible contribution to (as distinct from confusion with) psychopathology can be evaluated.

Some ingredients of a possible research design to solve this problem might consist of the following:

1. A probability sample of subjects unselected for psychopathology and, preferably, drawn from the general population.
2. Baseline measures of their psychiatric condition, including measures of various types of psychopathology and related role functioning.
3. Restrospective measures that sample and date key or landmark events from each of the three event populations over the major developmental stages of the subject's life history. (I realize here that there are major problems of recall that increase as one goes back in time. Thus this retrospective sample of events characteristic of the life history of the subject would focus on those occurrences from each event population that are most likely to be remembered: for example, from event population 2, hospitalizations for physical illness, extended periods of absence from usual activities for physical illness. From event population 3, death of parents or spouse, other separation from parents during childhood, hospitalizations of spouse.)
4. A short-term follow-up—say after one year—at which time the following would be secured:
(a) Postmeasures of the psychiatric condition of the respondents.
(b) Intervening measures of the most important events that occurred during the year from each of the three populations, with each event carefully dated with respect to every other in terms of time occurrence. Here the short-term follow-up would maximize accurate recall so that the coverage of both number of events and details of the events reported could be much more extensive. The relation of these to the retrospective life history sample of landmark events described above would give us some indication as to whether this brief one-year sample of the respondent's life included events that were typical or atypical of his life history of events.

In this design the key variables whose etiological significance would be evaluated are the events from event populations 2 and 3 (physical illness and injury and objective events outside the subject's control) that occur between the premeasures and postmeasures of psychiatric condition. The events from event population 1 that occurred between the premeasures and postmeasures would be used as control variables to test for possible early onset or exacerbation of psychopathology if they preceded the events from event populations 2 and 3 or as part of the postmeasure of psychiatric condition if they followed the events from event populations 2 and 3.

If you were interested in studying the etiological significance of life events in physical illness rather than in psychopathology, a similar strategy could be used. In such an investigation the subjects sampled would be unselected for physical illness; the baseline and postmeasures would be of physical illness; and the intervening events whose etiological significance would be evaluated would be drawn from event populations 1 and 3 rather than 2 and 3.

As should be evident, the variables of physical illness and psychopathology are key ones in both strategies. The reason, of course, is that the strong positive relationship between them makes it impossible to ignore either regardless of whether interest is mainly in the relation of life events to physical illness or in the relation of life events to psychopathology. The fact of the matter is that the two main groups of contributors to this book, one concerned more with physical illness and the other more with psychopathology, have much to learn from each other and ample warrant on the basis of the research to date to make the effort to do so.

REFERENCES

Antonovsky, A., & Kats, R. The life crisis history as a tool in epidemiological research. *Journal of Health and Social Behavior,* 1967, **8,** 15–21.

Brown, G. W., & Birley, J. L. T. Crises and life changes and the onset of schizophrenia. *Journal of Health and Social Behavior,* 1968, **9,** 203–214.

Brown, G. W., Sklair, F., Harris, T. O., & Birley, J. L. T. Life-events and psychiatric disorders, Part I: Some methodological issues. *Psychological Medicine,* 1973, **3,** 74–87.

Coates, D., Moyer, S., & Wellman, B., Yorklea study: Symptoms, problems and life events. *Canadian Journal of Public Health,* 1969, **60,** 471–481.

Cochrane, R., & Robertson, A. The life events inventory: A measure of the relative severity of psycho-social stressors. *Journal of Psychosomatic Research,* 1973, **17,** 135–139.

Dohrenwend, B. P., Chin-Shong, E. T., Egri, G., Mendelsohn, F. S., & Stokes, J. Measures of psychiatric disorder in contrasting class and ethnic groups: A preliminary report on on-going research. In E. H. Hare & J. K. Wing (Eds.), *Psychiatric Epidemiology: An International Symposium*. London: Oxford University Press, 1970. Pp. 159–202.

Dohrenwend, B. P., Egri, G., & Mendelsohn, F. S. Psychiatric disorder in general populations: The problem of clinical judgment. *American Journal of Psychiatry,* 1971, **127,** 1304–1312.

Dohrenwend, B. S. Life events as stressors: A methodological inquiry. *Journal of Health and Social Behavior,* 1973, **14,** 167–175. (a)

Dohrenwend, B. S. Social status and stressful life events. *Journal of Personality and Social Psychology,* 1973, **28,** 225–235. (b)

Eastwood, M. R., & Trevelyan, M. H. Relationship between physical and psychiatric disorder. *Psychological Medicine,* 1972, **2,** 363–372.

Fleiss, J. L., Spitzer, R. L., Endicott, J., & Cohen, J. Quantification of agreement in multiple psychiatric diagnosis. *Archives of General Psychiatry,* 1972, **26,** 168–171.

Hinkle, L. E., & Wolff, H. G. Health and the social environment. In A. H. Leighton, J. A. Clausen, & R. N. Wilson (eds.), *Explorations in Social Psychiatry.* New York: Basic Books, 1957. Pp. 105–137.

Holmes, T. H., & Rahe, R. H. The social readjustment rating scale. *Journal of Psychosomatic Medicine,* 1967, **11,** 213–218.

Hudgens, R. W., Morrison, J. R., & Barchha, R. G. Life events and onset of primary affective disorders. *Archives of General Psychiatry,* 1967, **16,** 134–145.

Langner, T. S., & Michael, S. T. *Life Stress and Mental Health.* New York: The Free Press of Glencoe, 1963.

Leighton, D. C., Harding, J. S., Macklin, D. B., Macmillan, A. M., & Leighton, A. H. *The Character of Danger.* New York: Basic Books, 1963.

Masuda, M., & Holmes, T. H. The social readjustment rating scale. *Journal of Psychosomatic Research,* 1967, **11,** 219–225.

Murphy, G. E., Robins, E., Kuhn, N. O., & Christenson, R. F. Stress, sickness and psychiatric disorder in a "normal" population: A study of 101 young women. *Journal of Nervous and Mental Disease,* 1962, **134,** 228–236.

Myers, J. K., Lindenthal, J. J., Pepper, M. P., & Ostrander, D. K. Life events and mental status: A longitudinal study. *Journal of Health and Social Behavior,* 1972, **13,** 398–406.

Rahe, R. H., & Arthur, R. J. Life change patterns surrounding illness experience. *Journal of Psychosomatic Research,* 1968, **11,** 341–345.

Rahe, R. H, McKean, J. D., & Arthur, R. J. A longitudinal study of life-change and illness patterns. *Journal of Psychosomatic Research,* 1967, **10,** 355–366.

Shepherd, M., Cooper, B., Brown, A. C., & Kalton, G. W. *Psychiatric Illness in General Practice.* London: Oxford University Press, 1966.

Spitzer, R. L., Endicott, J., Fleiss, J. L, & Cohen, J. The Psychiatric Status Schedule: A technique for evaluating psychopathology and impairment in role functioning. *Archives of General Psychiatry,* 1970, **23,** 41–55.

Srole, L., Langner, T. S., Michael, S. T., Opler, M. K., & Rennie, T. A. C. *Mental Health in the Metropolis: The Midtown Study,* Volume I. New York: McGraw-Hill Book Company, 1962.

Theorell, T. *Psychosocial Factors in Relation to the Onset of Myocardial Infarction: A Pilot Study*. Stockholm: Department of Medicine, Seraphimer Hospital, Karolinska Institute, 1970.

Thurlow, H. J. Illness in relation to life situation and sick-role tendency. *Journal of Psychosomatic Research,* 1971, **15,** 73–88.

PART 5

Conclusion

CHAPTER 18

Overview and Prospects for Research on Stressful Life Events

BARBARA SNELL DOHRENWEND AND BRUCE P. DOHRENWEND

The contributors to this book have presented evidence that supports the general hypothesis that stressful life events play a role in the etiology of various somatic and psychiatric disorders. There is considerable disagreement among them, however, as to the nature of this role. For example, Holmes and Masuda concluded that a clustering of life events sufficient to be labeled a "crisis" will have "etiologic significance as a necessary, but not sufficient, causes of illness and accounts in part for the time of disease onset (p. 48)." In explaining the etiological role of life crises Holmes and Masuda postulated "that life-change events, by evoking adaptive efforts by the human organism that are faulty in kind and duration, lower 'bodily resistance' and enhance the probability of disease occurrence (p. 68)." In contrast, Hinkle emphasized the primary role of predisposing factors and the secondary role of life events, at least with respect to certain types of illness. Other authors more or less explicitly assigned varied weights to stressful life events as a threat to health in general or in relation to particular illnesses.

EFFECTS OF STRESSFUL LIFE EVENTS

Because of its complexity, the issue of the pathogenic potency of stressful life events probably cannot be resolved by head-on attack. However, advances have been made and, we think, will continue to be made by researchers focusing on specific questions that underlie this general issue. One such specification concerns the variety of the correlates of stressful life events.

Variety of Correlates

A question for which we have a fairly clear answer is: Are the correlates of stressful life events limited to specific types of pathology? A review of earlier chapters in this book will provide a partial but useful set of evidence on this question.

The greatest variety of effects was described by Holmes and Masuda. In addition to reporting that overall changes in health were related to stressful life events, they cited studies showing the following specific correlates: heart disease, fractures, childhood leukemia, pregnancy, beginning of prison term, poor teacher performance, low college grade point average, and college football players' injuries. Among specific somatic disorders associated with stressful life events Hinkle and Theorell focused attention on coronary heart disease, both fatal and nonfatal, but with more equivocal results than those reported by Holmes and Masuda. Paykel, Hudgens, and Brown each added evidence that various psychiatric disorders may follow stressful life events, specifically acute schizophrenia, depression, suicide attempts, and neurosis.

The range of psychological correlates was expanded by evidence from the epidemiological research with community samples reported by Markush and Favero and by Myers and his colleagues. Markush and Favero found that relatively mild symptoms of depression as well as an index of general level of mental health were related to measures of stressful life events. Myers and his colleagues showed that a slightly different index of mental health was also related to the stressfulness of life events. Gersten and her colleagues extended the association between mental health indexes and measures of stressful life events to children in a community sample.

This evidence from recent clinical and epidemiological studies of extremely heterogeneous effects is consistent with Hinkle's appraisal that early experimental research suggested "that there would probably be no aspect of human growth, development, or disease that would in theory be immune to the influence of the effect of a man's relation to his social and interpersonal environment," and that "subsequent experimental investigations . . . have strongly supported [this] conclusion (p. 10)." Thus the answer to the question of whether the correlates of stressful life events are limited in kind seems to be that almost any disease or disability may be associated with these events.

Magnitude of Risk

But "may" is not "will," so the next question is: What is the risk that illness or disability actually will follow stressful life events? Unfortunately, this question cannot be answered definitively from the evidence that is currently available.

There are two major reasons for this lack of information. The first is that many investigators have not designed their research to provide an answer to this question. The second is that as yet unresolved methodological issues raise, at the very least, serious doubts about the accuracy of the answers that have been provided.

The majority of studies of effects of stressful life events have started with a set of cases that had been given clinical diagnoses and compared them with a set of controls, usually healthy persons matched to the clinical cases on some background characteristics (cf. MacMahon & Pugh, 1970, Ch. 12). Relatively few studies have started with cohorts of individuals who differed with respect to their experience of stressful life events and examined them to determine the consequences of this experiential difference (cf. MacMahon & Pugh, 1970, Ch. 11). In the first type of study the finding that, compared to their controls, the clinical cases had an excess of stressful life events prior to the onset of illness implies that such events are a factor in the etiology of the diagnosed illness. However, only studies of cohorts who differ with respect to stressful life events provide any information about the magnitude of the risk that illness or disability will actually follow these events, information without which the practical implications of research on stressful life events is far from clear.

A number of studies using the cohort design were reported in this book. However, the only one that provided a straightforward estimate of the risk of illness was a study by Rahe and Holmes reported in the chapter by Holmes and Masuda. The results of this study, presented in Table 6 of that chapter, imply that the risk of illness following stressful life events is very high. Specifically, Rahe and Holmes found in a study of physicians that 55% of all "life crises" (our calculation) and 79% of major life crises were followed by health changes. These figures rest on a number of somewhat arbitrary procedures, however.

First, the definition of "life crisis" was determined after the fact on the basis of the distribution of the 96 health changes reported by the subjects of this study: "Eighty-nine of the 96 major health changes reported (93 percent) were associated temporally with a clustering of life changes whose values summed to at least 150 LCU per year. A life crisis was, thus, defined as any clustering of life-change events whose individual values summed to 150 LCU or more in 1 year." Second, as Holmes and Masuda noted, "On the basis of the previous studies . . . , an *arbitrary* criterion was established for the temporal association of an illness or health change with life-change events: a reported change in health must occur within the 2-year period following the occurrence of a cluster of life changes" (p. 59, our italics). Third, a point that we will return to, the list of life events used here appears to contain items that might more properly be classified as symptoms of illness than as antecedent life events, thus spuriously inflating the size of the relation between reported events and illness. Finally, the application of these figures to individuals is problematic since the base for the percentages was number of life crises rather than number of persons with a given LCU score. All of these considerations suggest that these figures overestimate the risk of illness following stressful life events.

This interpretation is supported by a follow-up study in which Rahe and Holmes used the life events reported for an 18-month period by 84 of their original subjects to predict illness during a subsequent 9-month period. They found that "49 percent of the high-risk group (300+ LCU) reported illness; 25 percent of the medium-risk group (200–299 LCU) reported illness; and 9 percent of the low-risk group (150–199 LCU) reported illness (p. 64)." Since most of the problems present in the first part of this study were not solved in this prospective follow-up, even these lower figures are probably overestimates.

Seriousness of Effects

Assessment of the effects of stressful life events depends not only on establishing what proportion of individuals suffer adverse health changes of one kind or another following these events, but also on the seriousness of these changes. For example, how often do stressful life events lead to a heart attack and how often to a cold? Although this question cannot be answered directly from available data, Mechanic inferred from the prevalence rates for different disorders that the latter is probably the more common kind of outcome: "Studies dealing with illness in general come to depend disproportionately on common instances of illness, particularly acute respiratory disease, which overshadow more important types of morbidity that occur with lower prevalence in the population (p. 92)."

A similar inference with respect to symptoms of psychological disorder is suggested by the longitudinal study reported by Myers and his colleagues. As they showed in Tables 7 and 8 in their chapter, changes in psychological symptom scores over a two-year period tended to reflect changes in their subjects' life events. The implication of these data is that psychological symptoms associated with stressful life events are often labile. These results are consistent with Hudgens' caveat, based on his clinical experience, that "we should remember that most people do not become severely disabled psychiatrically when terrible things happen to them, and that those who do become disabled regain their equilibrium in a reasonably short time (p. 119)."

Factors that Mediate Responses to Stressful Life Events

A major question, and for some investigators the central problem concerning the effects of stressful life events, grows out of the observation that one individual may become ill and another remain healthy after both experience the same life event. The most general formulation of the research question generated by these individual differences is: What are the factors that mediate the impact of stressful life events on the individual? In practice, this question tends to be divided along disciplinary lines into three parts:

1. What are the physiological processes that mediate the individual's response to stressful life events?

2. What are the psychological processes that mediate the individual's response to stressful life events?

3. What are the social processes that mediate the impact on the individual of stressful life events?

Research directed at answering the first question is illustrated by the studies of heart disease reported by Theorell and by Hinkle. On the basis of work in progress Hinkle suggested that "New cases of coronary heart disease rarely if ever occur except among men who have some combination of hyperlipidemia, abnormalities of carbohydrate metabolism, hypertension, cigarette smoking, and a family history of this disease (p. 37)." Thus although Hinkle also found that heart attacks were sometimes associated with stressful experiences, he emphasized their limited importance compared to predisposing physiological factors in the etiology of heart disease. A similar point was made by Hudgens, without explicitly specifying possible mediating factors, with respect to serious psychiatric disorder: "it does not seem to me that investigators have yet convincingly demonstrated that life stress can cause madness in a person previously of sound mind" (p. 120; cf. Dohrenwend & Dohrenwend, 1969, Ch. 8).

Psychological processes that might mediate the effects of stressful life events were discussed by a number of authors. This topic was, for example, the focus of Antonovsky's chapter. He hypothesized that a set of personality characteristics, which he labeled resistance resources, explains differences between individuals in general vulnerability to the ill effects of stressful life events, but he has not yet carried his research to the point of testing this hypothesis. Using a related but somewhat different concept Rahe included psychological defenses as a component in his lens model of factors that determine the outcome of stressful life events, and he cited a study of parents of children dying of leukemia as evidence that the ability to mobilize these defenses mediates physiological responses to stressful life events. Theorell reviewed a number of studies that indicate associations between various personality characteristics and heart disease, with the implication that these traits may make individuals more vulnerable to heart attack following stressful life events.

In general, the results of psychological research suggest that personality differences probably mediate the effects of stressful life events. However, this research has not yet provided estimates of the extent to which these differences modify the risk of general or specific effects of stressful life events.

The third question, concerning social factors that mediate the impact of stressful life events on individuals, was addressed by Brown in his chapter. His ratings of contextual threat represent an attempt to develop a global measure of social processes leading to individual differences in response to stressful life events. This global approach was implicitly rejected by Cobb, however, who suggested a set of specific social supports to be studied as possible factors intervening between stressful life events and illness. Estimates of the extent to which either social processes measured globally or any specific processes modify the risk of illness following stressful life events have yet to be developed, however.

Hypotheses Concerning Effects of Stressful Life Events

From the specific questions concerning effects of stressful life events with which researchers have been concerned, and from the varying positions that have been taken by contributors to this book on these questions, alternative hypotheses can be derived:

1. Compared to other physiological, psychological, or social factors, stressful life events account for a relatively large proportion of the risk of illness.
2. Compared to other physiological, psychological, or social factors, stressful life events account for a relatively small proportion of the risk of illness.

These hypotheses can be applied either to illness in general or to more or less specifically defined categories of illness. Whether applied to general illness or specific disease, neither hypothesis represents precisely the position taken by any particular researcher. Instead, these hypotheses serve to point up issues that have been generated by recent research.

As they stand, however, the hypotheses are not sufficient to provide a basis for resolving the overall issue of the pathogenic power of stressful life events, for they leave this basic term undefined. Since there is considerable controversy about the conceptualization and measurement of life events, let us review the major theoretical controversies and methodological issues to see what specific questions need to be answered.

CONCEPTUALIZATION AND MEASUREMENT OF STRESSFUL LIFE EVENTS

On the question of how to measure the stressfulness of life events the most obvious point of divergence among the contributors to this book concerns the issue of whether life events are stressful in objective terms or whether, as Hudgens argued, "what is stressful for one person may be of little consequence to another (p. 131)." In support of the latter position Hinkle reported that "there was . . . evidence from the personality studies which indicated that those who had experienced the greater amount of illness had, in general, perceived their environment as more threatening, challenging, demanding, and frustrating than the healthier people. The more healthy members of the group tended to describe their life situations in a much more benign manner, even though these experiences 'objectively,' in the eyes of the examiner, seemed to be very like the experiences of the frequently ill (p. 29).'' In contrast, Holmes and Masuda presented extensive research based on a system that assigns a standard score to describe the stressfulness of a given life event, and this scoring system was also used in research reported in several other chapters (Gersten et al.; Markush & Favero; Miller et al.; Myers et al.; Theorell).

Underlying the highly visible disagreement about subjective versus objective definitions of stressfulness, however, is a prior issue on which there appears to be considerable agreement. Specifically, before becoming concerned with criteria for determining whether or to what extent life events are stressful, investigators have of necessity designated, at least implicitly, an objectively defined domain of events to which this question applies: the domain of life events that are possibly stressful.

The Domain of Possibly Stressful Life Events

In laboratory studies of responses to stressful stimuli the domain from which stimuli are drawn is usually defined in terms of apparent noxiousness (e.g., Frankenhaeuser, 1971). This straightforward definition has not generally been used for research on stressful life events, however. Instead, most studies on this topic have investigated events that change a person's life, no matter whether the change appears to be for better or for worse. Conversely, stimuli that elicit habitual activities have not generally been included in studies of stressful life events, no matter what their quality.

The wide acceptance of life changes as the domain of possibly stressful life events is illustrated by the fact that it was used in most of the studies reported in this book despite their other theoretical and methodological differences. At the same time, this definition of the domain was challenged by Gersten and her coauthors as both too narrow and too broad, and by Hudgens and by Brown implicitly, and by Paykel and by Theorell explicitly, as possibly too broad.

Gersten and her coauthors implied that life changes was too narrow a domain when they suggested, ''Perhaps we should include as an event on an event list a nonevent. A nonevent is an event that is desired or anticipated and does not occur; thus nonevents could be either desirable or undesirable (p. 169).'' The authors also noted, however, that this addition to the domain is incompatible with measurement procedures, based on the concept of readjustment, that are used in a considerable portion of current research on stressful life events. The modification they suggested therefore may not be readily incorporated into ongoing programs of research.

The suggestion that the domain of possibly stressful life events should be narrowed was implied by Hudgens in his study of depression when he limited his sample of events to "personal catastrophes." A somewhat ambiguous limitation was implied by Brown's decision in studies of schizophrenia and depression to investigate events "which on commonsense grounds are more likely than most to produce marked emotional arousal (p. 227)." Neither of these investigators examined a wider domain in order to determine whether the set of events that they selected was especially closely associated with the psychiatric conditions under study.

In contrast, Paykel investigated the relation of a wide selection of life changes to several types of psychiatric disorder. The results of these studies led him to conclude that "events that can be regarded as desirable do not appear to occur excessively before any of the psychiatric disorders examined, but undesirable events do. An additional distinction, that between exits and entrances, appears particularly relevant to clinical depression: exits precede depression but entrances do not (p. 148)." Thus the evidence from Paykel's research suggests that when the effects being studied are certain major psychiatric disorders only undesirable life changes should be included in the domain of potentially stressful life events, and when depression in particular is the effect under investigation the domain might be narrowed to include only events that involve the exit of someone from the social field of the subject.

In their study of child behavior Gersten and her coauthors obtained results that supplement and are generally consistent with Paykel's findings. Their analysis showed that most of the childhood disorders they investigated, and the disorders that they considered to have the most serious long-term implications for the child, were related to undesirable but not to desirable life changes. They also found, however, that one of their measures, regressive anxiety, was affected by life changes of the desirable as well as the undesirable kind.

The chapters by Paykel and by Gersten and her colleagues have, then, focused attention on the hypothesis that the domain of possibly stressful life events is limited to particular categories of life changes, specifically, either undesirable changes or exits, at least when the predicted outcomes are certain types of psychiatric disorder. In contrast, Rahe pointed out in his chapter that studies concerned with a wider variety of illnesses have yielded positive relations between desirable life events and illness reports. He also noted, however, that none of the results to date concerning effects of desirable events can be considered definitive since so few events in this category have been studied (cf. Kellam, this volume, p. 213).

Classifying events in terms of a different set of categories, the type of activity involved, Theorell found that despite the fact that myocardial infarction patients and their nonpatient controls did not report different numbers of events, "41% of the patients compared to 17% of control subjects ($p < .01$) were found to have reported changes at work during the year investigated (p. 107)." Furthermore, Theorell noted, ''The observed tendency of premature MI patients to report problems and changes at work is probably related to this patient group's 'work addiction' tendency (p. 110).'' Although he cautioned that because these results are based on a retrospective study, ''the fact that the patient has known about the disease may have contaminated the answers to the question (p. 107),'' it is interesting to note complementary findings from studies reported by Paykel which also involved retrospective reporting—specifically, psychiatric patients, when compared to matched general population controls, did not, in general, report an excess of events in any particular area of activity. Thus although Theorell's results are not definitive, they point to a type of classification that may provide a useful limitation on the domain of possibly stressful life events in relation to myocardial infarctions.

In general, then, the question still to be answered is whether limited domains of possibly stressful life events will be found for some types of disorder, or whether the domain of possibly stressful life events encompasses all life changes for all or nearly all outcomes. The prospect of finding that relatively narrow domains of life events are related to specific disorders is an attractive one, either from a theoretical or a practical perspective, that deserves systematic investigation.

Issues Raised by Procedures for Sampling Possibly Stressful Life Events

The various lists of life events that have been used by investigators are samples drawn from the domain of possibly stressful life events, defined usually, as we have noted, as life changes. In drawing these samples, as in assembling items for most psychological measures (cf. Nunnally, 1967, p. 175), investigators have depended heavily on subjective judgment. Such judgments seem, for example, to be the basis for what is probably the first published life-events list, Adolf Meyer's suggestion that a diagnostically useful life-chart should include ''the changes of habitat, of school entrance, graduations or changes, or failures; the various 'jobs'; the dates of possibly important births and deaths in the family'' (1951, p. 53). These categories of life events are included in most subsequent lists, presumably in part because of investigators' agreement with Meyer about their importance. Unfortunately, although there may well be biases built into these subjective judgments there is no way to analyze them to determine what these biases might be.

Life-event lists have not, however, been limited to items selected by means of investigators' subjective judgments, but in two cases that we know of have been composed in part or in whole of a sample of events drawn by objective procedures. In one case B. P. and B. S. Dohrenwend supplemented an intuitively chosen list by adding events reported by a systematic sample of community respondents in answer to the question, ''What was the last major event that, for better or for worse, changed or interrupted your usual activities?'' (Dohrenwend, 1970; Markush and Favero, this volume). This procedure had the advantage of broadening the sample of life events beyond the experience of the investigator. However, it also reflected the particular subcultures of the different groups in the community from which respondents were drawn rather than providing a representative sample of the entire universe of possible life changes. Thus, for example, no respondents in New York City reported life changes related to building a house, a category of events that would almost surely be reported by some rural and suburban respondents. This procedure may also have failed to represent adequately life events for all age groups, since respondents were all between 21 and 59 years of age. As Kellam pointed out in his chapter, ''The events chosen to represent stressful *events or conditions* during adolescence would be quite different from those at middle age, which in turn would be different from those at old age (p. 212).''

In another objective sampling procedure, Holmes and Rahe compiled a list of ''life events empirically observed to cluster at the time of disease onset'' (1967, p. 215). Like the Dohrenwend procedure, this explicit sampling technique can be examined for possible biases, a question that is particularly important in this case since Holmes and Rahe's list of life events has been widely adopted as a research tool.

The onset of disease is not an all-or-none process but may be more or less subtle and gradual. A list of life events that ''cluster at the time of disease onset'' is therefore likely to be biased toward symptoms or concomitants of incipient disorder. Events on Holmes and Rahe's list such as ''Major change in sleeping habits'' and ''Major change in eating habits'' are suspect on this count for a wide range of illnesses, and many other events ranging from ''Sexual difficulties'' to ''Being fired at work'' must be considered suspect at least in relation to psychological disorders. The seriousness of the problem is suggested by Hudgens' finding that, by his count, 29 of the 43 events on this list ''are often the symptoms or consequences of illness (p. 131).'' As Brown and B. P. Dohrenwend pointed out in their chapters, this kind of bias in the sample of life events limits the kind of inference that can be drawn from a correlation between events and illness. Specifically, one cannot safely make the etiological inference from this correlation that life events cause illness since it is also possible that the correlation is due at least in part to the onset of illness causing certain life events or to a common factor causing both.

In research concerned specifically with the etiology of psychological disorders this problem has led investigators to examine the effects of the subset of life events over which the respondent probably had no control, their reasoning being that any events for which he was responsible in part or in whole might reflect the respondent's psychological state (e.g., Brown & Birley, 1968;

Brown & Birley, 1970; Dohrenwend, 1973; Myers, Lindenthal, Pepper, & Ostrander, 1972; Paykel, this volume). In addition, as B. P. Dohrenwend pointed out in his chapter, it is important in testing etiological hypotheses concerning stressful life events and psychological disorder to give separate consideration to the respondent's own illnesses when they are reported as life events, given the strong interrelation among somatic and psychological disorders (e.g., Eastwood & Trevelyan, 1972). This point was also suggested by Hinkle as applying to somatic disorders when he wrote, "The occurrence of an episode of one disease increases the likelihood that episodes of other diseases will occur. Thus obesity increases the likelihood that latent diabetes mellitus will become manifest; the presence of diabetes mellitus increases the likelihood that infections of the urinary tract will occur; infections of the urinary tract increase the likelihood that serious kidney disease will occur; kidney disease increases the likelihood that hypertension will occur; hypertension increases the likelihood that coronary heart disease will occur; and so on. Thus the presence of one disease may imply the presence of other diseases and beget yet other diseases (p. 39)." The procedures adopted by some investigators together with discussion of the problem of etiological inference by others leads to the conclusion, first, that events which may have been under the respondent's control should be excluded from the domain of life changes sampled and, second, that within the domain sampled the respondent's illnesses should be treated as a separate subset because of their distinctive etiological implications.

The bias toward symptoms or concomitants of illness in the sample of events on Holmes and Rahe's list is a problem in research intended to test etiological hypotheses, but it is an advantage for another type of study. As B. P. Dohrenwend emphasized in his chapter, if the investigator's objective is to develop an instrument for predicting the onset of illness, without necessarily explaining it, Holmes and Rahe's procedures for sampling life events is optimal, and the more closely the sample of events is tied to the onset of a particular illness the more effective it will be. Thus, in general, the appropriate procedure for sampling life events as well as the domain from which they are sampled depends on the purpose of the study.

Perception of Life Events as a Measure of Their Actual Stressfulness

The most obvious point of disagreement among contributors to this book concerning the measurement of stressful life events, as we noted earlier, appears to be the issue of whether the actual stressfulness of life events can be measured objectively or whether, on the contrary, it must be assessed in subjective terms. However, despite the fact that the opposition between objective and subjective measures of stressfulness has been argued in the literature, this statement of the controversy is misleading. In fact, all investigators seem to start from the premise that the stressfulness of life events depends on how they are perceived. Where those who have been concerned with the issue of how to measure stressfulness appear to differ with each other is in the amount of perceptual consensus about life events that they assume exists. They take three general positions:

1. The perception of the extent to which a particular life event is stressful is idiosyncratic, differing from individual to individual.
2. The perception of the extent to which a particular life event is stressful is the same within culturally or otherwise homogeneous groups but differs from group to group.
3. The perception of the extent to which a particular life event is stressful is the same universally.

Let us consider first the theoretical arguments and empirical evidence for idiosyncratic as against group or universal perceptions of the stressfulness of life events.

Idiosyncratic versus Group or Universal Perceptions of the Stressfulness of Life Events

If the stressfulness of a life event is indicated by how it is perceived and the effect of a stressful life event consists of illness or some other disturbance in functioning, one index of the accuracy of a perceptual measure of stressfulness should be the strength of its relationship with illnesses or other outcomes. By this criterion the evidence suggests that idiosyncratic perceptions of the stressfulness of life events are superior to group or universal perceptual measures. Earlier in this chapter we quoted references by Hinkle to personality studies that support this point indirectly. More directly, Theorell reported in his chapter that he found the largest significant difference between myocardial infarction patients and nonpatient controls when their recent life events were weighted according to ratings made by each individual of the "upsettingness" of his own recent events. By contrast, when standard weights were applied to all subjects' recent life events the event scores of MI patients and nonpatients did not differ significantly (p. 111).

The apparent advantage in accuracy of idiosyncratic perception as the indicator of the stressfulness of life events is not sufficient, however, to dictate its adoption for, if this indicator is used, the question of whether stressful life events figure in the etiology of illness takes on a special, limited meaning. Consider, for example, Theorell's further finding that "the *normal* way of reacting in scaling performance to a fresh experience of an event is to give it a *lower* score. This tendency, however, is not observed in the MI patient groups where the fresh experience did not affect the weights given to the events significantly. Thus the patients seemed to have a more rigid way of scaling changes (p.

113)." At the same time, as we just noted, Theorell found that these idiosyncratic weights yielded the largest difference in recent life-event scores between MI patients and nonpatients and that standard weights yielded a nonsignificant difference between the two groups. It appears, then, that the significant difference in life-event scores was due not to differences in the actual events in the lives of MI patients and nonpatients but to the difference in their perception of these events. The implication is that their recent life-event scores did not identify environmental pressures on the MI patients that contributed directly to their infarctions but, instead, suggested a perceptual style associated with vulnerability to this illness. In general, if individuals' perceptions of the stressfulness of particular life events are the best predictors of whether their life events will be followed by illness or not, the implication is that no prediction can be made from the events as such. Instead, given the occurrence of life events, it is the perceptual response to them that is significant in etiology.

When a study based on idiosyncratic perceptions of events is retrospective in design even this etiological inference may not be valid, for the report that the life events that preceded an illness were particularly upsetting (Theorell, p. 110, this volume) or particularly "threatening, challenging, demanding, and frustrating" (Hinkle, p. 29, this volume) may be an after effect of the illness (cf. Brown, p. 218, this volume; Paykel, p. 135, this volume). Only prospective studies using idiosyncratic perceptions to indicate the stressfulness of life events, which have not yet been done so far as we know, would establish the validity of individual perceptual responses to life events as a component in the etiology of illness or other outcomes.

Even positive results from such prospective studies would not, however, support the hypothesis that stressful life events constitute environmental pressures which contribute directly to the onset of illness. A test of this hypothesis would require a measure of the stressfulness of life events that is anchored in the environment rather than generated by the individual whose illness is to be explained. Different investigators have suggested environmentally anchored measures based on universal human perceptions of life events or, alternatively, on consensus within particular groups. Let us review the evidence bearing on these two possibilities.

Universal versus Group Perceptions of the Stressfulness of Life Events

In their chapter in this book Holmes and Masuda reviewed the large body of methodological and substantive studies of the measure of the stressfulness of life events first published by Holmes and Rahe (1967). The rationale underlying this measure was derived from the psychophysical research of S. S. Stevens which showed that "there is a general psychophysical law relating subjective magnitude to stimulus magnitude, and that this law is simply that equal stimulus ratios produce equal subjective ratios'' (1957, p. 153). Stevens and his coworkers demonstrated that this relationship holds, for example, between the intensity of sound and loudness, between physical distance and visual distance, between physical length and visual length. Not only do these observations support the theory but, in turn, the validity of the measurement of these and other subjective dimensions is strongly supported by the fact that they are congruent with a parsimonious theory.

In contrast, the validity of the general perceptual measure of stressfulness of life events cannot be evaluated by determining whether ''equal stimulus ratios produce equal subjective ratios,'' since there is no measure of the stimulus dimension available. However, as Stevens noted, it has been demonstrated that this problem does not preclude development of valid scales.

Nor is the large individual variability in judgments of the stressfulness of particular events a reason for dismissing the measure as invalid, since experience has shown that no matter what the stimulus dimension, ''The judgment of subjective magnitude is inherently a 'noisy' phenomenon. . . . Patience and experimental skill can probably clean up part of the variance, but there will always remain irreducible dispersions to set a level below which we sink into uncertainty'' (Stevens, 1957, p. 167). In judgments of the stressfulness of life events, moreover, we have no reason to assume that ''irreducible dispersions'' have been reached. For example, although it has been shown that judges who have experienced a given life event tend to rate it lower on stressfulness than those who have not experienced it (Theorell, this volume, p. 113), this source of variability has not been controlled in published measures of the stressfulness of life events. In addition, contextual factors, such as whether the event was anticipated or not, or the extent to which the subject was in control of the event have been almost completely ignored in attempts to secure standard perceptual measures of stressfulness (cf. Averill, 1973; Brown, this volume, p. 221–222; Stevens, 1957, p. 168). Until the relevant experiential and contextual variables are controlled we will not know how much inherent variability there is in individual perceptions of the stressfulness of particular life events.

At present therefore the validity of a universal perceptual measure of the stressfulness of life events cannot be seriously questioned on the basis of evidence of unreliability among individual judges. In contrast, some of the systematic variations in ratings by judges from different social backgrounds do pose a serious challenge to the validity of this measure.

Evidence of group differences was described in detail by Miller and his coauthors in their chapter comparing ratings of life events by judges from a rural area in the southeastern United States with ratings by judges from urban areas in the United States. Differences have also been observed between Americans on the one hand and Swedes (Rahe, Lundberg, Theorell & Bennett, 1971) or Japanese (Holmes & Masuda, this volume, Table 5) on the other hand. In these studies discrepancies were found both in the level of readjustment perceived to be required by all life events and in rankings of particular life events on this dimension.

The variations in overall level of readjustment ratings are not related to cultural differences in any obvious way and may, at least in some instances, be an artifact of measurement (Miller, Bentz, Aponte, & Brogan, this volume, p. 268–269). In contrast, the discrepancies in the ratings of particular events in relation to each other do seem in many cases to reflect differences in the values and practices of the groups involved and hence, by implication, real differences in judges' perceptions of their stressfulness. For example, among the 40 events whose geometric mean ratings were compared by Miller and his coauthors, "Mortgage greater than $10,000" ranked twenty-second when rated by urban judges and sixth when rated by rural judges. In discussing the relatively high level of readjustment that rural judges attributed to this event, Miller and his coauthors noted, "In the rural South, a general pay-as-you-go philosophy still prevails. This is particularly true for families where the money base is small. It is not at all unusual to find all or most members of a family doing 'public work,' investing their weekly income in building materials, and spending weekends and spare time building their home. Such a house might take years to build but would be completed, financially as well as materially, as soon as it was finished (p. 271)." In obvious contrast, such a procedure would be unusual if not impossible in an urban setting.

Congruences of this kind between group values and experiences on the one hand and ratings of the stressfulness of relevant life events on the other hand suggest, as Miller and his coauthors indicated, that the burden of proof now rests with those who would argue for the validity of universal human perceptions of the stressfulness of all life events. There may be universal agreement about some events, or there may be agreement within quite broad sociocultural groupings about events in certain crucial domains. At present, however, all we know is that we must be wary of generalizing measures of the stressfulness of life events beyond the particular sociocultural group from whom the ratings of events were obtained.

SUMMARY: CONCEPTUALIZATION AND MEASUREMENT OF THE STRESSFULNESS OF LIFE EVENTS

We have suggested that the process of measuring the stressfulness of life events involves three decisions and that each investigator makes these decisions within the framework of his research purpose, his theoretical assumptions, and certain available research findings. The questions requiring decisions are:

Table 1. Decision Making in Definition and Measurement of Stressful Life Events

Considerations Determining Decisions	Decisions to be Made		
	Definition of Domain of Possibly Stressful Life Events	Procedure for Sampling Domain of Possibly Stressful Life Events	Measure of Stressfulness of Life Events
Generally accepted practice without explicit rationale	Life changes		
Research purpose:			
Actuarial prediction without explanation of outcome	No further limitation indicated	Select events that are empirically associated with outcome to be predicted	
Etiological explanation of outcome	Limit to events whose cause is independent of outcome under study	Select events by procedure that is independent of outcome to be explained	
Conceptualization of stressfulness of life events:			
Stressfulness of life events is generated by idiosyncratic perception of event			Subject's perception of his life events
Stressfulness of life events is generated by social norms			Environmentally anchored universal or group perceptions of life events
Research findings:			
Correlations between particular types of event and particular outcomes	Limit to indicated types of events if related outcome is of interest		
Differences between groups in judgments of stressfulness of life events			Appropriate group perceptions of life events

1. How is the domain of possibly stressful life events defined?
2. How is a sample of events to be drawn from that domain?
3. How is the actual stressfulness of events to be reliably measured?

Table 1 presents a summary of considerations that affect these decisions and the specific nature of their effects. This table does not describe an ideal decision-making model but is instead an attempt to provide an empirical description of the current practices followed more or less explicitly in defining and measuring the independent variable in research on stressful life events. With progress in this research this description should become out of date.

THE FUTURE

Life events are, in and of themselves, eminently researchable. They are things that are important to the subjects whom we study, that they know about, are interested in, and, though sometimes painful, can tell us about. Herein lies their advantage as strategic phenomena on which to focus in the study of the role of social factors in health and illness.

The problem, however, is to ask the right questions about such events and their effects under circumstances in which the answers will provide clear demonstrations of whether and to what extent they are causally implicated in the disorders in which we are interested. It is by no means clear that we have yet done so, though the fascinating tangle of correlations thus far reported virtually demand, in our opinion, a major increase in research efforts toward clarification. What form should such efforts take? What ingredients should they include? If we have read our colleagues correctly, we think that they should involve the following:

1. More use of prospective designs.
2. Procedures for reliably measuring attributes of life events other than the perceived amount of change that they entail and their positive or negative valence. Especially important would be assessment of whether they are within or outside the control of the individual and whether they were anticipated or unanticipated.
3. Specification of relevant populations of life events and systematic sampling of the events from each—both events contemporaneous in the lives of the individuals being studied and events in their past. Such sampling would permit us to seek answers to questions such as:

(a) What are the roles of primacy, frequency, and recency for different types of event in the life of the individual?

(b) What are the relations among events from different event populations?

(c) Are there combinations and sequences of events that fit a stress-strain model of stress and illness?

(d) Do some types of events at different developmental stages of the individual have inoculation effects for some types of disorder?

4. Expansion of research designs to include larger numbers of possible outcome variables—involving both physical illnesses and psychopathology.

5. Provision for controlled comparison of the contribution of stressful life events by contrast with the contributions of variables suggested as relevant by other theories or empirical findings concerning the disorders being studied (e.g., cigarette smoking and family history of heart disease vis-à-vis cardiovascular disease).

We have seen that controversies abound concerning how to conceptualize and measure stressful life events, and what effects they have. These controversies are a sign of progress beyond common sense assumptions such as "take it easy; you'll live longer," and they can be expected to continue to generate imaginative research. Their resolution will depend in considerable part, we believe, on judicious combination of the ingredients, outlined above, that we have distilled from the work reported in this book.

REFERENCES

Averill, J. R. Personal control over aversive stimuli and its relationship to stress. *Psychological Bulletin,* 1973, **80,** 286–303.

Brown, G. W., & Birley, J. L. T. Crises and life changes and the onset of schizophrenia. *Journal of Health and Social Behavior,* 1968, **9,** 203–214.

Brown, G. W., & Birley, J. L. T. Social precipitants of severe psychiatric disorders. In E. H. Hare & J. K. Wing (Eds.), *Psychiatric Epidemiology: Proceedings of the International Symposium Held at Aberdeen University 22–25 July 1969.* New York: Oxford University Press, 1970. Pp. 321–325.

Dohrenwend, B. P., & Dohrenwend, B. S. *Social Status and Psychological Disorder: A Causal Inquiry.* New York: John Wiley & Sons, 1969.

Dohrenwend, B. S. Social class and stressful events. In E. H. Hare & J. K. Wing (Eds.), *Psychiatric Epidemiology: Proceedings of the International Symposium held at Aberdeen University 22–25 July 1969.* New York: Oxford University Press, 1970. Pp. 313–319.

Dohrenwend, B. S. Social status and stressful life events. *Journal of Personality and Social Psychology,* 1973, **28,** 225–235.

Eastwood, M. R., & Trevelyan, M. H. Relationship between physical and psychiatric disorder. *Psychological Medicine,* 1972, **2,** 363–372.

Frankenhaeuser, M., Experimental approaches to the study of human behaviour as related to neuroendocrine functions. In L. Levi (ed.), *Society, Stress, and Disease*. New York: Oxford University Press, 1971.

Holmes, T. H., & Rahe, R. H. The social readjustment rating scale. *Journal of Psychomatic Research,* 1967, **11,** 213–218.

MacMahon, B., & Pugh, T. F. *Epidemiology: Principles and Methods*. Boston: Little, Brown and Company, 1970.

Meyer, A. The life chart and the obligation of specifying positive data in psychopathological diagnosis. In E. E. Winters (Ed.), *The Collected Papers of Adolf Meyer. Volume III, Medical Teaching*. Baltimore, Md.: The Johns Hopkins University Press, 1951. Pp. 52–56.

Myers, J. K., Lindenthal, J. J., Pepper, M. P., & Ostrander, D. R. Life events and mental status. *Journal of Health and Social Behavior,* 1972, **13,** 398–406.

Nunnally, J. C. *Psychometric Theory*. New York: McGraw-Hill Book Company, 1967.

Rahe, R. H., Lundberg, U., Theorell, T., & Bennett, L. K. The social readjustment rating scale: A comparative study of Swedes and Americans. *Journal of Psychosomatic Research,* 1971, **15,** 241–249.

Stevens, S. S. On the psychophysical law. *Psychological Review,* 1957, **64,** 153–181.

Author Index

Subject Index